# Unity in Mission

## THEOLOGICAL REFLECTIONS ON
## THE PILGRIMAGE OF MISSION

Edited by

## Mitzi J. Budde and Don Thorsen

NATIONAL COUNCIL OF THE CHURCHES
OF CHRIST IN THE USA

**FAITH & ORDER COMMISSION**
THEOLOGICAL SERIES

Paulist Press
New York / Mahwah, NJ

Cover photo by Pattie Steib / Shutterstock.com. All rights reserved.
Cover design and book design by Sharyn Banks

Library of Congress Cataloging-in-Publication Data

Unity in mission : theological reflections on the pilgrimage of mission / edited by Mitzi J. Budde and Don Thorsen, National Council of the Churches of Christ in the USA.
    pages cm. — (Faith and Order Commission theological series)
Includes bibliographical references.
ISBN 978-0-8091-4830-1 (alk. paper)
1. Missions—Interdenominational cooperation. I. Budde, Mitzi J., editor of compilation. II. Thorsen, Donald A. D., editor of compilation.
    BV2082.I6U55 2013
    266—dc23
                                                                        2012046109

ISBN: 978-0-8091-4830-1 (paperback)
ISBN: 978-1-58768-332-9 (e-book)

Published by Paulist Press
997 Macarthur Boulevard
Mahwah, New Jersey 07430

www.paulistpress.com

Printed and bound in the
United States of America

# CONTENTS

# CONTENTS

# INTRODUCTION

*Mitzi J. Budde and Don Thorsen*

Understanding mission is perhaps the best path to unity. Mission is central to the church's existence as well as to its ministries. Emil Brunner said, "The Church exists by mission, just as the fire exists by burning."[1] In addition to the cruciality of mission, Jesus wanted his followers to be unified. He prayed that "they may be one" (John 17:11), and this unity extends to all dimensions of their witness to Jesus and to the Gospel.

Mission is transformational in both personal and social dimensions of life. The implications are that the church has a prophetic vocation in the world, a calling to be an agent of renewal within the wider community of humanity that inhabits the world, without the world becoming coextensive with the church. The church is to be "in" the world without being "of" the world. What is the mission of the church in relation to and even in community with the rest of humanity?

This book focuses on the topic of "unity in mission." We investigate various aspects of the church's mission: serving the purpose of God as a gift given to the world in order that all may believe; proclaiming the Gospel in word and deed; reconciling all things to God and to one another through Jesus Christ, transforming the world; caring for those suffering and in need, suffering on their behalf; and advocating on behalf of the poor, needy, and marginalized. In the power of the Holy Spirit, the church seeks faithfully to proclaim and live the love of God for all, and to fulfill in unison Jesus' mission for the salvation and renewal of the world, to the glory of God.

1

# APPROACH TO UNITY IN MISSION

Over a four-year period, members of the Faith and Order Commission met to study the nature of mission and how it may serve to unite Christians and churches. Although Faith and Order represents a Commission of the National Council of Churches of Christ in the USA (NCC), its participants include representatives from member churches of the NCC as well as nonmembers. Faith and Order includes representatives from Catholic and Orthodox Churches, European-born Protestant and American-born Protestant Churches, Evangelical and Pentecostal Churches. To be sure, the breadth and variety of discussion about ministry traditions in Faith and Order can be remarkable. Yet, the mutual desire for unity in mission brings about dialogue, understanding, appreciation, and cooperation that transcend their differences.

The Faith and Order Study Group was entitled Unity in Mission, and its work was co-chaired by Mitzi J. Budde and Don Thorsen. In the spring of 2008, the Study Group began its four-year (or quadrennium) project of presenting papers about the approach to Christian mission representative of their respective church traditions. In sharing with one another, participants distilled areas of agreement as well as disagreement with regard to how a growing unity in mission contributes to visible Christian unity as well as to loving service to God and others.

It is difficult to describe how inspiring and convicting it is to hear about the manner in which churches go about Christian mission and ministry. Successes as well as failures all contribute to a more mature and useable approach to church life. Not only differences in church traditions, but differences in ethnicity and gender, language and culture contributed to the work of the Study Group.

Diversity in mission is not in and of itself problematic. The apostle Paul used the analogy of the body of Christ to describe the church (see 1 Cor 12:12–27; Eph 4:1–16). He understood that, by the grace of God, it is the diversity of Christians within churches that overall help make the church successful. All *parts*—or Christians—within churches contribute their particular gifts, talents, and skills so that the *whole* of its mission might be fulfilled to the glory of God. Likewise, God uses the diversity of churches in helping them successfully fulfill God's will throughout the entire world.

## THEMES OF UNITY IN MISSION

As the Study Group met, several unifying themes or motifs emerged as group members presented papers to one another. They represented various aspects of their work toward visible Christian unity and how the particular search for unity in mission shaped around central themes. They included themes of journey, pilgrimage, and accompaniment that emphasize the dynamic, emergent processes involved with both mission and unity. For example, in many papers, a common theme was how we are journeying as churches as well as individual Christians. For some contributors, the concept of journey or pilgrimage is a strong theme; for others, not so much. But it serves as a leitmotif that undergirds the entire book.

Other themes that arose included the use of story, witness, or other accounts from members' personal and ecclesial contexts. Almost every chapter in the book includes stories that help readers focus upon the challenges as well as the opportunities for Christians to minister broadly and effectively in churches, and how their stories may serve to unite one another in mission. Overall, the book is a work of narrative theology, rather than analytical or systematic theology. Unity in mission is a huge, complex issue. In response to this complexity, we sought to bring out new approaches and new voices through story and through the conceptualizing of experience.

The Study Group intentionally wanted to show the variety of ways to approach unity in mission. Members did not attempt to formulate one way that might ring true for all our traditions, or to seek the development of a unified consensus statement. Yet, we saw the need to recover ways of thinking that preserves and makes manifest a unity of mission through ecumenical cooperation.

## FINDING UNITY IN MISSION

The papers that resulted from our investigations in the Study Group present the mission of God in a way that includes the varieties of ministries in which churches are involved. Once more, diversity is not considered an inescapable hindrance to cooperation for the sake of God's mission in the world. Thus, the chapters in this book promote both the unity and the diversity of church ministries, and they emphasize the ecumenical benefits of focusing together on the missional dimension of the church. The authors explore the diversity of ministries, while advocating a greater unity and effectiveness that may emerge as a result. Just as churches are thought to represent different parts of the body of Christ, the church worldwide represents a marvelous wholeness that provides opportunities for greater understanding, appreciation, and cooperation in ministry. The Study Group saw mission as an occasion for ecumenical hope among Christians and churches in the world.

Members of the Unity in Mission Study Group included Mitzi J. Budde (Evangelical Lutheran Church in America) and Don Thorsen (Wesleyan Theological Society), co-chairs; Anton C. Vrame (Greek Orthodox Archdiocese of America); Susan E. Davies (United Church of Christ); Lyndon Harris (The Episcopal Church); Dale E. Luffman (Community of Christ); Young Lee Hertig (Presbyterian Church, U.S.A.); Kevin Park (Presbyterian Church, U.S.A.); John T. Ford (United States Conference of Catholic Bishops); Ernest Falardeau (United States Conference of Catholic Bishops); Matthew D. Lundberg (Christian Reformed Church); Antonios Kireopoulos (Greek Orthodox Archdiocese of America); Young-Ho Chun (United Methodist Church); Leonard Lovett (Church of God in Christ); Donald Dayton (2009–11,Wesleyan Theological Society); Shirley Paulson (2010–11, The First Church of Christ, Scientist); Tony Richie (2010–11, Society for Pentecostal Studies); Tamara Rodenberg (2008-9, Christian Church, Disciples of Christ); and Richard Jeske (2008–9, American Bible Society).

Early writings by the Study Group were published in the *Journal of Ecumenical Studies*. Included were articles by Mitzi J. Budde ("The Marks as Signposts"), Susan E. Davies, John T. Ford ("Unity and Mission: A Pilgrimage"), Antonios Kireopoulos, Anton C. Vrame, and an earlier version of the article by Matthew D. Lundberg.[2] The articles are copyrighted by the *Journal of Ecumenical Studies*, and are reprinted with permission.

# INTRODUCTION

The chapters in this book represent work done by members of the Study Group. During the quadrennium of study, Michael Kinnamon and S. Wesley Ariarajah spoke to the Faith and Order Commission on topics relevant to the subject of unity in mission, and writings were solicited from them for this volume.

## APPLYING UNITY IN MISSION

How do we apply the content in this book for the sake of both Christian mission and unity? The chapters have been arranged in five sections, and they follow a logical progression of ideas relevant to unity in mission. However, the chapters are not arranged in an argumentative style that requires reading the chapters sequentially. Thus, if readers find some chapters to be of greater interest than others, then there is no problem in reading them out of order. Indeed, we encourage readers to study those topics that are of most interest to them, or that they desire most to apply to their lives, churches, and ministries. At the same time, we encourage readers to study the entire book because we believe that it contains practical as well as conceptual insights for promoting both the mission and unity of churches.

The first section is entitled "Foundations of Unity in Mission," and its chapters introduce the subject matter as well as talk about how both mission and unity are founded upon God, the writings of Scripture, and input from church history. The second section is entitled "Word and Sacrament," and its chapters talk about proclaiming the Gospel and the role of the sacraments. The third section is entitled "The Way of Reconciliation," and its chapters deal with some of the difficult questions and issues that have arisen in church history that challenge mission and unity, and for which Christians and churches need reconciliation. The fourth section is entitled "Experiential Journeys of Mission," and its chapters contain a wide variety of personal experiences related to mission and unity, which contain insights needed for future ecumenism, for healing among churches as well as people and nations, and for the need to focus on racial and ethnic dynamics related to unity in mission. The fifth section is entitled "Biblical Reflections," and its chapters consist of Bible studies related to mission and unity.

Finally, we encourage readers to approach unity in mission not just as a subject to be studied, but a calling about which they should pray, meditate, and act. The issues, indeed, are complex, and we shun simplistic answers to solve them. But we believe in a God who, through the presence and power of the Holy Spirit, gives us hope about the ways in which Christians and churches may increasingly minister together in unity for the sake of the mission of Jesus Christ and of the Gospel.

## NOTES

1. Emil Brunner, *The Word and the World* (London: SCM Press, 1931), 11.

2. See the *Journal of Ecumenical Studies* 45, no. 2 (Spring 2010): 178–248.

# FOUNDATIONS OF UNITY IN MISSION

# 1

# UNITY AND MISSION
## A Pilgrimage of Accompaniment

*John T. Ford*

## VIA CRUCIS

On Good Friday afternoon on New Hampshire Avenue in the Washington, DC, metropolitan area, thousands of people participate in the annual *via crucis*, "the way of the cross," a processional reenactment of the final steps of Jesus' carrying his cross along the *Via Dolorosa*—"the Street of Sorrow," "the Way of Suffering," the "Route of Pain"—winding through the streets of Jerusalem that Jesus walked on his way to his crucifixion on Golgotha.[1] An example of *religiosidad popular*—popular religious devotion[2]—this dramatization of the "execution walk" of Jesus dates back to the time of St. Francis of Assisi in the thirteenth century, with roots that go back centuries earlier.[3]

At the time of St. Francis, a pilgrimage to the Holy Land was expensive, difficult, and dangerous. For those who could not afford a journey to a distant land, replicas of the sacred sites in the Holy Land were built at various locations in Europe and Russia.[4] Yet, visiting these shrines was not always easy or convenient. St. Francis introduced the Stations of the Cross[5] so that people could reenact the final journey of Christ close to home in their local churches. While the Stations were a new devotion, the dramatization of the final steps of Jesus paralleled other types of medieval religious theatre: *las posadas*, "the inns," which reenact the search of Joseph and Mary for lodging on their journey to Bethlehem; *las pastorelas*, "the visit of the shepherds" to the newborn Jesus; *los tres reyes*, the search of "the three kings" for the newborn king.[6] Processions that symbolize the spiritual journeys, not only of biblical persons, but also of present-day participants are the central feature of these three celebrations, as well as for the *via crucis*.

In medieval religious drama, many of the principal events in the life of Jesus and the saints were reenacted—sometimes in church, at other times in public places; in fact, many churches in colonial Spanish America included huge outdoor spaces for the celebration of religious pageants.[7] People today are often surprised that such reenactments continue to be staged in many Hispanic communities in the United States. What is the reason for the continued popularity of such practices of medieval piety? One important factor is that the Stations—like *las posadas*, *las pastorelas*, and *los tres reyes*—are not merely stage productions to be watched but religious activities in which the spectators also become participants. In other words, religious theatre is both catechetical—a means of instructing people about the great events of Christianity—and "sacramental"—a way of providing people with an opportunity for participating in the history of salvation.[8]

A variation on the individual Stations of the Cross is evident, for example, in *Scenes from the Passion of Christ* by Hans Memling (c. 1433–94), who incorporated a number of events—including the Last Supper, the carrying of the cross, the crucifixion, the burial, and the resurrection—into a single painting.[9] As is typical in Renaissance religious art, the donors are depicted in the picture, in this case as praying at opposite sides in the lower corners of the painting; symbolically, the donors, like all Christians, are called to be witnesses of the passion and resurrection of Christ.[10]

Another familiar example of popular reenactments of the last hours of Jesus is through passion plays, which date back at least to the thirteenth century and continue to be performed in many different countries, including the United States.[11] Yet, as forms of *religiosidad popular*, passion plays have sometimes been vitiated by serious problems and prejudices.[12] There have been cases where church authorities have reproved performers for their coarse language and excessive cruelty, which occasionally has led to the serious injury and even the death of the Christ-actor.[13] In addition, passion plays have all too often reflected the antisemitic prejudices of both the participants and the populace[14]—prejudices that have been repeatedly repudiated by church authorities in recent decades.[15]

Like Hans Memling, who painted his *Scenes from the Passion of Christ* with a fifteenth-century Flemish background, in celebrating the *via crucis* in the Washington, DC, area, many of the sites chosen for Stations are locations where the local community has experienced some type of violence or tragedy: the place of a murder or robbery, a corner for criminal activity, the site of a fatal accident, a burned-out home, etcetera. The parallel is both intentional and instructive; just as Jesus experienced suffering and sorrow during the final hours of his life, so Christians today experience pain and hardship in their journey through life. Thus, the drama of the crucifixion of Jesus takes on personal meaning: The way of the cross followed by Jesus is salvific, not only in a theologically abstract way, but also concretely here and now today. We as Christians are participants in the history of salvation, even though the crucifixion happened nearly two millennia ago.

The Stations of the Cross are not simply a reenactment of an important historical event, as if the people in procession were like the reenactors of Civil War battles. The *via crucis* is not simply a historical representation but a religious *re*-presentation—a spiritual activity, a dramatized prayer, which helps the participants experience the crucifixion of Jesus as a salvific event that gives significance and purpose to their lives. As the title of a popular Spanish edition of the Bible—*Dios Habla Hoy*—indicates: "God speaks today."[16] Accordingly, the Bible is not an ancient and outdated document; the words of the Bible are a living message for today. We understand biblical events through the events of our lives, and, reciprocally, the events of the Bible enable us to understand the events of our lives.

Simultaneously, the Stations of the Cross evoke the biblical theme of pilgrimage. In the Hebrew Bible, the chosen people, under the leadership of Abraham, were called by God to journey to a promised land. At the time of Moses, the chosen people were led to a land flowing with milk and honey; at the end of the Babylonian exile, the chosen people pilgrimaged back to their homeland. Similarly, in the Christian Scriptures, Jesus called his disciples to journey with him throughout Galilee and then to Jerusalem; after his

11

resurrection, the first Christians were known as followers of "the Way"—a simple yet singularly evocative description of Christianity as essentially a pilgrimage.[17]

Going on pilgrimage has long been an important part of Hispanic piety. Every year—for more than a millennium—thousands of people journey, many walking across northern Spain on foot, to the Shrine of St. James at Santiago de Compostela.[18] Even more popular as a pilgrimage destination is the Shrine of Our Lady of Guadalupe in Mexico, where over 1,000,000 pilgrims gather to celebrate her feast day each year,[19] yet one need not travel to a distant pilgrimage center; practically every village in the Hispanic world has a shrine that is a local pilgrimage center. Similarly, the Stations of the Cross found in Catholic Churches worldwide make it possible for every Christian to follow the final footsteps of Jesus in prayer.

The Christian conviction that life is a journey resonates with the Spanish saying—"*el camino se hace caminando*" (the road is made by traveling), a reminder that "one's life is made by the way one lives."[20] Not surprisingly, this theme of life-as-journey is woven into the celebration of the Stations of the Cross. For example, one popular hymn that is frequently sung while making the Stations has the refrain—"*Caminemos con Jesús*" (Let us walk with Jesus).[21] This hymn points to the transformative aspect of the *via crucis*: By walking along with Jesus on his road to death, Jesus becomes our companion as we journey through life toward our own death. Moreover, because we are companions of Jesus, we become companions with each other; Jesus is the companion of all who follow "His Way." The Stations of the Cross, then, are not simply a private devotion; the Stations emphasize that the road to salvation is communal as well as personal. As Christians, we are all called to walk with Jesus as a community of believers.

This communal aspect of salvation is evident in another hymn that is often sung during the celebration of the Stations of the Cross: "*Perdona a tu pueblo, Señor*" (Pardon your people, O Lord).[22] This prayer not only emphasizes the belief that Christ's crucifixion is the source of salvation but also that Christians need the Sovereign's pardon in order to attain salvation. Moreover, the Spanish word *pueblo* has a dual meaning: It can mean "people" in a generic sense—all people need the pardon of God given through Christ; it

can also refer to a particular town or village—the people participating in the Stations are praying for forgiveness for their community: themselves, their families, and their neighbors.

Thus, the celebration of the Stations of the Cross has a "sacramental" aspect in the sense that it is a visible sign of a divine event
of grace; divine redemption is both manifested by and realized
through the death of Jesus. By celebrating the Stations of the Cross,
the mystery of salvation confronts the contemporary human situation in spite of the fact—as well as because of the fact—that the
human condition is filled with sin and suffering. The Stations allow
us to participate in the mystery of salvation, even though we need
God's forgiveness in order to journey with Jesus and even though
we need divine pardon in order to journey with each other as companions of Jesus. The Stations of the Cross are then a concrete
exemplification of the belief that the salvific event—"the Word
became flesh and dwelt among us"—was not merely a historical
fact in the past but must also be a salvific reality for every Christian
in the present.

## *VIA UNITATIS*

The ecumenical movement has often been described as a pilgrimage—comparable to such biblical examples as Abraham's seeking the land of promise and Moses' leading the chosen people
through the desert. Like the people of the Old Covenant, Christians
are quintessentially pilgrims—seeking to fulfill Christ's prayer of
unity for his disciples (John 17). Yet, as was the case for the people
following Abraham and Moses, the destination of the ecumenical
movement is vague, and its route is problematic.

First, with regard to the destination, while the goal of "visible
unity" among Christians is generically clear, its precise determina-
tion remains a matter of disagreement. Is the ecumenical goal one
of "organic union," so that all churches become one church? Is the
goal "full communion," in which all churches admit each other's
members to the celebration of the Eucharist? Is the goal "reconciled
diversity," in which all churches recognize each other as churches,
without necessarily resolving all theological difficulties and eccle-

siastical dissimilarities? Or, is there some other format for unity that is still to be discerned?[23]

Insofar as ecumenists have been unable to agree about the destination of the ecumenical pilgrimage, it is hardly surprising that there is also disagreement about the route. For example, some ecumenists feel that unity demands basic doctrinal agreement, while allowing for differences in nonessential matters; accordingly, during discussions, Faith and Order advocates have devoted considerable time to working out consensus statements on various church-dividing issues, both theological and ecclesiastical.[24] Other ecumenists, however, feel Christian unity is not so much a matter of achieving theological agreement and ecclesiastical complementarity as it is in living, working, and testifying together as followers of Christ. Accordingly, advocates of Life and Work have devoted considerable effort to designing and implementing cooperative projects of Christian ministry, service, and witness—projects that unite Christians in their lives and ministries.

In other words, ecumenists have different strategies for both mapping and traveling the road toward Christian unity. On the one hand are those who want the ecumenical pilgrimage to be charted well in advance; all major difficulties should be resolved and all essential structures specified prior to, and as a precondition for, visible unity. On the other hand are those who feel that the ecumenical pilgrimage is necessarily a voyage of exploration; the good ship *Oikoumene* needs to maneuver in response to the winds and waves of life, so that ecumenical explorers will eventually, perhaps even unexpectedly, reach the promised goal of unity—if they are willing to take appropriate risks in the ecumenical venture.[25]

Although the ecumenical pilgrimage route is still a matter of dispute, like that of the original *Via Dolorosa*,[26] it must be a *via unitatis*—a "road of unity"—in two ways. The ecumenical pilgrimage must be both a road toward unity and also a journey uniting its participants. Like the celebration of the *via crucis*, the ecumenical movement as a *via unitatis* brings together people of different places and races, who are called to achieve both a common sense of direction and a common experience of fellowship: "*el camino ecuménico se hace caminando*" (the ecumenical road is laid out en route).

Nonetheless, the ecumenical movement to date has often been a matter of theological dialogues and cooperative charitable projects—and only coincidentally a spiritual experience. The lack of an "ecumenical spirituality" seems to have been a basic lacuna that has resulted in a kind of ecumenical travel fatigue: On the one hand, ecumenists often find themselves repeatedly refining and redrafting the same consensus document, which may ultimately suffer death by a thousand emendations; on the other hand, ecumenists may expend considerable effort on charitable projects that are not welcomed by the people for whom they were designed. In parallel with the *via crucis*, the *via unitatis* needs not only to engage in doctrinal discussion and practical projects but also to have a spiritual dimension: The ecumenical movement needs to address the heart as well as the head.[27]

As the Second Vatican Council (1962–65) pointed out, ecumenism requires both a "change of heart and holiness of life";[28] the ecumenical pilgrimage needs to unify Christians not only intellectually and pragmatically but also spiritually. Paralleling the dynamics of the *via crucis*, the *via unitatis* must unite its participants in a journey both with Christ and with other Christians. The *via unitatis* must have not only a horizontal dimension of Christians journeying together but also a vertical dimension of Christians responding to the guidance of the Spirit—just as the chosen people were united by following the "pillar of cloud" (Exod 13:21).[29]

In the past, ecumenical dialogue has often tended to be an intellectual pursuit—a dialogue about doctrine and discipline, about Faith and Order.[30] In the future, ecumenical dialogue, while continuing its efforts at resolving doctrinal differences and ecclesiastical disparities, must also bring Christians closer together in their life and work, in fellowship and witness. Ecumenical agreements reached through dialogue need to be implemented at every level of the shared life of the churches. In other words, ecumenical discussions, like the stories shared on a journey, must help create Christian community.[31]

As a way of creating community, Christians should "act together in all matters except those in which deep differences of conviction compel them to act separately."[32] Nonetheless, whenever the ecumenical pilgrimage is focused solely on matters of Life and

Work, it may become like a tour that is well organized and efficient but lacking in intellectual content and meaningful relationships: Most Christians enjoy the experience of working together on projects but are sometimes surprised when disagreements about policy and procedures arise—among people of evident goodwill. In other words, acting without thinking is seldom satisfying in the long term and often merely postpones crucial questions that eventually will need answers. In fact, some ecumenical projects have run aground because the participants presumed that practical cooperation would resolve theoretical issues, only to discover that they were really more divided than they initially suspected.

Accordingly, the *via unitatis*, like the *via crucis*, needs to be interactive not only cognitively and practically but also spiritually. The good news about doctrinal agreements is that they represent the consensus of the participants in a particular ecumenical dialogue. The bad news about such statements is that they may be unintelligible to people in the pews who have neither the knowledge nor the experience of the people who produced these statements. In other words, ecumenical agreements are the product of a select group of pilgrims who have had the privilege of interacting together; without such shared dialogue, there never would have been a consensus statement.

Yet, if such agreements are to be accepted by people other than those who wrote them, there must also be a parallel process for readers of these documents. To be meaningful, every text needs a context; what has often happened with ecumenical documents is that the text has been published, but the context is missing. If ecumenical statements are to be meaningful, and so accepted by other Christians, the recipients need to replicate the dialogue process that produced the consensus; the recipients of consensus statements need to participate in the ecumenical pilgrimage.[33]

As a spiritual journey, an ecumenical pilgrimage should ideally bring out the very best in people. Yet, one might recall that medieval pilgrimages were in fact both difficult and dangerous. Medieval pilgrims traipsed over poor roads, suffered at the mercy of the elements, and endured poor lodging and indigestible food; medieval pilgrims ran the risk of contracting diseases at a time when hospitals were few and medical knowledge primitive; pilgrims were cheated by dishonest merchants, robbed by thieves, and attacked by predators. Worst of all, medieval pilgrims sometimes lost sight of the purpose of their journey, and, instead of being practitioners of pardon and peace, they engaged in controversy and even conflict.[34]

If the modern ecumenical pilgrimage is not as physically hazardous as its medieval antecedents, there are still some major risks involved. First of all, ecumenists are sometimes viewed with suspicion by their denominational colleagues. Ecumenical involvement is sometimes misconstrued as dissatisfaction with one's own denomination: "Aren't there plenty of opportunities and needs within our church?" Even if a denomination is officially committed to ecumenism, ecumenical celebrations are usually occasional events arranged by "ecumenical officers" at such times as Easter, Thanksgiving, or the Week of Prayer for Christian Unity.[35] Not only is ecumenism ordinarily not part of the regular experience of most Christians, many clergy have little or no ecumenical involvement—and some have virtually no ecumenical experience.

Even for ecumenists, ecumenical involvement includes risk factors. For example, in the writing of ecumenical agreements, there is the temptation of "theological perfectionism." In fact, some potentially promising consensus statements seem to have been defeated by hundreds of qualifications. Ecumenists may need to be reminded that, while agreement on fundamentals is absolutely necessary, the absolutely perfect ecumenical statement will not be produced until the eschaton. At the opposite extreme is the quagmire of ambiguity; some ecumenical statements seem so vague that they can mean anything and may end up meaning nothing. Travelers on the *via unitatis* need an ecumenical hermeneutics that clearly expresses points of both agreement and disagreement, as well as areas where further study and prayer are necessary.[36]

Perhaps the major obstacle encountered on the *via unitatis* is denominationalism. People with vested denominational interests seemingly try to detour the ecumenical pilgrimage by a variety of tactics: appeals to denominational polity, historical tradition, theological perspectives, biblical hermeneutics, and so on, so that every answer is turned into a new question. While such a hermeneutical procedure is an essential part of theological investigation, practically speaking, it may have the effect of continually stopping the pilgrimage to ask directions; even if the directions are useful, the ecumenical pilgrimage is repeatedly delayed, and little progress is made. Moreover, achieving consensus is not only a matter of crafting theological statements but also of entering into a spiritual relationship.

Another and more widespread obstacle on the *via unitatis* is simply ecumenical ignorance. Lack of knowledge about the meaning of consensus statements can lead to disinterest and benign neglect; most people have heard about pilgrimages, but comparatively few people actually make them. Similarly, lack of information makes consensus statements susceptible to misinterpretation and rejection; insofar as ecumenism ultimately involves various changes—theological, ecclesiastical, spiritual—many people resist. Conversion is never easy. To overcome denominational defensiveness, ecumenical leaders need to convince people that ecumenism is a pilgrimage that benefits all churches. Ecumenism needs to be seen as enriching, not destroying, denominational traditions.

Finally, pilgrims on the *via unitatis*, like the participants in the *via crucis*, should find their journey transformative. A person who devoutly participates in the Stations of the Cross should be drawn closer to both Christ and the Christian community; similarly, an ecumenical pilgrim should be drawn closer to Christ and closer to other Christians. For ecumenical pilgrims, the *via unitatis* should be a conversion experience. Unfortunately, there is no guaranteed incentive to persuade people to join any pilgrimage; there are people in every church who are content to be where they are or who are upset by doctrinal discussion and ecclesiastical change or who want to be spectators, not participants, in the ecumenical pilgrimage.

In sum, the *via unitatis* is essentially heuristic: It opens new theological vistas, offers new opportunities for Christian cooperation, and affords the possibility of deeper spiritual relationships. For example, most ecumenists return from an ecumenical conference both challenged by the insights gained through doctrinal discussion and also invigorated by the ecumenical fellowship they have experienced. Ways must be found to provide a similar experience of the *via unitatis* for all Christians. As part of the ecumenical pilgrimage, the *via unitatis* needs to be a visible foretaste of the unity that Christ intended for his followers.

## VIA MISSIONIS

In the Bible, the journeys mandated by God always had a purpose in the divine plan of salvation: Abraham's journey led the chosen people to the promised land; Moses' journey brought God's people back to Israel. Biblical journeys included a providential message, an assurance of divine guidance, and a salvific mission: deliverance from bondage, creation of a new people. This duality of message and mission is part of every pilgrimage: a message, God's guidance sought by the pilgrims in their prayers, and a mission, the pilgrims' journey of faith to a place of blessing. These two dimensions are also evident in the ecumenical pilgrimage, which is motivated by a divine message, "that all may be one," and a divine mission, achieving the visible unity of Christ's church.

The starting point of the ecumenical pilgrimage in the twentieth century is customarily traced to the Edinburgh Missionary Conference, June 14–23, 1910. Convoked as a meeting of Protestant missionary societies, the conference was motivated by the hope of evangelizing the world in a generation. Although the conference leadership decided in advance that, "no opinion on ecclesiastical or doctrinal questions would be expressed by the Conference," one of its commissions did discuss the topic of "Cooperation and the Promotion of Unity."[37] The participants soon came to the realization that they could discuss doctrinal differences and ecclesiastical disparities in nonpolemical ways. The ecumenical commitment generated by the Edinburgh Conference led to the founding of three organizations: the International Missionary Council, Faith and Order, and Life and Work—all of which eventually became components of the World Council of Churches.[38]

Along with these organizational results, the Edinburgh Conference provided a compelling insight that has continued to motivate ecumenical endeavors: The divisions among Christians contradict the will of Christ, scandalize the world, and seriously impede the preaching of the Gospel.[39] In other words, the divisions among Christians have not only resulted in a great deal of interdenominational rivalry and polemics, but these divisions have also proved to be a major obstacle to evangelization. How can Christians really claim to preach a gospel of love, if they do not welcome each other to their churches, or, even worse, if Christians attack one another?

The participants at Edinburgh were convinced that the missionary work of the church requires the unity of the church, but how can this relationship between mission and unity be achieved? The Third World Conference on Faith and Order, at Lund, Sweden, in 1952, issued the following challenge: "Should not our churches ask themselves whether they are showing sufficient eagerness to enter into conversation with other churches, and whether they should not act together in all matters except those in which deep differences of conviction compel them to act separately?"[40] This so-called Lund Principle makes a double demand. The first is the need for ecumenical conversations that attempt to reconcile doctrinal differences and ecclesiastical dissimilarities; this task is one that has generally been undertaken by Faith and Order. The second demand is ecumenical cooperation. The history of the ecumenical movement in the twentieth century shows the Lund Principle at work in many different ways in many different places. Throughout the world, Christians have cooperated on numerous projects in response to natural disasters, such as earthquakes and floods, as well as to human calamities, such as wars and persecutions. Christians have also cooperated in responding to human needs, such as adequate housing, fair employment, legal aid, and care for the poor, the sick, and the homeless. More recently, Christians have become concerned about defending human rights in political situations, alleviating the effects of economic crises, along with advancing environmental issues and advocating the stewardship of creation. Such Life and Work projects have brought Christians together to express their faith by sharing their blessings, while being blessed by sharing.

Nonetheless, some ecumenical projects cause confrontation rather than consensus. For example, Christian sponsors of projects aiding pregnant women sometimes are at odds because of opposing views regarding abortion—which some churches approve and others forbid. Similarly divisive is the question of the church's involvement in political matters: some Christians feel that churches must speak out against current social ills and take a stance against political corruption; other Christians feel that there should always be an unbridgeable separation between church and state.

These practical differences—rooted in moral convictions—sometimes carry over to the celebration of the Eucharist. For example, Christians who have cooperated on a project may find that they cannot express their unity at the most basic level—celebrating the Eucharist together—since some churches invite all Christians to receive communion, while other churches restrict the reception of the Eucharist to their own members. On the one hand, churches with a policy of "open communion" often affirm that Christ is the host, who invites all to share in the Eucharist; thus, all Christians should gather around Christ at the Lord's table. On the other hand, churches that basically restrict the reception of the Eucharist to their own members usually understand the Eucharist as a sign of existing visible unity; accordingly, sharing the Eucharist together would be a false sign of a visible unity that really does not yet exist.

In any case, like people on a pilgrimage who disagree about how things should be done, the *via missionis* sometimes promotes unity and sometimes frustrates unity. Yet, by its very nature, participation in mission is transformative in at least three different ways. Theologically speaking, the *via missionis* reflects both the immanent life of the Trinity—the Son and Spirit proceed from the Father—and the economic life of the Trinity—the Son is sent into the world to redeem it, and the Spirit continues to sanctify it. Correspondingly, every Christian is a participant in trinitarian life both by grace and by good works.

Second, historically speaking, the *via missionis*, which began with the sending of the apostles by Christ to preach the Gospel to all people, continues in the present with the sending of missionaries to preach the Gospel to those who have not yet heard of Christ. All Christians are called to be missionaries, to be participants in the apostolic work of evangelization—a pilgrimage of proclamation—by living the Gospel in their daily lives. Finally, the *via missionis* is sacramental in the sense that the community of the church is to be a visible sign of the unity of the Trinity. All are called to be one in Christ, as the Son is one with the Father. This oneness is manifested through the coming of the Son into the world and the world's sanctification through the Spirit. All Christians are then called to be ministers of both word and sacrament, ministers of both proclamation and sanctification.[41] Such cannot happen unless Christians are also ministers of unity and mission.

## CONCLUDING REFLECTIONS

The ecumenical movement has many dimensions and so can be seen from many different perspectives. In viewing the ecumenical movement as a pilgrimage of accompaniment—Christians on a journey with Christ and with their companions in Christ—the interrelated dynamics of unity and mission loom large.

In looking at the ecumenical movement from the perspective of pilgrimage, many biblical examples of journeys come to mind—Abraham, Moses, Jesus, Paul, and more—yet, these biblical pilgrimages should be seen not merely as past events but as sacramentally present realities: "*Dios habla hoy*" (God is speaking today). Like the *via crucis*, which is not only a reenactment of the last journey of Jesus but also a re-presentation of that journey, participants in the *via unitatis* must be convinced that they are called to be one in Christ; participants in the *via missionis* must be committed to sharing the one Gospel both with each other and with all others.

Such a commitment to ecumenical pilgrimaging does not mean that the many issues that presently separate Christians—disagreements about the interpretation of the Bible, differences in ecclesiastical structure, obstacles to the mutual recognition and reconciliation of ministry, restrictions about eucharistic sharing, divergent views about a host of moral and sexual issues, and so forth—will be easily resolved or even resolvable. What an ecumenical pilgrimage can provide is not a solution, but a venue where such issues can be honestly discussed by Christians journeying together.

Like the *via crucis*, the *via unitatis* brings Christians together in a pilgrimage that unites them not only as "wayfarers" but also as "way-sharers," as companions on a journey in search of unity. The participants' experience of searching for unity together is part of the process of achieving unity. Similarly, participants on the *via missionis*, by proclaiming the Gospel together, deepen their personal understanding of the Gospel and this deeper understanding brings them closer together.

As a result of pilgrimaging together, participants on the *via unitatis* should grow closer to each other and so grow closer to Christ; reciprocally, by growing closer to Christ, the participants should grow closer to each other. Almost inevitably, participants on the *via unitatis* will want to reach out and share their experience of Christian unity with others; they will want others to be blessed as they have been blessed. In effect, companionship on the *via unitatis* naturally leads people to the *via missionis*.

Accordingly, participation on the *via unitatis* is transformative. Ecumenism must be more than producing consensus statements— however necessary such agreements may be. Ecumenism must be more than collaborative projects—however much needed such charitable projects may be. Ecumenism must also bring people together through living, working, worshiping, and testifying together as Christians. This transformation will affect not only the participants as individuals but also their churches; the *via unitatis* must lead to *koinonia*—a genuine ecumenical fellowship that is inclusive, a companionship that joins others in Christ and reaches out to others through Christ.

Nonetheless, at least until the eschaton, the *via unitatis* is heuristic; it is a road whose horizon is continually expanding by providing both personal enrichment for each Christian pilgrim and spiritual renewal for the Christian community as a whole. Just as participants in the *via crucis* invite others to join the procession, so, too, participants on the *via unitatis* must reach out to others by inviting them to join the ecumenical pilgrimage that seeks the unity of all Christians in faith, hope, and love and that seeks to incorporate all people into the Christian community. In effect, the *via unitatis* and the *via missionis* naturally merge.

Finally, although the *via crucis* might be described as an occasion of grace, a time when participants making the Stations of the Cross seek God's grace, they are acutely aware that grace is always God's to give. Similarly, pilgrims on the *via unitatis*, while seeking the unity that Christ willed for his followers, must humbly recognize that unity is not a human achievement but a grace, God's gift. Similarly, agents of evangelization on the *via missionis* must humbly acknowledge that it is God's grace that must work in them and through them to touch the lives of those being evangelized. Like the participants in the *via crucis* whose commitment is expressed in the refrain—*"Caminemos con Jesús"* (Let us walk with Jesus)—ecumenical pilgrims on the *via unitatis et missionis* must commit themselves to searching together for unity by working together in mission.

## NOTES

1. After Christianity became a recognized religion under Constantine (emperor: 306–37 CE), Christians began retracing the steps of Jesus during the last hours of his life—from the Garden of Gethsemane to the Holy Sepulcher. Since retracing the route came some three centuries after the event, and since the urban geography had changed in the interval, the reconstructed route was both conjectural and disputed.

2. The literature on *religiosidad popular* is abundant. For a theological interpretation, see C. Gilbert Romero, *Hispanic Devotional Piety: Tracing the Biblical Roots* (Maryknoll, NY: Orbis Books, 1991); for a multidisciplinary set of essays, see Anthony Stevens Arroyo and Ana María Díaz Stevens, eds., *An Enduring Flame: Studies on Latino Popular Religiosity,* PARAL (Program for the Analysis of Religion among Latinos) 1 (New York: Bildner Center for Western Hemisphere Studies, 1994).

3. E.g., Egeria (Aetheria) a Spanish (Gallic) woman wrote a detailed record of her pilgrimage to Jerusalem (ca. 381–84) in a text known as *Itinerarium Egeriae* or *Peregrinatio Aetheriae;* see http://go.owu.edu/~o5medww/egeria/index.htm (accessed July 12, 2012).

4. An early example in Bologna is the replica of the Holy Sepulcher in the Church of San Sepolcro, which was once part of a complex of seven churches dating back to the fifth century. Similarly, in the seventeenth century, Patriarch Nikon (1605–81) constructed a replica of Christ's burial place/resurrection site in the Church of the Resurrection at Voskresensk (renamed Istra in 1917)

outside Moscow. An American example can be visited at the Franciscan Monastery in Washington, DC.

5. At each of the fourteen Stations of the Cross are depictions—paintings, sculptures, images—of various scenes from the final hours of the life of Jesus. Most Catholic churches have a set of stations; stations are also erected outdoors. Prior to the eighteenth century, the number of stations varied; in1731, Pope Clement XII fixed the number at fourteen: (1) Jesus is condemned to death; (2) Jesus accepts the cross; (3) Jesus falls the first time;* (4) Jesus meets his mother;* (5) Simon of Cyrene helps Jesus carry the cross; (6) Veronica wipes the face of Jesus;* (7) Jesus falls the second time;* (8) Jesus meets the women of Jerusalem; (9) Jesus falls the third time;* (10) Jesus is stripped of his garments; (11) Jesus is nailed to the cross; (12) Jesus dies on the cross; (13) the body of Jesus is taken down from the cross; (14) the body of Jesus is laid in the tomb. Sometimes a fifteenth station commemorating the resurrection of Jesus is added. The asterisked stations are not mentioned in the Gospels.

6. See, e.g., "*Auto de los Reyes Magos* (ca. 1200)," in *Antología general de la Literatura Española*, ed. Ángel del Río and Amelia A. de del Río, 3rd ed. (New York: Editorial Mensaje, 1982), 1: 18-20.

7. See the detailed and abundantly illustrated treatment by Jaime Lara, *City, Temple, Stage: Eschatological Architecture and Liturgical Theatrics in New Spain* (Notre Dame, IN: University of Notre Dame Press, 2004).

8. Although these religious reenactments are not "sacraments" in the proper sense of the term, they are "sacramental" in the sense of being a "visible manifestation of a salvific reality" (author's definition).

9. A copy of Memling's painting (1470–71, Galleria Sabauda, Turin) may be viewed at http://www.artbible.info/art/large/351.html (accessed July 12, 2012).

10. The donors have been identified, respectively, as Tommaso Portinari, a Florentine banker in Bruges (lower left-hand side) and his wife Maria Baroncelli (lower right-hand side) on the grounds of their resemblance to bust portraits of the couple painted by Memling; see http://www.wga.hu/frames-e.html?/html/m/memling/1early2/04passi.html (accessed July 12, 2012).

11. A list of plays is available at http://en.wikipedia.org/wiki/ Passion_play (accessed July 12, 2012).

12. Insofar as *religiosidad popular* attempts to present biblical events in a specific context, human distortion—presuppositions, preferences, prejudices, etc.—of the biblical original is inevitable, though not excusable.

13. See "New Mexico's Passion Play: The Penitentes and Their Self-Inflicted Tortures"; available at http://sacred-texts.com/bib/cv/ pch/pch86.htm (accessed July 12, 2012).

14. E.g., Adolf Hitler praised the internationally famous *Passionsspiel* at Oberammergau as a convincing portrayal of "the menace of Jewry"; see Collin Hansen, "Why Some Jews Fear the Passion," available at http://www.christianitytoday.com/ch/news/ 2004/feb20.html?start=1 (accessed July 12, 2012).

15. See, e.g., the statement of the Bishops' Committee for Ecumenical and Interreligious Affairs of the National Conference of Catholic Bishops, "Criteria for the Evaluation of Dramatizations of the Passion" (1988); available at http://www.sacredheart.edu/ pages/12452_criteria_for_the_evaluation_of_dramatizations_of_ the_passion_1988_.cfm (accessed July 12, 2012).

16. For *Dios Habla Hoy*, see http://www.biblegateway.com/ versions/index.php?action=getVersionInfo&vid=58 (accessed July 12, 2012).

17. The description of the Christian community as "The Way" is found in the Acts of the Apostles (9:2, etc.). "The Way" was also used as a self-descriptive term by the Qumran community.

18. There are numerous accounts of pilgrimages to Santiago de Compostela; see, e.g., Cees Nooteboom, *Roads to Santiago: A Modern-Day Pilgrimage through Spain*, trans. Ina Rilke (Orlando, FL: First Harvest, 2000).

19. The Náhuatl version of the apparition of Our Lady of Guadalupe was recorded in the *Nican Mopohua* (available at http://weber.ucsd.edu/~dkjordan/nahuatl/nican/NicanMopohua. html [accessed July 12, 2012]); a historical-critical analysis of the apparitions is given by Stafford Poole, *Our Lady of Guadalupe: The Origins and Sources of a Mexican National Symbol, 1531–1797* (Tucson, AZ: University of Arizona Press, 1995).

20. This saying has a variety of forms, e.g., "*se hace camino al andar.*"

21. For a more detailed discussion of "accompaniment," see Roberto S. Goizueta, *Caminemos con Jesús: Toward a Hispanic/Latino Theology of Accompaniment* (Maryknoll, NY: Orbis Books, 1995).

22. Lyrics are available at http://letrasyacordes.net/cancion/38351 (accessed July 12, 2012).

23. For a discussion of different models of unity, see William G. Rusch, *Ecumenical Reception: Its Challenge and Opportunity* (Grand Rapids, MI: William B. Eerdmans Publishing Co., 2007).

24. The major ecumenical agreements in the U.S. are available in Joseph A. Burgess and Jeffrey Gros, eds., *Growing Consensus: Church Dialogues in the United States, 1962–1991* (New York: Paulist Press, 1995); and Lydia Veliko and Jeffrey Gros, eds., *Growing Consensus: Church Dialogues in the United States, 1992–2004* (Washington, DC: U.S. Conference of Catholic Bishops, 2005).

25. A cross and boat, early Christian symbols of the church that embody faith and unity, have long served as the logo of the World Council of Churches; see http://www.oikoumene.org/en/resources/wcc-logo.html (accessed July 12, 2012).

26. One of the anomalies of the *Via Dolorosa* in Jerusalem is that, during the Middle Ages, Eastern pilgrims followed one route, while Western pilgrims followed another.

27. See Walter Kasper, *A Handbook of Spiritual Ecumenism* (Hyde Park, NY: New City Press, 2007); also see E. Glenn Hinson, ed., *Spirituality in Ecumenical Perspective* (Louisville, KY: Westminster/John Knox Press, 1993).

28. Vatican II, *Unitatis Redintegratio* (Decree on Ecumenism), §8a: "This change of heart and holiness of life, along with public and private prayer for the unity of Christians, should be regarded as the soul of the whole ecumenical movement, and merits the name, 'spiritual ecumenism'"; available at http://www.vatican.va/archive/hist_councils/ii_vatican_council/documents/vat-ii_decree_19641121_unitatis-redintegratio_en.html (accessed July 12, 2012).

29. See, e.g., the poem, "The Pillar of the Cloud," by John Henry Newman (1801–90), which is sung as a hymn, "Lead, Kindly Light"; available at http://www.newmanreader.org/works/verses/verse90.html (accessed July 12, 2012).

30. "Faith and Order" refers to matters of doctrine and "order" in the sense of church organization or structures.

31. See John T. Ford, "Koinonia and Roman Catholic Ecclesiology," *Ecumenical Trends* 26 (March 1997): 10–12.

32. The phrase cited is from the Third World Conference on Faith and Order at Lund, Sweden (1952); available at http://ecumenism.net/archive/encounter.htm (accessed July 12, 2012), #3.

33. A classic, but unfortunate, example of the popular rejection of ecumenical consensus statements is the case of the pre-Reformation Council of Florence (1439), whose agreements attempting to resolve the schism between the Eastern and Western Churches were promptly repudiated by Eastern Christians. See Joseph Gill, *The Council of Florence* (Cambridge, U.K.: University Press, 1961).

34. The most notorious example of a pilgrimage gone awry is the Fourth Crusade (1202–04), which set out as a pilgrimage to liberate the Holy Land but, en route, sacked the Byzantine Christian capital of Constantinople, thereby creating a long-lasting animosity between Eastern and Western Christians.

35. Originally known as the Church Unity Octave, the Week of Prayer for Christian Unity was initiated by Fr. Paul Wattson, S.A., at Graymoor, New York, in 1908; see http://www.geii.org/week_of_prayer_for_christian_unity/index.html (accessed July 12, 2012).

36. John T. Ford, "Theological Language and Ecumenical Methodology," in *Ancient Faith and American-Born Churches: Dialogues between Christian Traditions*, ed. Ted Campbell, Ann K. Riggs, and Gilbert W. Stafford, 15–23 (New York and Mahwah, NJ: Paulist Press, 2006); available at http://www.ncccusa.org/unity/fandoford.html (accessed July 12, 2012).

37. Edinburgh Conference, Commission VIII; see http://www.archive.org/stream/reportofcommissi08worluoft#page/n5/mode/2up (accessed July 12, 2012), 2–3, 5.

38. "Faith and Order" united with "Life and Work" to form the World Council of Churches (WCC) in 1948; the International Missionary Council became part of the WCC in 1961; the World Council of Christian Education joined the WCC in 1971.

39. E.g., Vatican II, *Unitatis Redintegratio* (§1), after declaring that, "The restoration of unity among all Christians is one of the principal concerns of the Second Vatican Council," echoed the

teaching of Edinburgh that the division among Christians "openly contradicts the will of Christ, scandalizes the world, and damages the holy cause of preaching the Gospel to every creature."

40. See http://ecumenism.net/archive/encounter.htm (accessed July 12, 2012), #3.

41. See the section on "The Calling of the Whole People of God" *Baptism, Eucharist and Ministry*, Faith and Order Paper 111 (Geneva: World Council of Churches, 1982); available at http://www.oikoumene.org/en/resources/documents/wcc-commissions/faith-and-order-commission/i-unity%20-the-church-and-its-mission/baptism-eucharist-and-ministry-faith-and-order-paper-no-111-the-lima-text.html (accessed July 12, 2012).

# 2

# SCRIPTURE AND MISSION

*Michael Kinnamon*

One way of approaching my assigned topic—Scripture and mission, in the context of Faith and Order's historic concern to promote the visible unity of the church—is simply to ask: What does the Bible say about mission? Are there scriptural themes or paradigms that can be commonly affirmed by the various Christian traditions?

My focus, however, is less on context than on methodology: How has Scripture been used by different "camps" in the contemporary debate over mission? More specifically, I want to compare the understanding of biblical authority and interpretation set forth in the series of mission conferences identified with the Lausanne Continuation Committee (often referred to as "Evangelical") with the understanding found in those conferences sponsored by the World Council of Churches' Commission on World Mission and Evangelism (often referred to as "ecumenical").[1] To what extent have divergent understandings of biblical authority contributed to interchurch tension? How might the churches move beyond current divisions over the Bible as a source for theologies of mission?

What follows is based on a fundamental assumption: Christians agree—at least in their churches' official statements!—that Scripture holds a unique place of authority in shaping the faith and practice of the church. Scripture, in the words of the Second World Conference on Faith and Order (Edinburgh, 1937), "affords the primary norm for the church's teaching, worship, and life."[2] This affirmation implies that the church must continually test its witness, its understanding and practice of mission, against the witness of Scripture. Both the World Council of Churches (WCC) and the National Council of Churches (NCC), in their respective "basis" statements, name Scripture as the source of the churches' shared confession and common mission, which is certainly in line with the Lausanne Covenant and associated mission conferences.

The problems come when we consider how Scripture is related to other possible sources of authority and how (and whether) it is interpreted. These are the issues to which I now turn.

## LAUSANNE MOVEMENT

I will begin with the Evangelical position, since it is the easier of the two to describe. The authors of the Lausanne Covenant, a key document created by the Lausanne movement, in its second paragraph, state their belief in "the divine inspiration, truthfulness, and authority of both the Old and New Testament scriptures in their entirety as the only written Word of God, without error in all that it affirms, and the only infallible rule of faith and practice."[3] The Holy Spirit still speaks to Christians today, but does so preeminently *through the Bible*, illuminating the minds of believers in order that they might perceive the truth set forth on its pages.

Thirty-six years later, the Evangelical world mission conference in Cape Town (2010) reaffirmed that the whole Bible is the word of God, "supremely and uniquely authoritative," "true and trustworthy in all it affirms." It nuanced these statements, however, by acknowledging that the Bible is "spoken and written through human authors," and that Christians love Scripture because of the one who is revealed through it.[4]

Both Lausanne and Cape Town support their discussion of mission with a myriad of specific biblical verses. This, I take it, is not simply "proof-texting" but a reflection of the participants' conviction that Scripture is trustworthy in all its parts, and that all theology must be grounded firmly and solely in the Bible. Both acknowledge, at least in passing, that the testimony of Scripture is diverse, although the emphasis is far less on such diversity than on the essential unity of the biblical narrative.

What I am calling the ecumenical understanding of mission is presented in two by-now-standard texts from the WCC: "Mission and Evangelism—An Ecumenical Affirmation"[5] (ME), sent to the churches for study in 1982, and "Mission and Evangelism in Unity

Today"[6] (MEUT), published in 1999. Neither document offers the kind of general statement about the authority of Scripture found in Lausanne and Cape Town, but it is clear that the Bible is not seen as the only source for a theology of mission. For example, ME refers in several places to "the biblical stances and ancient creeds"[7]—an indication that the WCC includes Orthodox as well as Protestant Churches in its membership.

Particular passages of Scripture are cited in ME, but infrequently. Instead, the text points toward overarching scriptural themes ("the church of Jesus Christ is called to preach Good News to the poor following the example of its Lord who was incarnated as poor, who lived as one among them and gave to them the promise of the Kingdom of God"[8]) or echoes Scripture without explicit acknowledgment ("the Spirit of God is constantly at work in ways that pass human understanding and in places that to us are least expected"[9]). The 1999 text makes a greater effort to show the biblical foundation of its argument, but only in its opening section. In both documents, there is a good deal of emphasis on the church's dialogue with its contemporary context.

This appeal to other sources of authority is continued in the meeting that paralleled the Evangelical gathering in Cape Town, known as Edinburgh 2010.[10] The "Listening Group Report"[11] from that conference contains almost no direct biblical references (the two citations are, predictably, from Luke 4 and John 17); and a background paper for the conference, entitled "Foundations for Mission,"[12] helps explain why. According to the paper, a holistic mission practice will be grounded not only in the Bible but in experience. In fact, experience is stressed because, as the authors put it, this allows us to hear those who have long been denied a voice in discussions of mission "due to the politics of power," and helps overcome the tendency to prioritize the theoretical over the practical.[13] Of course, not all experience is as authoritative, but "only that which resonates with the life, ministry, death and resurrection of Jesus Christ"[14]—which implies the need for experience to be in constant dialogue with Scripture.

The other great emphasis in the paper is diversity. Biblical texts, it argues, are generally "polysemic"[15]—that is, they have multiple layers of meaning that are not exhausted by any single interpretation. And the Bible as a whole is astonishingly diverse, reflecting the plurality of its human authors and their contexts. Attempts to reduce this diversity are often simply efforts of those with power to impose their standards or understandings on others—efforts that have been the cause of great conflict in the church, undermining its mission.

Again, however, this does not mean there are no limits to the diversity of interpretation. The norm, according to the paper, is this: "God's unconditional love shown in the cross and resurrection of Jesus Christ"[16]—the definitive witness to which is found, of course, in the Bible.

Let me venture beyond the words of these texts we have been examining. The authors of the Lausanne Covenant, if I am not mistaken, are suspicious of approaches to Scripture, including an overemphasis on historical criticism, that can undermine the Bible's authority in the life of the church and lead to a loss of what they call "biblical substance" (something which they see, especially, in the more liberal Protestant Churches). The authors of the "ecumenical" reports, particularly Edinburgh 2010, insist on bringing Scripture into dialogue with experience and underscoring its diversity because they are suspicious of approaches that, in their judgment, allow the Bible to be used by those with social and political power for their own purposes. To put it another way: One group fears that the Bible will be turned into an inflexible rule book that inhibits our ability to follow the creative leading of the Spirit—or, worse, that it will be used as a club to beat up on ideological opponents. The other fears that the God-given norms of Christian faith will be lost sight of in favor of our own agenda, that the emphasis on diversity will undercut the authoritative mandate to proclaim the Gospel.

# WORLD COUNCIL OF CHURCHES

The understanding of Scripture and its authority set forth in the reports from WCC-sponsored mission conferences is more fully explored and defended in a series of reports from Faith and Order conferences or working groups in the 1960s and 70s. I do not mean to suggest that the ecumenical movement is a wholly consistent enterprise! It is quite likely that drafters for Edinburgh 2010 knew little of these earlier statements on biblical authority and hermeneutics. But it still may be useful to review their conclusions in order to discern trends in the movement.[17]

The first report I want us to note is from the Fourth World Conference and Faith and Order (Montreal, 1963). This meeting, which was the first WCC-related conference to welcome a delegation from the Roman Catholic Church, dealt head-on with a central Reformation Era dispute: the relationship of Scripture and Tradition. Tradition is here understood as "the Gospel itself, transmitted from generation to generation in and by the church, Christ himself present in the life of the Church."[18] The Bible is, as it were, Tradition written down at an early stage of its development, and, as such, is the criterion—the plumb line—by which subsequent Tradition is measured. This means that Scripture and Tradition "are so intertwined that neither of them, taken in itself, can simply be used as authoritative."[19] Talk of *sola scriptura* is, at best, unduly polemical. The church exists, in the language of Montreal, "by the Tradition of the Gospel (the *paradosis* of the *kerygma*) testified in Scripture, transmitted in and by the Church through the power of the Holy Spirit"[20]—a formulation that has been foundational to the shared work of Catholics, Orthodox, and Protestants on such documents as *Baptism, Eucharist and Ministry*. It seems to me that it has also had an impact on the mission statements discussed above, especially ME.

Four years after Montreal, the WCC's Faith and Order Commission met in Bristol, England, where it considered a working group report entitled, "The Significance of the Hermeneutical Problem in the Ecumenical Movement." While earlier reports on the subject had regarded diversity as a problem to be overcome in order to discern the common biblical testimony, Bristol affirmed the theological importance of scriptural diversity. Indeed, any responsibly, biblically grounded theology, it suggests, will not gloss over diversities, even contradictions, in the texts, and will avoid forced harmonization.[21] This need not detract from the underlying unity of the Bible, but it does entail a particular approach. A participant in this work, Ellen Flesseman-van Leer, summarizes some of the implications:

> [T]oday, greater store is set on Faith and Order documents being imbued with a biblical spirit than giving many textual quotations. The hermeneutical studies have helped us to realize that the diversity of traditions in the bible makes it difficult to work with proof texts. They have taught us, moreover, that a careful analysis of the literary and contextual background of each text is required before it can be quoted and that no text is directly applicable to any present-day dogmatic or ethical [or missional] question. It can be said that, as a consequence, the Faith and Order Commission has become more restrained but also more responsible in quoting the Bible, so that fewer explicit textual quotations will be found in recent documents.[22]

We clearly see this same restraint as well in documents having to do with mission.

A third study in this series, this one on "The Authority of the Bible," was ready in time for the Commission's next meeting, which took place in Louvain in 1971. The main assertion is that authority is not a quality inherent in the Bible per se, but is a relational concept: the Bible is authoritative in so far as it leads people to faith. The report goes on to insist that the Bible is not "a standard to which we must conform in all the questions arising in our lives... a norm for every problem and every situation."[23] The Bible does have a place of priority for the church's thought and action; but that is because it is "witness to the God who gives us freedom in Christ."[24] It follows that Scripture must be read in the context of the major issues of our day, a dialogical process that begins in the Bible itself.

Faith and Order returned to this "ecumenical reflection on hermeneutics" in the 1990s, producing a study booklet entitled *A Treasure in Earthen Vessels*. I will simply note that this more recent work, as I read it, shows greater sensitivity to the dangers pointed to by Evangelical colleagues. The following captures the flavor of the text: "Although embedded in the life and times in which it was given written form, scripture, as inspired testimony, provides a measure for the truth and meaning of human stories today. In this sense, hermeneutical priority belongs to the Word of God, which has critical authority over all traditions....In the process of interpretation, which involves the particular experiences of the reader, scripture is the primary norm and criterion."[25]

## NEED FOR BETTER BIBLICAL EXEGESIS

It is now time to be clear about my own perspective. I am convinced, following a careful study of these texts, that both the Evangelical and ecumenical camps have important concerns regarding the use of Scripture, but that *neither* actually engages Scripture, "wrestles" with it, in a way that allows the Bible to challenge our prejudices and presuppositions. In other words, we need to do better biblical exegesis in our ecumenical work. William Sloan Coffin once wrote that Christians often use Scripture the way a drunk uses a lamp post—more for support than illumination. I have the same feeling after my review of these otherwise often impressive texts.

The Lausanne stream obviously claims that Scripture is important in its thinking about mission, listing numerous passages at the end of each paragraph (Lausanne) or in the notes for each paragraph (Cape Town). But we are seldom, if ever, told *how* these particular texts support the argument of the paragraph or *why* these texts are cited and others ignored. It is hard not to conclude that biblical texts are selected because they reinforce a theological or, worse, ideological position.

For example, the Lausanne Covenant, while affirming that Christians should share in God's concern for justice and reconciliation throughout human society, also makes clear its opposition to liberation theology when it declares that "reconciliation with man is not reconciliation with God, nor is social action evangelism, nor is political liberation salvation."[26] It is hardly surprising, therefore, that out of 138 biblical texts cited, only four are from the prophets—a favorite part of Scripture for liberation-oriented Christians.

Or, let us take the divisive question of the place of other religions in God's plan of salvation. The Lausanne Covenant is unambiguous in its theological position: "There is no other name by which we must be saved...those who reject Christ repudiate the joy of salvation and condemn themselves to eternal separation from God"[27] and bolsters this with such predictable texts as Acts 4:12 and John 3:16–19. Liberal Christians should not ignore these passages! But neither should conservatives overlook Matthew 25 (the parable of the Last Judgment in which the separation of sheep and goats is not dependent on confessing Christ) or Romans 11 (where Paul declares that God has not rejected God's people, the Jews)—neither of which is cited in Lausanne. Matthew 11:28 is in the list ("Come to me, all you that are weary...."), but not Matthew 7:21 ("Not everyone who says to me, 'Lord, Lord,' will enter the Kingdom of heaven, but only the one who does the will of my Father in heaven"). Ephesians 1:20–21 is cited (God has raised Christ above all rule and authority), but there is no wrestling with how this might apply to individual decisions of faith.

The WCC documents do no better when it comes to taking Scripture seriously. In some places, the Bible is used as mere ornamentation ("From the experiences of 'so great a cloud of witnesses' [Hebrews 12:1] over the centuries, it is therefore imperative to convey the message that Christian spirituality leads to holistic healing"[28]). More often, however, it is introduced to support an argument ("The Good News of the Kingdom is a challenge to the structures of society [Eph. 3:9–10, 6:12]"[29]), without exploring whether or how the cited texts are appropriate in that context. To take only one other example, MEUT, the WCC text from 1999, in a paragraph arguing that the mission of God has no limits or barriers, invokes the parable of the sheep and the goats (Matthew 25),[30] even though scholars generally agree that "the least of these" is a reference to the followers of Christ, not all of humanity. It may, of course, be appropriate to extend the parable for that theological purpose, but a case needs to be made. We need "to wrestle" with the text.

In short, there is no real exegesis in any of the documents that allows us to hear the voice of Scripture in its entire nuance. I do not doubt that many of the authors of these texts have, themselves, engaged in serious biblical study, but this does not come through the mission statements. Readers are left with the impression that Scripture is used to bolster predetermined positions, not listened to on its own terms.

I have two rather obvious suggestions for addressing this problem. First, insist on being attentive to the whole of Scripture, not just those parts we find most compatible. The surest guard against proof-texting is to take seriously—even argue against!—those passages we find problematic. In particular, WCC texts emphasize the diversity of the Bible, but then do not show it. Allow that diversity to speak. Invite readers into the conversation found in Scripture itself. Simply listing diverse texts is obviously not a theological argument; but no biblically grounded theology can pretend that the Bible speaks with univocal voice.

Of course, the brevity of corporately produced statements does not give much space for exegesis. Readers could, however, be directed to such work in scholarly volumes that have wide acceptance. David Bosch's extensive treatment of mission in Paul and the Gospels (Part I of his germinal book, *Transforming Mission*) comes quickly to mind, as does the *Biblical Foundations for Mission* by Catholic scholars Donald Senior and Carroll Stuhlmueller.[31] Another example of importance to me is Walter Brueggemann's essay, "The Bible and Mission: Some Interdisciplinary Implications for Teaching," in which he examines 1 Kings 4:20–28, Deuteronomy 19:1–10, 1 Samuel 2:1–10, Hosea, 2:2–23, and Isaiah 46 and 47 as diverse models for mission.[32] As Brueggemann writes, "Church practice…tends to reduce the Bible to a set of simple moves which can be made in an identifiable, predictable way. Against that, scripture study must insist on a range of alternative moves which remain in deep tension with each other but are all biblical."[33]

Second, insist on reading the Bible in the widest possible community of interpreters, including those from other theological "camps." If I dare say it this way, there is something very unbiblical about reading the Bible in like-minded enclaves! Listening to others as they interpret is the surest way to guard against hearing only what we want to hear.

This suggestion points toward what the long-time director of the WCC's department of biblical studies, Hans-Ruedi Weber, calls "ecumenical spirituality." Let the Bible speak to us together, he urges, even when we do not agree on how to understand its authority. Talking *about* the Bible can be divisive; listening *to* it in common can be converting and uniting. We need not acknowledge that the other group is more correct than we are to acknowledge that the witness of any group, including our own, is inevitably partial in light of the fuller truth to which we may be led through study of the word of God.[34]

I will end by suggesting three other points that may offer common ground when it comes to the scriptural basis for mission (or anything else). They are as follows:

1. I hope Christians can commonly affirm that, while the Bible is not the only source for constructing a theology of mission (Tradition and experience are inevitable partners), it is the *privileged* source, the one to which we must appeal in making our case. The Montreal report acknowledges that the criterion for determining "genuine Tradition" is "the holy scriptures rightly interpreted."[35] And Edinburgh 2010 affirms that experience must be tested by Scripture if there are to be limits to the diversity of missional practice.[36] The real point, however, is deeper. People will not know how to interpret their experience as experience of God unless they know something of the biblical narrative that gives language and concepts for such interpretation.

2. The pendulum in the church swings between an emphasis on diversity and an emphasis on unity—showing the need, in my judgment, for them to be held in tension. The biblical treatment of mission is demonstrably diverse (Senior and Stuhlmueller conclude their exhaustive study with these words: "In the Bible, there is no fixed pattern for mission but a plurality of responses to different circumstances"[37]); but beneath this is a unifying narrative of the Father who has sent the Son that, through the power of the Holy Spirit, the church might be sent forth in mission. Scripture itself— for example, in the account of creation or in the image of the body of Christ—paints not simply a picture of diversity but of a unity that is wondrously diverse.

3. All of this underscores my conviction that the Bible is authoritative for the life and mission of the church. But I also hope we can affirm that there is no simple, direct move from the

Bible to contemporary mission practice—a point reinforced by all of the scholars to whom I earlier referred.[38] Its best use, as Weber suggests, is to provide vision, not specific strategy.[39] This is of great ecumenical importance. Christians can divide over strategies—indeed, it seems to be a law of human nature that the more concrete the issue, the stronger the conviction!—without undermining the essential unity we have through our shared commitment to participate in God's (diverse) mission in allegiance to Jesus Christ, testimony to whom we find preeminently in Scripture.

## NOTES

1. Evangelical mission conferences were held in Lausanne in 1974, Manila in 1989, and Cape Town in 2010. During this same period, conferences organized by the Commission on World Mission and Evangelism were held in Bangkok (1973), Melbourne (1980), San Antonio (1989), Salvador (1996), Athens (2005), and Edinburgh (2010).

2. Leonard Hodgson, ed., *The Second World Conference on Faith and Order* (New York: MacMillan, 1938), 229.

3. "Lausanne Covenant," in *The Ecumenical Movement: An Anthology of Key Texts and Voices,* ed. Michael Kinnamon and Brian E. Cope (Geneva: WWC, 1997), 359. It is par. 2 in the Covenant.

4. The "Cape Town Commitment" is available at www.lausanne.org/ctcommitment. These quotations come from section 6, "We Love God's Word" (accessed March 18, 2012).

5. "Mission and Evangelism—An Ecumenical Affirmation," in *The Ecumenical Movement: An Anthology of Key Texts and Voices,* ed. Michael Kinnamon and Brian E. Cope (Geneva: WWC, 1997), 372–83.

6. "Mission and Evangelism in Unity Today," *International Review of Mission* 88, nos. 348–349 (January-April 1999): 109–27.

7. For example, see "Mission and Evangelism—An Ecumenical Affirmation," par. 19.

8. Ibid., par. 32. A famous example of supporting an argument by appeal to broad scriptural themes came at the WCC's

assembly in Uppsala, Sweden (1968), where a session on racism was juxtaposed to a dance/drama of the life and message of the prophet Amos.

9. Ibid., par. 43.

10. The report of the meeting is published as Kirsteen Kim and Andrew Anderson, eds., *Edinburgh 2010: Mission Today and Tomorrow* (Oxford: Regnum Books, 2011). This conference, like that in Cape Town, was intended to commemorate the great 1910 world mission conference, also held in Edinburgh. That event gave rise to the International Missionary Council and is often cited as the symbolic beginning of the modern ecumenical movement.

11. *Edinburgh 2010*, 309–20.

12. Daryl Balia and Kirsteen Kim, eds., *Edinburgh 2010: Witnessing to Christ Today*, vol. 2 (Oxford: Regnum Books, 2010), 10–33.

13. Balia, *Edinburgh 2010: Witnessing,* 12. The paper suggests throughout that the experiences of those at the margins of society should be privileged as being foundational for mission and theology.

14. Ibid., 17. The report from the conference (*Edinburgh 2010*, 12) indicates that the heavy emphasis on experience was a highly contested part of the "Foundations for Mission" paper.

15. Ibid.

16. Ibid.

17. There is no room in this short paper to summarize adequately these reports on biblical authority and hermeneutics. The full reports can be found in Ellen Flesseman-van Leer, ed., *The Bible: Its Authority and Interpretation in the Ecumenical Movement* (Geneva: WCC, 1980). This booklet is Faith and Order paper no. 99.

18. "Scripture, Tradition and Traditions," in *The Bible: Its Authority and Interpretation in the Ecumenical Movement,* ed. Ellen Flesseman-van Leer (Geneva: WCC, 1980), 19. It is par. 39 in the Montreal report.

19. Ibid., 3. The words are those of Flesseman-van Leer in her "Introduction" to the volume.

20. Ibid., 20 (par. 45 in the report).

21. "The Significance of the Hermeneutical Problem in the Ecumenical Movement," in *The Bible: Its Authority and Interpreta-*

*tion in the Ecumenical Movement,* ed. Ellen Flesseman-van Leer (Geneva: WCC, 1980), 31–32. It is not coincidental, I think, that this new appreciation for diversity in Scripture came at a time when *koinonia* was first being explored as a model for (understanding of) unity in ecumenical dialogues. The Bristol report was the first to suggest that "the awareness of the differences within the Bible will lead us towards a deeper understanding of our divisions and will help us to interpret them more readily as possible and legitimate interpretations of one and the same Gospel" ("The Significance of the Hermeneutical Problem," 40).

22. Ibid., 11.

23. "The Authority of the Bible," in *The Bible: Its Authority and Interpretation in the Ecumenical Movement,* ed. Ellen Flesseman-van Leer (Geneva: WCC, 1980), 56.

24. Ibid.

25. *A Treasure in Earthen Vessels: An Instrument for an Ecumenical Reflection on Hermeneutics* (Geneva: WCC, 1998), 19, 20–21. This booklet is Faith and Order paper no. 182.

26. "Lausanne Covenant," par. 5.

27. Ibid., par. 3.

28. "Mission and Evangelism in Unity Today," 34.

29. "Mission and Evangelism—An Ecumenical Affirmation," par. 14. Ephesians 3 is a particularly curious choice in this context, since it speaks of the wisdom of God being made known "to the rulers and authorities in the heavenly places."

30. Ibid., par. 11.

31. David J. Bosch, *Transforming Mission: Paradigm Shifts in Theology of Mission* (Maryknoll, NY: Orbis, 1991); and Donald Senior and Carroll Stuhlmueller, *The Biblical Foundations for Mission* (Maryknoll, New York: Orbis, 1983).

32. Walter A. Brueggemann, "The Bible and Mission: Some Interdisciplinary Implications for Teaching," in *Missiology: An International Review* 10, no. 4 (October, 1982): 397–412. The mission reports we have been examining generally affirm that the whole Bible should be used as a foundation for mission, but there are few references in them to the Old Testament. The Hebrew Bible is never cited, for example, in "Mission and Evangelism in Unity Today."

33. Brueggemann, The Bible and Mission, 397.

34. Hans-Ruedi Weber, "The Bible in the Ecumenical Movement," in *A History of the Ecumenical Movement*, ed. John Briggs, Mercy Amba Oduyoye, and Georges Tsetsis (Geneva: WCC, 2004), 3:195–215. See esp. 210–11.

35. "Scripture, Tradition and Traditions," 19. It is par. 51 in the Montreal report.

36. Balia, *Edinburgh 2010: Witnessing*, 17.

37. Senior, *The Biblical Foundations for Mission*, 343.

38. For example, see Bosch, *Transforming Mission*, 24.

39. See also Senior, *The Biblical Foundations for Mission*, 343.

# 3

# THE MARKS AS SIGNPOSTS OF THE JOURNEY TO UNITY IN MISSION

*Mitzi J. Budde*

## I. THE MARKS AS SIGNPOSTS OF THE JOURNEY TO UNITY IN MISSION

Several years ago, I was invited to be a guest lecturer on the ecumenical agreements of my denomination for a class at a Protestant seminary. As I taught the class, it became clear to me that the students were well-informed about the Reformation divisions of the church, so much so that they became quite concerned to realize that their church had entered into full communion agreements with some of the modern-day denominational descendants of these divisions. Finally, I said to them, "You're talking about the Reformation as if it were yesterday." One of the students responded, "For us, it is like yesterday. We just finished the course two weeks ago!" At that moment, I realized that they had internalized the sixteenth-century divisions of Christianity for themselves as the key component of their identity, as the norm whereby they, as future clergy, would measure others, both inside and outside the church. Each new generation rediscovers and redraws the battle lines of division.

The marks of the church—"one, holy, catholic, and apostolic," as we confess in the Nicene Creed—challenge us to bridge the battle lines. The marks, classically considered to be notes or signs of the substance of faith, should not be considered merely a static definition of church. Rather, they are a process. We might view them as signposts on the pilgrimage, the Global Positioning System, if you will, guiding us on the journey to dialogue, witness, and engagement. The marks can be considered action verbs by which we encounter God (holiness) and engage the people of God (catholicity) in order to reveal the deep unity that exists in Jesus Christ (oneness) and transmit the faith of the church in ways that will speak to future generations, while remaining faithful to the tradition (apostolicity). The marks delineate the ways by which the Christ event becomes the church event, the way Christ's mission becomes the church's mission. No individual church can have the fullness of the marks of the church within itself; these marks "relate both to the nature of God's own being and to the practical demands of authentic mission,"[1] in the context of the whole church. This is the gift and the call of ecumenism: to guide us to unity in mission.

The journey of ecumenism is to discern how fully one's own tradition reveals the marks of the church in its pilgrimage and to learn from fellow pilgrims how other traditions might broaden our own understanding of the ways and works of God. Pilgrims journey together for sharing and for safety. The church's pilgrimage provides sustenance through Word and Sacrament and safety through discernment and discipline. The church is the place created by Christ for a reliable encounter with the Holy Spirit through the Gospel proclaimed, the sacraments celebrated, the fellowship of prayer and worship, and mutual affirmation and admonition. Church is the place where we are challenged to grow in our Christian walk, a place to be hallowed as a Christian people, a place where we are being made holy day by day, a place to be formed more deeply into the *imago Dei* we were created to be and to root out the sin that clings so closely. God leads God's people on the pilgrim way through the work of the Spirit, the apostolic ministry, and the priesthood of all believers, as God's people seek to discern the road and travel faithfully together with one another, in order to reach out to and engage the world. Our ecumenical work, thereby, draws us into mission, challenging us to deep listening, authentic engagement, and deepening trust and understanding in our pluralistic society.

Mission is first and foremost God's work in calling the church to share its message with others. It is God's event in creating, calling, converting, claiming, and caring for God's people as individuals and as the faith community that is the church. The church participates in God's mission (*missio Dei*) and is sent out in thankful response to God's activity. The "sent-ness" is part of the very being of the Christian Church. The mission of the church is to provide for faith through a community of believers bearing Christ's name, sustained by the

Holy Spirit, accompanying one another on the pilgrimage of faith, and journeying together from generation to generation and across the globe. Yet, this call to mission challenges the Christian Church at several levels: how we effectively engage the cultural context in which we live, how we bear witness to those who have not heard the Gospel, how we dialogue with other religions in a pluralistic society.

In their recent book, *God is Back: How the Global Revival of Faith is Changing the World*, John Micklethwait and Adrian Wooldridge have observed that the American capitalist paradigm prevails in the religious marketplace in American society. They note that parishes and megachurches—and their "pastorpreneur" leaders—have to compete with one another to keep and grow their market share of available practicing Christian consumers for their product: a particular form of practicing religion. This competition, the authors assert, has had a positive influence upon religious commitment in America, which has effectively exported this model of religiosity to the rest of the world. They argue that American society models for the rest of the world a place where religion and modernity and popular culture can thrive side-by-side, each informed by the other, citing multiple examples from their research on the intersections among strong religious identity, outreach (mission), and pluralism (respect for the other who believes differently). However, they also acknowledge the complicated role that religion plays in international politics today and the level of ignorance about others' religious beliefs that characterizes American society today.[2] These are some of the challenges that confront us as Christian people in a pluralistic context, who seek both unity in Christ and communication with those of other faiths and those of no faith at all.

## II. THE MARKS OF THE CHURCH IN ACTION

### A. Oneness—To Reveal the Unity That Exists in Jesus Christ

The first mark of the church, "one," identifies the deep unity that exists as a gift of God, a gift given by the power and presence of Christ's life-giving Spirit. It is modeled on the perfect unity that is the relationship of the persons of the Holy Trinity with one another (John 17). Through Christ, the people of God are invited to share in that relationship. The church is the earthly expression, a dim reflection, of the relationship between the persons of the triune God. Human participation in this relationship is a pure gift of grace.

By gathering around Word and Sacrament as the church, we bear witness to the world that we are joined and knit together with other Christians. In ecumenical work, we proclaim and make visible the deep unity that we share in Christ. We cannot create unity, but as Christian communities, we can create a witness to the unity that is given to us in Christ as a gift of the Holy Spirit. The mission of the church is the way in which it responds to the call to make that unity visible: in our lives and our words, in our actions and our worship, the ways in which we live together faithfully in shared witness to that ultimate reality that is our true unity in Christ.

In the late 1980s, the National Council of the Churches of Christ in the U.S.A. study group on the Unity of the Church and the Renewal of the Human Community explored how the church needs to be inclusive of the poor, the marginalized, those suffering with AIDS, and those of ethnicities traditionally excluded, in order to have authentic unity. "In the view of the working group on AIDS, the test of how well the church lives out its witness to unity in Christ is *how well it breaks down barriers* at points where people are being excluded."[3] There is no place for caste distinctions in the church. True unity is expressed when diversities are honored and oppression based on class, race, or gender is overthrown, when the voices of all who bear the name of Christ are heard and honored as fully representative of the Christian experience.

Oneness is about being clear about one's own identity, as an individual and as a church, in order to be in relationship with integrity with other Christians and with those of other faiths. It is about understanding who we are, what we stand for, bearing witness to what we know to be true, in order to encounter and engage the "other" honestly, openly, and noncoercively. We make the pilgrimage of faith an ecumenical journey together, "so that the world may believe" (John 17:21), so that those who do not profess Christ might discern in us the deep unity that we claim in Christ, despite the powerful visible evidence of the church's brokenness. The rich history of our individual denominational forms of witness in the past can join together and become more coherent through the bridges built from the results of theological dialogue and ecumenical relationships, guided through prayer.

## B. Holiness—To Encounter God

God alone is holy; the church's holiness derives from God's. "For you are a people holy to the Lord your God; the Lord your God has chosen you out of all the peoples on earth to be his people...because the Lord loved you" (Deut 7:6, 8). The church is holy as it reflects God's holiness as the body of Christ, and even that is a dim reflection, clouded by sin. The church reflects God's holiness as faithful stewards of God's gifts to the church: Word and Sacraments, which are, in Orthodox phraseology, "God's holy gifts for God's holy people." The church is called to use these gifts both to *be* disciples and to *make* disciples.[4] Thereby, the people of God are equipped and empowered for the work of mission through Word and Sacrament, doxology and prayer.

Baptism is the sacrament of unity and the call to mission. Baptism sends Christians out to "participate in the mission of witness and service which is the continuing work of the Spirit of Christ."[5] To be united with Christ through baptism means to be united with Christ's church in all of its expressions, from local parish to universal church, across divisions and across denominations, and to be united with all those who are also baptized into Christ. Each Christian is "baptized *by* a particular church *into* the one church."[6] That sacramental unity, however, is not yet complete, since as yet not all churches recognize one another's baptismal practices and since some churches have chosen to use baptismal formulas that are not accepted by the church universal. And, while some parts of the body of Christ have found theological expression that provides for shared Eucharist and recognition of ministries, the majority of Christian bodies have not yet reached ecumenical achievement in one or both of these areas.

The theological principle that we are simultaneously saints and sinners applies both to Christians as individuals and to the corporate body, the church. Protestants understand the church as always in a process of reformation: *ecclesia semper reformanda*, the church must always be reformed and reforming. Pope Benedict XVI reflects on the church's holiness in this way: "It is holiness that radiates as the holiness of Christ from the midst of the Church's sin…One could actually say that precisely in her paradoxical combination of holiness and unholiness the Church is in fact the shape taken by grace in this world."[7]

Joint prayer with each other feeds the hunger that impels us to keep at the ecumenical work that will lead to unity in baptism, Eucharist, and ministry. Prayer for one another sustains the bonds of holy friendship in Christ in the absence of sharing the Lord's Supper together. A century of prayer for Christian unity has brought about great ecumenical accomplishments in the twentieth century. Holy practices guide us on the journey of spiritual ecumenism.

Many Christians have had the experience that I did recently of worshiping in a cathedral halfway around the globe from home and participating in the liturgy in a totally unfamiliar language. The familiarity of the liturgical *ordo*, the recognition of the name of Jesus, the sense of unity with the unknown Christians all around provide an encounter with the holy and an awareness of the catholicity of the faith. A form of Pentecost takes place as strangers from various places and stations in this life become friends in Christ and fellow pilgrims on the road, sharing one meal.

The church encounters and engages the holiness of God through penitence, prayer, praise, pilgrimage, patience, and petition. Prayer empowers the mission of the church, and prayer with and for each other is at the heart of the ecumenical vocation.

## C. Catholicity—To Engage the People of God in Seeking Unity in Mission

The classic definition of catholicity comes from Vincent of Lerins in the fifth century: "that which is believed everywhere, always, and by everyone." This definition defines the mission of ecumenism, seeking the truth of the Gospel that transcends denominational ideology and human boundaries. Measuring one's own theological convictions against Vincent's classic definition can be a useful mile marker on the journey to unity in mission. Yet, in a post-modern age, one wonders whether there is anything that is still believed everywhere and by all in the twenty-first century.

Michael Root has observed that the least ecumenical thing in a local parish is the new members' class, because there the church tends to focus on those things that make that denomination distinctive from others, which are second-order matters of the faith, rather than on what all Christians share in common: the biblical, doctrinal, liturgical, and spiritual foundations of the faith that are definitive and constitutive, first order, catholic matters. Part of the complexity is that various churches define first order and second order differently, and diversity in our hierarchies of truth can be more difficult to reconcile. A key problem faced in the ratification process of the Lutheran-Roman Catholic accord, the Joint Declaration on the Doctrine of Justification, was that, while the two churches had come to agree upon a differentiated consensus on the theological nuances of justification, the two traditions' respective understandings of that doctrine's place in the theological hierarchy of truths remained quite different. That continuing disagreement almost scuttled the agreement. Ecumenists wrestle with the question of whether the importance of a doctrine has to be part of the agreement in order for an agreed statement to become an ecumenical accord.

Full catholicity, like the other marks, can only be an attribute of God that the church reflects only dimly. The universal church is fragmented, and an ecumenical commitment is integral to catholicity. Canon Paul Avis, General Secretary of the Church of England's Council for Christian Unity, asserts, "We should not credit any ecclesial body with participating in catholicity unless it is not only open in relationship and dialogue to other churches, but is manifestly striving to heal the wounds of division in the body of Christ."[8] Discerning catholicity means seeking the underlying universal truths of the faith in the fresh interpretations that each new age demands, so as to create a living, active, dynamic tradition. This catholicity must be true to the church of the apostles, responsive to the needs of the present day, and congruent with the eschatological realm of God, that is, diachronic unity. This catholicity must also be true to the church in every place, the local and the universal church: synchronic unity. The two together are catholicity.

In ecumenical dialogue, the dialogue of healing of memories is critically important. In twenty-first-century American society, healing the wounds of racial or ethnic discrimination is an equally important part of catholicity. Ecumenism should not imply any kind of melting pot, merged identity, or uniformity. Injuries and offenses of the past cannot be forgotten, but we trust that they can be forgiven. Diversity of cultural expression, liturgical forms, theological emphases, and spiritual practices are all elements essential to our human identities, and we can celebrate them through the ecumenical gift exchange. Recognizing the *imago Dei* in the diversity of races, ethnicities, and historical circumstances in which we live can help us to celebrate our distinctives as members of the one body that is Christ Jesus. For example, at a prayer service with Ecumenical Orthodox Patriarch Bartholomew of Constantinople on November 27, 2004, Pope John Paul II returned relics of St. Gregory of Nazianzus and St. John Chrysostom to the Orthodox Communion. These relics of two of the Orthodox Church's most revered saints had been lost to Constantinople in the early 1200s. Such a powerful gesture of goodwill contributes substantially to reconciliation for the future and honors the holiness inherent in the other tradition. Pilgrims bear the image of the crucified one, through whom our own wounds are healed.

Parts of the North American Church today are experiencing an opposite flow of traditional missionary activity, wherein Christians from Africa or Asia are coming to the United States to witness to their own forms of Christianity, sometimes even within the same denominational family. Sometimes these provide positive experiences of the universality of the church, such as those provided by many international Roman Catholic priests serving in U.S. parishes today. Other instances are received as incursions and are fraught with difficulty, as the Episcopal Church has recently received sometimes undesired and uninvited mission outreach from the Anglican Church from Uganda, Nigeria, and the Southern Cone. Issues of culture, contextualization, biblical interpretation, and theological expression are new ecumenical challenges of this form of reverse mission. How far can or should catholicity stretch in such cases?

## D. Apostolicity—To Transmit the Faith of the Church in Ways That Speak to Future Generations Yet Remain Faithful to the Tradition

"So then you are no longer strangers and aliens, but you are citizens with the saints and also members of the household of God, built upon the foundation of the apostles and prophets, with Christ Jesus himself as the cornerstone" (Eph 2:19–20). Nearly every church considers itself "built upon the foundation of the apostles." The ecumenical question is how to measure what a given church's expression of Christianity is in continuity with "the faith that was once for all entrusted to the saints" (Jude 3). A church is apostolic to the degree to which it "stands firm in fidelity to the witness of the Apostles and lives from the gifts of the Spirit."[9] How the church spreads that witness and shares those gifts with others in this generation and the next is the call of the church to mission. The church's mission is its apostolicity.

The Roman Catholic, Orthodox, and Anglican traditions have traditionally understood apostolicity in terms of succession in the historical episcopal office. This is a key issue between these churches and their Protestant dialogue partners; this is also the chief barrier to mutual recognition of ordained ministry. For Protestants, apostolicity has been understood more generally as continuity in apostolic faith and life. The 1982 World Council of Churches' *Baptism, Eucharist and Ministry* document described historic episcopate as "a sign, though not a guarantee," of the continuity and unity of the church.[10] This language was later used in the full-communion agreement between the Episcopal Church and the Evangelical Lutheran Church in America. This bilateral full-communion agreement is the first time in the United States that a church in historic episcopate and a nonhistoric-episcopate church have been able to reconcile their ordained ministries. The dialogue came to agreement that "apostolic succession" and "historic episcopate" are not synonyms but, rather, that historic episcopate is *a* way—not the *only* way—in which a church can demonstrate that it is in apostolic succession. The two churches will value and maintain this ministry of oversight as *one* of the ways in which the apostolic succession of the church is visibly expressed and personally symbolized in fidelity to the Gospel through the ages. In the ecumenical agreement, the Evangelical Lutheran Church in America bound itself to bringing its bishops into historic episcopate henceforth, while the Episcopal Church recognized and acknowledged that the Lutheran tradition has maintained continuity in apostolic succession since the Reformation, despite the fact that many parts of Lutheranism lost the historic episcopate through historic happenstance.

*The Niagara Report* from the international Anglican-Lutheran dialogue related the crucial theological issue of the dialogue—the nature of ministry and episcopacy—to the issue of mission:

> Mission indeed comes to special expression in the church's apostolicity. For apostolicity means that the Church is sent by Jesus to *be* for the world, to participate in his mission and therefore in the mission of the One who sent Jesus, to participate in the mission of the Father and the Son through the dynamic of the Holy Spirit.[11]

In *The Pullach Report* of 1972, the two communions defined the signs of apostolicity expansively. While the exercising of pastoral care and oversight are one mark of apostolicity, the report also included Scripture, creeds, confessions, liturgies, preaching, teaching, the sacraments, ordination to Word-and-Sacrament ministry, common life of the church, and "engagement in mission to and for the world."[12] These elements are all ways by which a church might demonstrate to the church catholic its continuity in apostolic teaching and unity in faith, whether or not it had maintained the historic episcopate.

Apostolicity finds expression through the liturgical continuity of the church's sacramental life through baptism and Eucharist. Apostolic succession comes "not only from the past but also from the future, from the eschatological community with which the Eucharist relates each local church at a given time in history."[13] Apostolicity validates a given tradition's version of *anamnesis*—its own way of recounting the Christian journey—for the sake of sharing that story with those whose identity is based in an alternate faith odyssey and with those whose individual explorations are not connected to any chosen religious narrative.

# III. CONCLUSION: THE PILGRIMAGE OF UNITY IN MISSION

Ecumenism and mission are constitutive of the life of the church and a reflection of life of the Trinity as it has been revealed to us through Jesus Christ. One, holy, catholic, and apostolic are "promises of what the church can be in the power of the Holy Spirit."[14] We are challenged in the twenty-first century to continue to bear witness to the world in ways no longer denominationally defined, in an ecumenical pilgrimage of unity.

The four marks of the church serve as the boundary-markers of the faith, keeping us honest in our Christian identity. They serve as bridges for both interreligious dialogue and evangelical outreach in our churches, communities, cultures, and contexts. They free us for mission in ways congruent with the past, informed by the present, and hopeful for the future. The marks of the church serve as signposts of the journey of faith and witness as they both measure how well the church bears Christ's name in the world and empower us as Christians for outreach and dialogue, bridging the denominational battle lines that have been used to position our various traditions in the religious marketplace. Rather than forming seminarians into denominational "pastorpreneurs," God can transform them into ecumenical leaders who are both appreciative of the diverse expressions of the faith inherited from previous generations and articulate in their own theological commitments.

The marks of the church provide sharing, safety, and sustenance to the pilgrims of mission and unity. They create boundaries to keep us from straying too far from the pathway. They serve as beacons toward unity, pointing toward the future even while grounding us in the doctrines and liturgies of the tradition. They help pilgrims to discern the road, define the mission, and discover the way forward. They link us to all those of every time and place who have confessed Christ and who will confess Christ in the words of the creed.

## NOTES

1. World Council of Churches, *The Nature and Mission of the Church* (Geneva: WCC Publications, 2005), par. 35.

2. John Micklethwait and Adrian Wooldridge, *God Is Back: How the Global Revival of Faith Is Changing the World* (New York: Penguin Press, 2009).

3. Letty M. Russell, *The Church in the Round: Feminist Interpretation of the Church* (Louisville, KY: Westminster/John Knox Press, 1993), 133; emphasis in the original.

4. William J. Abraham, "On Making Disciples of the Lord Jesus Christ," in *Marks of the Body of Christ*, ed. Carl E. Braaten and Robert W. Jenson (Grand Rapids, MI: William B. Eerdmans Publishing Co., 1999), 155.

5. Michael Root and Risto Saarinen, *Baptism and the Unity of the Church* (Grand Rapids, MI: William B. Eerdmans Publishing Co., 1998), 22.

6. Ibid., 15.

7. Pope Benedict XVI, *Introduction to Christianity* (San Francisco, CA: Ignatius Press, 2004), 341–42.

8. Paul Avis, *Beyond the Reformation* (London: T & T Clark, 2006), 204.

9. James F. Puglisi, "Catholic Learning concerning Apostolicity and Ecclesiality," in *Receptive Ecumenism and the Call to Catholic Learning: Exploring a Way for Contemporary Ecumenism*, ed. Paul D. Murray (Oxford, U.K.: Oxford University Press, 2008), 185.

10. World Council of Churches, *Baptism, Eucharist and Ministry* (Geneva: World Council of Churches, 1982), par. 38.

11. Anglican-Lutheran International Continuation Committee, *The Niagara Report* (London: Church House Publishing, 1988), 14.

12. "Report of the Anglican-Lutheran International Conversations, 1970–1972: Pullach, 1972," in *Anglican-Lutheran Agreements*, ed. Sven Oppegaard and Gregory Cameron (Geneva: Lutheran World Federation, 2004), 34.

13. Puglisi, "Catholic Learning," 188.

14. William J. Abraham, "I Believe in One, Holy, Catholic, and Apostolic Church," in *Nicene Christianity: The Future for a New Ecumenism*, ed. Christopher Seitz (Grand Rapids, MI: Brazos Press, 2001), 186.

**4**

# RELATIONAL UNITY IN MISSION
## Reflecting God's Life

*Susan E. Davies*

## PROLOGUE

My life has been a complex journey surrounded, supported, and challenged by the life of Christ as I have found it in the church. I went to nursery school at Bushnell Congregational Church in Detroit, and continued in Sunday school. The first time I heard a link between the biblical perspectives I was learning at church and the scientific world I was discovering in school was in our seventh-grade class (in the kitchen). The teacher was an amateur astronomer, who talked about the confluence of comets that occurred in 6 to 4 BCE, just at the time the Magi were said to have followed a bright star to Bethlehem. It was earthshaking information. Bible stories might be about real people who had lived on the same planet I inhabited. I could be a Christian and live in the "modern" world, two cultures that spoke very different languages.

I continued in church school, walking each Sunday the many blocks past my grandmother's house on the way to church. Junior and senior Pilgrim Fellowship followed, as well as citywide and statewide Pilgrim Fellowship. I was Fellowship Commissioner. Girls could not be president in school or church those days, but we could help foster community. In 1959, I participated in a life-changing, ten-day pilgrimage to colleges and schools for slaves and freed people founded in southern states by the American Missionary Association during and after the Civil War.

The late 1950s were Jim Crow, the Montgomery bus boycott, whites-only bathrooms and drinking fountains, church bombings, shut-down public-school systems, covert FBI surveillance of Dr. King's Southern Christian Leadership Council and the Nation of Islam's Malcolm X, voter registration drives, and lynchings. Mack Charles Parker was taken from jail, beaten, and hung from a tree in Mississippi the month after our pilgrimage.

In the midst of this swirling, deadly, hope-filled turmoil, white kids from Detroit were being welcomed to school dances we could not tell our occasional white hosts about, lest we endanger our "Negro" hosts, welcomed into homes and churches in black communities in southern Indiana, Tennessee, and Alabama, and discovering the challenging history, strength, and gifts of Fisk University, Tuskegee Institute (now University), and Talladega College. I discovered a complex, strong, extended, and oppressed culture, a world about which my white public schools had taught me nothing. My church, however, was part of the Michigan Congregational Christian Conference, which thought it essential that white kids know something of black culture and community in order to work for justice in our society. The culmination of that leg of my journey was my time as a youth delegate to the Second Uniting General Synod of the new United Church of Christ in Oberlin, Ohio, in 1959.

I knew nothing then of the long preparations for the church union and its deep roots in the conciliar ecumenical movement, but I remember clearly the arguments at Bushnell about whether organic union with the Evangelical and Reformed Church (horror: they had bishops!) would dissolve our local independence as a congregation. Yet, Bushnell voted to join the new United Church of Christ, and they and the Michigan Conference of Congregational Christian Churches sent me to Oberlin, where the new church's Statement of Faith was adopted.

Two years ago, during the fiftieth anniversary celebration of Faith and Order in the United States, I sat in the Finney Chapel in Oberlin, hearing the rafters echo the "Gloria" when the new Statement of Faith was confirmed. In its fiftieth anniversary year, and in recognition of the broader ecumenical journey that gave birth to the United Church of Christ, it seems appropriate to use sections of that Statement to address the church's unity in mission.

## UNITY

Church unity appears in the second paragraph of the Statement: "You bestow upon us your Holy Spirit, creating and renewing the church of Jesus Christ, binding in covenant faithful people of all ages, tongues, and races."[1] No matter how divided by culture; languages; marginality and centrality; liturgical traditions; ethnic, racial, and tribal identities; sexualities; and theological and ecclesiological differences and disputes, the church is one. The body of Christ is one, whether we will it or not. Our divisions run deep, wounding the body, but they cannot divide Christ.

The languages, images, and logic we use in discussing unity affect the possibilities and outcomes of our conversations and our common mission. Biblical images of Christian unity, such as the "body of Christ," "the people of God," "the temple of the Holy Spirit," and "*koinonia*/communion" are deeply relational in their theological implications. Unity in Christ is a spiritual reality that finds expression in relationships, struggle, crossing boundaries, and embracing the other, the stranger.[2]

For many years, Christian unity has been defined in a philosophically based "logic of noncontradiction," which too often causes "an exclusivist understanding of truth and easily leads to the stigmatization of the irregular as heresy."[3] The thousands of different Christian Churches in the United States alone give witness to the divisive nature of this logic, especially when embedded in an individualistic culture.

Konrad Raiser has noted that the word *unity* is rarely found in the Christian Scriptures:

> What we find instead is the concern for building and maintaining communion between people and communities who remain different. Unity in biblical terms is not something empirically given but rather a continuous, living process which presupposes existing diversities. The image of the body and its members comes to mind immediately to exemplify this relational understanding of unity over against the hierarchical tendencies of the dominant pattern [then and now].[4]

At the "Ecumenism from the Margins" panel presentation to the Faith and Order Commission in October 2009, Dr. Anne Joh of Garrett Evangelical Theological Seminary offered the Commission a variation on Raiser's theme. She urged us to remember, as churches engaged in our part of the ecumenical movements, that we must be constantly aware of the ways in which certain European and Euro-American forms of church and types of theologizing have been made normative in our Faith and Order study topics, our bilateral dialogues, and our interchurch relationships. Joh suggested that we think of Christianity as a hybrid, not as a single form in this post-Christendom, neocolonial context. She suggested we decenter and destabilize the "common sense" that says that the cultural form and norm of Christianity are defined always by the West. "Is it good enough," she asks, "that we allow for contextual theologies to diversify our Christian tradition? What would happen if Christian theology was a contextual theology? What would it mean if Christianity had [a] multiplicity of margins and centers?"[5]

If we take our cues from Raiser's "relational understanding of unity," Joh's "hybridity," and the covenantal language in the UCC Statement of Faith, we may move more easily into unity in mission. If unity does not mean subjugation, denial of difference, a hierarchy of historical origins, or theological supremacy, then unity may well mean a covenant for pilgrims who are united in Christ while retaining the integrity of their differences, who celebrate the hybridity of their companionship, who struggle together for the common good, who eat together, and, indeed, who suffer and die together.[6]

## REFORMED DISUNITY

My journey from Bushnell Congregational Church, UCC, to a more global perspective has in recent years led to my role on the Executive Committee of the World Alliance of Reformed Churches (WARC). It has been quite a pilgrimage from the prideful horror of bishops. I have been pushed to see the world and the church from perspectives not easily found in the United States. For the last five years, I have been Co-Moderator of the WARC Covenanting for Justice Global Network, which has worked with Reformed

Churches and congregations around the world to implement a document adopted by the 24th General Council in 2004 in Accra, Ghana: the Accra Confession, or, more formally, "Covenanting for Justice in the Economy and the Earth."[7] Two ecumenically neuralgic terms in the Confession are "confession"[8] and "empire." I address "empire" in this essay because the term has continued to divide Reformed Churches, and a recent meeting in South Africa has brought some hope for common understanding.

The Accra Confession regards the economic and ecological disasters that have resulted from current global economic structures as theological issues affecting the integrity of Reformed faith [16].[9] The document describes the reigning neo-liberal philosophy as "an ideology that claims to be without alternative, demanding an endless flow of sacrifices from the poor and creation. It makes the false promise that it can save the world through the creation of wealth and prosperity, claiming sovereignty over life and demanding total allegiance which amounts to idolatry" [10].

It goes on to use the term *empire* [11] to describe a "global system that defends and protects the interests of the powerful. It affects and captivates us all. Further, in biblical terms such a system of wealth accumulation at the expense of the poor is seen as unfaithful to God and responsible for preventable human suffering and is called Mammon. Jesus has told us that we cannot serve both God and Mammon (Lk 16:13)" [14].

Patterning itself after the 1934 Barmen Declaration that theologically opposed Nazism and the 1986 Belhar Confession that theologically opposed apartheid, the Accra Confession alternates statements of Christian faith and rejections of injustices, concluding with a "covenant in obedience to God's will…and in accountable relationships [which] binds us together to work for justice in the economy and the earth…" [37]. Here, the Accra Confession makes the church's mission a matter of unity, faith, and justice.

# EMPIRE

*Empire* has been a church-dividing word when used to describe our current global economic and ecological context, because it names the economic, political, cultural, and military power of the nations and corporations of the North Atlantic. Most of the European nations had empires during the five hundred years of colonial expansion, which ended its occupation phase in the mid-twentieth century. The United States has never acknowledged its international possessions as part of an American Empire, although the neoconservatives who came to political prominence and power in the 1990s and 2000s proudly used that language in their writings. The United States currently retains possession of Puerto Rico, Guam, American Samoa, the Northern Mariana Islands, and the U.S. Virgin Islands. Former U.S. possessions include Cuba, the Philippines, Micronesia, and Palau.

The "empire" spoken of in the Accra Confession, however, is much more complex than simple possession of lands. It is a web of allied and competing nations and international corporations that own land; other corporations; natural resources; buildings; factories; ranches; oil and natural-gas fields; water and water rights; diamond, gold, and other precious-metal mines; and transportation and production facilities in almost every corner of the world. At times, they have "owned" whole countries. (Think "Banana Republic"—not the retailer, but the origin of the term.) The corporations are beyond the control of any one nation-state, but the militaries of many nations are used to protect their interests. They have immense influence in international financial and commodity markets, and their legally defined responsibility in the United States is to make a profit for their investors. The current international economic system is called "neo-liberal economic globalization," and it depends on ever-increasing consumption of goods and services, metals and grains, plastics and computers.

As these structures have developed over the last fifty years, resources and profits have flowed out of the global south into the global north, destroying the lands and impoverishing the peoples, while enriching elites in the global south and north and providing much of the comfortable lifestyles of Europeans and North Americans. The policies of the World Bank, the International Monetary Fund, and now the World Trade Organization have been structured to benefit the international corporations rather than the peoples of the earth—or the earth itself. Very little of this analysis appears in news sources in the global north, although it does peek its nose through the tent in books and book reviews in various places, in opinion pieces in the *New York Times*, and occasionally in films. It can be found on the Web, but not in local newspapers. It can be found in union newspapers, but not on the nightly news. People in the United States neither hear it nor wish to accept it when they do.

When, in 2004, the Accra Confession used "empire" in its description of the evil being done in the world, most European and white North American Reformed Christians who were aware of it objected vehemently. They/we looked only through the eyes of our world and were unable to see what the rest of the world—Africa, South and Southeast Asia, the Caribbean, Central and South America, the Pacific, and most of the Middle East—was experiencing. We were not living in covenantal pilgrimage with our sisters and brothers in Christ. The Accra Confession was born in the agonies of Reformed Churches in the global south, and its adoption vindicated their cries of rage and despair.[10] For many in the global north, the Accra Confession threatened our self-understandings and our deepest beliefs about ourselves and our good intentions.

Among those most offended by the "imperial" language in the Accra Confession were German Reformed Christians. They were widely connected with their former colonial churches and aware of the ways Germans were working to ameliorate the effects of neo-liberal economic globalization. They had also been working in Germany to welcome and integrate "guest workers" into their own economy. Their strong history of philosophical theology did not include conceptualizing a headless "empire." Many German Reformed Christians did not want their American liberators from the Nazis to be attacked in a church document. World Alliance of Reformed Churches gatherings were wracked with dissension over the term and its usage. Thus, it was that a German Church and a Southern African Church entered into dialogue about "empire."

## JOURNEY TO RELATIONAL UNITY

For the last three years, the Evangelical Reformed Church in Germany (EKD) and the Uniting Reformed Church of Southern

Africa (URCSA) have been in dialogue as part of the Globalization Project of the Beyers Naude' Institute of the University of Stellenbosch, supported by the German Institute and directed by Dr. Allan Boesak. The South African Reformed Churches have been among the strongest supporters of the Accra Confession, while the EKD has been among those whose members have most vociferously objected to it. The Confession had become the occasion of division rather than unity among the churches.

Representatives of the EKD and URCSA have spent the last several years engaged in deep and sustained theological conversation, in person and online, seeking to understand each other's position on the Confession, seeking unity where there has been painful division. They met face-to-face twice yearly, engaging in historical and economic analyses of globalization and empire, seeking the guidance of the Holy Spirit. They listened to economists and theologians, historians and local people's stories. They used a relational understanding of unity, while respecting the hybridity of the church. They prayed with one another, ate together, celebrated communion together, and learned each other's languages of faith and justice.

Together the South African and German Churches have accomplished a small miracle: a definition of empire with which Reformed Christians in the north and the south can agree. Their definition of empire is more complex than that found in the Accra Confession, reflecting the global economic and social realities of after-the-crash 2009:

> We speak of empire because we discern a coming together of economic, cultural, political and military power in our world today, that constitutes a reality and a spirit of lordless domination, created by humankind, yet enslaving simultaneously; an all-encompassing global reality serving, protecting, and defending the interests of powerful corporations, nations, elites and privileged people, while imperiously excluding, even sacrificing humanity and exploiting creation; a pervasive spirit of destructive self-interest, even greed—the worship of money, goods and possessions; the gospel of consumerism, proclaimed through powerful propaganda and religiously justified, believed and followed by the colonization of consciousness, val-

ues and notions of human life by the imperial logic; a spirit lacking in compassionate justice and showing contemptuous disregard for the gifts of creation and the household of life.[11]

The unity they sought arose through intentionally sustained dialogue, which provided opportunity for building relationships. The dialogue partners could then recognize and affirm difference while seeking common language and understanding. Their willingness to recognize the multiple margins and centers of the church allowed them to hear one another more clearly. Their unity on this painfully neuralgic issue demonstrates that unity in Christ is clearly not subjugation of one by the other, nor is it a denial of difference. It is, rather, seeking to live into the relationships we have been given by God in the body of Christ.

## TRINITARIAN *PERICHORESIS:* UNITY IN RELATIONSHIP

Our calling as Christians is to live into the unity God has given us in Christ for our common mission. Following the example of the early church, living as it did in an earlier empire, our journey in mission may be enriched if we seek to build unity in relationships that emulate the *perichoresis* of the Trinity. This term, developed most fully by John of Damascus, the eighth-century Arab monk, means literally going around and through each other. John also spoke of fellowship and intimacy as characteristics of the Trinity. Trinitarian theology is a multifaceted subject of much academic and ecclesiological interest in the last decades. Western and Eastern Christian traditions have taken different, yet intersecting, paths over the generations. My use of trinitarian imagery for Christian unity differs from Roman Catholic and Orthodox theology, as my approach to and understanding of the Trinity has been shaped by feminist and womanist theologies, as well as theologies in and from the global south.

In a very helpful article in the June 2009, issue of *Ecumenical Trends,*[12] Ryan Patrick McLaughlin noted three major dimensions of trinitarian ecclesiology: constitutional, reflective, and participatory.[13] When I speak of Christian unity that reflects the trinitarian *perichoresis* within and between the churches, I am using his "reflective dimension," which he described as the "attempt to establish precedence for relationships within the church [and between the churches] based on the relationships of the Father, Son, and Holy Spirit to each other."[14] McLaughlin also cited Kevin Giles's description: "[T]he inner life of the divine Trinity provides a pattern, a model, an echo, or an icon of Christian communal existence in this world."[15]

In the context of our work on Unity in Mission, the reflective dimensions of trinitarian understandings are crucial for the life of the church and the world. If the nature of all things, the core of all being—the Trinity—is mutual relationship in which both unity and difference are part of the very essence of being, of God, then the church and human societies on this small planet in one obscure corner of the universe need to pattern our lives in accordance with this reality. Brazilian theologian Ivone Gebara has written of the "trinitarian structure of the universe," which she terms "the reality that constitutes the entire cosmos and all life-forms—a reality marked simultaneously by multiplicity and by unity, by the differences among all things and by their articulated interdependence."[16]

For an increasing number of theologians in many social locations, in both the global south and north, the social model of the Trinity requires that we live within and among the churches in mutual respect, love, and relationship. North American Reformed theologian and pastor Cynthia Rigby put the matter this way, "To confess that God is triune is to know that God is for us in God's very being. To reflect God's triune image in relationship to one another, then, is not to lord it over one another. To be God-like, when God is understood to be a community, is not to be self-sufficient but to live in relation."[17]

If God is community, relational at the very core, and if difference is embedded in the Trinity, then Joh's descriptor for the church—"hybrid, not a single form"—begins to offer us a way to value theologically the wide variety of forms the church has taken for the last two thousand years throughout the globe. My early intercultural experiences—church/school, and white dominant culture/black oppressed culture—began to give me some inklings of these possibilities. To be God-like, says Rigby, is "not to Lord it over one another." Rather, it is to respect and value the Christian cultural and theological complexities that make up the church, the body of Christ. With Raiser, I am reminded of Paul's body images in 1 Corinthians 12.

In discussing the triune God, Elizabeth Johnson summarized the essential values inherent in the immanent divine as: "Mutual relation/friendship;[18]…Radical equality—a community of equals, patterns of differentiation that are non-hierarchical;…[and] Community in diversity; in classical theology expressed with the term perichoresis, a picture of an eternal divine round dance."[19] Theologians who use such language are aware, with Miroslav Volf and McLaughlin, that "perichoresis—as experienced by the divine persons—is not possible for human beings who are separate subjects. However, the Spirit indwells these separate subjects and forms a communion between them *and* communion with them."[20]

However we express this moving, many-layered, differentiated, hybrid, constantly experienced, and renewed relationship, unity and/in difference are at the heart of our trinitarian faith, our ecclesial relationships, and our human identity. They are part of our covenantal pilgrimage toward the future God is bringing toward us. That pilgrimage includes new creation of history and the cosmos, as Jong Chun Park puts it: "Korean Christian women, who decide to participate in the *oikonomia* of God who continues the new creation of history and the cosmos, are the ones who invite all of us to the trinitarian *perichoresis* of God for interliving. Despite living in the still divided and interkilling world, we are obliged to be open to "New Encounter" for peace and interliving brought by the power of the Holy Spirit."[21] Yes, we are so obliged, both in the church and in the wider societies in which we all live.

The authors of WARC's "Mission and Evangelism in Unity Today" put it this way: "Created in the image of the triune God—who is by definition an eternal communion of life and love—human beings are by nature relational. The relational dimension of human life is a given, ontological reality…. The Trinity, the source and image of our existence, shows the importance of diversity, otherness and intrinsic relationships in constituting a community."[22] Unity in relationship is a pilgrimage that requires and enables liberating companionship across denominations, geography, ethnicity, race, and species. It is a unity in relationship that recognizes shifting margins and centers and embraces the whole of the worlds God has called into being.[23]

## TRINITARIAN *PERICHORESIS:* UNITY IN MISSION

A trinitarian relational understanding of mission is frequently found in recent ecumenical documents, as can be seen, again, in "Mission and Evangelism in Unity Today":

> The mission of God (*missio Dei*) has no limits or barriers; it has been addressed to and has been at work within the entire human race and the whole of creation throughout history....
> A trinitarian approach to the *missio Dei*...promotes a more inclusive understanding of God's presence and work in the whole world and among all people, implying that signs of God's presence can and should be identified, affirmed and worked with even in the most unexpected places....The mission of God (*missio Dei*) is the source of and basis for the mission of the church, the body of Christ. Through Christ in the Holy Spirit God indwells the church, empowering and energizing its members. [11–13][24]

An understanding of mission that is fundamentally relational, rooted within the immanent Trinity as well as in God's trinitarian relationship with the world, puts relations of love, mutuality, and justice at the heart of mission as we seek to reflect the being of God in the world.

The UCC Statement of Faith says we are called into the church to "accept the cost and joy of discipleship, to be God's servants in the service of others, to proclaim the gospel to all the world and resist the powers of evil, to share in Christ's baptism and eat at his table, to join him in his passion and victory...[to live in God's promise of] courage in the struggle for justice and peace." Love, mutuality, and justice underlie the Statement's description of Christian mission, connecting proclamation and justice. In a broken, bleeding world, the good news of Christ cannot be preached or lived without resisting the powers of evil, without struggling for justice and peace. That struggle must have at its heart the decentering, de-norming of Western forms of Christianity, until we all recognize the multiple centers and margins of our ecclesiologies and theologies. However earnestly we attempt to reflect the trinitarian dance in the world, our churches are temporal institutions, refracting in cracked human mirrors the love, mutuality, and justice of God.

Mission is and must be deeply engaged in accompanying the billions who suffer, resisting the powers of evil in whatever personal, economic, ecological, political, or social forms they are found. "Mission means risking our identity for the sake of the gospel, losing and saving our life in order to discover, once more, who God is calling us to be."[25]

## CONCLUSION: RELATIONAL UNITY IN MISSION

Relational unity in mission requires that we recognize and respect intercultural, ecclesial, and theological differences. It requires that we understand the church as having many centers and margins, with multiple forms throughout the history of the church around the globe, all of them shaped by particular cultural and philosophical structures, many imposed by colonial powers. It requires careful and long, mutually respectful listening, prayer, and speaking (in that order), particularly for those who are accustomed to being easily heard and respected. The URCSA–EKD dialogue and its results give us hope that, within and across theological traditions, reconciliation and new insight into God's truth can be achieved.[26]

While the church on this planet can never fully reflect the immanent trinitarian relationships of equality, mutuality, and love, we can hold *perichoresis* before us as a "model, an echo, or an icon of Christian communal existence in this world."[27] Relational unity in mission is centered in the divine *perichoresis*, in the love, mutuality, and justice that lie at the heart of the one who continually journeys with us, creating, sustaining, and redeeming the universe and all its inhabitants. The Trinity is the core of all things: difference in relationship, which is mutual, nonhierarchical, loving, and justice-seeking. It is our prime example of relational unity, from which and toward which we live and move and have our being. Perhaps, as we enter a new time in the life of the church, we might enter a covenant as pilgrims who are united in Christ while retaining our differences, celebrating the hybridity of our companionship, and struggling together for respectful unity in relationship.

The UCC Statement of Faith concludes:

> You promise to all who trust you forgiveness of sins and full-ness of grace, courage in the struggle for justice and peace, your presence in trial and rejoicing, and eternal life in your realm which has no end.

> Blessing and honor, glory and power be unto you.

So let it be.

# NOTES

1. "United Church of Christ Statement of Faith in the Form of a Doxology," in *The New Century Hymnal* (Cleveland, OH: The Pilgrim Press, 1995), 885.

2. Some material in the "Unity" section is derived from "Bible Study on Ephesians 4:1–3," presented in Johannesburg on September 7, 2009, by Prince Moiseraele Dibeela and Susan E. Davies; publication forthcoming.

3. Konrad Raiser, "Ecumenism in Search of a New Vision, 1992," in *The Ecumenical Movement: An Anthology of Key Texts and Voices*, ed. Michael Kinnamon and Brian E. Cope (Geneva: WCC Publications; Grand Rapids, MI: William B. Eerdmans Publishing Co., 1997), 73.

4. Ibid., 74 (bracketed material added).

5. Anne Joh, "N.C.C.C. Commission on Faith and Order," (unpulished manuscript, Garrett Evangelical Theological Seminary, October 15, 2009), 4–6.

6. Dibeela, "Bible Study," 2.

7. "Covenanting for Justice in the Economy and the Earth," available at http://www.warc.ch/documents/ACCRA_Pamphlet.pdf (accessed July 16, 2012).

8. In the Reformed tradition, "confessions" have been understood primarily as Christian doctrinal declarations by which ecclesiological unity is maintained. They are also understood as standing always under the higher authority of the Bible, not as single, absolute statements of Reformed faith for all people in all times and places. See Shirley C. Guthrie, *Christian Doctrine* (Louisville, KY: Westminster/John Knox Press, 1994), 25.

9. Bracketed numbers refer to paragraphs in the Accra Confession (see n. 7).

10. See, e.g., Rene Kruger, ed., *Life in All Fullness: Latin American Protestant Churches Facing Neoliberal Globalization* (Buenos Aires: Instituto Universitario, ISEDET, 2007).

11. "Message," Global Dialogue on the Accra Confession, Johannesburg (September 3–8, 2009). The definition of empire is from the Globalisation Project of the Uniting Reformed Church in Southern Africa and the Evangelical Reformed Church in Germany, 2.

12. Ryan Patrick McLaughlin, "Church in Transit: Developing the Already/Not Yet of Miroslav Volf's Trinitarian Ecclesiology," *Ecumenical Trends* 38 (June 2009):1–7, 14–15.

13. Ibid., 1–2.

14. Ibid., 2 (bracketed material added).

15. Kevin Giles, *What on Earth Is the Church? An Exploration in New Testament Theology* (Eugene, OR: Wipf & Stock Publishers, 1995), 222; cited in McLaughlin, "Church in Transit," 2.

16. Ivone Gebara, *Longing for Running Water: Ecofeminism and Liberation* (Minneapolis, MN: Fortress Press, 1999), 156.

17. Cynthia Rigby, "Scandalous Presence: Incarnation and Trinity," in *Feminist and Womanist Essays in Reformed Dogmatics*, ed. Amy Plantinga Pauw and Serene Jones (Louisville, KY: Westminster/John Knox Press, 2006), 64.

18. See also Eleanor H. Haney: "'Friend' gathers up much of the feminist reflection and my own experience; it is a preeminently nonhierarchical image, preeminently suggestive of mutuality,

shared power, openness, trust, and fidelity. It captures much of what is also suggested in parental images without the unequal power relationship" (Eleanor H. Haney, *The Great Commandment: A Theology of Resistance and Transformation* [Cleveland, OH: The Pilgrim Press, 1998], 70).

19. Elizabeth Johnson, *She Who Is: The Mystery of God in Feminist Theological Discourse* (New York: Crossroad Publishing, 1993), 216–19, as cited in "Elizabeth Johnson: A Feminist Interpretation of the Triune Symbol," in Veli-Matti Karkkainen, *The Trinity: Global Perspectives* (Louisville, KY: Westminster/John Knox Press, 2007), 207.

20. McLaughlin, "Church in Transit," 4.

21. Jong Chun Park, *Crawl with God, Dance in the Spirit! A Creative Formation of Korean Theology of the Spirit* (Nashville, TN: Abingdon Press, 1998), 135.

22. "Mission and Evangelism in Unity Today" [38, 39], *"You are the Light of the World" (Matthew 5:14), Statements on Mission by the World Council of Churches, 1980–2005* (Geneva: WCC Publications, 2005), 74–75.

23. UCC Statement of Faith.

24. "Mission and Evangelism in Unity Today," 65.

25. Setri Nyomi, "Together in Mission: A Letter on Mission Renewal," Document 13 in O. P. Mateus, *Theology: Mission and Ecumenism Documents, 1997–2004* (Geneva: WARC Department of Theology, 2004), 42.

26. The "Joint Declaration on the Doctrine of Justification" by the Lutheran World Federation and the Catholic Church is a historic example of what such inter-cultural dialogue can achieve; available at http://www.vatican.va/roman_curia/pontifical_councils/chrstuni/documents/rc_pc_chrstuni_doc_31101999_cath-luth-joint-declaration_en.html (accessed July 16, 2012).

27. Giles, *What on Earth*, 222.

# WORD AND SACRAMENT

# 5

# UNITY IN PROCLAMATION

*Don Thorsen*

Christian proclamation has its beginning in Jesus Christ. After John the Baptist prepared the way of the Lord, Mark 1:14–15 says: " Jesus came to Galilee, proclaiming the good news of God, and saying, 'The time is fulfilled, and the kingdom of God has come near; repent, and believe in the good news.'" The "good news" is also known as the Gospel, or evangel (Greek, *euangelion*), and it heralds the new covenant Jesus established for the salvation of people (Luke 22:20).

The disciples bore witness to Jesus throughout their lives and ministries. After Pentecost, the disciples "did not cease to teach and proclaim Jesus as the Messiah," that is, Christ—the "anointed one" of God (Acts 5:42). The apostle Paul also proclaimed the Gospel by witnessing, evangelizing, and serving as a missionary throughout the ancient world. He said: "I handed on to you as of first importance what I in turn had received" (1 Cor 15:3); for Paul, there was unity among believers in their proclamation of Christ's death and resurrection. He said: "Whether then it was I or they, so we proclaim and so you have come to believe" (1 Cor 15:11).

Unity in proclamation is, of course, aided by the presence and power of the Holy Spirit. When asked to give testimony of believers' hope in God, Jesus said: "...do not worry about how you are to speak or what you are to say; for what you are to say will be given to you at that time; for it is not you who speak, but the Spirit of your Father..." (Matt 10:19–20). Paul confirms this unity, saying that believers should make "every effort to maintain the unity of the Spirit in the bond of peace. There is one body and one Spirit..." (Eph 4:3–4).

Christians throughout church history have continued to proclaim the Gospel of Jesus Christ by preaching, teaching, and other means of advancing the reign of God. There has been unity among Christians and churches with regard to their ongoing proclamation. Christians proclaim the Gospel weekly (if not daily) in churches through preaching and teaching. Observance of the sacraments proclaims the Gospel: "For as often as you eat this bread and drink this cup, you proclaim the Lord's death until he comes" (1 Cor 11:26). Witnessing, testifying, evangelizing, missionary work, serving others, advocacy on behalf of the poor, and numerous other means have been used for proclaiming the Gospel of Jesus. Indeed, one may say that Christians *cannot not* proclaim the Gospel. They must simply choose the ways in which they do so.

Christians have never ceased their intended proclamation of Jesus Christ, though they have not always gone about it the same way. Over time, Christians and churches have preferred certain means over others. Some means to proclamation have been considered out of date, inadequate, unproductive or, at times, unjust and hurtful. So, Christians and churches have been careful about how they go about proclaiming Jesus in word and deed. Certainly, if Christians do not embody (or incarnate) the Gospel in their actions, then their words will be ineffective in communicating Jesus to others.

## BUILDING UNITY

Christians and churches may build unity as they partner in proclaiming Jesus as part of the mission of God (Latin, *missio Dei*). Of course, not all Christians understand God's mission precisely the same way. Be that as it may, the mission of God is thought to be holistic, holding in creative balance divine grace and human responsibility, faith and works, Scripture and Tradition, Word and Sacrament, conversion and discipleship, charisms and charismata, and compassion ministries and social advocacy. *Although proclamation of the Gospel represents only one aspect of the mission of God, Christians and churches may build unity with one another in proclaiming Jesus to others because of similarity in their ministries that supersede their differences.* In exploring the ecumenical dimensions of proclamation, it will be helpful to talk about the varieties of proclamation. In particular, it is important to talk about evangelism, proselytism, and their implications in a world increasingly aware of other religions, and the need for developing constructive interreligious relations.

In talking about the Bible and historic Christianity, it is important to remember the need for critical thinking and study of the historical and literary contexts in which they developed. Unanimity does not exist among Christians with regard to the nature and interpretation of the Bible. The same may be said for understanding theological and ministerial developments in church history. However, it lies beyond the scope of this paper to engage in scholarly investigation into all the issues underlying the formation of biblical texts and subsequent interpretations of them by Christians and churches. Be that as it may, it is possible to make general statements about historic emphases that occurred, related to issues of proclamation. The following discussion intends to focus on those emphases and some of their implications for understanding unity in mission among churches. Such understanding may then help us today in integrating proclamation in ways that are more holistic, relevant, and effective as well as faithful to the Bible and historic Christianity.

To be sure, faithful incorporation of proclamation into the mission of the church represents a process, a journey, a pilgrimage that involves all dimensions of Christian beliefs, values, and practices. It is not enough for people to develop right beliefs (orthodoxy) or right practices (orthopraxis); it involves the development of a right heart (orthokardia), right community (orthocommunitas), right society (orthosocietas), and other ways that rightly reflect God's will. Certainly, trying to maintain balance among these priorities is difficult, intellectually as well as spiritually. This is why Christians need to look upon the pursuit of unity in proclamation as a kind of pilgrimage that involves one's whole heart as well as mind, and soul as well as strength (see Mark 12:28–31). The pilgrimage may not be easy; it may not be completed in our lifetime. But it is a pilgrimage worthy of undertaking, and by the grace of God, it is a pilgrimage overflowing with hope by faithfully and lovingly fulfilling God's mission in the world.

# MISSION, PROCLAMATION, AND EVANGELISM

Understanding mission is perhaps the best path to Christian unity. Mission is transformational in both personal and social dimensions of life. The implications are that churches have a prophetic vocation in the world, a calling to be agents of transformation within the wider community of humanity that inhabits the world, without the world becoming coextensive with churches. Churches are to be *in* the world without being *of* the world (John 17:11, 16; 1 John 2:15–17).

Various aspects of the church's mission include the following: serving the purpose of God as a gift given to the world in order that all may believe; proclaiming the Gospel in word and deed; reconciling all things to God and to one another through Jesus Christ; transforming the world; caring for those suffering and in need, suffering on their behalf; and advocating on behalf of the poor, needy, and marginalized. In the power of the Holy Spirit, the church seeks faithfully to proclaim and live the love of God for all, and to fulfill Jesus' mission for the salvation and transformation of the world, to the glory of God.

Evangelism represents one part of God's mission. Yet, it plays an important role in Scripture, church history, and churches' ministry today. Evangelism, also known as evangelization, represents proclamation of the Gospel of Jesus Christ for the salvation of people. Scripture talks about evangelists; they share the Gospel in both word and deed (Eph 4:11). Throughout church history, Christians have proclaimed the good news of salvation. Evangelism has been a part of all church traditions—Catholic, Orthodox, and Protestant.

Evangelism is inextricably bound up with what it means to be Christian and a church. How can one help but speak about what one believes and values, and how can one's life not help but be influenced by them? How can Christians pass on the Gospel from one generation to the next without communicating it in churches, ministry, social advocacy, academic institutions, within families, among friends, and neighbors? Evangelism represents the intentional proclamation of Jesus and salvation to whomever, whenever, and in whatever way thought appropriate. Although it is God who saves, Christians are called upon to "make disciples," which includes sharing one's beliefs, values, and practices in both word and deed (Matt 28:16–20).

## VARIETIES OF EVANGELISM

Evangelism, like the mission of God, occurs in a variety of ways. Perhaps it is best to remember that there is more than one way to proclaim Jesus to others. Francis of Assisi is famously remembered as having said, "Always proclaim the Gospel. If necessary, use words." Obviously, he did not think that words were always necessary in proclaiming the Gospel, and that a godly life communicates God best to others. Just the same, Christians speak all the time about Jesus, and some of them are more intentional than others in sharing the good news.

Historic ways of evangelizing include the churches' worship (Latin, *leitourgia*), service (*diakonia*), witness (*martyria*), and preaching (*kerygma*). People most often associate preaching with evangelism, but that is not necessarily the case. To be sure, Peter called people to repentance (*metanoia*) and baptism for the forgiveness of sins and reception of "the gift of the Holy Spirit"—new life in Jesus Christ (Acts 2:38). But evangelism does not always occur in this direct, public, provocative manner. Indeed, most often it occurs in slower, more progressive ways.

Routinely, evangelism occurs within the context of churches, worship, sacraments, families, friendships, and other interrelational means. Yes, preaching and calls for decision may occur, but conversions (or the making of disciples)—more often than not—occur through a process of nurture, rather than decisive events. People are evangelized through family relationships and conversations, interaction and sharing among friends, neighbors, and others with whom they come into contact. Evangelism may occur by inviting others to church or related ministries; it may occur inadvertently as well as intentionally. Since it is the Holy Spirit who convicts people of sin and the need to repent, believe, and be baptized, who are we to limit the work of the Holy Spirit?

Missions and missionary work have been prominent ways that Christians have undertaken the worldwide proclamation of the Gospel of Jesus Christ and the evangelism of others. Since the first century, apostles such as Paul have traveled throughout the world evangelizing, planting churches, and providing for the needs of those who are impoverished in so many ways (see Acts 15). Ministries of reconciliation, compassion ministries, and social advocacy on behalf of others have been characteristic of missionary work throughout church history. Such practical ministries have not sidetracked Christians from fulfilling their calling. Despite different missiological methods used by missionaries, their ministries have often been at the forefront of uniting Christians and churches. For example, many consider the 1910 World Missionary Conference to be one of the key events in the modern ecumenical movement. Missionaries met from around the world in order to share, challenge, encourage, and collaborate with one another in their ministries. To be sure, the ecumenical spirit of the Conference was not perfect; not everyone was invited to participate. Nonetheless, it became apparent that cooperation in missionary work at home and abroad, evangelism, educational instruction, compassion ministries, and social advocacy could be improved quantitatively and qualitatively through Christians who worked collaboratively rather than competitively in the world.

## EVANGELISM AND PROSELYTISM

Christians have not always proclaimed the Gospel in ways considered compatible with biblical teachings of justice as well as compassion. Deceptive and coercive methods have been used, and the distinction between acceptance of Jesus Christ and that of a particular culture have not been made satisfactorily. Western Christians, for example, have made acceptance of their culture, politics, and economics as central to their proclamation and evangelism as of the Gospel. Indeed, physical and military coercion have been used, which compromised the *good news* of Jesus. Certainly, centuries of Western colonial practices have severely hindered the ways in which people from the so-called majority world (or two-thirds world countries) assess Jesus, Christians, and churches. Such deceptive and coercive methods are known as proselytism, which starkly contrasts with evangelism. Although evangelism and proselytism have sometimes been used synonymously, the two are increasingly thought to contrast with one another.[1] Indeed, if one accepts the contrasting definitions between the two terms, then their methods are mutually exclusive. Evangelism should be done as openly and honestly as possible, without resorting to unjust methods that take advantage of those who are vulnerable, for one reason or another. Of course, it is not always easy to distinguish between evangelism and proselytism, since some people consider any proclamation, contrary to what is already believed by others, to be unwarranted and unwelcome.

In order to avoid the deceptive and coercive methods of proselytism, some have advocated the cessation of the proclamation of Jesus Christ altogether. However, that is not possible, since proclaiming the Gospel is inextricably bound up with the mission of God. Can one silence Christians, or expect them not to act in Christlike ways? Can one or should one silence the church, whether it speaks of spiritual or social transformation? It is not realistic to silence God, Jesus, and the Holy Spirit; and it is not realistic to think that Christians will be silent about their beliefs, values, and practices or that they will no longer proclaim the Gospel through their deeds. Christians can no more cease to "bring good news to the poor" than they can cease "to proclaim release to the captives and recovery of sight to the blind, to let the oppressed go free, to proclaim the year of the Lord's favor" (Luke 4:18–19). Just as Christians believe they must speak prophetically against sin, evil, and injustices in the world, they must speak evangelistically about Jesus, who wants to save and restore everyone and everything.

During the past century, Christians have become increasingly sensitive to cultural realities related to how they proclaim the Gospel of Jesus Christ. In particular, missionaries have become more aware of the contextual nature of what they think, say, and do. Consequently, missionaries and missiology have become less deceptive and coercive in how they proclaim Jesus through their heightened awareness and sensitivity to the social, political, and economic contextuality of their ministries. But these changes have not stopped missionaries from proclaiming the Gospel. Likewise, Christians have not stopped preaching and teaching; they have not stopped worshipping God and performing the sacraments; they have not stopped meeting people, developing relationships, and caring for others in all dimensions of their lives. To be sure, some Christians have put less emphasis on missionary and evangelistic ministries; however, others have not. Be that as it may, their heightened awareness and concern to follow the Golden Rule of loving one's neighbor as oneself (Mark 12:28–31) has complemented their corresponding concern to follow the Great Commission, which involves going, making disciples, baptizing, and teaching (Matt 28:19–20). In making known the Gospel, Christians do not want their witness marred by inattentiveness to others, since they want to listen to others as well as have others listen to them. Christians want their preaching heard in ways that are clear and persuasive, and not deceptive or coercive. Such forms of proclamation are interested in hearing as well as being heard.

A variation of proselytism involves unjust and unloving methods of evangelism directed toward other Christians. Evangelism does not preclude anyone to whom the Gospel of Jesus Christ may be shared, but it does preclude deceptive and coercive methods, especially directed against fellow believers from other church traditions. For example, Protestants have sometimes targeted Catholic and Orthodox Christians around the world, rather than those who have not heard of Jesus. Such tactics prey upon those who are vulnerable due to ignorance, gullibility, or misinformation. This competitive approach to missionary work and evangelism (or "sheep stealing") has done more to hurt than help the mission of God, especially when the needs of the world remain so vast and varied.

A great deal of ecumenical literature is available with regard to what proselytism is and how to avoid it. The World Council of Churches talks about it; so does the National Council of Churches.[2] Proselytism is not a new dilemma. Christian discussion of the topic occurred in the Faith and Order Commission as early as 1920, so proselytism certainly is not new to ecumenical concern.[3] In the interim, many Christian gatherings have met in order to talk about the nature and extent of proselytism, how to prevent it from occurring, and how to continue evangelizing in ways that are biblical, just, and worthy of the mission of God.[4] As important as evangelism is, Christians ought not to use unjust and unloving methods for spreading the Gospel. They also need to evaluate their intentions, since ulterior motives may hinder the mission of God. Christians do not want the Gospel needlessly obscured by unholy motives and methods.

## EVANGELISM AND INTERFAITH RELATIONS

Evangelism becomes more precarious when understood in light of increased interaction with and interest in dialoging with people from other religions or faith traditions. It is a truism nowadays that the world is shrinking; people from different cultures and religions increasingly come into contact with one another. Such contact does not require travel abroad, since people—in the United States, at least—are becoming increasingly diverse, religiously as well as other ways. So how ought Christians to view proclamation (in general) and evangelism (in particular) in relationship to those from other religious traditions?

Paul Knitter wrote a provocative book in identifying several models of how Christians and churches relate to people from other religions. He presents four models: 1) The Replacement Model ("Only One True Religion"); 2) The Fulfillment Model ("The One Fulfills the Many"); 3) The Mutuality Model ("Many True Religions Called to Dialogue"); and 4) The Acceptance Model ("Many True Religions: So Be It").[5] Knitter subdivides these models into numerous sub-models, reflecting a variety of Christian viewpoints with regard to interacting with people from other religions, including how proclamation and evangelism should occur.

It lies beyond the scope of this work to analyze and assess, theologically, the various models. However, it is noteworthy that Knitter categorizes the World Council of Churches (WCC) in the first model: The Replacement Model. He notes that the WCC made landmark decisions in the 1970s to encourage dialogue with people from other religions; however, according to Knitter, "while the WCC was pushing dialogue beyond the Replacement Model, its theology was still located in a perspective of total replacement."[6] To be sure, members within the WCC have suggested more progressive views of other religions, but nothing officially has changed. Knitter concludes: "And that's where things seem to remain within the WCC: strong appeals to Christians to engage persons of other religions in serious dialogue and cooperation, but theological positions that retain their roots in the Replacement Model—either total or partial."[7]

The National Council of Churches has carefully nuanced the nature of its dialogue with people from other religions. For example, the Interfaith Relations Commission actively engages in building and maintaining interfaith relationships and advancing theological reflection upon their relationships.[8] In order to accomplish these goals, the Commission emphasizes both theological reflection and building relationships with individuals and organizations of other faith traditions, and encouraging similar involvements by other Christians.

Value placed upon interfaith relations highlight the value of getting to know people from other religions, without an evangelistic agenda. Indeed the command to love our neighbor as ourselves requires that Christians listen sincerely and receptively to others; it is what we would expect as loving toward ourselves. People created in the image of God, regardless of their religious convictions, deserve to be heard, understood as best as possible, appreciated, and learned from, since all truth—so to speak—is God's truth. Christians impoverish themselves when they do not listen to others. Christian love demands that we love others as we love ourselves, and interfaith relations importantly remind us of the need to communicate in ways that are open, honest, and fair in relationship to everyone.

A growing missiological concern is to understand and appreciate the faith of those in other religions. Too often, ignorance has damaged opportunities for Christians to relate positively with those who do not share their beliefs, values, and practices. Understanding comes largely through willingness to dialogue without an agenda other than to know and communicate with one another. This openness to dialogue may include talking with those most unlike Christianity, whose extreme and sometimes violent views may be due as much to misunderstanding as to malevolent motives. Such dialogue does not easily occur; Christians ought not to be naïve in how they relate with others. But open and honest communication with people from other religions seems far more loving than alternatives that disdain dialogue.

Growth in understanding and appreciation of people from other religions may lead to collaboration in areas of mutual concern. For example, religious freedom is a theme beneficial to people around the world. Too many martyrs have died, when their deaths were preventable. People would benefit from efforts by those from all religions to reduce the marginalization, oppression, and violence done to others, especially when it occurs in the name of religious conviction. The universality of human rights is an issue that may unite people from different religions around the world. Indeed, there are many issues for which people from different religious traditions may collaborate for the sake of equal rights for women, children, and others who are unjustly treated.

In light of interfaith relations, how should Christians view proclamation of Jesus Christ, the Gospel, and evangelism? Regardless of interfaith relations, Christians will continue to witness and proclaim—in word and deed—about their beliefs, values, and practices. It is God's will that they do so, and proclamation is considered part of their love toward others. No doubt, evangelism will still occur, since people will continue to be drawn to faith, repentance, baptism, and churches. However, Christians should become more wise and loving about sharing the Gospel and not peripherals related to their cultural, political, and economic preferences. Such wisdom and love should also beware of ministry methods that deceptively or coercively take advantage of people in other religions. Proselytizing tactics are as wrong directed toward such people as they are when directed toward Christians, who are vulnerable in one way or another.

## CONCLUSION

Proclamation remains essential to God's mission in the world. It does not represent the only dimension of the mission of God, but proclamation in word and deed is inextricably bound up with how

Christians give witness in the world. To be sure, proclamation occurs in many ways; it does not always include words. Proclamation needs to be incarnate, that is, our actions need to be holy if we are to speak words about a God and savior who are holy, and who want to become reconciled with the world and restore it. Christians *cannot not* help but proclaim the good news of the Gospel to others; but they can be wise and loving in how they go about doing so.

Likewise, evangelism remains crucial to the mission of God. It is as important today for people in the world as it was in the early church. Christians ought to be engaged in evangelism in ways that are faithful to the Bible and prudent (temperate, just, and courageous) in communicating the Gospel to others. Certainly it is becoming more difficult to share about Jesus Christ, given the varying social, political, and economic contexts in the world. Likewise, increasing interaction with and sensitivity to those from other religions challenge God's call to bear witness for the salvation and transformation of the world. With the help of the Holy Spirit, Christians may be emboldened to share God's good news, which includes the totality of apostolic faith, life, and witness.

Rather than being divisive among Christians and churches, proclamation and evangelism may contribute to ecumenical understanding, cooperation, and unity. Working toward mutual understanding may not necessarily lead to agreement. But dialogue and collaboration can grow as Christians recognize and appreciate each other's understanding of God's mission in the world. Like Paul's analogy of the church as a body, Christians around the world may function as a catholic or universal body (Eph 4:1-16). Not every part of churches worldwide need to understand and act exactly the same way in order for God's reign to occur. Their diversity may contribute to unity as well as the richness of Christian witness, since the mysterious workings of God's Spirit occur in so many ways. Unity in proclamation and unity in evangelism may only occur gradually in incremental steps. But such unity can occur, and unity among Christians in the future may come about best when considering and contributing to the holistic mission of God.

# NOTES

1. The meaning *of proselytism* comes originally from Greek and Roman words that mean "coming to a place" or "convert." A proselyte, for example, was someone who had converted to a new religion. In the New Testament, "proselytes" were usually Gentile (or pagan) converts to Christianity. Initially, the words *proselyte* and *proselytism* were neutral terms, used synonymously with *evangelism*. However, over time, the negative aspects of evangelistic practices were associated more and more with proselytism. Although *evangelism* and *proselytism* have been used synonymously in this chapter, the unjust and unloving practices of converting people are identified more with proselytism than evangelism. That does not mean, of course, that negative practices may still take place when Christian evangelistic practices occur, but it is important to distinguish between words when they help to contrast very different approaches used to convert people.

2. For example, see "The Challenge of Proselytism and the Calling to Common Witness," World Council of Churches, available at http://www.oikoumene.org/en/resources/documents/wcc-commissions/joint-working-group-between-the-roman-catholic-church-and-the-wcc/challenge-of-proselytism.html (accessed July 12, 2012).

3. For example, see "The concern about proselytism as an ecumenical issue antedates the establishment of the WCC. The 1920 Encyclical of the Ecumenical Patriarchate, which proposed the foundation of a *koinonia* of churches, asked for the cessation of proselytizing activities. In the preliminary Faith and Order and Life and Work meetings, which took place in the same year, the issue of proselytism was again raised. Since the very establishment of the WCC the issue of proselytism has been identified as one of the hindrances to Christian unity. As early as 1954, the Central Committee in Evanston decided that in view of difficulties that were affecting relationships between WCC member churches, a commission should be appointed to study further the issue of proselytism and religious liberty. After a number of years of laborious study, a statement on "Christian Witness, Proselytism and Religious Liberty in the Setting of the World Council of Churches," drafted by the com-

mission and revised twice by the Central Committee (1956 and 1960), was received by the WCC Third Assembly (New Delhi, 1961).

"Issues of proselytism and common witness have also been on the agenda of the Joint Working Group between the Roman Catholic Church and the World Council of Churches, which has elaborated three important study documents: "Common Witness and Proselytism" (1970); "Common Witness" (1982); and "The Challenge of Proselytism and the Calling to Common Witness" (1996)"—in "Towards common witness: A call to adopt responsible relationships in mission and to renounce proselytism," World Council of Churches, September 19, 1997, available at http://www.oikoumene.org/gr/resources/documents/wcc-commissions/mission-and-evangelism/towards-common-witness.html (accessed February 15, 2010).

4. For example, see: Pontifical Council for Promoting Christian Unity, "The Evangelical-Roman Catholic Dialogue on Mission, 1977-1984: A Report," in *Information Service*, no. 60 (Vatican City: Vatican Press, 1986), 71–97; Pontifical Council for Promoting Christian Unity "Summons to Witness to Christ in Today's World: A Report on the Baptist-Roman Catholic International Conversations, 1984-1988," in *Information Service*, no. 72 (Vatican City: Vatican Press, 1990), 5–14; Pope John Paul II, "Letter to European Bishops on Relations Between Catholics and Orthodox in the New Situation of Central and Eastern Europe (31 May 1991)," in *Information Service*, no. 81 (Vatican City: Vatican Press, 1992), 101–03; Pontifical Commission for Russia, "General Principles and Practical Norms for Coordinating the Evangelizing Activity and Ecumenical Commitment of the Catholic Church in Russia and Other Countries of the Commonwealth of Independent States," ibid., 104–08; Joint International Commission for Theological Dialogue between the Roman Catholic Church and the Orthodox Church, "Uniatism: Method of Union of the Past and the Present Search for Full Communion," in *Information Service*, no. 83 (Vatican City: Vatican Press, 1993), 96–99; "US Orthodox/Roman Catholic Consultation at the Holy Cross Orthodox School of Theology" (Brookline, MA: May 26–28, 1992), in *Origins*, vol. 22, no. 5 (11 June 1992), 79–80; "Towards Koinonia in Faith, Life and Witness," discussion paper

for the fifth world conference on Faith and Order. Santiago de Compostela, 3–14 August 1993, published in the conference report, T. F. Best and Gunther Gassmann, eds., *On the Way to Fuller Koinonia*, Geneva, WCC, 1994 (Faith and Order paper no. 166), 263ff.—in "The Challenge of Proselytism and the Calling to Common Witness," available at http://www.oikoumene.org/en/resources/documents/wcc-commissions/joint-working-group-between-the-roman-catholic-church-and-the-wcc/challenge-of-proselytism.html (accessed July 12, 2012).

5.  Paul F. Knitter, *Introducing Theologies of Religions* (Maryknoll, NY: Orbis Books, 2002), vii–x.

6.  Ibid., 43.

7.  Ibid., 44.

8.  See Interfaith Relations Commission, Interfaith Home, National Council of Churches, available at http://www.ncccusa.org/interfaith/ifrhome.html (accessed July 12, 2012).

# 6

# BAPTISM
## Sacrament of Unity,
## Sacrament of Mission

*Mitzi J. Budde*

Our Christian identity is established in baptism. Baptism is a call, a commission, and a new creation. Through baptism, we are publicly named and claimed as Christ's own and the journey of our lives becomes one of accompaniment to his, in the context of a community of faith with pilgrims who are likewise committed to the same journey, called to a similar path, commended for the same destination, offering one another strength and sustenance on the way.[1] Each of the baptized has a Christian vocation for unity and mission, given in baptism, guided through regular encounter with Scripture, fed through the Eucharist and sustained in community. This call to unity and mission is not unique; rather, we are individually commissioned in baptism to participate with the church catholic in Christ's mission.

I offer two vignettes related to the call and claim of baptism on our lives:

Vignette #1: As I drove past Calvary United Methodist Church in Great Cacapon, West Virginia, on an early August afternoon, I was captivated by the sign outside the church: "Need to be baptized? River baptisms 8/28 2pm. Call 258-6263." The town's name derives from its location at the confluence of the Cacapon and Potomac Rivers; that convergence is actually the town's *raison d'être*. But the church building is not on the river, so any one who wanted to accept the invitation to baptism would need to contact the church to find out where on the river, and on which river, this baptismal event would take place. What an unusual invitation: "Need to be baptized?" Not a cajoling message like "You should be baptized." Nor a threatening one like "Want to be saved? You must be baptized!" But an invitation: driving by on State Route 9, do you feel a need to be baptized? Is God stirring the water in your life?

Vignette #2: Being a librarian can, at times, resemble being a bartender or a priest; one never knows what type of inquiry the next phone call or the next patron will bring. A long time ago, while I was working in a seminary library, an anonymous caller urgently wanted to know, "Do you have a liturgy for unbaptism? I was baptized as an infant. How do I get rid of it?"

What these two stories—one inviting baptism, the other rejecting baptism—have in common is the question of what claim the baptismal act has on our life's journey. Is God claiming an allegiance through baptism? Does God require a response? What is God's call to the baptized? What does the church's practice of baptism mean? What is the individual's responsibility as a baptized person? What is the church's responsibility to the baptized person? What is our baptismal mission, and how does it correlate to the church catholic?

This article seeks to address how baptism relates to the unity and mission of the church and to explore the missiological opportunities and challenges of ecumenical mutual recognition of baptism. In 1982, the World Council of Churches Faith and Order convergence document *Baptism, Eucharist and Ministry (BEM)* called the church to account for its baptismal disunity:

> The inability of the churches mutually to recognize their various practices of baptism as sharing in the one baptism, and their actual dividedness in spite of mutual baptismal recognition, have given dramatic visibility to the broken witness of the Church....The need to recover baptismal unity is at the heart of the ecumenical task as it is central for the realization of genuine partnership within the Christian communities.[2]

It should be acknowledged that some Christians and churches will choose to remain apart from any effort toward mutual recognition of baptism. Some Christians and churches view baptism as an ordinance done in obedience to Christ's command, but not as a sacrament. Some other traditions do not practice water baptism at all, such as the Society of Friends who considers all of life as sacramental and the Church of Christ, Scientist, whose understanding of baptism is a nonmaterial baptism of the Holy Spirit and fire found within the heart rather than in an outward ritual. The theological distinctives of these traditions provide a perspective that bears witness that no human act, including baptism, is a work necessary for salvation and that all Christian acts are responses to the prompting of the Holy Spirit. The church has achieved ecumenical convergence on the doctrine of justification; salvation comes through Jesus Christ alone.[3] Christians and churches that choose to work toward mutual recognition of baptism do so in order to overcome the fractured witness of nonrecognition of the church's act of initiation and in order to fulfill the creed of the church: "we acknowledge one baptism for the forgiveness of sins...."

Much of the ecumenical literature on baptism since *BEM* has focused on ecclesiology and sacramentology, on baptism within the church. Susan K. Wood's recent book, *One Baptism: Ecumenical Dimensions of the Doctrine of Baptism*, for example, is a remarkable ecumenical text. Like most such resources, however, the book does not address mission.[4] Understandably so: there is a sense in which we need to get our own internal house in order as Christians so that we might give a credible witness to the world as to why anyone should need or want to be baptized and to stay baptized.

I want to assert that the call of baptism is a call to mission, to service from the church outward to the world: bearing witness to unbelievers, reaching out to those in need (both baptized and unbaptized), working for justice in this world through the power of the Holy Spirit until Christ establishes his ultimate justice in the culmination of time, a new heaven and a new earth.[5] Baptism links us to Christ's truth—Christ, who is "the way, the truth, and the life" (John 14:6)—to Christ's justice and Christ's mercy, the human journey of life lived joyfully in accord with God's will, the unknown future unfolding before us in the cathedral that is the world, the creation all around us, the kingdom of God within us, fighting the good fight with the armor of Christ in whatever corner of the cosmic war of good and evil we find ourselves. The literature on baptism generally focuses on the ecclesiology of the visible and invisible church; we should talk about the visible and invisible kingdom of God around and within, present and future. Would we be citizens of that kingdom? In baptism, we individually and collectively answer yes.

## HOW BAPTISM RELATES TO THE UNITY AND MISSION OF THE CHURCH

In baptism, we are individually and corporately commissioned for mission. The liturgy of baptism in the worship book of the Evangelical Lutheran Church in America, *Evangelical Lutheran Worship*, is framed theologically with an explicit connection between baptism, unity, and mission. The presiding minister opens the liturgy with these or similar words: "God, who is rich in mercy and love, gives us a new birth into a living hope through the sacrament of baptism...We are united with all the baptized in the one body of Christ, anointed with the gift of the Holy Spirit, and joined in God's mission for the life of the world."[6] Then, following the renunciation of evil, the confession of faith in the Apostles' Creed, the baptism in the triune name Father, Son, and Holy Spirit with water, and the anointing with oil, the baptismal liturgy closes with the gathered assembly of the people of God welcoming the newly baptized with words that define this mission: "We welcome you into the body of Christ and into the mission we share: join us in giving thanks and praise to God and bearing God's creative and redeeming word to all the world."[7] The baptismal mission is two-part: first, to give thanks and praise to God, and second, to bear God's creative and redeeming word to all the world, in the context of the gathered people of God.

This is the call to all the baptized. *The Nature and Purpose of the Church*, a Faith and Order document of the World Council of Churches, calls baptism "the 'ordination' of all believers"[8] and defines the church in this way: "As the communion of the baptised [sic], the Church is a priesthood of the whole people of God."[9]

With these considerations in mind, I would like to suggest six aspects to baptismal mission in the unity of the church. First, our baptismal mission is derived from and united with Jesus' own mission and ministry. Mark 1:9–15 describes Jesus' baptism by John the Baptist in the Jordan River. This biblical account is one of the few biblical occurrences in which the three persons of the Trinity appear together. Each plays a crucial part: Jesus presents himself for baptism; the Spirit descends on Jesus; and God the Father pronounces Jesus the beloved son. The heavens are torn apart, split open, rent from top to bottom—God is decisively entering human time and space.[10] The text makes us witnesses to this event, and we are allowed to see the relationship of the Trinity. We get a glimpse into the interior life of God. The church's unity, given by the power and presence of Christ's life-giving Spirit, is modeled on the perfect unity that is the relationship of the persons of the Holy Trinity with one another as through Christ, and we are invited to share in that relationship. The church is the earthly expression, a dim reflection, of the relationship between the persons of the triune God. Our participation in this relationship is a pure gift of grace.

Jesus submits to a baptism of repentance for the forgiveness of sins in solidarity with us, each one of us, and with all of sinful humanity. By doing so, he links his baptism with our own. "We have been buried with him by baptism into death, so that, just as Christ was raised from the dead by the glory of the Father, so we too might walk in newness of life" (Rom 6:4). The apostle Paul reminds us that it is by living and dying with Christ through the waters of baptism that we become Christians.

Baptism initiates God's people into the ministry of Christ. Just as Jesus was immediately driven into the wilderness by the Spirit after his baptism, so the church is called to mission in Christ's name, through the ongoing work of the Spirit in us and through us to reach out to a hurting and sinful world. Through baptism, the Spirit has an avenue through which to drive us out into the wilderness places: to the highways and byways of the journey of life, to "participate in the mission of witness and service which is the continuing work of the Spirit of Christ."[11]

Second, our baptismal mission is linked to the commissioning of the disciples after Jesus' resurrection: "Go therefore and make disciples of all nations, baptizing them in the name of the Father and of the Son and of the Holy Spirit, and teaching them to obey everything that I have commanded you. And remember, I am with you always, to the end of the age" (Matt 28:19–20). Jesus sent the disciples out—and sends us—in solidarity with all and in service to all who are thirsty, to share his living water with a wilted and weary world.

We "come to the unity of the faith and the knowledge of the Son of God, to maturity, to the measure of the full stature of Christ" (Eph 4:13) through that grace. And the variety of gifts that enrich the church and its witness comes out of that unity in Christ: "some would be apostles, some prophets, some evangelists, some pastors and teachers" (Eph 4:11). This diversity advances the witness of unity through different types of messengers who bear the Gospel message to a variety of settings and situations and audiences. This is the apostolic succession that has borne the witness of the Gospel through the generations in faithful unbroken continuity, each proclaiming his or her own unique witness to Christ, in harmony with all the others. Each gift for ministry, whether that of an individual or of a denomination, is measured and tested by its faithfulness to "one Lord, one faith, one baptism" (Eph 4:5).

Third, our baptismal mission calls us to participate in the great cosmic battle of good and evil and challenges us not to sit on the sidelines. Through faith, we know that ultimately God will prevail, but until the kingdom comes, we are called to work for justice and mercy for all people. The Bible uses the imagery of water to signify the powerful forces of evil, over which God claims authority and subdues—the story of Noah and the flood, the parting of the Red Sea that allowed the people of Israel to escape in Exodus and drowned Pharaoh's army. In his catechisms, Martin Luther connects baptism with repentance and faith and the daily battle with sin that all humans must wage:

> Christians always have enough to do to believe firmly what Baptism promises and brings–victory over death and the devil, forgiveness of sins, God's grace, the entire Christ, and the Holy Spirit with his gifts…Thus, we must regard baptism and put it to use in such a way that we may draw strength and comfort from it when our sins or conscience oppress us, and say, "But I am baptized!"[12]

The biblical writers also use water and baptism as symbols of social justice: "Let justice roll down like waters, and righteousness like an everflowing stream" (Amos 5:24). We are called to discern how to live out our baptisms wherever we are situated in life: whether it is to challenge unjust business practices in the workplace, or to work for a just and lasting peace in the Middle East, or to advocate for the reopening of the government-shuttered Greek Orthodox Holy Trinity Seminary in Turkey, or to donate to disaster relief efforts, or to become a missionary in distant lands. "As many of you as were baptized into Christ have clothed yourselves with Christ…[T]here is no longer slave or free, there is no longer male and female; for all of you are one in Christ Jesus" (Gal 3:27–28). Through our baptismal mission, we live in a perpetual advent of hope, waiting and wonder, bearing our cross, yes, but also assured of resurrection.

Fourth, our baptismal mission is grounded in the deep joy of life in Christ. In Acts, the story of the baptism of the Ethiopian eunuch by Philip culminates with the eunuch continuing on his way, rejoicing (8:39). The baptismal liturgy anticipates and celebrates this joy in Christian living. The collect pray over the newly baptized with the laying on of hands (also used in the service of affirmation of baptism) saying, "Sustain [name] with the gift of your Holy Spirit: the spirit of wisdom and understanding, the spirit of counsel and might, the spirit of knowledge and the fear of the Lord, *the spirit of joy in your presence*, both now and forever [emphasis added],"[13] and in the service of affirmation of baptism the people welcome the newly confirmed with these words: "We *rejoice* with you in the life of baptism."[14]

Near my home in West Virginia runs the Cacapon River, a tributary of the Potomac. The river is a living thing; it changes every time you see it. In summer, it can be a meandering stream of water; when it thaws in spring, it can be a raging torrent, straining to overflow its banks. But in winter, the river can seem to be completely frozen over and completely still. And yet, if you look and listen closely, you can see and hear, underneath the ice, the living current flowing steadily, inexorably toward the Chesapeake Bay and ultimately the Atlantic Ocean. Baptism is the living stream that flows through us, restoring and reviving us every day of our lives.

"Yes, everything is for your sake, so that grace, as it extends to more and more people, may increase thanksgiving, to the glory of God" (2 Cor 4:15). So God's living waters of baptism can refresh, strengthen, renew, and empower God's people through all the seasons of life, as grace extends further and further, for the joyful work of the kingdom.

Fifth, our baptismal mission is the foundation of the life of faith: "you were washed, you were sanctified, you were justified in the name of the Lord Jesus Christ and in the Spirit of our God" (1 Cor 6:11). Baptism is a gift of grace and a call to the vocation of being a Christian. The gift does not spare us from the wilderness as it did not spare Jesus. Conflict, pain, and evil are still all around. In the Lord's Prayer, we pray to be saved from the time of trial, and because Jesus faced and ultimately vanquished temptation in the wilderness, we are spared from trials that are more than we can bear. As Luther says in the *Babylonian Captivity of the Church*, "In [baptism] the penitent has a shield against all assaults of the scornful enemy, an answer to the sins that disturb his conscience, an antidote for the dread of death and judgment, and a comfort in every temptation—namely, this one truth—when he says: 'God is faithful to his promises, and I received his sign in baptism.'"[15]

Baptism forms us in the Christian life and transforms us by God's grace and the work of the Holy Spirit into God's own family: sisters and brothers to Christ himself. This once-in-a-lifetime event initiates a lifelong process of growth in discipleship and faith in us. The baptismal mission is worship and witness. Like the pull of a deep but unseen current, the Holy Spirit guides us through our baptism to shield and comfort us through the trials and temptations of our own journey. Baptism is the daily death of the sinful self and the daily resurrection of the new person in Christ, in order to bear witness to the world, "so that the life of Jesus may be made visible in our mortal flesh" (2 Cor 4:11). Baptism grafts an individual into the community of faith, the church, and links that person with all the baptized people of God. To be baptized into Christ is to be baptized into the church, which is Christ's body. This baptism into Jesus' death and resurrection is the bond that we share with all Christians everywhere. As people made in the image of God, we too are inherently a people in relationship with one another.

Sixth, our baptismal mission is future-oriented, located within the church and then directed outward to the world, pointing always to the kingdom of God. Karl Barth wrote in his *Church Dogmatics*: "The future has not to be merely a being after baptism; it must be a being from baptism."[16] Baptism brings the eschatological future of the one being baptized into the present. The promise of salvation is given.

In summary, baptism is the gateway to participation in the community that is the church, the body of Christ, through which the Holy Spirit leads us into a life-long Christian faith journey, bearing witness to our neighbors, upholding our fellow Christians and the church in prayer, forgiving and being forgiven in a life of reconciliation, caring for the poor and needy, welcoming the stranger as Christ has welcomed us, offering hospitality to all of God's people, growing in knowledge of the faith in lifelong catechesis, participating in worship, eating the Eucharist meal, and seeking full communion with the whole church until the kingdom of God is fulfilled.[17]

## MISSIOLOGICAL IMPLICATIONS OF ECUMENICAL MUTUAL RECOGNITION OF BAPTISM

Baptism is the sacrament of unity. Christians are "baptized *by* a particular church *into* the one church,"[18] and, thereby, Christians are united in "one Lord, one faith, one baptism" (Eph 4:5). We are knitted and yoked together with all those who have been sealed with the Sign of the Cross in baptism. We are to bear one another's burdens and share in one another's joys and sorrows. We are to care for each other in the wilderness, even as the angels tended Jesus in the wilderness. Our unity with Christ in baptism is also then unity with everyone else who is baptized into Christ.[19] *Baptism, Eucharist and Ministry* made the bold claim: "when baptismal unity is realized in one holy, catholic, apostolic Church, a genuine Christian witness can be made to the healing and reconciling love of God."[20] To be united with Christ through baptism means to be united with Christ's church in all of its expressions, from local parish to universal church, across divisions and across denominations.

The 1982 Lima document (*Baptism, Eucharist and Ministry*) further asserted:

> Churches are increasingly recognizing one another's baptism as the one baptism into Christ when Jesus Christ has been confessed as Lord by the candidate or, in the case of infant baptism, when confession has been made by the church (parents, guardians, god-parents and congregation) and affirmed later by personal faith and commitment. Mutual recognition of baptism is acknowledged as an important sign and means of expressing the baptismal unity given in Christ. Wherever possible, mutual recognition should be expressed explicitly by the churches.[21]

Twenty-five years later, the ecumenical movement has begun to make notable strides in responding to *BEM*'s call for the churches to develop an explicit expression of mutual recognition of baptism. The 2006 World Council of Churches General Assembly "affirmed together that baptism is the basis of their commitment to one another within the ecumenical movement."[22] Some recent accomplishments toward this end include:

- The Joint Working Group between the Roman Catholic Church and the World Council of Churches released a common statement on baptism in 2005 entitled *Ecclesiological and Ecumenical Implications of a Common Baptism: A JWG Study*.[23] In it, the Joint Working Group identified eleven specific "ways in which the convergences achieved on baptism can be consolidated and received into the life of the churches so that further steps forward towards unity can be built on solid foundations," such as incorporating the theological significance of baptism into the theological basis for ecumenical bodies, encouraging ecumenical study of baptism and the use of common baptismal certificates in local regions, having church representatives at each other's baptismal events, praying regularly in worship for those newly baptized in all traditions, and cooperating in advocating for sacramental understanding of baptism in media depictions of the rite.[24]

- In Germany, on April 29, 2007, an agreement on the mutual recognition of baptism was signed between eleven churches: The Council of Anglican Episcopal Churches in Germany, The Ethiopic Orthodox Church, the Armenian Apostolic Church in Germany, The Evangelical-Old Reformed Church in Lower Saxony, The Herrnhuter Brethren, the Independent Evangelical Lutheran Church, the Evangelical Church in Germany, the Evangelical Methodist Church, the Orthodox Church in Germany, the Roman Catholic Church, and the Old Catholic Diocese of Germany. It stated, "therefore we recognize every baptism carried out according to Jesus' teaching in the Name of the Father and of the Son and the Holy Ghost with the symbolic submersion in water or pouring of water and rejoice in every single person who is baptized. This mutual recognition of baptism is an expression of the bonds of unity in Jesus Christ."[25]

- In 2010, the United States Conference of Catholic Bishops (USCCB), the Christian Reformed Church in North America, the Presbyterian Church (USA), the Reformed Church in America, and the United Church of Christ adopted a *Common Agreement on Mutual Recognition of Baptism*, which states: "For our baptisms to be mutually recognized, water and the scriptural Trinitarian formula 'Father, Son, and Holy Spirit' (Mt 28:19-20) must be used in the baptismal rite."[26] Seven years in the making, the common agreement is based upon eight points of agreement specified in an eighty-two-page dialogue document, *These Living Waters*, from the Seventh Round of Reformed-Catholic Dialogue.[27]

- A trilateral conversation on baptism was authorized and established in 2011 between the Lutheran World Federation, the Pontifical Council for Promoting Christian Unity of the Roman Catholic Church, and the Mennonite World Conference.[28]

- The World Council of Churches published a study text entitled *One Baptism: Towards Mutual Recognition* in 2011. The document is not a convergence document, as *Baptism,*

*Eucharist and Ministry* was in 1982, but rather it is a study text intended as a resource to further the churches' dialogues on this issue. The text "is offered in the hope that fresh perspectives will help the churches (a) to clarify the meaning of the mutual recognition of baptism, (b) to put the consequences of mutual recognition fully into practice, and (c) to clarify issues which still prevent such recognition."[29]

Mutual recognition of baptism allows churches and individual Christians to unite our voices and to use our diversity of gifts to make a fuller and more coherent witness, in order that all may "know Christ and make him known," in the words of the *Book of Common Prayer*.[30] Our ecumenical agreements flow out of the common mission that we share with the saints of the church and with all faithful Christians, ordained and lay. And as unity is made manifest, the Spirit continues to heal the breaches in the church.

In *The Cost of Discipleship*, Dietrich Bonhoeffer wrote, "The body of Christ becomes visible to the world in the congregation gathered around word and sacrament."[31] By gathering around Word and Sacrament as the community of faith, we bear witness to the world that we are joined together to the communion of saints across time and space—those who have blessed the Eucharist through these same words, across the centuries and around the globe. The church, broken as Christ's own body was broken, is being resurrected even as Christ's own body was resurrected. While unity is not something that can be created by human effort, it is our baptismal mission to make the unity of the church given by Christ visible and recognizable in our lives and our words, in our service and our worship.

## THREE SPECIFIC CURRENT ISSUES

The recent ecumenical work toward mutual recognition of baptism has brought a number of current baptismal practices and issues to the fore. In this final section, I wish to focus on three of them: the traditional division over the validity of infant baptism, the use of alternate formulas for the triune name, and the recent trend in some churches of serving the Eucharist to the unbaptized. Those churches that desire to support mutual recognition of baptism seem to be moving toward a consensus in these three areas.

First is the divide between those who practice baptism for all age groups and those who restrict baptism to persons making an individual profession of faith at an age of accountability. This has been the most difficult impasse of mutual recognition of baptism. The WCC study document *One Baptism*, the Roman Catholic–WCC Joint Working Group text *Ecclesiological and Ecumenical Implications of a Common Baptism*, and various bilateral dialogues, such as the International Conversations between the Anglican Communion and the Baptist World Alliance, have variously proposed that these differences might be bridged "by seeing baptism as part of a larger process of initiation, or one stage on a journey of beginning in the Christian life."[32] Baptist theologian S. Mark Heim developed this further in an essay published in 2007 in the book celebrating the twenty-fifth anniversary of *Baptism, Eucharist and Ministry*, entitled *BEM at 25*. In it, he explains the theological and ecclesiological issues at stake for churches that reject infant baptism and challenges his own tradition "to demonstrate that we can participate in acts of common confession with the wider church," while simultaneously inviting churches that practice infant baptism "to consider whether there are ways to understand the mutual recognition of baptism that would preserve the distinctive strengths of gathered church ecclesiology."[33]

The gift of churches that practice baptism of people of all ages, including infants, is their emphasis on the primacy of God's claiming act in lives of faith and the assertion that faith is predicated upon the gift of God's grace. The conundrum these churches face is the prevalent disregard of many of those thus baptized for the church and the life of faith thereafter. The recidivism rate, if you will, is quite high.

The gift of churches that require personal confession of faith prior to baptism is their emphasis on the accountability of the individual before God and the assertion of the individual's right to reject God's proffer of grace. The Three Self Patriotic Movement Church in China, for example, practices primarily adult baptism so that an individual makes an informed choice about the personal costs of confessing the Christian faith. Even in a country like the United States that has a constitutional commitment to freedom of religion and (historically) a predominantly Christian society, there can be personal costs to professing Christ publicly. The conundrum these churches face is the evidence through the ages and across the globe of millions who were baptized as infants who have demonstrated with their lives that they have claimed their baptisms and seek to walk in the way of Christ, living lives of witness and service. To claim that such Christians are not validly baptized, or even that they are irregularly baptized, seems to question the work of the Holy Spirit.

In the liturgy of confirmation (or affirmation of baptism) in *Evangelical Lutheran Worship*, each confirmand is asked to affirm that, with God's help, he/she intends "to continue in the covenant God made with you in holy baptism." That covenant has five parts: "to live among God's faithful people, to hear the word of God and share in the Lord's supper, to proclaim the good news of God in Christ through word and deed, to serve all people, following the example of Jesus, and to strive for justice and peace in all the earth."[34] When individuals have claimed their baptism as their own through a catechetical process that culminates in a public affirmation of this covenant, might that life journey of faith be recognized by all as valid baptismal faith? Reciprocally, that journey of faith, especially the rite of affirmation of baptism, could be viewed as an integral part of the sacramental act, even when it is separated by a number of years. The Orthodox Churches exemplify this sacramental unity by integrating baptism, confirmation, and chrismation in the same liturgical act. Faith in the word of promise is the fulfillment of baptism.[35]

Second, mutual recognition of baptism is based upon the invariable use of the traditional triune formula—Father, Son, and Holy Spirit. The effort to identify creative alternatives that avoid the exclusive use of male imagery for God is appropriate and edifying in many avenues of church life, such as preaching, teaching, and Bible study. Sacramental sharing among a variety of denominations, however, is predicated on the use of the biblical and creedal terminology used by Christ (e.g., "Abba, Father"; the Great Commission) and the church catholic for two millennia. The Joint Working Group of the Roman Catholic Church and the World Council of Churches requests that churches refrain from utilizing alternative baptismal formulas and administering the Eucharist to those not baptized.[36]

Third, a new challenge has emerged in those parishes that have embraced a practice of open table or open communion, meaning an open invitation to all to receive the Eucharist, whether or not they have been baptized in any tradition and whether or not they identify themselves as Christians. Baptism has traditionally been the church's sacrament of initiation and has been normatively a prerequisite to admission to the Eucharist. Methodists, for example, sometimes speak of communion as a converting ordinance, with the expectation that participation in the Lord's Supper will impel the inquirer toward baptism into Christ's life, death, and resurrection. By contrast, offering open communion indiscriminately to everyone, without seeking to follow up that hunger for Christ's body and blood as an invitation to baptism can seem like a failure of witness. The WCC study document *One Baptism* suggests, "As a general principle, the historic order of reception of baptism before reception of the Eucharist should be observed for the sake of the unity of the church."[37] Mutual recognition of baptism is imperiled when Christians and churches no longer communicate a need for baptism.

Baptism is not primarily an act of joining a particular parish but rather claiming God's sacramental grace for oneself, being grafted into the body of Christ which is the church catholic, and committing oneself to make the life of Jesus visible in our mortal flesh (2 Cor 4:11). The church's baptismal mission is to hold open the invitation to all people to be incorporated into the life of Christ.

It should also be acknowledged that not all Christians and churches would choose to conform to these criteria in order to achieve an ecumenical recognition of baptism. Those who wish to stand outside these agreements also present an important witness: to new ways of engaging God beyond the mainstream (Society of Friends, for example) and to continuity with historical protests that form the identity of certain groups (such as Baptists). It would be helpful if all Christians and churches could be clear about the level of recognition that a particular choice about baptism would receive from the wider church. If a person seeking baptism, or a parent presenting a child for baptism, and the clergy and congregation of a particular church together agree that they wish to use alternative baptismal formulas, for example, it seems appropriate that there be full disclosure about the possible implications if at some point in the future they wish to change church affiliation.

Although innovators will perhaps stand apart from the terms of these agreements, can those participating in these agreements find room to consider the theological perspectives they bring and continue a search for mutual understanding, even if mutual recognition is not possible at this time? Can all traditions at least dialogue with one another about baptism and through that dialogue expand our understandings of the ways in which God may continue to be at work through the Spirit today?

# CONCLUSION

Need to be baptized? Trusting in the promise that "if you confess with your lips that Jesus is Lord and believe in your heart that God raised him from the dead, you will be saved" (Rom 10:9), we do not presume to take God's place as judge. We baptize in obedience to Christ's example and his command. Through Christ, baptism becomes the defining aspect of Christian life, "for our whole life should be baptism, and the fulfilling of the sign or sacrament of baptism, since we have been set free from all else..."[38] It is a daily call to repentance, reconciliation, and return to God's love and forgiveness. And it is the proleptic in-breaking of the kingdom of God into the present life until it finds its ultimate consummation at the end of human life when all Christians are brought into the eschatological kingdom.

The Christian answer to the caller who wished to undo baptism is that one can never be completely free of it; there is no liturgy of unbaptism. Baptism isn't magic, but it does have an objective reality and content. Though one can reject its benefits, the person will always be baptized into Christ. In a sermon on baptism, St. Augustine said:

> See then, how it can come to pass that a man may have the baptism of Christ and still not have the faith or the love of Christ; how it is that he may have the sacrament of holiness and still not be reckoned in the lot of the holy. With regard to the mere sacrament itself, it makes no difference whether someone receives the baptism of Christ where the unity of Christ is not. For, in the case of desertion from the Church by someone who had been baptized in the Church, the deserter will be deprived of the holiness of the life, but he will not lose the sacramental character...A military deserter is deprived of membership in the army, but he is still marked as a soldier of the king.[39]

Just as a baptized Christian can confirm and affirm his or her own baptism, so a person may insist upon repudiating and rejecting one's own baptism; God does not force anyone into relationship with him. The Spirit will keep trying to woo one back into relationship with Christ, but, like the prodigal son of Luke's Gospel, one can turn from the fold of faith.

"For we walk by faith, not by sight" (2 Cor 5:7). By faith, we know that ultimately God's will is being done and will be done. By praying the words, "Thy will be done," in the Lord's Prayer, we are really praying that through our baptism as individuals and as a Christian community, we will receive the grace to be part of Christ's ministry and mission, seeking the accomplishment of God's will and not the thwarting of it, reflecting the unity of the Trinity, and loving and serving all people—those who are baptized, those who have affirmed their baptism, those who have rejected baptism, and those of other faith traditions or of no faith at all. Throughout the lifelong journey of living out the mission of the sacrament of baptism, Christians are called to be a people united in grace and mercy, love and justice.

## NOTES

1. See the theme essay of this book, John T. Ford, "Unity and Mission: A Pilgrimage of Accompaniment."

2. World Council of Churches, *Baptism, Eucharist and Ministry*, Faith and Order Paper No. 111 (Geneva: World Council of Churches, 1982), 6.

3. See the Joint Declaration on the Doctrine of Justification, available at http://www.vatican.va/roman_curia/pontifical_councils/chrstuni/documents/rc_pc_chrstuni_doc_31101999_cath-luth-joint-declaration_en.html (accessed July 16, 2012).

4. Susan K. Wood, *One Baptism: Ecumenical Dimensions of the Doctrine of Baptism* (Collegeville, MN: Liturgical Press, 2009). An exception however, is the useful section on mission in Michael Root, "Baptism and the Unity of the Church: A Study Paper," in *Baptism and the Unity of the Church,* ed. Michael Root and Risto Saarinen (Grand Rapids: Eerdmans, 1998).

5. For a dynamic educational program for middle schoolers based on the theme of mission as a way of life given in the baptismal covenant, see Lauren R. Stanley, *OMG, Y'all! An Exploration of Living Our Lives On a Mission From God* (Doctor of Ministry Project, Virginia Theological Seminary, forthcoming).

6. Evangelical Lutheran Church in America, *Evangelical Lutheran Worship* (Minneapolis: Augsburg Fortress, 2006), 227.

7. Ibid., 231.

8. World Council of Churches, *The Nature and Purpose of the Church* (Geneva: World Council of Churches, 1998), 76.

9. Ibid., 83.

10. M. Eugene Boring, *Mark: A Commentary* (Louisville, KY: Westminster John Knox Press, 2006), 45.

11. Root, "Baptism and the Unity," 22.

12. Martin Luther, "The Large Catechism," in *The Book of Concord: The Confessions of the Evangelical Lutheran Church,* ed. Robert Kolb and Timothy J. Wingert (Minneapolis: Fortress Press, 2000), 461–62.

13. Evangelical Lutheran Church in America, *Evangelical Lutheran Worship*, 231, 237.

14. Ibid., 236.

15. Martin Luther, "The Babylonian Captivity of the Church," in *Word and Sacrament II*, vol. 36, *Luther's Works* (Philadelphia: Fortress Press, 1959), 60.

16. Karl Barth, *The Christian Life (Fragment): Baptism as the Foundation of the Christian Life*, vol. 4, pt. 4, *Church Dogmatics* (Edinburgh: T & T Clark, 1969), 202.

17.  This summary was informed by the early church material in Gordon Lathrop, "The Water That Speaks: The *Ordo* of Baptism and Its Ecumenical Implications," in *Becoming a Christian: The Ecumenical Implications of Our Common Baptism,* Faith and Order Paper No. 184 (Geneva: WCC Publications, 1997), 18–21.

18.  Root, "Baptism and the Unity," 15. Emphasis in the original.

19.  Ibid., 13.

20.  World Council of Churches, *Baptism, Eucharist and Ministry,* 6.

21.  Ibid., 15.

22.  World Council of Churches, *One Baptism: Towards Mutual Recognition: A Study Text.* Faith and Order Paper No. 210 (Geneva: World Council of Churches, 2011), 109.

23.  Joint Working Group between the Roman Catholic Church and the World Council of Churches, "Ecclesiological and Ecumenical Implications of a Common Baptism: A JWG Study," Eighth Report, 1999–2005, available at http://www.oikoumene.org/fileadmin/files/wcc-main/documents/p1/8thjointworkinggroup.pdf (accessed July 16, 2012), 45–72, App. C.

24.  Ibid., 100–12.

25.  See http://www.ekd.de/english/mutual_recognition_of_baptism.html (accessed July 16, 2012).

26.  USCCB and Four Protestant Communities, "Common Agreement on Mutual Recognition of Baptism," *Origins* 40, no. 25 (November 25, 2010): 390.

27.  These Living Waters, Baptism Document, 7th Round Reformed-Catholic Dialogue, available at http://www.ucc.org/synod/resolutions/gs28/Resolution-on-Common-Agreement-on-Mutual-Recognition-of-Baptism.pdf (accessed July 16, 2012).

28.  "LWF Council Agrees to Plans for Trilateral Dialogue with Roman Catholics and Mennonites," 17 June 2011, available at http://www.lutheranworld.org/lwf/index.php/trilateral-dialogue-catholic-mennonite.html (accessed July 16, 2012).

29.  World Council of Churches, *One Baptism,* 1.

30.  The Episcopal Church, *The Book of Common Prayer* (New York: Church Hymnal Corp, 1979), 836.

31. Dietrich Bonhoeffer, *The Cost of Discipleship*, revised and unabridged edition (New York: Collier Books, 1963), 281.

32. "International Conversations between the Anglican Communion and the Baptist World Alliance, McClean [sic], Virginia, USA, 2000-2005," in *Growth in Agreement III: International Dialogue Texts and Agreed Statements 1998-2005*, ed. Jeffrey Gros, Thomas F. Best, and Lorelei F. Fuchs (Geneva: WCC Publications; Grand Rapids: William B. Eerdmans, 2007), 367.

33. S. Mark Heim, "Baptism and Christian Initiation in Ecclesiological Perspective," in *BEM at 25: Critical Insights into a Continuing Legacy*, ed. Thomas F. Best and Tamara Grdzelidze, Faith and Order Paper No. 205 (Geneva: WCC Publications, 2007), 26.

34. Evangelical Lutheran Church in America, *Evangelical Lutheran Worship*, 236.

35. See Luther, "The Babylonian Captivity," 66: "Thus it is not baptism that justifies or benefits anyone, but it is faith in that word of promise to which baptism is added. This faith justifies, and fulfils that which baptism signifies."

36. Joint Working Group, "Ecclesiological and Ecumenical Implications," 109.

37. World Council of Churches, *One Baptism*, 92.

38. Luther, "The Babylonian Captivity," 70.

39. Saint Augustine, "On Baptism," in *Commentary on the Lord's Sermon on the Mount: with Seventeen Related Sermons,* The Fathers of the Church: A New Translation, vol. 3 (New York: Fathers of the Church, 1951), 333–34.

# 7

# BREAD FOR THE JOURNEY
## The Challenge of the Eucharist to the Churches

*Ernest Falardeau, SSS*

## INTRODUCTION

In *Baptism, Eucharist and Ministry,* the Faith and Order Commission of the World Council of Churches (WCC) indicates the pivotal role of the Eucharist in the search for unity in Christ for the Christian Churches.[1] It asks that the churches find some way to bridge the differences that have divided Christians for centuries so as to make more visible the unity that is ours "in the breaking of the bread." Continuing on this trajectory, the WCC convergence statement on *The Nature and Mission of the Church* urges the churches to see the challenge that the Eucharist presents as a moral imperative to worship God and "search for appropriate relationships in social, economic and political life (Mt 5:23ff; 1 Cor 10:14; 1 Cor 11:20-22)."[2]

Ecumenism, the search for Christian unity, is an experience more than an idea. It is a conversion of heart and mind more than a concept to be understood and communicated to others. The hope is that the Holy Spirit who inspires us may inspire others. As a Roman Catholic, I find that the Eucharist presents a constant challenge, a moral imperative in the command of the Lord Jesus to "do this in remembrance of me" (Luke 22:19), both to celebrate the Lord's Supper and to serve one's brothers and sisters as Jesus did in washing the feet of his disciples. Rather than an "either/or," the

Eucharist is a "both/and." It is, therefore, a challenge to all Christians and their churches to worship God and love one's neighbor.

## Bread for the Journey

The Eucharist is bread for the journey; it is not a reward for our goodness. We do not receive it because we are holy but because we need God's grace to become holy. We need the constant inspiration of God's word and the power of God's grace to transform us into what we are to become: the image of God resplendent on the face of Jesus Christ, the risen Lord. As John T. Ford suggests, the journey is made by walking, and we learn what the unity of the church is by being open to God's continual conversion and transformation of who we are into what we are to become: the body of Christ, one in Christ and in God.

This is why "being is communion," and it is becoming the "other" that is God in Christ, and the church. It is the day of the Lord, continually becoming the reality in a world that is God's, "in [whom] we live and move and have our being" (Acts 17:28). God's world is awash in grace and goodness, yet ever in need of redemption and of the unity in Christ that only can come by the grace of God on a world ever in need of forgiveness and transformation.

As we pray for unity, we know we are on sacred ground. We reflect on the gift of God that is the body and blood of Christ given once, for all, for the world's redemption, becoming the food on God's table before which God and man "at table are sat down." Bread for the journey: we dare to accept Jesus' invitation to "do this in remembrance of me"(Luke 22:19), knowing that by doing so we accept the challenge to forgive our neighbor and our enemy, and we must serve everyone because Jesus washed the feet of all the disciples, knowing they were about to betray him, deny him, and flee his presence.

Seeing the Eucharist as a moral challenge and as the necessary food for our journey to the Father, I am reminded of the family meals that were at the heart of my own family's life and existence. I believe those meals illustrate the kind of love, forgiveness, and acceptance that the Eucharist requires and provides so that we may continue our journey homeward to the Father with Christ.

## One Man's Family

Every family is different and has different ways of doing things. Every family is human and, therefore, part of sinful humanity with its strengths and weaknesses. My family is no different. But looking back on our family meals when I was a child, I can say that they were very special. Though we were ten children, Dad found ingenious ways of seeing that everyone had his or her place at the table. All were not only welcomed around the table, but meals would not begin until everyone found their place (we were six boys and four girls). Dad made a special bench so that the three youngest members of the family could sit comfortably on it—huddled together a bit, but comfortably—and high enough to reach the food on their plate. Coming to dinner was not considered a reward; it was a privilege we would not want to miss.

The meal was the place where everyone was at home. Events of the day were recounted. All was forgiven and forgotten as we approached the table. Each person was respected and could have their say. We enjoyed one another's company, our jokes or stories, and accomplishments. Even embarrassing moments could be laughed at together. No one was excluded from the table or "sent off to bed without dinner." Exclusion was not a part of the family discipline or experience.

While I can understand the concept of excommunication and its use by the churches, I also understand that Jesus did not exclude sinners from his table. St. Peter Julian Eymard, the founder of the Blessed Sacrament Fathers and Brothers (of which I am a member), though he grew up in the Jansenistic world of nineteenth-century France, advocated far in advance of his time the admission of Catholics to frequent Holy Communion and of children to the Sacrament at an early age. He saw the Eucharist as the remedy for our human weakness, not a reward for our virtue.

In my ecumenical journey, I have found the example of my family of birth and my religious family an insight into the Eucharist, which has helped me to appreciate the Eucharist as a sacred sign of God's saving grace. Can we not learn from the Scriptures and lives of the saints to see in the Eucharist God's merciful and loving forgiveness of sins for which he died and rose? There

112

will be eternity for God's judgment. For the moment, it is time to see and imitate his mercy.[3]

# I. THE EUCHARIST AND THE TRANSCENDENCE OF GOD—THE CHALLENGE OF WORSHIP

Jesus explained that there are two commandments and they are very much alike. One is the command to worship God because he alone is Lord. The other is the command to love one's neighbor as oneself. There were two tablets of the law, the Decalogue: one referred to what was due to God, and the other what was due to one's neighbor. And so the challenge of the Eucharist is both to love God and worship him because he is Lord and to honor one's neighbor because he/she is a child of God, made after God's image and likeness. As Jesus said, these commandments are alike because they concern love. They are also alike because they are moral imperatives.

Thomas Aquinas is one of the great thirteenth-century teachers of moral and systematic theology. His treatment of the virtue of religion (*servitium Dei*) is especially enlightening and clear in its exposition of why we must worship God. He treats this subject in his IIa IIae (part two, section two) of the *Summa Theologica*. We can only summarize his exposition briefly.

## Thomas Aquinas on Worship

In his masterful treatment of the virtues, Thomas Aquinas singles out worship (service of God) as the first among the moral virtues. He places this virtue immediately after the theological virtues of faith, hope, and charity. He understands the virtue of religion as something required of all human beings because God is Lord and Creator. As such, it is God's right and our obligation to give him the worship that is his due.[4]

Aquinas recognizes that worship is something that we cannot do without God's grace and help. Only a divine being can give God due worship. We can only do our best and give him all we can.[5] Moreover the relationship between God and humanity is one of sonship. And so the element of filial piety and devotion enters into the picture.[6]

In the *Summa Theologiae,* Thomas Aquinas asks whether the Eucharist is necessary for salvation.[7] He indicates that it is, but differently from baptism. And in his response, he describes the Eucharist as the sacrament of unity with a reference to St. Augustine's teaching on the same subject. Aquinas says that the "*res*" of the Eucharist is "the unity of the body of Christ" and gives the context of 1 Corinthians, "because there is one bread, we who are many are one body, for we all partake of the one bread" (10:17).

In the course of his answer, Aquinas has some interesting considerations about the desire to receive the Eucharist and its value. These remarks are in the context of the unity of the church, which is the fruit of the Eucharist. This entire section has ecumenical relevance even today.

## Common Ground and Continuing Differences

The theologians who framed the World Council of Churches document on *Baptism, Eucharist and Ministry,*[8] indicated the long ancient tradition of the Eucharist as a sign of worship and a means of grace and salvation. While Christian Churches repeat the sign that Jesus gave and commanded to "do this in remembrance of me" ( Luke 22:19), they interpret the way this is to be done differently, with different emphases and implications. It would be useful to say a few words about what they share in common and some of their differences.

### The Catholic and Orthodox Tradition

For Orthodox and Catholics, the Eucharist is at the heart of Christian worship. The Eucharist is the sign of the once and forever offering that Jesus made of himself to the Father in obedience to his will, to suffer for the ransom of the many in the human race. He died once and for all and for all humanity. His sacrifice was accepted by the Father, as demonstrated in the resurrection of Jesus from the tomb on Easter morning. "To do this in his memory" is to celebrate, in ritual and worship, what Jesus had done. The overtones of this Christian Passover are the Jewish Seder or Passover Meal with its rich concepts of covenant, liberation, and salvation.

114

In this ancient Christian tradition, the Eucharist is liturgical worship, the action of the people led by their duly ordained clergy, for the glory of God and "for the forgiveness of sins." In the Orthodox perspective, especially, the Eucharist is salvation in action, the church—the body of Christ—becoming what it is through the power of the Holy Spirit (*epiclesis*). This view is shared by Catholics.

### The Church Is Essentially Eucharistic

The Orthodox-Roman Catholic Dialogue, in its ecclesiological consensus statement, affirms that the church of Christ is essentially Eucharistic.[9] Indeed, where there is Eucharist, there is the church. John Zizioulas, in his theology of communion, affirms that the heart of the matter is a sharing in the divine life of the Trinity.[10] This communion is established by faith and baptism and is nurtured by Eucharist. Without the Eucharist, the Christian life is both incomplete and impossible. "Unless you eat the flesh of the Son of Man and drink his blood, you have no life in you" (John 6:53).

"At the Last Supper, Christ stated that he was giving his body to the disciples for the life of 'the many.' In the Eucharist this gift is made by Christ to the world, in sacramental form. From that moment the Eucharist exists as the sacrament of Christ himself. It becomes the foretaste of eternal life, the 'medicine of immortality,' the sign of the kingdom to come. The Eucharist is the sacrament which incorporates us fully into Christ."[11]

The Second Plenary Meeting of the Catholic-Orthodox Theologians picked up the topic of the church as mystery. In the opening paragraphs of the document, the nature of the church is described in terms of the nature of the mystery of Christ and the Trinity. Stressing the role of the Holy Spirit in that mystery and in the mystery of the Eucharist, the Commission emphasizes the importance of the local church and its sacramental connection with the Eucharist and the bishop in Apostolic succession.

It is from this vantage point that the nature of the church is understood and expressed. It is the faith of the apostolic church, the church down the ages, and which continues to this day. The unity of the church is built on this solid foundation, and the church continues to build it through the ages. The main thrust of this statement of faith and theology is that the church needs reformation in every age, because it is a human institution that easily falls into sin. But as a divine institution that is identified with Jesus Christ and his body both sacramental and institutional, it continues to the end of time, as Jesus Christ promised (Matt 28:20).

In this view of the church as mystery, the Eucharist is both the sign and means of unity. Concern for genuine unity requires that Christians must be one for the authenticity of the Eucharist. While that unity will always be frail and require nourishment, the Eucharist ought not to be neglected as a means of unity. Pope Benedict XVI continues to encourage the church to see, in every effort to celebrate the Eucharist in every Christian Church, a longing for the *res sacramenti* (the reality/realization) of the grace of the sacrament, which is the unity of the church in its members through Christ in the Father.[12]

The visible structures of the church must be evaluated by its inner reality as the mystery of Christ given for the life of the world, by the Father through the saving grace of the Spirit. This *epicletic* dimension of the Eucharist and of the Christian mystery is never to be forgotten. John Zizioulas has written very well from this perspective, and influenced the WCC documents, particularly *The Nature and Mission of the Church*, as well as the Roman Catholic-Orthodox Theologians' Dialogue.[13]

## *Other Christian Perspectives*

In the course of this study, I have learned that all of the Christian Traditions celebrate the Lord's Supper. As a result of *Baptism, Eucharist and Ministry* and the years of dialogue and implementation of its convergence and recommendations, there has been a better understanding of the centrality and importance of the Eucharist to Christian life and practice. Cecil (Mel) Robeck, professor of Ecumenics, Church History and Pentecostalism at Fuller Theological Seminary, recommended to me an outstanding book that studies five views of Eucharistic theology and their Christological and ecclesiological implications.[14] The exchange and the variety of views that are presented, even within each tradition, shows that in addition to contributions by numerous Reformation pioneers, the understanding of each tradition is a wide spectrum developed by contributions, reflecting a long history of theological reflection on the Scriptures and the theology of the Eucharist.

One can only be impressed by the search for truth represented by this wide range of thinkers over hundreds of years. What exactly did the Lord Jesus offer when he held the loaf and the cup and said "This is my body, this is my blood. Take and eat; take and drink"? None of the traditions represented believes he meant "Here is a mere symbol of my body and blood." All agree there is a special presence of risen Lord in the Eucharist, and a *koinonia* with Christ in God and in the body of Christ, which is the church. There is *anamnesis* and *epiclesis*. And there is a spiritual communion, which is the work of the Holy Spirit. There are different faith traditions and different theological perspectives. But there seems to be a common thread of belief and a common effort to understand the truth of what Jesus did and said as he offered the Bread of Life for the spiritual hungers of the world.

## II. THE MORAL IMPERATIVE

The second challenge of the Eucharist is one that is more readily grasped, yet perhaps less easily implemented in its concrete living. It is one that Matthew 25 urges us to reflect upon constantly, since it will be the standard of the final judgment: whatever we have done to the least (or failed to do) will be the reason for our shame or reward. Paul's challenge to the Christians of Corinth is similar.

## Paul's Challenge to the Corinthians

Paul's challenge to the Corinthians is to come to the Lord's Supper with a clear understanding of its moral imperative. He reproached the Corinthians for coming to the table without understanding that communion "in the Lord" requires recognition not only of his physical body, but also of his mystical body, which is the church. To abuse one's brother or sister by one's conduct at the table, or away from it, is a failure to recognize the body of Christ, which we are and which the Eucharist nurtures.

Christian Churches—East and West, Protestant and Catholic—interpreted Paul's admonition in terms of ritual purity and "worthiness" to receive the Eucharist. Though the Reformers wanted a more frequent reception of the Eucharist than was present either in Orthodox or Catholic practice in the sixteenth century, they were unable to shake the popular view that one must be holy and prepared to receive the Eucharist before approaching it.

The Catholic breakthrough came with the decrees of Pope Pius X on frequent communion and the communion of children at the beginning of the twentieth century[15] and was confirmed by the Liturgical Movement of the 1950s and the decrees of the Second Vatican Council in the mid 1960s.

Protestant practice continues to evolve in the wake of the WCC *Baptism, Eucharist and Ministry* (1982) as well as a more pastoral view of the Eucharist as a need rather than a reward. All Christians are challenged by the Eucharist, and it is appropriate that each Christian Church and all its members ask what response it is giving to Paul's letter to the Corinthians. As *The Nature and Mission of the Church* puts it:

> Because the Lord's Supper is the Sacrament which builds up community, all kinds of injustice, racism, estrangement, and lack of freedom are radically challenged when we share in the body and blood of Christ. Through Holy Communion the all-renewing grace of God penetrates the human personality and restores human dignity. The Eucharist, therefore, obliges us also to participate in the ongoing restoration of the world's situation and the human condition. God's judgment demands that our behavior be consistent with the reconciling presence of God in human history.[16]

## III. THE CONSEQUENCES OF THE MORAL IMPERATIVE OF THE EUCHARIST

The moral imperative of the Eucharist is to bring about the social, economic, and political consequences for the body of Christ, which is the church and which flows from the mystery of God in Christ and is celebrated in the Eucharist. A discussion of these consequences in detail would take us beyond the scope of this essay, but the urgency and the immediate need for their implementation continues to press us for action.

Let me briefly outline some of the areas where such implementation is more obviously needed. We can list them under three headings: social, economic, and political consequences of the nature and mission of the church.

## Social Consequences

As Christians we believe that the will of the triune God is that the whole human race should be saved by God's grace in Jesus Christ. The Father and the Son sent the Holy Spirit so that the people of God and the family of God could be formed into the body of Christ, which is the church. The human family, divided by sin, is to be united by God's grace. This is the prayer of Christ at the Last Supper, "that they may all be one. As you, Father, are in me and I am in you, may they also be in us, so that the world may believe that you sent me" (John 17:21).

We must recognize the body of Christ in the Eucharist and in all those who share the life of Christ through baptism and eating and drinking the body and blood of Jesus Christ. We are one family, members of one body, and members of one another. And this reality is the foundation of all our decisions about the social order.

## Economic Consequences

Jesus tells us that we will always have the poor among us (John 12:8) and that whatever we do for the least and most needy among us, we do for him (Matt 25:40). In this context, our efforts for peace and justice must flow from our love and compassion. We are fed with the best of wheat, the bread from heaven, the Eucharist. Christ, who feeds us and loves and saves us through the Eucharist, commands us to do as he has done: serve one another, wash one another's feet. We must be compassionate as the Father is compassionate. Economic decisions must flow from our communion with God in Christ. The poor, the immigrant, the hungry, and the needy are all one with us, and we with them. It is from this vantage point that economic consequences must be seen and implemented.

119

## Political Consequences

George Washington regretted the formation of political parties in the United States. He believed that they would cause division and polarize the political energies of the country. While bipartisan action has been seen as the solution to such division and polarization, the current situation in our country (indeed worldwide) has proven Washington's intuition to be correct. The greatest division in the history of the United States was over the question of slavery and state's rights, leading to a civil war. The present political impasse is largely the fruit of a growing failure to dialogue among political adversaries. The Eucharist is not a solution to this problem. However, the Eucharist, the sign of Christian unity in Christ, and our communion in Christ into his body, which is the church, does challenge us to solve our political problems in the light and with the strength of God given to us through his Spirit in the sacrament of unity.

The purpose of the Eucharist is to unite us in the one body through the one cup and loaf that we share, which is Jesus Christ. To live in him is to live as brothers and sisters in the family of God; to share a common table, God's table, is to share a common life on a single journey—to the Father's home. One in Christ, with one faith, one Lord, one baptism, we share a common life and a common destiny.

Hence, in the consequences of civil rights, racial and ethnic equality, equal opportunity, and justice under the law, we are one people. Segregation at the altar rail is as unacceptable as segregation in heaven. God's will on earth should reflect his will in heaven. And, thus, the consequences for the political world must constantly challenge us to see in the Eucharist and the Lord Jesus, one who lives for others, one who lives in God.

# IV. NEXT STEPS

The path to unity points to genuine possibilities in the foreseeable future. Full communion agreements among Anglicans and Lutherans as well as Methodists give great hope for the unity of Christians. The Churches Uniting In Christ (CUIC) conversation and movement also promises a degree of unity that is unprecedented.

On the Catholic side, agreements between the Assyrian and West Syrian Churches and the Roman Catholic Church make Eucharistic sharing already mutually possible.[17] Eastern Orthodox and Roman Catholic understanding also is very promising.

More difficult, but no less urgent, are breakthroughs in the dialogue between the Catholic Church and Anglican, Lutheran, Methodist, and Presbyterian Churches. The work of theologians in dialogue point to ways in which obstacles can be surmounted and progress can be made.[18]

Evangelical, Holiness, and Pentecostal Christians show an interest in ecumenical affairs and Christian unity. They have been involved with the Faith and Order Commissions of the World Council of Churches and of the National Council of Churches in the United States. Their participation in the dialogue about *The Nature and Mission of the Church* is very helpful and promising.

## CONCLUSION

*"Caminando se hace el camino."* (The journey is made by walking.) We use the metaphor of a pilgrimage for our work as Faith and Order representatives on the nature and mission of the church. Underlying this proverb is the experience that we learn what the journey is like by walking it. We understand what Christian unity is like by walking together on the path of Christian unity. Christian unity is an experience rather than a lesson that one learns. It is a conversion or change of heart and mind closer to the mind and heart of Christ. Or as *Unitatis Redintegratio* puts it, drawing closer to Christ, we draw closer to God and one another in Christian unity.[19]

In our reflection on the Eucharist, we have discovered two essential challenges. The first challenge is to see the Eucharist as worship, praise, and thanksgiving to God for his marvelous works. It is the praise and worship of Jesus Christ, head and members. This worship is due to God because he is Lord. It is the worship of the whole body of Christ, head and members. It is our worship, which we make in our own name and in the name of all creation to God our Creator.

God does not need our worship; we do. To be fully human is to recognize who we are and who God is. In our effort to recognize our own humanity, we also recognize the body of Christ in the celebration of the Eucharist and the sharing of his body and blood. The Eucharist is Jesus Christ offering us his life, death, and resurrection, the mystery of Christ, for our salvation.

The Orthodox understanding of the church as essentially Eucharistic, underscores that as we worship, we recognize the presence and the saving action of Jesus Christ, who gives us his Spirit to make us the body of Christ, which is the church. We and all humanity become one in the sign of the body and blood of Jesus Christ by which our sins are forgiven and we are saved.

The second challenge of the Eucharist is the moral imperative. All our decisions in the sphere of social, economic, and political realities must flow from our understanding of who we are as church. The church is the body of Christ. As members of that body and sharing the name of Jesus Christ, we Christians must live what we pray and what we profess. *Lex orandi, lex credendi,* the rule of faith establishes the rule of prayer, and our prayer demonstrates what we believe. Our life must correspond to our faith. "The one who is righteous will live by faith" (Rom 1:17). Thus our faith, hope, and love are the foundation of the kind of actions we take in our daily lives whether in social, economic, or political spheres.

As American Christians, we have a distinct contribution to make to the church and to the dialogue about the nature and mission of the church. We have experienced over two centuries of religious freedom and religious tolerance in our country. Here, ecumenism is a daily experience literally everywhere. Our landscape is not only a mosaic of Christian Churches, it is a mosaic of interreligious diversity known uniquely in our country. The separation of church and state is not a wall of separation, but an avenue for ecumenical and interreligious collaboration and greater understanding. In this experience, we realize that without religion, our democracy would cease to exist. We also know that in this setting, religion flourishes.

The next steps on our pilgrimage toward unity are clear. The long road and its twists, turns, and difficulties are beyond our horizon. But we walk by faith and not by sight. We walk with hope, and with the joy that comes from knowing that the Spirit that hovered over the waters in creation and over the birth of Jesus Christ and his church, also guides our steps forward. The Spirit will guide us on our way and give us the strength to persevere. We must have the will and the courage to seek God's will and his help toward the goal. The Eucharist is "Bread for the Journey."

The inclusive experience and welcoming atmosphere of a family meal gives some insight into the spirit that should guide us forward. The spirit of the Eucharist that is Jesus Christ welcoming each of us, nourishing and sustaining us on our journey, and urging us to recognize him in the breaking of bread and the poor stranger in our midst, will help us to find our way on our pilgrimage home. That is the way of love and unity, the way of the Eucharist, which makes the church and celebrates its birth and its resurrection to glory.

## NOTES

1. World Council of Churches, *Baptism, Eucharist and Ministry*, Faith and Order Paper #111 (Geneva: WCC, 1982).

2. World Council of Churches, *The Nature and Mission of the Church: A Stage on the Way to a Common Statement*, Faith and Order Paper #198 (Geneva: WCC, 2005), 81.

3. With Vatican II and other Catholic theologians, I believe the Eucharist is both a sign of unity and a means to it. This view would be supported by the permission for Eucharistic sharing by Catholics and Oriental Orthodox Christians (Assyrian and West Syrian), which were developed in 1984 and 1994 between Pope John Paul II and the patriarchs of these two churches. The experience of Lutherans, Anglicans, and Methodists in the United States as well as those in Churches Uniting in Christ (CUIC) would concur.

4. Thomas Aquinas (St.), *Summa Theologiae* (Latin text and English translation, introduction, notes, appendices and glossaries, New York/London: McGraw-Hill/Blackfriars, c1968), II–IIae, Q. 80–100.

5. Ibid., Q. 81, Art. 5, ad 3m.

6. Ibid., Q. 82, Arts. 1–2.

7. Ibid., IIIa, Q. 73, Art. 3. See also *The Catechism of the Catholic Church* (Washington, DC: English Translation for the United States US Catholic Conference, 1994), 1396.

8. World Council of Churches, *Baptism, Eucharist and Ministry*, esp. E2–13.

9. Joint Commission for Theological Dialogue Between the Roman Catholic Church and the Orthodox Church (Second Plenary Meeting, Munich, June 30–July 6, 1982), *The Mystery of the Church and of the Eucharist in the Light of the Mystery of the Holy Trinity* (Rome: Pontifical Council for Promoting Christian Unity), 4–6, available at http://www.vatican.va/roman_curia/pontifical_councils /chrstuni/ch_orthodox_docs/rc_pc_chrstuni_doc_19820706_munic h_en.html (accessed May 21, 2012).

10. John D. Zizioulas, *Being as Communion: Studies in Personhood and the Church* (Crestwood, NY: St. Vladimir's Seminary Press, 1985) and *Communion and Otherness: Further Studies in Personhood and the Church,* ed. Paul McPartlan (London: T&T Clark, 2006).

11. Joint Commission for Theological Dialogue, *The Mystery of the Church,* 4–6.

12. Benedict XVI, *The Sacrament of Charity (Sacramentum caritatis),* Post-Synodal Apostolic Exhortation. February 22, 2007 (Washington, DC : USCCB; Vatican City : Libreria Ed. Vaticana, 2007), 14.

13. John D. Zizioulas, *Eucharist, Bishop, Church: The Unity of the Church in the Divine Eucharist and the Bishop During the First Three Centuries*, trans. Elizabeth Theokritoff (Brookline, MA: Holy Cross Orthodox Press, 2001). Gaëton Baillargeon, *Perspectives Orthodoxes sur L'Église Communion: L'œuvre de Jean Zizioulas* (Montréal: Éditions Paulines & Médiaspaul, 1989).

14. *The Lord's Supper: Five Views*, ed. Gordon T. Smith. (Downer's Grove, IL: IVP Academic, 2008). The book examines Roman Catholic, Lutheran (Missouri-Synod), Reformed, Baptist, and Pentecostal views with responses from each of the other participants for each presentation.

15. Pope Pius X, *Sacra Tridentina Synodus* (Dec. 16 & 20, 1905) encouraging frequent reception of Holy Communion, and *Quam Singulari* (Aug. 8 & 15, 1910) determining the appropriate time for children to receive the Eucharist for the first time.

16.  World Council of Churches, *Nature and Mission*, 78.

17.  Joint agreed statements between the Assyrian Orthodox Church and Rome, 1984 and between the West Syrian (Malabar) Church and Rome, 1994 and 2001. See also *The Code of Canon Law*, Latin-English ed. (Washington, DC: Canon Law Society of America, 1983), Canon 844.

18.  *Lutherans and Catholics in Dialogue*, 10 vols. (Washington, D.C.: Bishops' Committee for Ecumenical and Interreligious Affairs, 1965–2005), esp. vol. 3, *The Eucharist as Sacrifice* (1967) and vol. 4, *Eucharist and Ministry* (1970).

19.  Vatican II, *Unitatis Redintegratio,* in *Vatican Council II: The Conciliar and Post Conciliar Documents*, ed. Austin Flannery, OP (North Port, NY: Costello Publishing, 1981), 7.

# THE WAY OF RECONCILIATION

# 8

# INTERSECTIONS OF THE CONCERNS OF MISSION AND INTERFAITH DIALOGUE IN THE ECUMENICAL MOVEMENT

## A Historical Survey and Analysis

*S. Wesley Ariarajah*

The question of how Christian faith should relate to other religions in the context of its missionary vocation has been there from its very beginnings. Christianity was born within Judaism. But when Jesus' followers began the mission of proclaiming Jesus as the expected Messiah, tensions rose between the Jewish followers of Jesus and those who did not accept the message of the apostles. This early tension between Christians and Jews would continue through the centuries. When Christianity eventually moved into the Greco-Roman world and became a religion of the Gentiles, the early Christian theologians had to struggle with the religious and philosophical traditions of the Greco-Roman context, and one could have an interesting study of the tensions and interactions between dialogue and mission already in this early period of the history of Christianity. This discussion, however, seeks to deal with the history of the intersection between dialogue and mission within the Modern Ecumenical Movement, especially since the first World Missionary Conference in Edinburgh, 1910.

It should be noted that the word *dialogue,* as a formal concept employed in Christian relation to people of other religious traditions, emerged only since the late 1960s. Until then the issue was discussed primarily in terms of what the Christian attitude and approach to people of other religious traditions should be as they seek to be in mission to them. The missionary mandate was never in question at that time; the issue was how best it can be carried out to people who lived by other faiths. It is, therefore, important to study the history of the intersection between Christian approaches to other religions and the missionary mandate out of which the concept of dialogue would gradually emerge.

## INITIAL QUESTIONING OF MISSIONARY ATTITUDES

The agenda of the first missionary conference at Edinburgh was the evangelization of the world in that generation. John R. Mott, the pioneer of the Edinburgh meeting, was convinced that if the missionary agencies and movements pooled their human and material resources, study together the issues involved in reaching the non-Christian world, and developed common strategies, the task could indeed be achieved. "This is a decisive hour for Christian missions," he wrote, in the Forward of the *Report of Commission I* of the conference, "The call of providence to all our Lord's disciples, of whatever ecclesial connections, is direct and urgent to undertake without delay the task of carrying the gospel to all the non-Christian world…The opportunity is inspiring; the responsibility is undeniable."[1] One of the tasks of this commission was to "survey the unoccupied sections of the world, with the view to the speedy and complete occupation of these areas."[2]

The unbridled confidence that the whole world could be evangelized in that generation came from three realities. The first and the foremost was that most of the non-western world was under colonial powers; it was thought that what had been achieved politically could be extended to the religious sphere as well. Second, the Christianization of the whole of Europe and much of Latin America gave the confidence that this would also happen in Asia, Africa, and Oceana; an all embracing Christendom was still the vision and hope that drove the missionary movement. And the third, other religions and civilizations were considered inferior and in error, and it was thought that the "superior" Western culture and religion would be welcomed by the "heathens." The only issue then was how to reach all who had not heard the message, and how best to present it to them.

It is of interest that the bulk of the initial opposition to this line of thinking came not so much from the "natives" but from the missionaries that had been sent to carry out this vision. Dissent was already present at the Edinburgh meeting, as found in the work of *Commission IV* on "The Missionary Message in Relation to Non-Christian Religions." The Commission had decided to organize its work by sending a questionnaire on matters related to its work to missionaries in the mission fields: What are the doctrines and observances in other faiths that seem to give genuine help and consolation to the devotees in their religious life? What are the chief moral, intellectual, and social hindrances to their responding to Christianity? What should be the attitude of the Christian preacher to the religion of the people among whom he or she works? What are the points of contact with other religions, and what are the aspects of Christianity that appeal to others? There were more questions, but the last question had two forms. One, sent to Western missionaries working among other faiths, asked whether the person's work as a Christian missionary among people of other faiths had, either in form or content, altered his or her understanding of "What constituted the most important and vital elements in the Christian gospel." The other, sent to converts, asked what in Christianity had made a special appeal to them and whether the Western form in which Christianity was preached had perplexed them. This questionnaire was sent, according to the Commission report, for the purpose of "discovering the realities of the situation."

More than two hundred sets of answers, some in considerable length, were received. Sixty-one answers came, for instance, from those who worked in the context of Hinduism alone, including from some of the well-known names in the missionary movement, such as J. N. Farquhar, A. G. Hogg, Francis Kingsbury, Bernard Lucas, T. E. Slater, C. F. Andrews, and others.[3]

The Commission was overwhelmed by the number, length, and quality of the responses received. No one doubted the need to witness to the Gospel, and a number of them were quite clear about the negative aspects and limitations on other religious traditions.

But almost all of them, for instance from India, questioned some of the basic assumptions on which missions were geared to other religions, and asked for a more sympathetic approach to them. The Commission report says that the responses from the field in India called for prolonged and patient study of Hinduism, so that such sympathy "may be based on knowledge, and not to be the child of emotion or imagination." In the Commission's view, "more harm has been done in India than in any other country by missionaries who have lacked the wisdom to appreciate the nobler side of the religion which they have labored so indefatigably to supplant."[4] "It is a reasonable demand," one of the respondents had said, "to any man who tries to tackle so difficult a problem as that of changing another man's faith that he should know what he is talking about, not only his own religion, but also that which he desires to lead the people away from."[5]

F. W. Steinthal claimed in his response that Christian knowledge of Hinduism should go well beyond familiarity with its history, rituals, philosophy, etcetera, to the point of grasping, as far as one is able, the "real life" that throbs within: "Below the strange forms and hardly intelligible language, lies life, the spiritual life of human souls, needing God, seeking God, laying hold of God so far as they have found him."[6]

It is not my intention to summarize the responses of the fascinating *Report of Commission IV*. In summary, it claimed that the encounter of Christianity with these religious traditions should be seen as parallel to the encounter of the early church with Hellenism. It called on the movement to recognize the obvious relationship that people of these religions had with God, and to be challenged by the spirituality found in them:

> It may be here there will be the richest result of it all, that whether through the Christianized mind of India or through the mind of the missionary stirred to its depths by contact with the Indian mind, we shall discover new and wonderful things in the ancient revelation which have been hidden in part from the just and faithful of the Western world.[7]

I have discussed the *Report of Commission IV* in some length because it is not common knowledge that already in 1910, at the very heart of the first World Missionary Conference, there were strong voices calling for radical change in the assumptions about other faiths that motivated the missionary imperative. But this was only one of eight commissions into which the twelve hundred delegates were divided into, and the other commissions were primarily devoted to the main purpose of the conference. The final report of the Conference, therefore, followed Mott's line and issued the call for the evangelization of all the non-Christian lands.

In the post colonial context today, it is common to speak of some of the negative aspects of the nature of missions and attitudes of missionaries in the "third world" countries. It is indeed true that aspects of mission have been insensitive, judgmental, and suppressive of other religions and cultures. The discussion above, however, shows yet another side of the work of missionaries. Missionaries were also advocates of new approaches to people of other cultures and religions. By actually living with the people and entering into their daily lives, and by encountering their spiritual journeys from close quarters, they were able to discern the need for new thinking that the mission executives and theoretical missiologists could not visualize from their desks in the sending countries. Thus, even though there were some prominent "native" advocates for new approaches to other faiths, much of the early battles were fought by the missionaries themselves. This is also true in relation to the struggle against racism, slavery, and so forth in the United States, and advocacy for human and cultural rights in many parts of the world. Sensitive missionaries who lived among peoples of other cultures and religions have played an important ambassadorial role in pressing their constituencies back home to adopt progressive causes and policies that are yet to be fully recognized.

The success of the 1910 Conference led to the decision that such a conference should be called every ten years. Further, the decision was made to institutionalize the movement by constituting it into the International Missionary Council (IMC), which became a reality in 1921. It was the IMC that called the next World Missionary Conference in 1928 over Easter at the Mount of Olives in Jerusalem.

# EMBRACING THE VALUES IN OTHER RELIGIONS

The call for a new approach to other religions at Edinburgh that we noted came from lived experience of some of the missionaries in the mission fields and the gradual emergence of Comparative Religion as a new discipline in the universities in the early 1910s. Two additional major developments would impact the proceedings of the 1928 meeting. The first was the rise of secularism mainly in the west, which was also beginning to affect the east. Considerable alarm over this led some of the Christian thinkers to look upon secularism as the enemy that should be confronted by the spiritual resources of all the religious traditions. William Ernest Hocking, professor at Harvard, argued that this reality required a new alliance of religious forces and that this alliance is possible on the basis of the "substance of religion" everywhere. Hocking was using religion in an all embracing way, for in his view, all the religions "merged in the universal human faith in the Divine Being."[8]

In this context, the concept of "spiritual values" in other religious traditions came to the forefront at Jerusalem. The argument was made by some at the Conference that, even if we had reservations with other religious traditions, and are convinced of their need of the Gospel message, we should affirm the "values" they bring to the human community. The argument for a positive approach to other religions was now also being advocated by the increased Asians participants at the Conference. P. Chenchiah and K. T. Paul from India, and T. C. Chao and Francis Wei from China, challenged the missionary movement for its insensitivity toward other religions and cultures.

The European delegation, led especially by the German participants at the Conference, felt that the concept of "spiritual values" would eventually undermine the missionary mandate. Julius Richter, speaking on their behalf, claimed that he believed that the Gospel called for a faith "willing to sacrifice even the spiritual values of non-Christian religions." He held that instead of looking for real or imagined spiritual values in other faiths, it was the duty of Christians to "stand decidedly and even stubbornly with both feet" on the "unique way of salvation proclaimed with one voice in the Bible." G. Simons supported this view with the statement that "The

Gospel is not a supplement to the spiritual values in other religions, but the giving of new spiritual values to take the place of the old."[9]

The Jerusalem meeting was very divisive on the missionary approach to other religions, and Archbishop William Temple, who was chair of the committee that drafted the final message of the Conference, had a very difficult time at getting a consensus. The final message would have a clear statement of the urgency of spreading the Gospel message, but the tone changed from that found in Edinburgh. Speaking of the exercise of mission, it said:

> On our part we would repudiate any symptom of religious imperialism that would desire to impose beliefs and practices on others in order to manage their souls in their supposed interest. We obey God who respects our wills and we desire to respect those of others.

It went further to speak of the missionary activity as "sharing" the Gospel in humility, patience, and love. Even though its final message stayed with the missionary mandate, it went on to spell out the "noble qualities" and the "spiritual values" in other religions, which alienated some delegates at the conference:

> We recognize as part of the one truth the sense of the majesty of God and the consequent reverence in worship, which are conspicuous in Islam; the deep sympathy for the world's sorrows and the unselfish search for the way of escape, which are at the heart of Buddhism; the desire for contact with Ultimate Reality conceived as spiritual, which is prominent in Hinduism; the belief in the moral order of the universe and consequent insistence on moral conduct, which are inculcated in Confucianism; the disinterested pursuit of truth and of human welfare which is often found in those who stand for secular civilization but do not accept Christ as their Lord and Saviour.[10]

The *Jerusalem Message* was a patchwork compromise of many pressures that had gathered around the intersection of the missionary mandate and approach to other religions. It also shows the number of interests that had influenced the debate. On the one hand, there were still many within the mission constituency that saw mission as calling all peoples to the Christian faith. On the other, the urge to confront the rise of secularism, the growing interest in Comparative Religion, the emergence of liberal thinking especially in the United States, and the fuller involvement of Asian voices in the debate enormously complicated the mission agenda. It should also be noted that the world situation had also changed dramatically in the eighteen years between Edinburgh and Jerusalem. A. M. Chirgwin, writing an interpretation of the Jerusalem meeting in the *International Review of Mission*, puts these changes in a nutshell:

> In 1910 there had been no world war, no revolution in China, no non-cooperation movement in India, no demand of the coloured races for equal treatment by white races, no indigenous church firmly rooted in the life of the Eastern people.[11]

Thus, the internal struggles within the churches over the meaning and goals of mission, the changing world situation, and the pressure within the missionary constituency to continue the world mission made the *Jerusalem Message* a bundle of theological contradictions. Once the conference was over, the issues discussed in Jerusalem became a full-blown controversy.

The leaders of the missionary movement felt that it had become important to come up with a clear, well-considered, and theologically sound position on mission as related to peoples of other religious traditions. This concern would shape the agenda of the next World Missionary Conference in Tambaram, Madras, in 1938.

## CONTINUITY OR DISCONTINUITY?

The Tambaram Conference is considered by missiologists as one of the major milestones in mission history. This is partly because it was at Tambaram that the missionary outreach that had until then been the task of lay and voluntary missionary societies would be seen as the task of the church. It is said that Tambaram rediscovered the missionary nature and calling of the church. There were also other important developments, but Tambaram would become most famous for the herculean effort made by the missionary movement to give a strong biblical-theological basis for the missionary outreach to peoples of other religious traditions.

The task of doing this was given to Hendrik Kraemer, a Dutch theologian and missiologist. Kraemer was not only a missiologist but had been a missionary for prolonged periods among Muslims in Egypt and Indonesia. When this job was assigned to him, Kraemer first traveled in India and the United States to study the situation. In India, there were missionaries looking at Christianity as fulfillment of the Hindu aspirations. J. N. Farquhar had published the famous volume, *The Crown of Hinduism*; and others were locating "points of contact" within Hinduism for the presentation of the Gospel message. In the United States, Hocking had influenced the report of the Laymen's Foreign Mission Enquiry that published *Rethinking Mission*, calling on Christian missions to join with other religions in a "common search" for truth: "Look not at what is weak or corrupt in those faiths, but at what is strong and sound in them. That offers the best hearing for whatever Christianity may have to say."[12]

Having studied the situation, Kraemer wrote an epoch-making preparatory volume for the Tambaram meeting, of more than two hundred pages, *Christian Message in a Non-Christian World*, intended to answer the issues raised in Jerusalem and to put mission to people of other faiths on a firm biblical-theological foundation. It is not possible to summarize Kraemer's thoughts in a short article. But let me highlight the three basic principles at the heart of Kraemer's thesis, built on the theology of Karl Barth, which was also intended as a response to natural theology and liberal thought. Kraemer called his first argument "Biblical realism." By this he meant that the Bible is "realistic" about the human condition. As fallen creatures, humans can never hope to have knowledge or approach God by their own efforts. The only way one can have knowledge of God was by God's self-revelation in history (of Israel) and in Jesus Christ. Therefore, all religions, however spiritual, moral, and sublime they might be, are human attempts to grasp God, and remain as such. The only way to have saving knowledge is to respond to God's challenge to all humankind in Jesus Christ.

This led to his second main point that there is no "continuity" between the Gospel and the "values" in other religions. The Gospel is in total "discontinuity" with all religious teachings and values, however good and valuable they might appear to be. In any case, Kraemer argued, which was his third point, that religions are "totalitarian systems" that cannot be looked at in parts. One cannot isolate "values" and "points of contacts" in religions to relate to the Gospel or to build on them because they are internally coherent systems of thought. According to Kraemer, religions cannot be compared or their values isolated; they constitute "totalitarian" systems.

Karl Barth's theology was on the ascent in Europe, giving a new biblical and theological basis to the Protestant Churches that have been devastated by World Wars and plagued by the rise of natural theology and liberal thought. Kraemer did to missiology what Barth did to Protestant theology: to give a firm and well-argued biblical-theological basis. Kraemer was the star in Tambaram and was celebrated by those on the world mission side as one who put world missions back on track. But several Asian theologians and Asian missionaries challenged Kraemer's interpretation of the Bible, religion, revelation, and the Gospel, leading to one of the fascinating debates on the floor of any conference of that era.[13]

It is important to grasp what Kraemer did in Tambaram because it is this missiology, and the approach and interpretation of other religions that went with it, that has become the missiology of the Protestant Churches in general and the Evangelical movement in particular. Until the Tambaram meeting, the missionary movement took each religion as a separate entity and studied how the Gospel might be preached to each of them in their particularity. Kraemer put forward the concept that the Gospel was against all religions (including Christianity as a religion) because all religion is nothing but part of the human rebellion against God in their sinfulness. The practice of studying and attempting to understand the dynamics of each of the religious traditions as part of the missionary preparation came to an end with Tambaram. It was now Gospel versus religions, in their totality.

What was called the "Tambaram Controversy" over mission and other faiths continued in Asia, but soon after Tambaram, Europe became embroiled in the Second World War. The urgent need to care for the millions of refugees and displaced persons and the critical challenge to work toward peace and reconciliation precipitated the formation of the World Council of Churches (WCC) in 1948. The Faith and Order and the Life and Work movements merged into the WCC, but the IMC was still uncertain about joining the wider fellowship. However, the WCC and IMC decided to collaborate in their work. When the mission agenda was looked at, it became clear that moving toward world mission required that the "Tambaram Controversy" be resolved or at least adequately dealt with. The decision was made to do a study process rather than to call a conference. Accordingly, the WCC and the IMC prepared a study of "The Word of God and Men (sic) of Other Faiths" and requested the study centers around the world to help them with this study.

P. D. Devanandan, the Director of the Christian Institute for the Study of Religion and Society (CISRS) in Bangalore, India, engaged the Institute in the study process, but he did an innovation of calling some peoples of other religions for a "dialogue" on the matters raised in the study process. When the third Assembly of the WCC met for the first time in Asia, in New Delhi, Devanandan was one of the speakers and introduced the notion of dialogue into the WCC. The results of the extensive study process were eventually brought together in a major consultation in Kandy, Sri Lanka, in 1967. Here, Kenneth Crag took on Kraemer's position at Tambaram and challenged most of the propositions on which he had built his theses.[14] The consultation itself was called, "Christian Dialogue with Men of Other Faiths" and had Protestant, Roman Catholic, and Orthodox participants. It developed the concept of dialogue as a viable way of speaking about Christian relationship to people of other faiths:

> Meeting with men of other faiths or no faiths must lead to dialogue. A Christian dialogue with another implies neither denial of the uniqueness of Christ, or any loss of his own commitment to Christ, but rather that a genuinely Christian approach to others must be human, personal, relevant, and humble. In dialogue we share our common humanity, its dignity and its fallenness, and express our common concern for that humanity.[15]

THE WAY OF RECONCILIATION

The Kandy Report was not formally presented to the fourth Assembly of the WCC that met the next year (1968) in Uppsala, Sweden. But its ideas impacted the Assembly, and those who drafted the Uppsala Report followed the Kandy line of affirming the common humanity with peoples of other faiths, but without making any judgment on the theological significance of other faiths for Christian self understanding and mission. They also affirmed the presence of Christ in all dialogue situations:

> As Christians we believe that Christ speaks in dialogue, revealing himself to those who do not know him, and correcting the limits and distorted knowledge of those who do. Dialogue and Proclamation are not the same. The one compliments the other in a total witness.[16]

The Central Committee of the WCC meeting in 1971 in Addis Ababa, Ethiopia, would eventually follow up on the Uppsala affirmation of dialogue and further clarifications made on the purpose and goals of dialogue, to create a new program expression within the WCC, called the "Sub-Unit on Dialogue with People of Living Faiths and Ideologies," with Stanley J. Samartha as its first Director. After sixty years of debates and struggles within the missionary movement, the question of Christian relationship to people of other religious traditions had found its own place within the ecumenical movement in the concept of "dialogue" and a program structure related to it. However, the Sub-Unit was located just next to the much larger program unit within the WCC—The Commission on World Mission and Evangelism (CWME)—the successor of the International Missionary Council that had eventually come into the WCC in 1961. The terms of discussion would soon change from "World religions and mission" to "Dialogue and mission." How do they relate to each other? Is there room for both in Christian life and witness?

## DIALOGUE OR MISSION?

Once the concept of "dialogue" was established within the ecumenical movement, its intersection with the understanding of mission took place in two places. One was within the ecumenical movement represented by the WCC and its constituency of Churches and Councils of Churches. The other was outside this constituency represented by the World Evangelical Fellowship and the Lausanne Movement. Even though the WCC and the Evangelical constituencies overlap, they began to develop distinct theological approaches toward dialogue that would keep them theologically apart.

Already in 1948, the attempt to form the WCC by bringing together the Faith and Order, Life and Work, and the Missionary Movement (IMC) was resisted within the IMC by those who felt that becoming part of such wide concerns would undermine the urgency of mission. So, as mentioned earlier, only the Faith and Order and the Life and Work movements went into the formation of the WCC. But the ecumenically minded leaders, both within the newly formed WCC and within the IMC, kept the pressure on the IMC to join the WCC, and eventually succeeded in bringing it in 1961. The IMC became the Commission on World Mission and Evangelism (CWME), which was able to have its own bylaws and have in its Commission a constituency that was wider than that of the WCC. This marriage, however, remained an unhappy marriage to those within the IMC who had the sole focus on world mission.

The CWME inherited the IMC tradition of World Missionary Conferences every ten years, but within the WCC context, mission thinking at these conferences went in many directions, and concepts like "Mission of God," "Mission as resistance," "church of the poor," and so forth, emerged, all of which were seen by some within the missionary movement as undermining the primary task of announcing the good news to the still unevangelized peoples of the world. They were also unhappy with the newly created Interfaith Dialogue program which, in their view, sent the wrong signals to peoples of other religions.

All these led to the refounding of the World Evangelical Alliance in London (originally established in 1846). Further, concerned with the lack of focus of the ecumenical movement on evangelism, Billy Graham decided to call the first World Congress on Evangelism in 1966 in Berlin (followed by others), and later all those interested in world evangelism would come together at the first Lausanne Congress on World Evangelism in 1974 (with 2,700 delegates). The latest Lausanne Congress was held in Cape Town in 2010 with about four thousand delegates.

What is of interest to us here is the attitude of this movement toward dialogue. This is spelled out in the third and fourth articles of the Lausanne Covenant that holds the Evangelicals together:

### 3. The Uniqueness and Universality of Christ

We affirm that there is only one Saviour and only one gospel, although there is a wide diversity of evangelistic approaches. We recognise that everyone has some knowledge of God through his general revelation in nature. But we deny that this can save, for people suppress the truth by their unrighteousness. We also reject as derogatory to Christ and the gospel every kind of syncretism and dialogue which implies that Christ speaks equally through all religions and ideologies. Jesus Christ, being himself the only God-man, who gave himself as the only ransom for sinners, is the only mediator between God and people. There is no other name by which we must be saved. All men and women are perishing because of sin, but God loves everyone, not wishing that any should perish but that all should repent. Yet those who reject Christ repudiate the joy of salvation and condemn themselves to eternal separation from God. To proclaim Jesus as "the Saviour of the world" is not to affirm that all people are either automatically or ultimately saved, still less to affirm that all religions offer salvation in Christ. Rather it is to proclaim God's love for a world of sinners and to invite everyone to respond to him as Saviour and Lord in the wholehearted personal commitment of repentance and faith. Jesus Christ has been exalted above every other name; we long for the day when every knee shall bow to him and every tongue shall confess him Lord. (Gal. 1:6-9; Rom. 1:18-32; I Tim. 2:5,6; Acts 4:12; John 3:16-19; II Pet. 3:9; II Thess. 1:7-9; John 4:42; Matt. 11:28; Eph. 1:20,21; Phil. 2:9-11)

### 4. The Nature of Evangelism

To evangelize is to spread the good news that Jesus Christ died for our sins and was raised from the dead according to the Scriptures, and that as the reigning Lord he now offers the forgiveness of sins and the liberating gifts of the Spirit to all who repent and believe. Our Christian presence in the world is indispensable to evangelism, and so is that kind of dialogue whose purpose is to listen sensitively in order to understand. But evangelism itself is the proclamation of the historical, biblical Christ as Saviour and Lord, with a view to persuading people to come to him personally and so be reconciled to God. In issuing the gospel invitation we have no liberty to conceal the cost of discipleship. Jesus still calls all who would follow him to deny themselves, take up their cross, and identify themselves with his new community. The results of evangelism include obedience to Christ, incorporation into his Church and responsible service in the world.[17]

I have quoted this text at some length because this is one of the important intersections between the concern for dialogue and mission. The Lausanne Movement does accept dialogue as an important relational concept and as one that gives us a better understanding of peoples of other faiths, but is categorical in its belief that all persons of other faiths must be called to confess Jesus Christ as their Lord and savior. This approach, as a theoretical position, is widely held within the majority of the Protestant Church constituency and also within the member churches of the WCC.

We should now move to see the intersection of dialogue and mission within the WCC itself. It is clear that even though the Central Committee in Addis Ababa had agreed on the creation of the Dialogue Sub-Unit, not everyone was clear what it meant for the mission and evangelism concern, which was also firmly based within the WCC. This became obvious at the WCC Assembly held after the creation of the Dialogue Sub-Unit, in Nairobi in 1975.

The dialogue program had taken "Seeking Community" with people of other religious traditions and ideologies as the focus of its section work at the assembly. Five persons of other faiths were also invited as official guests at the assembly. When the report on Seeking Community came to the floor of the assembly, all the suppressed reservations that the mission constituency within the WCC had over dialogue broke out in the open, and the assembly floor had one of the most vociferous and polarizing debates on the floor. Dialogue would lead to syncretism, would betray the uniqueness and finality of Christ, and would undermine world mission were the sentiments

143

expressed. The report was sent back to be revised and was received later only after the addition of a preamble, which contained, among others, these statements:

> We all agree that the Great Commission of Jesus Christ which asks us to go into all the world and make disciples of all nations, and to baptize them in the Triune name, should not be abandoned or betrayed, disobeyed or compromised, neither should it be misused.... We are all opposed to any form of syncretism, incipient, nascent or developed, if we mean by syncretism conscious or unconscious human attempts to create a new religion composed of elements taken from other religions.[18]

The preamble displayed the fears as well as the unexamined assumptions about dialogue within the WCC constituency. We were back in Tambaram!

Bishop of Durham, David Jenkins, writing on the assembly, said that the attempts to move forward in dialogue in a religiously plural world led "to an outcry about syncretism and betrayal of the Gospel," and that the response of the drafting committee to the outcry left many Asian and others with the feeling that their insights and convictions were being trampled on and betrayed."[19]

It appeared that dialogue as a program within the WCC was in danger, but the WCC leadership saved the situation by requesting a special conference of all the main contenders at the assembly to sort out the issues in dialogue and mission and to bring a proposal to the Central Committee of the WCC. This special conference was held in Chiang Mai, Thailand, in April 1977, and the result was the "Guidelines on Dialogue," which rejected syncretism as a possible danger in dialogue, affirmed that dialogue and witness to the Gospel are not in contradiction to each other, and asked for further study of the theological issues raised by the practice of dialogue.[20] With these guidelines, concern for dialogue and mission continued to cohabit in the WCC, with some measure of interaction with each other, but not to the point of making a decisive difference to any one of them.

Having looked at this historical intersection between dialogue and mission, let me turn in this last section to the concerns and issues at stake here as I see it.

## ISSUES AND CONCERNS

A number of issues have emerged as the result of the history of the intersection between dialogue and mission, which in the first forty years of the modern ecumenical movement, were discussed as issues related to other religions and mission. I would highlight here five of those issues as needing attention in our day.

## 1. What Is Mission? What Are We after in Mission, and What Is the Final Goal of Mission?

In 1910, still in the colonial period, the Edinburgh Conference saw the evangelization of the whole world as its mandated mission. It was thought that, for instance in Asia, if India and China were brought to Christ, then the whole of Asia would eventually become a Christian continent like Europe. Much effort and resources were poured into this hope. A century later, not even 3 percent of India and, by any count, not more than 6 percent of the population of China has become Christian. With the exception of the Philippines and to some extent South Korea, Asia remains a non-Christian continent. Other religious traditions have revived and have a firm grip on the Asian peoples. What we are faced with is called irreducible or persistent plurality. It appears that, for the foreseeable future, religious plurality cannot be fought and overcome.

A large section within the Christian constituency, therefore, has moved, unannounced and often unconsciously, to dialogue as the way forward in pluralistic societies, but they are uncertain about its implications for mission, salvation, and the like. Within the mission constituency, there are two kinds of responses. One response sees the need to redefine mission in terms of the present realities. Another response still holds on to the task of calling every person of other religions to faith in Jesus Christ as their only savior. What we need, they believe, is greater commitment, larger resources, and more effective use of modern technology.

Yet, there is an unacknowledged deep crisis in mission thinking that many refuse to admit or look at. There is more conviction about our need to be in mission than of the need of the other to hear the Gospel. Further, Christianity is in crisis in nations that had traditionally been "Christian" continents, and much of the spread of Christianity in Africa, of which much is made these days, is based on "prosperity gospel"—an affront to Christ and his mission. The discerning, therefore, are able to see that all the questions related to mission need to be rethought: What is mission? Why are we in mission? What is the goal of mission, and when is mission accomplished? Mission, in my own thinking, needs an entirely new theological foundation than has been given in the past, which is based on other religions being in error and devoid of any relationship with God. Challenging the classic understanding of mission, however, has become a "political" issue within the Evangelical constituency, and few are willing to take this on.

## 2. What Does the Bible, in Fact, Say about Mission?

The second issue relates to what is claimed to be the "biblical basis" and "mandate" for mission. Unfortunately, much of the support for a mission of converting the whole world to the Christian faith is drawn from three or four isolated verses from the Bible: "Go out into all the world and proclaim the good news to the whole creation" (Mark 16:15); "I am the way, and the truth, and the life. No one comes to the Father except through me" (John 14:6); and other verses that claim Jesus as the "only mediator" (1 Tim 2:3–6) and the "only name" by which we would be saved (Acts 4:11–12). And much of the foreign mission is inspired by Paul's "missionary journeys." There is no doubt that an exclusive understanding of the Christian faith and a mandate for world mission of calling all persons to faith in Jesus Christ can be argued from Scripture.

However, very few in the mission constituency readily acknowledge that the evidence for world mission in the Bible is not so decisive and that a closer study of Scripture would bring out a much more complex picture. In the Hebrew Bible, which acknowledges God as the creator of the world and that God is working toward establishing God's shalom in the world, there was no anxiety to convert all nations to Judaism. While the Jewish people were called to be a "light to the nations," God remains the "God of the

Nations," and in all eschatological visions in the Hebrew Scripture (and in the Book of Revelation) nations remain intact.

The Book of Jonah is a correction to the view that God does not listen to the prayers of people of other religions. In the New Testament, Jesus never spoke against or tried to convert people of other religions of his time. The only religion he feared was the "Religion of Mammon," which unfortunately has become very much inculturated into the Christian faith practiced in our day. For Jesus, it is the false and misguided confidence that one places on wealth and power that can take one away from God.

It is also not true that St. Paul set out on a mission to the Gentiles in his "missionary journeys." Not allowed to give witness to his experience of Christ in Jerusalem, and his life under threat, he fled to the Diaspora Jewish communities to convince them that Jesus was indeed the Jewish Messiah. The Gentile mission was something he stumbled into and was totally unwelcome to the mother church in Jerusalem. Even though by force of circumstances he eventually became an "apostle to the Gentiles," nowhere in his letters does he ask the congregations he established to engage in a world mission, not even the suggestion that they should convert the immediate people around them. But he was relentless in his criticism if their life and conduct were a counter-witness to the Gospel message of love. He appears to still hold on to a version of the Jewish understanding of mission.

It is not my intention here to argue that the Bible has a decisive direction to give on this issue, because the opposite point of view could also be argued out. But it is clear that the "biblical mandate" for world mission needs a second look on the basis of the overall message of the Bible. I believe that both Jesus and Paul had the Jewish idea of mission, which is to be a "light to the Gentiles," "the city that is set on a hill," "the leaven in the lump," etcetera. The church was never intended to be majority, and whenever it was in majority and had power, it betrayed the Gospel. The desire to conquer the world for Christ is the result of Christianity becoming part of the Roman Empire, which was in the business of conquering and subduing neighboring countries. World mission that expected everyone to become Christian became a pattern when early Roman Catholic explorers found it "convenient" to force the "natives" to come under both political and religious rule so that they would give their undivided loyalty to the crown in Portugal or Spain. The Reformers were not interested in world mission. Nobler motives for mission would come with the rise of Pietism and Puritanism in Europe and the Great Awakening in the United States.

What the intersection between dialogue and mission has shown is that the anxiety to convert all persons to Christ may well be misguided and may not have the biblical and theological basis that is often claimed. At least, these need to be revisited with an open mind. One might stand strongly on the belief that God had done something decisively significant in Christ, and there is an undeniable witness to God in Christ that one needs to bear in the world. But what it involves, and what one hopes to achieve through it, needs further study in our day. Otherwise, the practice in the mainline churches of doing lip service to world mission as converting peoples of other religions will continue without any understanding of the relevant and urgent mission that needs to be done in the world that has increasingly come under the hold of Mammon.

## 3. Dialogue, Mission, and the Theology of Religions

Perhaps the most important issue that the intersection between dialogue and mission has raised is to the Christian Theology of Religions. Is God in a saving relationship to people of other religious traditions, or does God relate to people, especially for their salvation, only through Jesus Christ? The question also needs to be raised from the human side. Are all religions "heathen," "pagan," or as Barth would have it, "unbelief" in so far as it is part of human sin and rebellion against God? What does one make of the saints and sages in other traditions, and of the witness to experiences of liberation and of being touched by the grace of God?

Much of the early discussions on mission had an assumed theology of religions, which held that the other religions are "misguided" and in "error" or at best, can give some moral guidance and spiritual comfort, but not salvation. The emergence of dialogue has also not been able to help in resolving the question. This is because dialogue called upon Christians to respect and accept the "otherness of the other" and to be open to the witness that others have to give to their spiritual experiences. But because of the enormous pressure of the mission constituency, it was not in a position to give salvific value to other religious traditions. For this would have meant that the dialogue ministry has to be moved outside the churches. Therefore, in the beginning, there was a studied silence on this issue by the advocates of dialogue. However, the more established dialogue became within the church, the theology of religions questions became more and more serious. Eventually, the Dialogue Program of the WCC attempted to tackle this issue through two consultations in Baar, near Zurich, in Switzerland. The Baar consultation of 1990, made up of Protestants, Catholics, and Orthodox participants, attempted to move forward, by affirming God's saving presence in other religious traditions and discerning the activity of the Holy Spirit in the life of people of other faiths.[21] But it became evident that it had to remain a "consultation report" and not an official document of the WCC. It was deemed too controversial for the Central Committee to act on.

This is because attempts had already been made at the Vancouver Assembly of the WCC in 1983 to affirm God's presence in other religious traditions, but the mission constituency within the assembly refused to go with it. Finally, they agreed that God may be present in their "seeking for God" within their traditions, but refused to allow that God may indeed be "found" through them. A further attempt was also made to move on the issue at the World Mission Conference (of the CWME) in San Antonio, Texas, in 1989. But the final statement would only say that, while they cannot limit the saving activity of God anywhere, they can only point to Jesus Christ as the place they have found it! Today, Theology of Religions has also become an academic pursuit with a typology of Exclusivism, Inclusivism, and Pluralism with many related positions around them. However, these remain at the margins of Christian theology and missiology and appear to have little impact on them.

## 4. Rethinking Christian Theology

My own sense is that the real challenge is not so much to develop a new Theology of Religions, but to rethink Christian theology for religious plurality. Much of classic Christian theology emerged in the Middle Ages. Much of the Reformation theology had to do with the internal Christian faith and order issues than with missiology, and there was no awareness of world religions other than Judaism and Islam. Much of the post-Enlightenment theology was Euro-centered, and Barth, who had laid the foundations of the main thrust of the theology of the churches of the Reformation, was responding primarily to the developments in Germany. There had been no serious attempts to be informed by the theology of the Eastern Churches, and the "third world" theologies have been at the margins.

In other words, the reality of religious plurality and the experience of dialogue have not yet led to a radical rethinking of Christian theology or missiology.

## 5. Dialogue, Mission, and the World Situation

The last issue I wish to highlight relates to the relevance and effectiveness of both dialogue and mission in the world today. Looking from the perspective of the ministry of Jesus, the two most troubling developments in the world today are the "culture of Mammon" and the "culture of violence." If salvation is about bringing healing and wholeness to the human community, both dialogue and mission needs to address these issues with the seriousness they deserve.

There is a strong tendency within the dialogue movement to go beyond "relationships building" exercises to deal with the hard and divisive issues, and to begin to engage together as religious communities to build peace among themselves and in the world. There are some forms of mission that had always looked at humanizing life and bringing about healing and wholeness as its primary mandate. But the more conspicuous and more vociferous calls from another part of the Christian mission constituency to "win the whole world for Christ" is what many neighbors of other faiths hear, and are nervous about. The history of missions has been a mixed blessing. On the one hand, much had been done to bring healing, wholeness, and spiritual affirmation in many parts of the world. On the other, peoples of other religious traditions also fear

Christianity as a movement that seeks to invalidate and replace them. One of the Jewish Rabbis said: "Two thousand years of Christian love is enough to make anyone nervous." This image of Christianity needs to change. The interaction between dialogue and mission until now has not helped us to reach this goal.

## NOTES

1. World Missionary Conference, "Report of Commission I: Carrying the Gospel to All the Non-Christian World," in *Report of Commission I–VIII* (Edinburgh/London: Oliphant, Anderson, and Ferrier, 1910), 363.

2. Ibid., 279.

3. These answers are available in typed format in The World Council of Churches Library. See Hinduism, for instance, in: *Commission on Missionary Message: Hinduism,* Cat. no. 280.215w893c, Vol. 2–3.

4. World Missionary Conference, "Report of Commission IV: The Missionary Message in Relation to Non-Christian Religions, *Report of Commission I–VIII* (Edinburgh/London: Oliphant, Anderson, and Ferrier, 1910), 171.

5. Ibid.

6. Ibid., 172.

7. Ibid., 256.

8. International Missionary Council, *Report of the Jerusalem Meeting of the International Missionary Council, March 24th–April 8th, 1928*, vol. 1 (London: Oxford University Press, 1928), 369f, which reports on Hocking's contribution.

9. Ibid., 353–6, which reports on the speeches of Julius Richter and G. Simons.

10. Ibid., 491.

11. A. M. Chirgwin, "The Jerusalem Meeting and the Man in the Pew," in *International Review of Mission*, vol. 17, no. 3 (July 1928): 528–37.

12. Quoted in Norman E. Thomas, *Missions and Unity—Lessons from History, 1792–2010* (Eugene, OR: Cascade Books, 2010), 244.

13.  Unfortunately no minutes were taken of the "Tambaram Debate" as it was referred to in later years. However, recognizing the importance of the debate, a volume was brought out after the conference, as the first volume of the Tambaram Report, in which Kraemer wrote the first article on "Continuity and Discontinuity," outlining his ideas, followed by presentations by those who took part in the debate. See: *The Authority of Faith: International Missionary Council Meeting at Tambaram, Madras, December 12–29, 1938* (London: Oxford University Press, 1939).

14.  Kenneth Cragg, "The Credibility of Christianity," in the papers of the Kandy Consultation, published in *Study Encounter* 3, no. 2 (1967).

15.  Ibid., 73.

16.  Norman Goodall, ed., *The Uppsala Report 1968: The Official Report of the Fourth Assembly of the WCC, Uppsala, 4–20, July 1968* (Geneva: WCC Publications, 1968), 29.

17.  Michael Kinnamon and Brian E. Cope, eds., *The Ecumenical Movement: An Anthology of Key Texts and Voices* (Geneva: WCC Publications, 1997), 359.

18.  As quoted in Wesley Ariarajah, *Hindus and Christians—A Century of Protestant Ecumenical Thought* (Grand Rapids: William B. Eerdmans, 1991), 147.

19.  David E. Jenkins, "Nairobi and the Truly Ecumenical: Contribution to a Dialogue about the Subsequent Tasks of the WCC," *The Ecumenical Review* 28, no. 3 (July 1976), 281.

20.  For the text of the Guidelines, see Kinnamon, *The Ecumenical Movement*, 407–14.

21.  For the full text, see Ibid., 417–420.

# 9

# BITTER HISTORY ON THE CHURCH'S JOURNEY OF MISSION[1]

*Matthew D. Lundberg*

Mission is lived out at the level of the local and the specific—with particular denominations, congregations, and missionaries working for spiritual and social transformation in witness to the coming kingdom of God. But as a common practice of the Christian Church it always remains an ecumenical journey. At the deepest level, it is not the individual missionary or congregation that is the agent of mission. Rather, it is the one, holy, catholic, and apostolic church of Christ that is "sent" into the world as the community of disciples whose work in the world serves as a grace-driven extension of the mission of the triune God. It is, therefore, incumbent upon all of the world's churches to envision their efforts not as self-contained or ultimately competitive with other Christian bodies, but to see their missional work as a common journey undertaken with a myriad of companions. As a journey of accompaniment, each Christian tradition, communion, and denomination witnesses to the truth and life of the Gospel in a particular place and way, but in unity with Christian sisters and brothers across time and space.

Most journeys involve some amount of pain, adversity, and suffering as travelers move toward their destination. Companions on the way disagree about the route that should be taken; various obstacles present themselves; unforeseen difficulties, tragedies, and uncertainty cast shadows on the path. Failures experienced on the journey can tempt the pilgrims to turn back or seek shortcuts. The journey of the church's mission is no exception. The co-travelers of Christian mission have often found themselves at odds with regard to the message that they are trying to convey through their efforts, the means chosen to convey that message, and even the ultimate purpose of the journey. Rather than seeing it as a common pilgrimage of the one, holy, catholic, and apostolic church of Christ, the churches have often turned mission into an expression of competition and division, one that undermines the shared purpose of inviting non-Christians into the transformative Gospel community. Christian division is but one example of the fact that *sin* in its many manifestations has also accompanied the companions on the missional path.

Ecclesial sinfulness has not only corrupted the unity and fraternity of the church itself, leading to schism, denominational rivalry, and uncharitable proselytism. It is also, perhaps even more tragically, a force that has wounded countless parties and persons outside of the church—those to whom the church has been "sent" to convey the transformation of the Gospel. Whether the example be Christian support of slavery in the United States, prevailing silence and complicity in times of genocide in Europe or Africa, or the provision of theological arguments in favor of the evil of apartheid, the Christian Churches bear profound responsibility and culpability for some of the world's injustice and suffering. Moreover, many of the evils of which the church stands guilty have taken place in the course of its historic missionary project. In the course of "making disciples of all nations" the churches have aided imperialism, abetted the destruction of cultures, and afforded theological justification to racism and sexism. This is not to say, of course, that the church has *only* and *always* committed such sins in the course of the missionary enterprise. The history of mission of course includes its share of heroes, such as Bartolomé de Las Casas, its share of moral courage, as in the abolitionist movement, and its share of cultural sensitivity, as with some of the early Jesuit missions to Asia. But it is important to recognize that the history of Christian mission, as a reflection of the broader history of the church, is indeed a mixed bag that includes significant moral failure, social injustice, and imperial ambition. The only way for the ecumenical church to forge a true identity along its present journey of mission is to own its past.[2]

## SIN ON THE PILGRIMAGE OF MISSION

Before thinking theologically about what ecclesial sin might mean and how the church can own it on the ongoing journey, let us indwell the problem at greater length by entering briefly into two narratives of missional sin. First, the well-known story of the conquest, colonization, and "Christianization" of Central and South America by the imperial powers of Spain and Portugal in the fifteenth and sixteenth centuries. It is not necessary to assume that the Christian motives of the imperial powers were insincere (since, of course, we're talking about the era of "Christendom") to be able to acknowledge that many of the effects of this expression of colonial mission were horribly destructive, and that something of the character of the Gospel was forfeited in the process. It is not without reason that Luis Rivera Pagán describes this mission as "a violent evangelism."[3] H. McKennie Goodpasture's first-person history of Latin American Christianity provides an account of some of the violence that took place in this episode of Christian mission. It includes a policy document from Queen Isabella of Spain, which fuses an earnest desire for the evangelization of the "Indians" with an equally earnest desire to capitalize on the natives as a labor force while exploiting the gold found in the "new world." Starting with an acknowledgment that the Indians are free peoples, she quickly expresses chagrin that the Indians are "idle," not easily working with/for the Spanish, and resistant to the "Holy Catholic Faith." She then orders the governor of the Spanish community to "compel and force the said Indians to associate with the Christians of the island and to work on their buildings, and to gather and mine the gold and other metals, and to till the fields and produce food for the Christian inhabitants and dweller of the said island."[4] The queen emphasizes that the workers should be paid and should not be harmed, and repeats her desire that the Indians be "taught in matters of the Faith." But it is also clear that the key goal is that the whole process will "bring profit to my kingdom and subjects."

The story, with its ambiguous beginnings, takes a dreadful turn when the governor institutes the queen's policy with an eye only toward the enrichment of Spain, without the restraint required by the queen, and with little interest in the conversion of the natives.

# THE WAY OF RECONCILIATION

The Dominican priest Bartolomé de Las Casas, one of the more laudable figures of this story who displays the real possibility of a better way even in that historical context, observed that the governor "distributed Indians at his pleasure," parceling them out to Spanish landholders as a labor force that amounted to "an absolute servitude which killed them in the end."[5] The result was the division of families and the death of infants from starvation due to their mothers having no milk. The task masters, he writes, "treated the Indians with such rigor and inhumanity that they seemed the very ministers of Hell, driving them day and night with beatings, kicks, lashes and blows, and calling them no sweeter name than dogs."[6] He relates that the Indians were annually paid an amount that would buy them at most a trinket or two. In short, he writes, "the Indians were totally deprived of their freedom and were put in the harshest, fiercest, most horrible servitude and captivity which no one who has not seen it can understand. Even beasts enjoy more freedom when they are allowed to graze in the fields."[7] Interestingly, one of Las Casas's major complaints was that the queen's goal of bringing the Indians to Christian faith (in part, we must remember, by forcing them to work) was lost in this virtual enslavement. The original intent of evangelization along with enrichment and convenient labor degenerated into only slavery and the quest for gold, with genuine evangelization fading into the background as little more than a noble justification for such atrocities.

Examples of courage such as Las Casas should, of course, be remembered. Las Casas himself tells the story of another Dominican priest, António Montesinos, who preached an excoriating sermon to the colonial authorities at Hispaniola, in which he affirmed the full humanity of the native peoples and accused the colonial authorities of "mortal sin" due to their treatment of the Indians.[8] Another example, Toribio de Motolinía, emphasized the peacefulness and intelligence of the natives of Mexico, claiming that they were readier for the Gospel than most Spaniards.[9] Such exceptions, however, largely prove the unfortunate rule—that this colonial expression of mission ended up producing the decimation of the native peoples of Latin America through slavery, military murder, and disease.[10] And these atrocities committed centuries ago by no means belong only to the distant past, since they represent the beginning of a cultural and economic imperialism that produced the underdevelopment, dependence, and poverty that continues to afflict the Latin American world today.

A second example that follows a similar pattern is the plight of the natives of North America as they found themselves in the way of the inexorable western expansion of the United States toward its "Manifest Destiny." Although the idea of "manifest destiny" did not begin with overtly violent tones[11] and may not have represented the attitudes of most of the American people,[12] it is clear that the missionary presence of the church rarely accompanied American imperialism with a critical or prophetic voice. More often, in contrast, the church silently abetted or more overtly supported the kind of attitude conveyed by Francis Baylies, a U.S. congressman from Massachusetts who, in the 1820s, argued strongly for Manifest Destiny as a Christian imperative: "To diffuse the arts of life, the light of science, and the blessings of the Gospel over a wilderness, is no violation of the laws of God; it is no violation of the rights of man to occupy a territory over which the savage roams, but which he never cultivates, and which he does not use for the purposes for which it was designed—the support of man."[13]

At its Fall 2008 "Ecumenism from the Margins" consultation, the Faith and Order Commission of the National Council Churches of Christ, USA, heard from the Rev. Alvin Deer, a member of the Kiowa tribe in Oklahoma, and director of the Native American International Caucus of the United Methodist Church. In his telling of the stories of his people's suffering, Deer lamented the way in which mission was conducted in relation to Native Americans, since little attention and respect was given to their culture and heritage, and much violence was done in the process. But he also bemoaned the fact that the church hadn't been *more* interested in a true evangelization of American Indians. He claimed that Christian faith has been less embraced by Native American communities because of the violent form in which the Gospel came, something that he lamented given the Christian faith's potential for the social change and personal transformation that so many native communities need. Here we see that the criticism of Las Casas regarding the brutal Spanish enactment of Queen Isabella's decree can be applied to the U.S. policy of westward expansion no matter what lay in the way: Not only was Christianity used as a pretext for violence and imperialist ambition, but what evangelization *did* take place was often half-hearted and superficial, one that displayed but a meager witness to the God whose power is most resolutely displayed on Jesus' cross.

In both narratives, moreover, sins in which the Christian Churches and their historic mission were complicit contributed to systems, structures, institutions, attitudes, and practices that have continued to dehumanize the very people whom the church claims can find true humanity through Christ in the Gospel community. Like all sin, they produced consequences that travel subtly, yet, powerfully from the past into the present. This is the reason why the trend of focusing on the positive features of missionary presence and especially the indigenous *resistance* to the colonial aspect of missions in some recent explorations of the history of Christian mission, while understandable, may create a dangerous and subtle temptation for Christians who are members of the traditional missionary churches. For example, surely it is right to emphasize, as Lamin Sanneh has, the *African* role in the appropriation of the Gospel and to correct a one-sided focus on the flaws of missions and their colonial embeddedness—the myopic obsession of many versions of the history of missions. Sanneh is also certainly right to bring to focus the better face of the history of missions against the backdrop of colonial abuses.[14] But surely it involves a disturbing loss of memory and identity for the pendulum to swing too far in the opposite direction—a loss of memory that may strike some non-Christians as a failure of the churches to take responsibility for their past. Moreover, if the contemporary churches are to speak the Gospel in today's world with honesty, they must include an awareness of how past ecclesial sin has helped to shape contemporary injustice and oppression.

A recognition of the dark side of the Christian Church's presence in the world—a history that leaves a bitter taste in the mouth of its victims, both past and present—raises an important question as the churches accompany one another on the journey of mission in witness to the life-giving and life-changing Gospel: Where is the truth and life of the Gospel, when its proclamation has sometimes been accompanied by falsehood and death? This question spawns others: Where lies the credibility and integrity of the Gospel message when the community of its witnesses bears profound culpability for this bitter history? Do the Christian Churches possess the moral right to continue their mission of proclamation and social change when expressions of mission have often left their recipients worse off?

Some of the theological resources that have recently been offered on the ecumenical journey of mission have been appropriately mindful of the fact that Christian mission witnesses to the Gospel of life in a world of conflict, violence, and despair. Therefore, a great deal of scholarly and ecumenical energy has been devoted to the suggestion that the church adopt *reconciliation* as the key paradigm of Christian mission. One of the main proponents, Robert Schreiter, writes (reflecting on Ephesians 2):

> Ancient divisions are healed, and those once estranged are now fellow citizens in the household of God, together with the apostles and prophets, in a new society built upon Christ the cornerstone. This is an image of a new society that replaces and surpasses an old one that was marked by division and alienation. This, it seems to me, is a paradigm of what God's good news can mean and become for those displaced, alienated and excluded from the human community by ethnicity and want.[15]

The message of reconciliation, he argues, is "an important part of what Christian faith has to offer a world wracked by conflict and violence. It is the source of a profound hope that can sustain Christians who are now suffering. And it captures, although for us now dimly and opaquely, the very heart of Christ's mission to the world."[16] In no small part due to the influence of Schreiter, this way of conceiving of the missional task has also been conveyed powerfully in the ecumenical arena, for example, through a preparatory paper for the Athens 2005 mission conference that was titled "Mission as Ministry of Reconciliation."[17]

On the one hand, it makes much theological sense to view reconciliation as an appropriate paradigm and goal for Christian mission—given that the church's life flows from the triune God's primal act of reconciliation through Jesus Christ and is charged with witnessing to that reconciliation to the whole world, in part through its own fostering of social and interpersonal reconciliation. But in contexts where the church's misdeeds and historic complicity are particularly prominent, it must be asked whether reconciliation should be the first word on the church's lips. Aside from the church's obvious hope that it will be reconciled with those it has wronged, in such circumstances, reconciliation is not an event that the church has control over or even a right to expect. It seems, rather, that a more appropriate stance, and even a paradigm, for Christian mission, when the journey's story evokes memories of bitter history for which the church stands responsible, would be that of *repentance*.

## REPENTANCE AND MISSION

Repentance is a practice of faith that is simultaneously familiar to Christians and often overlooked in its radical significance. It is central in the Gospel message, and has received rich attention in the history of theology, but is sometimes understood in a rather reductionistic way. The centrality of repentance to the Gospel message is shown in a striking way by the beginning of the Gospel of Mark. John the Baptist's prophetic work in the wilderness centered around "a baptism of repentance for the forgiveness of sins" (Mark 1:4). And Jesus (in his initial words in Mark) announces the Gospel with an eye to repentance: "The time is fulfilled, and the kingdom of God has come near; repent, and believe in the good news" (1:15).

Repentance is a fundamental alteration in one's perception, a changed mind regarding the self, God, and the world that produces a vital re-patterning of one's life. In its broad sense, it refers to an all-encompassing conversion to a new way of thinking and living, a shift toward life-giving ways centering on commitment to God and neighbor, and a shift away from destructive and/or egocentric configurations of existence.

As an attitude of mind and a practice of the journey of mission, repentance is a deeply fitting stance of the church in view of past sins. Put differently, the ecumenical missional task of "shar[ing] the suffering of all by advocacy and care for the poor, the needy and the marginalised"[18] requires for its credibility the churches' frank

160

acknowledgement of and genuine repentance for their role in historical atrocities and contemporary systems of injustice.

An understandable response that many people have to this suggestion is that apologies have already been made and that we should move forward rather than dwell on a past that cannot be changed. To some extent, this may lie behind the previously mentioned trend among some historians of Christian mission to laud the fact that more recent discussion of mission is finally moving past the "colonialism paradigm."[19] But if it is true, as it surely is, that past sins travel perniciously into the present, as with the legacy of colonialist missions that is still felt in deeply embedded and systemic ways in the postcolonial world, it may be that the most genuine and credible expression of the church's mission will be the church's own act of repentance, including the confession of its sin to those persons and peoples who have been wounded and victimized by past manifestations of Christian mission, and may still feel its effects today.

Skepticism regarding the value of repentance as a paradigm of the church's continuing missional journey may be rooted in a one-sided understanding of what repentance involves, one that sees it as merely a negative stance, not capturing the forward-looking movement of the Gospel. In this sense, the term *repentance* perhaps brings to many people's minds first and foremost an attitude of sorrow, remorse, or mourning. This is why some theological traditions have termed repentance as *mortification*. In its broadest sense, mortification refers to the "putting to death" of the old, sinful self that is captivated by sinful inclinations and corrupt practices. It involves honest self-examination, forthright confession, and genuine contrition in the face of one's misdeeds and shortcomings.

The attitude of sorrow, remorse, and mourning, however, can all too easily become a fetishized end-unto-itself, a stultifying and consuming despair that erodes the church's confidence in the Evangelical message, which it is sent to proclaim and enact, by seeing only the false, misguided, and immoral ways in which the churches have acted in the past and often continue to act in the present. But the broader sense of "changed mind" reminds us that a full-orbed theological conception of Christian repentance must recognize that mortification is only one side of the reality of repentance, the negative condition of its positive dimension—namely, *vivification*. This forward-looking face of repentance refers to the new life and renewed patterns of the self that are cultivated by the power and presence of the Holy Spirit. It involves the Spirit-buoyed intent to carve out righteous and just patterns in one's life to the honor of God and "the integrity of creation."[20]

While not always put in precisely these terms, these interlaced backward- and forward-looking dimensions of true repentance have been broadly recognized in the theological discourse of the West. For John Calvin, repentance is the quintessence of sanctification by faith; and it cannot be understood without linking mortification and vivification to one another, just as the cross and resurrection are inseparably linked together in Christian faith and hope.[21] Calvin himself draws upon and modifies the portrait of penitence offered by Philipp Melanchthon, who correlates the two terms with the Lutheran law-Gospel distinction.[22] And it is the Catholic sacrament of penance that lies beneath these Protestant articulations, even if the latter alter the former in certain ways. While not using the terminology of mortification and vivification, the *Catechism of the Catholic Church*'s explanation of the sacrament includes this same twofold movement: "The movement of return to God, called conversion and repentance, entails sorrow for and abhorrence of sins committed, and the firm purpose of sinning no more in the future. Conversion touches the past and the future and is nourished by hope in God's mercy."[23]

These two aspects of repentance have usually been regarded as falling under the canopy of the individual Christian life. But the church's corporate culpability in the face of many of the world's evils points toward the need for a robust sense of repentance at the communal and even institutional level of the churches. As a systemic and structural power, in addition to being an act of the individual person, sin also infiltrates the behavior and patterns of the church itself. If, in the individual life, repentance is the natural Gospel-evoked response to a conviction of one's own sin, then also in the corporate life of the churches repentance is an appropriate response to the recognition of ecclesial sin. Indeed, in some circumstances, for example, in traditions whose complicity in the evils of mission-rationalized colonialism is particularly strong, or where the church has historically undergirded the social status quo to the detriment of the poor and powerless, it may be the *only* appropriate response. As Rwandan scholar Tharcisse Gatwa states in a theologically general way, but with a particular eye to Rwanda's experience of genocide: "For Christians to abstain from repentance resembles a denial of identity."[24]

It is in this sense of mortification *and* vivification that it is possible to conceive of repentance as a stance and even paradigm for the Christian journey of mission. If mission is the very being and life-blood of the church, and the church is honest about its past and present actions, then genuine repentance should be a prominent part of the church's ongoing work of witnessing in its own mission to the saving *missio Dei*. What Stanley Hauerwas writes about Christians can be applied corporately to the church:

> Memory is a moral exercise. We must be the kind of people capable of remembering our failures and sins if we are rightly to tell the story we have been charged to keep, for a proper telling requires that we reveal our sin. To acknowledge the authority of Scripture is also to learn to acknowledge our sin and accept forgiveness. It is only through forgiveness that we are able to witness to how that story has formed our lives.[25]

If memories are to be healed and reconciliation received in situations of *Christian* guilt in the social, political, and cultural arena, then the truth must be told and owned. The way for the church to tell the truth in the face of bitter memories is to adopt a stance of honest repentance. The mortification/vivification distinction reminds us of the need for authentic contrition and profound remorse, but also a forward-minded confidence in the Spirit that new patterns are possible and that the truth of the Gospel retains its power even in the face of the church's sin. Recognition of the sins of colonialist missions has led some in the Christian Church to hesitate to affirm the evangelizing mission of the church in any robust manner because it is difficult for them to imagine it taking place in a humanizing way. This attitude, however understandable, may represent mortification without vivification and, therefore, not repentance in the full sense of the term. Repentance is ultimately a future-minded attitude and practice. But it is a forward-looking attitude that refuses to gloss glibly over the past, one that involves honest and painful truth-telling. The vivification side of the coin means that repentance must be cultivated with an eye toward reconciliation, while mortification reminds us that it must always be one that takes sin and justice seriously. In short, such a Christian mission of repentance is a way of choosing a cruciform path on the journey of mission in the face of the ever-present temptation to seek out triumphalistic shortcuts.

A powerful example of the repentance paradigm, though one that comes from Christian ecumenism rather than Christian mission, is the Lutheran Churches' recent repentance for their sixteenth-century treatment of Anabaptists. The Anabaptists (Brethren, Mennonites, and Hutterites) were persecuted, often tortured, and sometimes executed by Catholic, Calvinist, and Lutheran authorities for what was received to be the "blasphemy" of their beliefs.[26] A joint study commission of the Lutheran World Federation and the Mennonite World Conference was formed in 2002 to examine this bitter history. The General Secretaries of these two bodies stated in the commission's report that even though there are ways for Lutherans to avoid the full force of blame (such as pointing out that Lutherans bear comparatively less blame than Calvinists and Catholics[27]), "finally all ameliorations and exculpations fails: the only adequate response is repentance."[28] The report emphasizes that the only right path in the present is for the Lutheran churches to express their regret and ask for forgiveness.[29] The Lutheran World Federation officially did repent and ask for forgiveness on July 22, 2010, in Stuttgart, Germany.[30]

While the Lutheran-Mennonite commission employs the language of reconciliation, perhaps because both sides of this situation are Christian and share a common theological impulse toward forgiveness, the report is first of all about repentance. It recognizes that the repentance of the Lutheran churches involves more than mere regret for the past. Ultimately, it is an "act of hope."[31] In other words, it includes vivification. Acknowledgement of the harm of the past is a first step, but it must change the way Lutherans live toward the future, including guarding their theological confessions from being used to persecute others for their different beliefs.[32] "The past cannot be changed, but we can change the way the past is remembered in the present. This is our hope. Reconciliation does not only look back into the past; rather it looks into a common future."[33] The study report is also clear that repentance, in this case a repentance that was met with reconciliation, is a way of proclaiming the Gospel: "Reconciliation with God and among Mennonites and Lutherans is, from the beginning to the end, only possible and real in Jesus Christ through the power of the Holy Spirit."[34]

As this case shows, one of the difficulties of accepting the unity of the missional journey is accepting this shadow side of the church's past and present. From an ecumenical perspective, the act of remembering and repenting that Hauerwas speaks about includes accepting as our *own* the "failures and sins" of our sisters and brothers, even those from the long past. To put it personally, there is a sense in which a sixteenth-century Calvinist act of drowning an Anabaptist belongs to me as a twenty-first-century Reformed Christian. The Lutheran-Mennonite study commission recognized the act of identification that is required for such an act of repentance. "Can Lutherans today ask for forgiveness for the harm that their confessional forebears did to the Anabaptists? Can Mennonites today grant forgiveness for something that their spiritual forebears had to suffer hundreds of years ago?"[35] Yet at the same time, it recognized that such an act of identification is necessary, since both parties in the contemporary scene of this story are profoundly cognizant of their connection to their spiritual forebears. For the Lutherans, this solidarity with the past includes "responsibility for addressing the 'dark sides' of the reformers' thoughts and actions, especially since the descendants of the victims have not forgotten them."[36] Such an act of identification is perhaps easier to handle when it takes place within a particular Christian tradition, as in these examples. It is a harder pill to swallow if I am thinking about how Christian unity in sin implies my *own* responsibility as a Christian for a Nigerian mosque burning, or for Spanish missionary colonialism in the West Indies in the early sixteenth century. How could such Christian deeds belong to me? But if the journey of mission in part includes accepting a sense of missional togetherness and accompaniment—if it really *is* a common journey—then the ecumenical unity that we are only learning to see must be understood not only to extend to the grace of the Gospel, but also our sin along the way. This point is implied by the Nicene affirmation of the theological unity and catholicity of the church. There is *one* church extended through space and time, so ecclesial misdeeds can be seen—at least theologically—as the common property of all the churches. An ecclesial expression of "bear[ing] one another's burdens" (Gal 6:2), then, must include an identification with one another's sins and guilt as burdens that the whole church takes upon itself on the journey of mission. Put differently, we must learn to perform an act of ecumenical identification. I have to learn to see as my own the Christian guilt and responsibility for others' sins that have wounded God's children in the world. That weight of guilt is perhaps mitigated by the fact that I can also begin to recognize that my guilt and that of my particular tradition are also borne by the whole church of Christ.

As the churches travel the path of mission, a common response on the part of those we meet along the way, those who are the intended "recipients" of mission, may be: Why were the German churches silent in the face of Nazi aggression and antisemitism? Why is Sunday morning the most segregated hour in American life? Isn't Christianity laughable when different churches can't even get along with each other and so each faction hides away in its own denomination? How can I believe in the Gospel when the theology of the Dutch Reformed Church in South Africa was a key ingredient in apartheid policy?

In the face of such questions, trite answers based on half-truths will always have a seductive appeal: Well, we shouldn't forget about the Confessing Church and the courage of folks like Bonhoeffer and Niemöller. Christians are looking for expressions of worship that resonate with their cultural worlds, so it's just natural that churches would be predominantly white or black. Christians agree on the big points, so their divisions are only skin-deep. The Afrikaner Christians were blinded by their cultural assumptions; their actions weren't representative of the church as a whole.

These answers, of course, express a significant moment of truth. The church has not acted *only* for evil in the world; it has not only been the tool of political and economic interests. The church's history and the history of its mission also include significant moments of courage, cultural sensitivity, missionary identification with the "least of these," and Evangelical transformation. We can indeed point to genuine moments of unity and reconciliation among divided churches, such as the Lutherans and Anabaptists. But in cases where the recipients of mission have a particularly acute sense of the church's moments of delinquency, the silver lining approach will likely appear to be an uncomfortable changing of the topic. In such cases, the churches would be better served by owning up to their responsibility and even Evangelical malpractice. Fortunately, such acceptance of Christian guilt does not imply an irredeemable, thoroughgoing Evangelical or missional failure, one that requires the conviction that past faithlessness deprives the church of any moral authority to live out its mission and witness to the Gospel. For the churches possess a powerful theology of repentance that brings sin and grace together in such a way that honesty about past sin becomes a forward-looking expression of confidence in the leading of God's Spirit, a way of living that simultaneously means truthful memory and future-minded transformation.

While the Lutheran-Mennonite case looks at repentance within the ranks of the churches, a good example of an outward-looking expression of mission through repentance is the apology that was issued to indigenous Canadians by the archbishop of the Anglican Church of Canada in 1993 for the church's significant role in Canada's practice of forcing indigenous children to attend residential schools, where many experienced abuse and neglect. In his apology on behalf of the church, an apology, notably, that came 15 years before the first forthright apology from a Canadian Prime Minister (in 2008), Archbishop Michael Peers hit a heavy note of mortification for the church's superintendence of the schools, the very theory of which assumed a condescending and coercive stance toward the native peoples and their cultures, and in which deplorable acts were committed against many children:

> I have felt shame and humiliation as I have heard of suffering inflicted by my people, and as I think of the part our church played in that suffering...I accept and I confess before God and you, our failures in the residential schools. We failed you. We failed ourselves. We failed God. I am sorry, more than I can say, that we were part of a system which took you and your children from home and family. I am sorry, more than I can say, that we tried to remake you in our image, taking from

you your language and the signs of your identity. I am sorry, more than I can say, that in our schools so many were abused physically, sexually, culturally and emotionally.[37]

Yet, nestled within this prominent note of contrition and sorrow is a significant future-minded note of hope and vivification: "I also know that I am in need of healing, and my own people are in need of healing, and our church is in need of healing. Without that healing, we will continue the same attitudes that have done such damage in the past...I also know that it is God who heals, and that God can begin to heal when we open ourselves, our wounds, our failures and our shame to God. I want to take one step along that path here and now." In the form of apology, what we see here is a short expression, even a proclamation, of the Gospel message of sin and grace, one couched in the form of repentance—interlaced mortification and vivification—a stance that is deeply and evangelically appropriate to the situation of the Canadian church.

The WCC's *Nature and Mission of the Church* document includes this rich and evocative statement: "In exercising its mission, the Church cannot be true to itself without giving witness (*martyria*) to God's will for the salvation and transformation of the world."[38] One possible implication of this statement is that that the church's missional message will be most compelling and full of integrity when the witnessing acts of the church embody, in both word *and* deed, the salvation of creation through Christ that the Gospel message hinges upon. The very character of the church's life, in other words, should be evangelical, pointing to the reality of God's life-giving ways through the fact that the church itself has been shaped and is continually being remodeled by those ways. The church's act of repentance, then, can serve as a parable of the Gospel message, as in the above examples of the Lutheran-Mennonite dialogue and the Canadian Anglican Church. If the Gospel centers on the Son's self-humiliation, which culminates on the cross and is transformed into the power of new life and fresh possibilities through the resurrection; if the Gospel invites all human beings to repentance and fuller life through the energies of the Spirit; and if the Gospel should characterize the whole life of the church, not merely its message, then the church should have confidence that the light of the

Gospel will shine through its own act of self-humbling in repentance. This ecclesial act of repentance will be especially resonant with the dynamics of the Gospel when it is graced with the response of forgiveness and reconciliation on the part of the victims of ecclesial sin. But since such a response can never be guaranteed or coerced, even the stance of repentance alone can be a poignant expression of the Gospel of new life. But, once again, it is important to underscore that this way of traveling the ecumenical journey of mission should not be interpreted only as a stultifying mortification that consumes itself in guilt for the past, but as a full-orbed repentance that ultimately vivifies the church in Spirit-guided practices of truth, justice, and love.

## NOTES

1. Parts of the second half of this essay, as well as its central argument, were previously published as "Repentance as a Paradigm for Christian Mission," *Journal of Ecumenical Studies* 45, no. 2 (Spring 2010): 201–17.

2. This is to adapt a point made by Stanley Hauerwas, *The Peaceable Kingdom* (Notre Dame, IN: University of Notre Dame Press, 1983), 41–44.

3. Luis N. Rivera Pagan, *A Violent Evangelism: The Political and Religious Conquest of the Americas* (Louisville, KY: Westminster John Knox, 1992).

4. H. McKennie Goodpasture, ed., *Cross and Sword: An Eyewitness History of Christianity in Latin America* (Maryknoll, NY: Orbis, 1989), 8.

5. Ibid., 9.

6. Ibid., 10.

7. Ibid.

8. Ibid., 11–12.

9. Ibid., 23–24.

10. See Rivera Pagan, *Violent Evangelism*, 170–9.

11. Robert W. Johannsen, "The Meaning of Manifest Destiny," in *Manifest Destiny and Empire: American Antebellum Expan-*

*sionism*, ed. Sam W. Haynes and Christopher Morris (College Station, TX: Texas A&M University Press, 1997), 10.

12. Frederick Merk, *Manifest Destiny and Mission in American History: A Reinterpretation* (New York: Knopf, 1963), 61.

13. Quoted in Robert J. Miller, *Native America: Discovered and Conquered*, Native America: Yesterday and Today (Westport, CT: Praeger, 2006), 140.

14. See Lamin Sanneh, "World Christianity and the New Historiography: History and Global Interconnections," in *Enlarging the Story: Perspectives on Writing World Christian History*, ed. Wilbert R. Shenk (Maryknoll, NY: Orbis, 2002), 100–2. Also see Sanneh, *Whose Religion is Christianity? The Gospel Beyond the West* (Grand Rapids, MI: Eerdmans, 2003).

15. Robert J. Schreiter, "Reconciliation and Healing as a Paradigm for Mission," *International Review of Mission* 94 (2005): 85.

16. Robert J. Schreiter, "Reconciliation as a Missionary Task," *Missiology* 20 (1992): 5.

17. Available at http://www.oikoumene.org/en/resources/documents/wcc-commissions/mission-and-evangelism/cwme-world-conference-athens-2005/preparatory-paper-na-10-mission-as-ministry-of-reconciliation.html (accessed July 14, 2012).

18. World Council of Churches, *The Nature and Mission of the Church: A Stage on the Way to a Common Statement*, Faith and Order Paper (Geneva: WCC Publications, 2005), §40.

19. E.g., Dana L. Robert, ed., *Converting Colonialism: Visions and Realities in Mission History, 1706-1914*, Studies in the History of Christian Missions (Grand Rapids, MI: Eerdmans, 2008), 3–4.

20. World Council of Churches, *Nature and Mission*, §40.

21. John Calvin, *Institutes of the Christian Religion*, ed. John T. McNeill, trans. Ford Lewis Battles, Library of Christian Classics (Philadelphia: Westminster, 1960), 3.3.3–9, esp. 8–9 on the cross-resurrection connection.

22. Philipp Melanchthon, *The Loci Communes of Philip Melanchthon*, trans. Charles Leander Hill (Boston: Meador, 1944), 250; also see 249–55.

23. *Catechism of the Catholic Church* (New York: Doubleday, 1994), 1490.

24. Tharcisse Gatwa, "Victims or Guilty? Can the Rwandan Churches Repent and Bear the Burden of the Nation for the 1994 Tragedy?" *International Review of Mission* 88, no. 351 (1999): 361; also see 349, 359–62.

25. Hauerwas, *The Peaceable Kingdom*, 70.

26. For a thorough telling of this story, see Lutheran-Mennonite International Study Commission, *Healing Memories: Reconciling in Christ* (Geneva: Lutheran World Federation; Strasbourg: Mennonite World Conference, 2010), 19–72. For example, a 1557 document from a group of Lutheran theologians stated that the "blasphemy" of the Anabaptists amounts to "sedition," and accordingly merits judgment and execution by the sword (Ibid., 67).

27. Ibid., 107.

28. Ibid., 6.

29. Ibid., 102, 108.

30. For an account, see "Lutherans Take Historic Step in Asking for Forgiveness from Mennonites," available at http://www.lutheranworld.org/lwf/index.php/lutherans-take-historic-step-in-asking-for-forgiveness-from-mennonites.html (accessed July 14, 2012).

31. Study Commission, *Healing Memories*, 5.

32. Ibid., 103–4.

33. Ibid., 108.

34. Ibid., 103.

35. Ibid., 102.

36. Ibid.

37. A Message from the Primate to the National Native Convocation, delivered at Minaki, Ontario, on August 6, 1993, available at http://www.anglican.ca/relationships/trc/apology (accessed July 14, 2012).

38. World Council of Churches, *Nature and Mission*, §37.

# 10

# THE ROLE OF ECUMENICAL CHARITY IN CHRISTIAN MISSION

*Antonios Kireopoulos*

In one of his most important and celebrated works, Jürgen Moltmann wrote, "Mission embraces all activities that serve to liberate man from his slavery in the presence of the coming God, slavery which extends from economic necessity to God-forsakenness."[1] This understanding of the church's mission raises both the spiritual ("God-forsakenness") and physical ("economic necessity") aspects of the impetus behind mission. In essence, Moltmann has pointed to the church's role in proclaiming eternal salvation and in bringing about earthly justice.

The church has indeed been involved in mission to proclaim this Gospel message of salvation and justice ever since Jesus' first followers heard his command to "Go therefore and make disciples of all nations" (Matt 28:19a). Subsequent generations of followers have carried this message throughout the world. Successive waves of missionary activity were characterized by different methods, depending on which churches were doing the sending. Over the last century, communities created through mission could be identified by the denominational logo of whichever church evangelized them. Today, with both short- and long-term missions that are sponsored by an array of nondenominational and other communities as well as mainline churches, this mission-field mosaic is even less orderly than in the past.

Sometimes these missionary efforts have complemented each other; sometimes they have clashed. Often these missionary efforts have introduced the crucified and risen Christ to people of other faiths; often they have introduced a differently packaged Christ to people who are already Christian. It is on the boundary line between these efforts that this essay focuses. My contention is that, in the absence of respectful relations between churches and with boundary lines marked with pain and anger, what results is a disfigured proclamation of the Gospel. Conversely, when ecumenical charity—understood here as care, concern, and affection of one church for another—characterizes these relationships, these boundary lines reveal an appreciation for one another's gifts and a willingness to share one another's burdens, and they illustrate how genuine evangelization can take place.

## PERSECUTION AND MISSION

John Meyendorff has taken the discussion about the nature of mission one step further by pointing to what such mission entails on the part of the church:

> Mission belongs to the very nature of the Church…This implies…the duty to propagate the Christian truth for the salvation of all men [sic]. However, mission is not only "preaching," not only talking about God, or promoting "our thing." Mission is not a Christian commercial. It is a witness and an act of love. It implies love for those to whom it is directed, and love means *self-giving*, not simply giving something.[2]

The church gives of itself so that those inside and outside the church can hear the good news of salvation and experience the first fruits of divine justice until Christ comes again.

This self-giving is to be understood as the very same self-emptying (*kenosis*) mentioned by Paul in Philippians 2:4–8:

> Let each of you look not to your own interests, but to the interests of others. Let the same mind be in you that was in Christ Jesus, who, though he was in the form of God, did not regard equality with God as something to be exploited, but emptied himself, taking the form of a slave, being born in human likeness. And being found in human form, he humbled himself and became obedient to the point of death—even death on a cross.

This most profound of scriptural passages, followed immediately as it is by Paul's theological conclusion—"Therefore God also highly exalted him and gave him the name that is above every name" (Phil 2:9)—lays out the Christian understanding of salvation: Jesus, through his crucifixion and resurrection, saves the world. The implication of the first part of this formula is that suffering may accompany the living out of one's faith, particularly as one shares this faith with others.

Living out the Christian faith can be characterized as a "journey." More specifically, this can be conceived of as a *via crucis*, a journey on which Christians carry whatever crosses are laid upon their backs.[3] Like the cross of Christ, these burdens (or sacrifices) mark the way to salvation. This is not a glorification of suffering; it is, rather, something that gives profound meaning to the experience of salvation. What does this imply for the church as a whole, as it carries out the "mission of God"? How does the church make its way on this journey? How does the church experience the cross?

On this missiological journey, to borrow themes from the World Council of Churches' study document, *The Nature and Mission of the Church*, the church brings a message of "transfiguration," "reconciliation," "compassion," "mercy," "repentance," and "healing."[4] This ecumenical text also ties this message, both in the proclamation and in *diakonia*, to the potential for persecution: "Because the servanthood of Christ entails suffering it is evident (as expressed in the New Testament writings) that the witness *(martyria)* of the Church will entail—for both individuals and for the community—the way of the cross, even to the point of martyrdom."[5] The point is that persecution, if it comes, may be the result of proclamation, or it may be the result of *diakonia*, neither one exclusive of the other but, in fact, only part of the way the church witnesses to the truth at any given point in time.

This would be the conclusion one would draw from the Scriptures used to support this paragraph. In Matthew 10:16–33, Jesus tells his disciples of the dangers that might await them from those who "will hand you over to councils and flog you in their synagogues; and [drag you] before governors and kings because of me." Further, he tells them, "Brother will betray brother to death, and a father his child, and children will rise against parents and have them put to death; and you will be hated by all because of my name." Jesus, here, even ties the proclamation to the persecution to come: "What I say to you in the dark, tell in the light; and what you hear whispered, proclaim from the housetops. Do not fear those who kill the body but cannot kill the soul; rather fear him who can destroy both soul and body in hell." In Matthew 16:24–28, Jesus goes further and ties the proclamation to the same fate that awaits him: "If any want to become my followers, let them deny themselves and take up their cross and follow me." These passages, which intersperse revelations of Jesus' true identity and, thus, the Gospel message with moments of *diakonia*, together form quite a dramatic confirmation of the type of persecution that may befall the community of believers as they seek to bear witness to the Gospel.

In the first centuries of Christianity, persecution was a very real threat to the believing community. Worship was done in secret, first for fear of Jews and Romans in Palestine and then for fear of the Romans and others as the religion spread, and martyrdom was a very real possibility. After Christianity became an officially recognized religion of the Roman Empire, persecution remained a threat only in lands at or beyond the edges of the empire, typically taking place in the context of mission. When Islam started to grow and spread, persecution came swiftly as civilizations collided, then more subtly in places where Christianity became the minority religion. Over the subsequent centuries, persecution took place in other contexts, most horrifically perhaps under the communist totalitarian regimes of the twentieth century.

In our era, individual cases of persecution still continue—churches caught up in violent conflict in Sudan, pastors killed for promoting human rights in the Philippines, house-church members prosecuted and imprisoned in China—though in many cases these are tied up with other factors as well. But, after centuries of Christian cultural domination in the West, with the majority of the church now living in the global South, with challenges to the Christian worldview coming from such things as secularism and pluralism, and with competition for members outstripping competition for souls in the mission field, as a matter of identity, the church must—with new urgency—ask what it means to "take up [the] cross."

Finding the answer will also entail distinguishing persecution from other types of suffering resulting from this competitive environment. This distinction can then help the church to discover a more meaningful proclamation of the Gospel. In other words, genuine mission may very well depend on the genuineness of ecumenical relations.

## REFLECTIONS THAT RAISE QUESTIONS

Two personal reflections—one based on first-hand experience and the other based on observation from a distance—will serve to illustrate how the state of ecumenical relationships can affect mission. The first describes a situation of conflict between church communities in post-Soviet Eastern Europe; the second describes an act of solicitude between church leaders in Turkey.

In Eastern Europe, Protestant (and other) communities face difficulties in response to their efforts to spread the Gospel. These difficulties typically come in the form of legal sanctions meant to prevent certain communities from attracting new members, operating churches, or even worshiping. In many, if not most, of these cases, these legal sanctions are supported by the local, usually Orthodox, church. While such violations of religious freedom are wrong in and of themselves, are claims of *persecution* justified when they may just be a natural backlash, resulting from a lack of ecumenical charity among Christian Churches?

In 1991, just weeks before the beginning of the fall of the Soviet Union, I was in Russia and Ukraine on a sort of pilgrimage. Having just graduated from St. Vladimir's Orthodox Theological Seminary and about to start working for the Orthodox Church in America, I was eager to learn first-hand about the history and then-present situation of the Russian Orthodox Church. Throughout both countries, I encountered American Evangelical missionaries, often running into the same groups in different locations. It seems we had similar touring itineraries overlapping with our respective overall agendas. I am guessing these were among the first of what would become a continuous wave of missionaries who would descend upon these and other Eastern European countries once the Soviet system collapsed.

In one of the great cathedrals—with walls covered with icons, beeswax candles burning and smelling sweetly, a small choir chanting the service—I went over to one of the pastors to whom I had spoken on other occasions along the way. With eyes half-closed, standing ramrod straight with his hands folded politely behind his back, he was swaying back and forth from one foot to the other ever so slightly and slowly to the sound of the music.

"Beautiful, isn't it?" I whispered to him as we stood together.

"You know," he responded, "I never realized the depth of Russian spirituality!"

I smiled cynically to myself. It was three years after the celebration of the thousandth anniversary of Christianity in Kieven Rus, and here was a Christian missionary who seemed to have missed this millennial milestone but was nonetheless in the region to evangelize the Russian and Ukrainian people!

A Russian Orthodox Christian, whose church had just been freed from seventy-five years of oppression, would see this pastor's attempts to evangelize as stealing sheep from one church, an impoverished one at that, to fill the lush green pastures of another. She would not feel conflicted for supporting restrictive legislation to limit the extent of such poaching. In her mind, this kind of exploitation is just one form of persecution following another. The pastor would see the legislation as a definite form of persecution, especially a decade or two after his initial visit to these countries. In his mind, he wonders how the Russian Orthodox Church can justify persecution of other churches after having experienced its own persecution in decades past.

There are questions we must ask ourselves. Is either of these situations "persecution"? How has mission been affected by an obvious absence of ecumenical charity? Have these churches carried one another's burdens, or have they placed additional burdens on each other's backs?

In Turkey, the Ecumenical Patriarchate of Constantinople is under constant pressure from the Turkish government. A prominent center of Christianity since the fourth century, its role of ecumenical primacy within Orthodoxy in modern times has been consistently denied by the civil authorities. For a community whose status is protected by the Treaty of Lausanne, which was signed after World War I, its presence is consistently undermined by the illegal confiscations of property and the closure of educational and other institutions as sanctioned by the courts. A repository of Byzantine art and architecture, its importance to Turkey's potential accession to the European Union is underestimated by the country's religious, cultural, and political elite.

Despite an officially secular society, this treatment of the Greek Orthodox community demonstrates the violation of religious freedom at best or religiously inspired persecution at worst. How can mission be positively impacted by ecumenical charity in this context?

In November 2006, Pope Benedict XVI visited Turkey. The visit came two months after his Regensburg address, in which he used an unfortunate quote about Islam from a fourteenth-century Byzantine emperor when making a point that violence is antithetical to reasonable faith—and in the process inflamed the Muslim world because of the quote's seeming disparagement of Islam. Most of the world's attention, therefore, was focused on how he would heal the wounds created by his address. However, of equal, if not more, significance on this visit was his meeting with Ecumenical Patriarch Bartholomew, the Orthodox Church leader and twenty-first-century heir of the Byzantine legacy.

To those who questioned the global leadership role of the ecumenical patriarch, the assertions of ecclesiastical parity with the pope certainly undermined their claims that he is the leader of only Turkey's 3,000 Greek Orthodox faithful. To those who dismissed the cultural significance of the Byzantine heritage, the support of a pontiff known for his defense of a "Christian Europe" was certain to figure into discussions about how a Muslim-majority country might fit into the European Union. Further, with regard to the confiscation of property and closure of institutions, the presence of these two prelates together in their liturgical garb undercut any rationale for the religious discrimination that is the result of such illegal actions.

This display of intimate kinship did more than just reveal the two churches' commitment to seeking unity, which is the goal of ecumenism. It also reflected the fruitfulness of ecumenical charity. Rather than demonstrate competition between churches, it showed that the two churches journey together on the same road toward the kingdom. The pope helped to carry the ecumenical patriarch's cross. This was a signal to the Muslim majority and government in Turkey and to all people everywhere that, in terms of mission, the Catholic and Orthodox Churches share and preach the same Gospel.

## UNITY AND MISSION

What do these reflections say to us about the connection between ecumenical charity and how we carry out mission? Can legitimate mission be realized in the absence of ecumenical charity? How is unity in mission served by ecumenical charity?

It was a joint working group of the Roman Catholic Church and the World Council of Churches that addressed this connection between mission and ecumenical charity in their joint 1995 text, "The Challenge of Proselytism and the Calling to Common Witness."[6] As noted in the foreword of the text, it was written "in response to concerns expressed by some of our churches in regard to the missionary outreach of other churches that would seem to bear some of the characteristics of proselytism" and "within the concern for full Christian unity and common Christian witness." The text further noted that "[t]here is the common conviction that central to the work of Christian unity is an urgent need for all Christians to be able to give a truly common witness to the whole Christian faith." The timing of this text, soon after the fall of the Soviet Union and the expansion of relative freedom in Eastern Europe, is not to be missed.

The strong link between Christian unity and Christian mission is also affirmed in the text. Specifically, any action that diminishes or works against one church works against both unity and mission. The lack of ecumenical charity is understood as any situation that denies the statement in the text that "[e]ven when churches are not in full communion with each other they are called to be truthful to each other and show respect for each other" (§10).

The lack of ecumenical charity is also a denial of what the churches have learned over the last century of ecumenical relations with regard to the reality of the "imperfect communion" (§12), a limited but nonetheless real union based on their common confession of Jesus Christ, already shared by them.

In terms of religious freedom, such a lack of ecumenical charity (that is, aggressive proselytism among other Christian communities, which here includes ridiculing another church or its beliefs, employing physical or psychological pressure, using political or economic power, extending inducements, and exploiting people's needs, all to gain converts from one church to another) "can violate or manipulate the right [of religious freedom] of the individual and can exacerbate tense and delicate relations between communities and thus destabilize societies" (§16). The document, therefore, suggests ways to overcome temptations to such bad behavior (including praying for one another, better Christian and ecumenical formation within their respective churches, and sensitivity to other cultural and ecclesial contexts).

If churches were able to apply these learnings, some of the road toward better relations—and even unity—would be paved. On this path, the respective gifts that each community brings to the proclamation and living out of the Gospel would be understood in terms of broadening the context for mission, rather than in terms of the "right" to assert one's individual prerogatives to the exclusion of another's. The latter understanding has historically resulted in the suffering of one community at the hands of another at a given time and place. The former would be an opportunity to bring healing and reconciliation "so that the world may believe" (John 17:21).

## NOTES

1. Jürgen Moltmann, *The Church in the Power of the Spirit: A Contribution to Messianic Ecclesiology,* trans. Margaret Kohl (New York: Harper and Row Publishers, 1977), 10.

2. John Meyendorff, *Witness to the World* (Crestwood, NY: St. Vladimir's Seminary Press, 1987), 188.

3. The author thanks John Ford, who wrote "Unity and Mission: A Pilgrimage of Accompaniment," which provides the

journey motif that holds this series of Faith and Order study group essays together.

4. *The Nature and Mission of the Church*: Faith and Order Paper 198 (Geneva: World Council of Churches, 2005): 24–27.

5. Ibid., 26.

6. This text is available at http://www.oikoumene.org/en/resources/documents/wcc-commissions/joint-working-group-between-the-roman-catholic-church-and-the-wcc/challenge-of-proselytism.html (Accessed July 15, 2012).

# 11

# BEYOND ORNAMENTAL MULTICULTURALISM
## Toward a Theology of the Beauty of God

*Kevin Park*

## PERSONAL STORY

Being of Korean descent, I did a double take recently while shopping in Costco when I found jars of *kimchi* in the refrigerated section side by side with pickles, cheese, and prepared pasta. When I was growing up in Toronto, *kimchi* was eaten only by Koreans and hidden well away from our white Canadian counterparts. Now, Costco in Louisville, Kentucky, is selling *kimchi* and giving out free samples!

Several months ago, my fourteen-year-old daughter, who is into Korean popular culture, was tickled to tell me that one of her white school friends texted her asking about a "cool" Korean boy band, which she had seen on YouTube, called "Super Junior."

Costco is selling *kimchi* and my daughter's white American friends are listening to Korean boy bands. This is a bizarre reality shift for me since the only source of Korean culture available to North Americans when I was growing up was the 70s TV show *M.A.S.H.* I am happy to acknowledge that America has come a long way in accepting Korean and other minority cultures. I am also happy that my children are growing up in a more welcoming environment than the one I grew up in...or are they?

Something else happened that put a wrinkle in all of this. My wife and daughter were walking the dog in a nearby park when a group of teenagers walked by loudly chanting, "Ching, chong, ching, chong...." My wife did not fully understand what was going on until after they had passed. When she realized that the gibberish was a racial slur, she became so angry that she wanted to tell them off, follow them to their houses, and have a talk with their parents. But she did not.

I asked my daughter if anything like this had ever happened to her before. She replied that sometimes she would hear similar taunts on the way home from school from kids passing by in a school bus. She said that it bothered her at first. But then she figured that those comments had nothing to do with her and that those boys were only embarrassing themselves. I was proud of how well she was able to process these negative and potentially traumatic experiences. I had thought there was a good chance that my girls would grow up unscathed from the kind of discrimination I had experienced as a young person, but I was wrong. Sure, Costco sells *kimchi* and white teenagers may be listening to Korean boy bands, but...[1]

I have to fight the cynicism this experience makes me feel. How much has North America really changed? We have a black president, for heaven's sake. Do we not live in a post-racial era?[2] I am not so sure. America accepts aspects of other cultures like ornaments on a Christmas tree. Korean culture and its advances are accepted, even celebrated, as long as they contribute to the American entertainment/music/technological/cultural/economic machine. But has there been any real structural change in the power system in order to accommodate minorities? Has the "aestheticization" of other cultures without corresponding structural accommodation actually made it more difficult for genuine cultural and racial reform?

This "ornamental multiculturalism" that treats other cultures as decorations to enhance the status of the dominant culture is at work in our churches and denomination as well. How can we move from a "cosmetic" and utilitarian understanding and use of multiculturalism to a deeper, genuine interrelationship that could beneficially transform us all?

## ORNAMENTAL MULTICULTURALISM

By ornamental multiculturalism I mean treating minority racial ethnic groups as ornaments that enhance the perceived value of the dominant culture. Ornaments do not exist on their own merit, but they exist to enhance something else. In ornamental multiculturalism, cultures are valued insofar as they contribute to the overall value of the dominant culture. In ornamental multiculturalism, minority cultures are celebrated by the dominant culture largely through rhetoric, aesthetics, and tolerance without affecting deeper change to the whole dominant cultural system.

In postmodern discourse, there is significant value given to "celebrating diversity." Given postmodernity's rejection of meta-narratives and foundational epistemologies, every narrative, no matter how "minor," is on a level playing field and, thus, "celebrated." On the surface, this looks like a good thing that can empower groups that have been historically marginal, but it does not take too much probing to find that this "celebration of diversity" is largely academic rhetoric, and those who are celebrating are the postmodern theorists rather than the minority communities.

In commenting upon David Bentley Hart's *The Beauty of the Infinite*, R. R. Reno says:

> Aging postmodern intellectuals do not read texts, nor do they attend to the subtle, nuanced textures of life. They use texts as occasions for what they imagine to be "liberative reading practices." All recalcitrant particularity is overawed by the sublime truths of Theory.
>
> Like the anxious Aztecs whose captives were ritually sacrificed to keep the sun on its course, countless literary professors are at their lecterns offering up the hearts of great poems, novels, and plays to keep their theoretical commitments alive. Worse still, theologians scavenge through the wreckage of the vivisected texts, trying to construct a postmodern theology. The ugliness of it all is depressing.[3]

Postmodern aestheticization of cultures has influenced not only society but mainline denominations as well. It can be a way to celebrate diverse cultures without committing to an adaptive change.

A quick comparison between the racial demographics of the United States and mainline denominations serves to point out the discrepancy in racial and ethnic diversity. Consider the following statistics:

- United States: 63.7% white (non-Hispanics), 12.6% black, 4.8% Asian, 16.3% Hispanic/Latino[4]

- Mainline Denominations: 91% white, 2% black, 1% Asian, 3% other/mixed (non-Hispanic), 3% Hispanic[5]

It is fair to say that all of the mainline denominations are not only aware of this discrepancy but are engaged in various programs. They include outreach and new church developments for new immigrants and racial ethnic communities. However, there are at least two pitfalls into which such programs can fall that can contribute to ornamental multiculturalism.

## TWO EXAMPLES OF ORNAMENTAL MULTICULTURALISM

### First Example: Racial Ethnic Communities as Utility for Church Growth

Given the decades of declining trend of mainline churches on the one hand and the growing statistics of racial ethnic demographics in the United States on the other, it is natural that outreach ministry programs for immigrant and racial ethnic communities be part of the larger church growth programs. Mainline denominations recognize that reaching out to these communities and growing immigrant churches are a crucial part of the survival of their institutions. This seems like an obvious truism that can give legitimate motivation for such programs. But such church growth strategies view racial ethnic communities as a means to an end—as church growth strategies to ensure the survival of the denomination. Such a utilitarian view of minority communities fall under the fallacy of ornamental multiculturalism. Racial ethnic population is viewed as ornaments to enhance the tree of "real" mainline institutions. Although such church growth programs seem like "natural" responses to the given demographic trends, they are void of sound, biblical, theological content.

There are no positive biblical examples of using minority cultures for the benefit of the dominant culture. Rather, biblical vision toward minorities and aliens is succinctly stated in Leviticus 19:33–34:

> When an alien resides with you in your land, you shall not oppress the alien. The alien who resides with you shall be to you the citizen among you; you shall love the alien as yourself, for you were aliens in the land of Egypt: I am the LORD your God.

This often-cited text for hospitality toward strangers says nothing about the usefulness of strangers for the host culture. The injunction moves from renunciation of oppression to loving the stranger. The text starts from the realistic premise that strangers will always be among us. It starts with "When an alien resides with you," not "If an alien resides with you." The text moves from negative injunction, "you shall not oppress the alien" to positive legal injunction; they "shall be to you as the citizens among you," to an injunction of love, "you shall love the alien as yourself." The main motivational incentive appeals to the memory of the Israelites as strangers in a foreign land.

This and other biblical texts on the treatment of strangers and aliens guard against a kind of pragmatic, utilitarian church growth approach to minority cultures. The biblical rhetoric toward strangers is not one of "use" but of radical hospitality that appeals to the vocation of the host culture as the people of God who experienced alienation but were delivered by God.

But memories of alienation are not part of contemporary American Christian consciousness in many denominations. Mainline denominations tend to long for the cultural influence and centrality they enjoyed generations ago. Many Americans cannot relate to being "aliens in Egypt," and, thus, the main biblical appeal of radical hospitality toward strangers itself seems alien to them. What will it mean for American mainline denominations to embrace the biblical imperative to remember that we were aliens in the land of Egypt? A lesson from the Waldensian Church in Italy can provide an inspiring example for us.

**The Case of the Waldensians:**[6] The Waldensian Church in Italy is a historically marginal church that, together with the

186

Methodists, makes up less than 0.001 percent of the population.[7] It is a Reformed denomination that predates the Protestant movement by more than three hundred years. The church's history is marked by oppression and persecution from its inception. I believe this historical marginality experienced by the Waldensians is enabling them to engage in remarkable hospitable ministry with the many Protestant immigrants in Italy.

Historically, Italy has been a country of emigration. Between 1870 and World War II, some twenty million Italians emigrated to different parts of the world, the majority of them coming to the United States. However, this trend has shifted radically from the 1970s. Since then, Italy has become a country of immigration.[8] Some five million immigrants, the majority of them from Eastern Europe and North Africa, have come to Italy, and immigrants now make up 8 percent of the population. Given Italy's strict immigration policy, many are undocumented; even legal immigrants have almost no access to becoming Italian citizens, including second-generation immigrant children born in Italy.

The Waldenisans and the Methodists in Italy formed a Union of Waldensian and Methodist Churches and have embraced this multicultural trend in a radical way through their visionary program called "Being Church Together." The name of the program is telling. They have intentionally chosen "Being Church Together" rather than "Being a Hospitable Church" or some variant. They realized early on that even using the word *hospitality* conjures up a power differential that points to the host church doing things for the guests. Rather, they wanted from the beginning to share church decision-making power with the immigrant communities. They spend 70 percent of their time and resources for Being Church Together. As a result, their church is changing in almost all aspects, including the visible multicultural presence of immigrants as well as styles of worship and polity. Their ethos is significantly different from how American mainline churches do multicultural church. Multicultural and immigrant ministry is not an option for the Waldensians; racial ethnic communities are not ornaments but part of the tree trunk of who they are. Paolo Nasso, the National Coordinator of Being Church Together, said, "When we're talking about migration we're talking about ourselves."[9] I believe that they are able to do this given their marginal history and identity. They know, experientially, what it is to be "aliens in the land of Egypt." I believe that their historical marginality gives them a particular epistemology of marginality that enables them to become a truly hospitable church that will change their very cultural and religious identity. What does it mean for American Churches to claim an epistemological vantage point of marginality that can also open us up toward being a radically hospitable church that will inevitably change the way we do church?

## Second Example: The Myth of Model Minority

In ornamental multiculturalism, the host culture praises the aesthetics, the beauty, and the usefulness of other cultures. For example, Asian Americans have been praised as a model minority in the United States, often cited by the white majority as paragons of a strong work ethic, high education, and American success.

However, this aestheticized view of Asian Americans is problematic on several levels. First, this view ignores the complexity of Asian American culture and invites a shallow, cosmetic understanding of their culture and history. Second, this view pits cultures against cultures, inviting crass ranking of cultures. If one culture is explicitly designated a "model" label, other cultures are implicitly seen as "reprobates." This competitive view of cultures tends to isolate cultural gifts and value them only from the point of view of the dominant culture. Thus, racism is downplayed and only acknowledged in personal terms and not acknowledged in corporate and systemic terms that need structural change. Third, such aestheticization glosses over the brokenness of culture. When the dominant culture's evaluation of a minority culture is only filled with positive, romanticized rhetoric, the broken aspects of both cultures are more easily covered up by both parties. Asian Americans are susceptible to accept, uncritically, the model minority myth as offered by the majority culture since it offers them some sense of praise and acceptance, no matter how cosmetic and shallow they may seem. When they have accepted such myths, the burden of perpetuating this model plays right into the aestheticization and ornamentalization of their culture that only help to perpetuate the codependent nature of ornamentalism. Stacey J. Lee writes:

> In all of its permutations the model minority stereotype has been used to support the status quo and ideologies of meritocracy and individualism. Supporters of the model minority stereotype use Asian American success to delegitimize claims of inequality made by other racial minorities. According to the model minority discourse, Asian Americans prove that social mobility is possible for all those who are willing to work. Asian Americans are represented as examples of upward mobility through individual effort. Charges of racial inequality are met with stories of Asian American success, thereby reifying notions of equal opportunities and meritocracy.[10]

This model minority myth is relevant for us as we seek to be a more multicultural church. Often, denominational publications and Web sites are full of praises for the racial ethnic cultures and how the future of the denomination depends on tapping into the robust spirituality of these faith communities of different cultures. Covers of denominational periodicals and event posters are strewn with pictures of racial ethnic peoples and congregations. These are welcome acts of acknowledgement and hospitality as long as they point to the kind of church we want to become. But without serious and costly dialogue toward structural change, such rhetoric, both in words and pictures, are in danger of remaining in the realm of aestheticization and ornamentalization.

## TOWARD A THEOLOGY OF BEAUTY

What is a theological counterpart to ornamental multiculturalism? I believe that a theology of the beauty of God has promise toward constructing a sound and faithful theology of marginality and diversity.

Contemporary theological aesthetics is indebted to Han Urs von Balthasar, who wrote a seven-volume series entitled *The Glory of the Lord*.[11] Balthasar wants to reclaim God's beauty, or God's glory, as an essential theological category. God's goodness is revealed as glory or beauty and is perceived by faith through a particular concrete form. God's glory is revealed in the form, most decisively in the form of Jesus Christ as God's self-expression. When we receive God's glory in Jesus Christ, we receive it more as beauty than rational truth. Rationality appeals to the mind, but beauty appeals to the whole person who is receiving God's goodness, truth, and love as expressions of God's glory.

> The infinite God of Christianity, as Trinitarian, is a God of love. This God of love is revealed in the person of Jesus Christ, and thus has a form of "logos" that is best termed beautiful. This God of love is revealed likewise in the entire cosmos that is created in Christ: all of creation, made in the entire cosmos that is created in Christ; all of creation, made in the image of God in Jesus Christ, thus bears, through an intrinsic relation interpreted analogously, the image of love and beauty.[12]

If God's love is revealed as the beauty of Christ, divine revelation is received, not primarily as rational propositions, but as an aesthetic experience that includes the rational. But rationality is only a part of the whole process of reception that must include the whole life of the Christian. God's beauty or glory is the starting point for Balthasar. William Placher writes in his review of Balthasar's work:

> Balthasar believed that in thinking about the true, the good and the beautiful, modern philosophy and theology had gone wrong by starting with theories of truth, turning then to ethics and getting to aesthetics at the end if at all. Beauty, he insisted, is not a decorative add-on. Rather, when we see the beauty of a bird in flight, of an act of love, of an old man's face or of the stars on a winter night, we grasp something of their essence otherwise unknown to us. Beauty gives us access to reality.[13]

That God's grace is received more like an aesthetic experience than a rational acknowledgment may be more apparent in racial ethnic communities of faith than mainline majority white communities of faith. When an African American church member exclaims, "We had church today!" or when a Korean congregant greets the pastor after worship saying, "I've received a lot of grace," they are describing an experience of God's grace and glory that moved their hearts. Alejandro Garcia-Rivera writes:

> Asking the question, *what moves the heart?*, I believe, brings us closer to the mysterious experience of the truly beautiful, and experience that transcends geological space and prehistoric time, and experience that holds the most persuasive claim to being what has become an *aporia* in our day, the real universal.[14]

Even Calvin, who defined faith as a kind of "knowledge," affirms this "heart" and "soul" aspect of the Gospel:

> [Knowledge of Christ] is a doctrine not of the tongue but of life. It is not apprehended by the understanding and memory alone, as other disciplines are, but it is received only when it possesses the whole soul, and finds a seat and resting place in the inmost affection of the heart...it must enter our heart and pass into our daily living, and so transform us into itself that it may not be unfruitful for us...its efficacy ought to penetrate the inmost affections of the heart, take its seat in the soul, and affect the whole man a hundred times more deeply than the cold exhortations of the philosophers![15]

> It now remains to pour into the heart itself what the mind has absorbed. For the Word of God is not received by faith if it flits about in the top of the brain, but when it takes rest in the depth of the heart.[16]

## AESTHETIC APPROACH TO CHRISTIAN THEOLOGY—HINTS FROM ASIAN THEOLOGIANS

If receiving God's grace is indeed more like an aesthetic experience than an intellectual consent, Asian theologians C. S. Song, Kosuke Koyama, and others have something to teach us. Song criticizes the traditional Western monopoly on Christian theology in the following:

And on account of the fact that Christianity has played an enormous role in Western civilization, the marriage between theology and Western norms or thought and life inevitably becomes the implicit assumption of doing theology in the West. It is the offspring of this marriage between theology and Western civilization that have largely defined the rules of the game called Christian theology.[17]

Rather than adhering to Western "rules," Song wants to transplant Christian theology in Asian soil such that Christian theology can develop free from Western philosophical-metaphysical categories, replacing them with Asian categories and worldview. Song criticizes Western theology of being guilty of "centrism," meaning that the West considers itself as the sole legitimate inheritor of Christian theology proper. Against such "centrism," Song calls for "multi-center theology," which affirms God's deep commitment for the salvation of all peoples.[18] Multi-center theology means that the Christian message must be articulated for each community in language and symbols a particular community can understand. Song is committed to an incarnational theology where the "Word" is assumed Asian flesh. He calls for a theology where the seeds of Christianity can be planted in Asian soil and grow in the "womb of Asia." Only then can theology be said to be truly Asian; only then can Christianity be a powerful prophetic voice in Asia rather than being a mere vehicle in the process of Westernizing Asia.

For Kosuke Koyama, like C. S. Song, contextualization of the Gospel is not a means-to-an-end process but an essential part of the Gospel itself. For Koyama, the very heart of the Christian message requires that every theology become an incarnational theology, thus, becoming "rooted" or incarnated in a particular culture in which the Gospel is to be expressed. According to Koyama, there is no such sequence as "the Gospel" and "the process of contextualization." The very process of contextualization is an inherent message of the Gospel itself. Without this process of incarnation of the Gospel, the Gospel is not the Gospel. There is no such thing as a "pure" theology separated from any concrete life situation. Therefore, when we speak of contextualization of theology, we are speaking of reappropriating one contextual theology into another context, or "rerooting" it as Koyama calls it.[19] The process of contextualization must begin from concrete life and symbols of the particular people. And so, Koyama could say the following concerning the water buffaloes in Thailand when he was teaching there:

> On my way to the country church, I never fail to see a herd of water buffaloes grazing in the muddy paddy field. This sight is an inspiring moment for me. Why? Because it reminds me that the people to whom I am to bring the gospel of Christ spend most of their time with these water buffaloes in the rice field. The water buffaloes tell me that I must preach to these farmers in the simplest sentence-structure and thought development. They remind me to discard all abstract ideas, and to use exclusively objects that are immediately tangible. 'Sticky-rice', 'banana', 'pepper', 'dog', 'cat', 'bicycle', 'rainy season', 'leaking house', 'fishing', 'cock-fighting', 'lottery', 'stomach-ache'–these are meaningful words for them.[20]

Koyama uses an imagistic and aesthetic style that incorporates everyday experiences of the culture in which he is immersed. His book titles denote his aesthetic style: *Water Buffalo Theology, Three Mile an Hour God,* and *No Handle on the Cross.*[21]

Song's and Koyama's source for theology, along with the biblical witness, is the suffering experience of the Asian peoples. Therefore, throughout their writings, they incorporate songs, poems, dances, and stories common to various parts of Asia. The result is an aesthetic style of doing theology, rather than a "systematic" style more familiar to the West. Song and Koyama make use of Asian images and symbols and limit their use of traditional Western theological language and categories. This lyrical style is an important part of these theologians' method; they want to join form and context together in formulating an Asian theology.

I have briefly outlined the theological methods of Song and Koyama in order to point out that theologians from non-Western backgrounds may be much more in tune with the aesthetic epistemology of the Gospel. This aesthetic way of communicating theology, in fact, may be much closer to the way Jesus taught than the way Western theology is done. Mark 4:34 records that Jesus "did not speak to them except in parables." Jesus' parables are not systematic doctrinal teachings but simple and memorable stories, often with everyday imagery, and yet conveying deep and central truths of God's kingdom. Parables are "aesthetic" teachings that appeal to the heart, mind, and life of the hearer. This is not simply to invalidate the way of traditional Western theological communication but to point out the imperative for Western theology to incorporate the aesthetic way of communicating Christian theology that is more of the norm in other cultures.

## THEOLOGY OF THE BEAUTY OF GOD AND THE THEOLOGY OF THE CROSS

The reception of grace and God's glory in Christ is a matter of the heart that is more like an aesthetic reception and experience than rational agreement and understanding alone. However, this reception of God's beauty is not read off from creation and then interpreted and extrapolated as divine revelation. Such a method can easily degenerate into what Luther called the "theology of glory," a kind of natural theology that deduced the nature of God from observations from nature. The divine self revelation is most decisively revealed in the cross of Jesus Christ that shatters all theologies of glory and ornamental theologies. Divine beauty, thus, pierces our veneer of crass ornamentalisms of all kinds. God's beauty, as revealed through the life, death, and resurrection of Jesus Christ, shatters our counterfeit aestheticizations through which we attempt to replace God's beauty with variations of our utilitarian ornamentalism. Brian Zahnd says:

> [I]n the present situation in which the American evangelical church finds itself, there is a desperate need to recover a theology of beauty. The way out of the mess and confusion of a politicized faith is to follow the path of beauty. It is the way of beauty that will lead us home to a more authentic Christianity. A theology of beauty is the antidote to the poison of pragmatism and the toxin of triumphalism.[22]

The decisive form of this beauty of God is the cross of Jesus Christ. Zahnd says, "Our form is the cruciform, and our beauty is the mysterious aesthetic of the crucified Savior."[23] Similarly, John Navone says:

> The Christian community affirms that Christ is the "true light that enlightens everyone" (John 1:9), and the Life that is the source of all authentic goodness. The same community believes that the beauty and glory proper to God who graciously communicates God's self to humankind as our ultimate fulfillment, may be seen fully with eyes of faith only in the form of Jesus Christ. His Cross, no form of beauty for worldly eyes, reveals what God's beauty and glory are really about. For those who see the Cross in the light of the resurrection, God's beauty appears as the glorious love which has extended its reign to include and transfigure what had been a kingdom of darkness and godlessness. The supreme beauty of Truth and Goodness Itself is seen in God's gracious love for God's creation. The crucified and risen Christ is the form and splendor of the Beautiful, the True, and the Good, which fulfills human desire and so brings humankind to communion with God.[24]

Divine beauty, then, is not something that starts with human preconceived notions of what beautiful is and then projecting that as a divine attribute. Rather, we know what divine beauty is through the life, teaching, death, and resurrection of Jesus Christ. Balthasar, with Luther, could affirm that God's beauty is revealed through the suffering love of the self-giving glory of God in the cross and resurrection of Jesus Christ; God's glory is the self-emptying of Christ in obedience to the Father through the Spirit. God's beauty, as such, penetrates though our facade of righteousness; God's glory exposes our ornamental aesthetics we attempt to project onto others and God. But counter intuitively, for the Christian faith, this glory of God is most powerfully revealed, not in the beauty of creation or in the power of nature, but in the cross of Jesus Christ. Zahnd says, "Our form is the cruciform, and our beauty is the mysterious aesthetic of the crucified Savior."[25] He continues:

> The Christ upon the cross, arms outstretched in the gesture of proffered embrace, refusing to call upon avenging angels but instead loving his enemies and praying for their forgive-

ness—this is the form and beauty of Christianity. The cruciform is the posture of love and forgiveness where retaliation is abandoned and outcomes are entrusted to the hands of God. The cross is laden with mystery. At first glance it looks like anything but success. It looks like failure. It looks like defeat. It looks like death. It *is* death. But it is also the power and wisdom of God. This is mysterious. It is also beautiful. This is the mysterious beauty that saves the world.[26]

It is important to point out that we are not glorifying the violence of the cross. As C. S. Song points out, the "cross, in short, is human violence and not divine violence."[27] The cross exposes the ugliness of human sin in all of its dimensions: personal, communal, religious, political, military. Sin, in all of its dimensions, had to cooperate and converge upon Jesus to have him crucified. Therefore, the cross of Jesus is a devastating revelation of the depth of human sin. This is not the part that is beautiful. What is beautiful is that, in spite of the full force of human sin upon Jesus, "the cruciform shows forth a transcendent beauty—the beauty of love and forgiveness. It is the beauty of Christ's love and forgiveness as most clearly seen in the cruciform that is able to save us from our vicious pride and avaricious greed."[28]

As such, the beauty or the glory of God, as revealed on the cross of Jesus as unquenchable love of God, allows for a critical theology of power that exposes human power as domination. Mary Solberg succinctly comments on this aspect of the epistemology of the cross:

> It may be fair to say that if an epistemology of the cross were about no other task, its contribution to the critique of power as domination would be sufficient.[29]

Furthermore, such a theology of the beauty of God has only one mode of communication: not of domination or power over the other, but only through persuasion. Zahnd comments:

> The third-century theologian Origen observed that "the marvel of Christ is that, in a world where power, riches, and violence seduce hearts and compel assent, he persuades and

prevails not as a tyrant, an armed assailant, or a man of wealth, but simply as a teacher of God and his love." Commenting on this, David Bentley Hart says, "Christ is a persuasion, a form of evoking desire…Such an account [of Christ] must inevitably make an appeal to beauty." I absolutely agree! Christ persuades, not by the force of Caesar, but by the beauty of love.[30]

As we receive this truth by grace through faith, the Holy Spirit ignites God's beauty that is in all of us as creatures created in the image of God as we live out the Christian life of discipleship. As we reflect God's beauty in this way, we are, thus, glorifying God in return.

However, as individuals and even as communities of faith, we cannot fully reflect God's glory by ourselves. We are limited and finite and broken, and thus, we reflect God's glory like broken and stained pieces of mirror. No one culture can hold or reflect all God's glory. We are just a part, and therefore, we need others, especially from other cultures, to see and reflect the fuller glory of God. This calls for contextual modesty for all cultures but especially for cultures that have been historically dominant. Balthasar himself recognized his cultural limitedness. He wrote the following in the Foreword of his first volume of *The Glory of the Lord:*

> The overall scope of the present work naturally remains all too Mediterranean. The inclusion of other cultures, especially that of Asia, would have been important and fruitful. But the author's education has not allowed for such an expansion, and a superficial presentation of such material would have been dilettantism. May those qualified come to complete the present fragment.[31]

## "THE HONOR OF THE NATIONS"

The biblical model of glorifying God is through multiplicity of nations and cultures as they bring glory to God more fully. In the Book of Revelation, it says:

I saw no temple in the city, for its temple is the Lord God the Almighty and the Lamb. And the city has no need of sun or moon to shine on it, for the glory of God is its light, and its lamp is the Lamb. The nations will walk by its light, and the kings of the earth will bring their glory into it. Its gates will never be shut by day—and there will be no night there. People will bring into it the glory and the honor of the nations (21:22–26).

The Greek word used for "nations" here is *ethnai*, where we get the English word "ethnicity." The implication is that nationalities and cultures and languages will not be erased in the New Jerusalem. The saints will retain their national and ethnic identities through which they will glorify God. Barry Ensign-George says:

> The glories generated by the nations (which are established out of God's blessing) are gathered in to God's new order… The nations have continued until the very end, and they will be drawn into the New Jerusalem with its new ordering of creaturely existence. The diversity that has arisen within creation as the embodiment of divine blessing is part of the divine purpose for creation, and it is glory that will be preserved by God. Across the history that stretches from the Garden of Eden to the garden city, the New Jerusalem, there are values to be gained that can only be gained by differentiation of the nations. God does not cast those values aside, but gathers them in. The divine pattern is not one of monocultures but of differentiation, of spaces created for the best realization of as full an array of particular goods as possible.[32]

Thus, multicultural ministry becomes more than a way to grow churches or a good option among other options of doing church. Multicultural ministry is nothing short of a way to more fully glorify God together. It is a faithful way to actualize what we pray every time we say the Lord's Prayer: "Your kingdom come. Your will be done, on earth as it is in heaven" (Matt 6:10).

Simply put, the way of peaceful, communal, mutually appreciative racial ethnic diversity is God's strategic plan to bring about God's kingdom on earth. Radical inclusive multicultural ministry corresponds to God's glory and is an important way to radiate the beauty of God in the world. Such multicultural dialogue that moves toward more full inclusion of racial ethnic peoples in all areas of ministry, including members, lay and ordained leaders, as well as executive leadership positions is an essential dimension of ecumenism in the twenty-first century as global migration becomes a norm. Any tendencies that hinder such deep multiculturalism that reflects God's glory, such as racism and ornamentalism, must be resisted personally, communally, and systematically. However, such true multicultural ministry, as attested in the story of the Pentecost and the early church, is no easy task. Multicultural ministry is difficult. But it is the way of the Gospel of Jesus Christ. The cross of Jesus Christ symbolizes his crossing of the boundaries of heaven and earth, divine and human, Jews and Gentiles. Peter Phan writes:

> Standing between the two worlds, excluding neither but embracing both, Jesus was able to be fully inclusive of both. But this also means that he is the marginal person par excellence. People at the center of any society or group as a rule possess wealth, power, and influence. As the threefold temptation shows, Jesus, the border-crosser and the dweller at the margins, renounced precisely these three things. Because he was at the margins, in his teaching and miracle-working, Jesus creates a new and different center, the center constituted by the meeting of the borders of the many and diverse worlds, often in conflict with one another, each with its own center which relegates the "other" to the margins. It is at this margin-center that marginal people meet one another. In Jesus, the margin where he lived became the center of a new society without borders and barriers, reconciling all peoples, "Jew or Greek, slave or free, male or female" (Gal 3:28). Strangers and guests as they are, missionaries are invited to become marginal people, to dwell at the margins of societies with marginal(ized) people, like Jesus, so as to be able to create with them new all-inclusive centers of reconciliation and harmony.[33]

Such a border-crossing ministry is the ministry of Jesus Christ exemplified most decisively on the cross. Such ministry requires suffering with the other and embracing the pain of the marginal peoples.

I end this paper with a story that Kosuke Koyama told of a lesson he learned about the nature of theology from his teacher Kazoh Kitamori shortly after World War II. Koyama says:

> Nineteen hundred and forty-six, right after the war, I was sixteen years old. I remember the war. And in some meeting, my teacher, Kitamori is his name, he spread out a handkerchief like this…and he put an egg inside it, a boiled egg. And he did it like this [lifting the handkerchief, enveloping the egg]. Now, handkerchief and boiled egg [are] having a good time because there's no friction, he said. No conflict. The handkerchief is holding a nice round-shaped egg. So they are having a nice time. This is nice time but we don't call this theology, he said. This is not [an] image of theology. Then he put up a very sharp object. [A] knife. And he did the same thing and he said, "You know, you see how this sharp object is hurting this silk handkerchief. It's embracing something which cannot be easily embraced. Embracing [is] conflict itself. It's a very painful embrace. And he said, "Would you please hold these two images. And the second one we call theology. First one we call just having a good time." He has written quite a serious theological treatise. There's a theological background to that. It's not a joke. Backbone is there.[34]

# NOTES

1. Derald Wing Sue at Teachers College, Columbia University, names such experiences as racial "microaggressions." Sue defines microaggressions as "the everyday verbal, nonverbal, and environmental slights, snubs, or insults, whether intentional or unintentional, that communicate hostile, derogatory, or negative messages to target persons based solely upon their marginalized group membership." See *Microaggressions and Marginality: Manifestations, Dynamics, and Impact,* ed. Derald Wing Sue (Hoboken, NJ: John Wiley and Sons, 2010), 3.

2. See criticism of *"Obamania"* in Eduardo Bonilla-Silva, *Racism Without Racists: Color-Blind Racism and Racial Inequality in Contemporary America*, 3rd ed. (Lanham, MD: Rowman & Littlefield, 2010), esp. chap. 9–10.

3. R. R. Reno, "Return to Beauty," review of David Bentley Hart, *The Beauty of the Infinite*, in *Touchstone: A Journal of Mere Christianity* (Sept. 2004), available at http://www.touchstonemag.com/archives/article.php?id=17-07-048-b (accessed May 21, 2012).

4. U.S. Census Bureau 2010, available at http://quickfacts.census.gov/qfd/states/00000.html (accessed October 1, 2011).

5. The Pew Forum on Religion and Public Life, available at http://religious.pewforum.org/portraits (accessed October 1, 2011). Note that Catholics are an exception to this trend. According to Pew, see the following statistics among U.S. Catholics: 65% White (non-Hispanic), 2% Black, 2% Asian, 2% Other/Mixed, 29% Hispanic. See http://religions.pewforum.org/portraits (accessed April 30, 2012).

6. This discussion on the Waldensians is from a lecture by Professor Paolo Nasso, the National Coordinator of Being Church Together (presented in London, U.K., March 3, 2011).

7. In 1975, the Waldensians and the Methodists joined to form the Union of Waldensian and Methodist Chruches. In Italy, there are about 30,000 Waldensians and 5,000 Methodists; the population of Italy is about 61 million people.

8. Paul Scheffer, *Immigrant Nations* (Cambridge: Polity Press, 2011), 180.

9. Ibid., 180.

10. Stacey J. Lee, *Unraveling the "Model Minority" Stereotype: Listening to Asian American Youth* (New York: Teachers College Press, 1996), 6.

11. Hans Urs von Balthasar, *The Glory of the Lord: A Theological Aesthetics,* 6 vols., ed. John Riches, trans. Andrew Louth, John Saward, Martin Simon, and Rowan Williams (San Francisco: Ignatitius Press, 1982).

12. David L. Schindler, "The Significance of Hans Urs von Balthasar in the Contemporary Situation," in *Glory, Grace, and Culture: The Work of Hans Urs von Balthasar,* ed. Ed Block Jr. (Mahwah, NJ: Paulist Press, 2005), 19.

13. William Placher, "Theo-Logic, Volume 3/Epilogue," in *Christian Century* 123, no. 11 (May 30, 2006).

14. Alejandro Garcia-Rivera, *The Community of the Beautiful: A Theological Aesthetics* (Collegeville, MN: Liturgical Press, 1999), 9.

15. John Calvin, *Institutes of the Christian Religion,* ed. John T. McNeill, trans. Ford Battles (Philadelphia: Westminster Press, 1960), bk. 3, chap. 7, par. 4 (3.7.4).

16. Ibid., 3.7.8

17. C. S. Song, *Third-Eye Theology: Theology in Formation in Asian Setting,* rev. ed. (Maryknoll, NY: Orbis Books, 1991), 20.

18. Song's methodology is developed at length in the *Third-Eye Theology* and *Theology in the Womb of Asia* (Maryknoll, NY: Orbis, 1986).

19. Kosuke Koyama, *Water Buffalo Theology* (Maryknoll, NY: Orbis Books, 1991), 115.

20. Ibid., vii-viii.

21. Kosuke Koyama, *Three Mile an Hour God* (London: SCM Press, 1979), and *No Handle on the Cross* (London: SCM Press, 1976).

22. Brian Zahnd, *Beauty Will Save the World: Rediscovering the Allure and Mystery of Christianity* (Lake Mary, FL: Charisma House, 2012), 27.

23. Ibid., 17.

24. John Navone, *Toward a Theology of Beauty* (Collegeville, MN: Liturgical Press, 1996), 19–20.

25. Zahnd, *Beauty Will Save the World*, 17.

26. Ibid., 7.

27. C. S. Song, *Jesus, the Crucified People* (New York: Crossroad Publishing, 1990), 99.

28. Zahnd, *Beauty Will Save the World*, 7.

29. Mary M. Solberg, *Compelling Knowledge: A Feminist Proposal for an Epistemology of the Cross* (New York: SUNY Press, 1997), 112.

30. Zahnd, *Beauty Will Save the World*, 10.

31. Balthasar, *The Glory of the Lord,* vol. 1, Forward.

32. Barry Ensign-George, "Denomination as Ecclesiological Category: Sketching an Assessment," in *Denomination: Assessing an Ecclesiological Category,* ed. Paul M. Collins and Barry Ensign-George (London: T&T Clark International, 2011), 10.

33. Peter Phan, "Crossing the Borders: A Spirituality for Mission in Our Times from an Asian Perspective," Service of Documentation and Study on Global Mission, available at http://sedosmission.org/old/eng/phan_2.htm (accessed April 30, 2012).

34. Kosuke Koyama, "The Future of a Jealous God," (lecture transcription, Princeton Theological Seminary, Princeton, New Jersey, December 2, 1980). See also *Water Buffalo Theology*, pp. 115–25, for Koyama's treatment of Kitamori as well as a more in depth discussion on the significance of God's painful embrace, which Kitamori calls a combination of two Japanese words, *tsutsumu* and *tsurasa,* which mean "to enfold" and "to feel pain deeply for others."

# EXPERIENTIAL JOURNEYS OF MISSION

# 12

# RECONCEIVING ECUMENISM
## Beyond Eurocentrism

*Donald W. Dayton*

## INTRODUCTION

For over a quarter of a century, I have been deeply involved in the ecumenical movement as a member of a church that does not affiliate with either the World Council of Churches (WCC) or the National Council of Churches (NCC). I have attended every WCC assembly since Vancouver (including Harare, Canberra, and Porto Alegre), and I have attended meetings of the Central Committee (Moscow), Faith and Order (Stavanger, Norway), Commission on World Mission and Evangelism (San Antonio and Geneva), a WCC consultation with Pentecostals (Lima, Peru), and so on. In the late 1980s, I spent a sabbatical term in Geneva at the special request of Emilio Castro, then head of the WCC, in a program designed to convince the WCC staff that non-members of the WCC can also be "ecumenical" and are not the reactionary ogres sometimes imagined. (I was expected to volunteer my services and suggested that this be in Faith and Order, but this offer was refused. I was shunted over to World Mission and Evangelism, a response that astounded me, but foreshadowed much of my later experience in European ecumenism.) I have served as a member of the Commission on Faith and Order of the NCC in this country for over a quarter of a century, chairing study groups, designing consultations, etcetera. I also have served for over a decade on the board of the North American Academy of Ecumenists.

In all of this immersion in the ecumenical movement, I have become increasingly disenchanted with "ecumenism" as we generally conceive and practice it. This alienation could be described in many different ways. For our purposes, I will describe it as a deep disenchantment with an incorrigible "Eurocentrism" of the ecumenical movement. This claim surprises my friends in Geneva who are often proud of ecumenical achievements in supporting the third world, claiming to be advocates of the "margins." All the same, I had little success in Geneva arguing this thesis: Whatever may be the case in the social and political arenas, the ecumenical movement remains, on the theological and ecclesiological levels, profoundly "Eurocentric" and needs to move to a more global perspective.

## ENLARGING OUR PERSPECTIVE BEYOND EUROPE

In my lecturing, teaching, and research in Asia (primarily in Korea, Japan, China, and Thailand, and usually with indigenous Christian Churches unrelated to Western mission boards), I like to emphasize that Christianity itself is one of the great Asian religions. A choice for Christianity is not to be, in the first place, identified with Westernization, modernization, or the adoption of European culture. The basic point here has been recently well made in Philip Jenkins' book, *The Lost History of Christianity*. The cover reprints an ancient map in the shape of a three-leaf clover with Jerusalem at the center and the leaves representing three trajectories: in Europe to the northwest, in Asia to the east, and Africa to the southwest. I believe it is correct to observe that, for the first millennium of Christianity, a majority of its adherents lived outside of Europe.

Merely to make (or remake?) this point about the non-European trajectories of Christianity opens (or reopens?) a Pandora's box of theological questions that we often assume are resolved. Christianity came to Korea, for example, first in its Nestorian form via China and only in the eighteenth century as Catholicism and a century later as Protestantism. Many ancient Asian churches are non-Chalcedonian and monophysite. Similarly in Africa, the Egyptian Coptic Church and the Ethiopian Church are also monophysite—or "miaphysite," as we are encouraged to say today to recognize that the one nature has both human and divine aspects. I am less interested in defending these traditions theologically than to point out the extent to which we tend to assume the finality of the European tradition for Christian theology, an assumption that results in a distorted "Eurocentric" perspective that has profound negative consequences. On the social and political level, for example, the suppression of this wider history often results in pitting Christian (European and Western?) culture against Arabic Islam, obscuring the extent to which Palestinians are often Christian and Iraq has had significant Christian communities largely driven underground or out of Iraq by turn-of-the-century invasions.

But I am really more interested in how a modern "Eurocentrism" distorts our perceptions of ecumenism and our choice of the questions that should be addressed. This could be illustrated in a number of ways. I choose the process of planting the Faith and Order movement in the North American context. This took place formally in 1957 at a meeting in Oberlin, Ohio. I was asked to give one of the keynote addresses at Oberlin II, celebrating fifty years of Faith and Order in the United States and the NCC. In preparation for this address, I studied the report of Oberlin I prepared for my Yale New Testament Professor, Paul Minear, and such limited archives of the Oberlin meeting as I was able to locate (at Oberlin College and Union Theological Seminary). I quickly concluded that the purpose of Oberlin I was *not* to plant an American Faith and Order movement to reflect theologically on its own context and reap the results for the illumination of global ecumenism. It was rather to transplant to America the Faith and Order movement as it is conceived of in Europe, assuming that the categories of that discussion are adequate for American ecumenism.

This theological "Eurocentrism" is clear in the report of Oberlin I. In the first place, there is *no* theological analysis of the American context and the distinctive ecclesiologies to be found. There is an extended sociological analysis that concludes with the somewhat trivial result that, because of a high degree of mobility in American society, there is less denominational loyalty and that Americans, therefore, change denominations more easily. It is, moreover, apparently assumed that the essential theological issues are well encompassed in the tripartite analysis of Orthodoxy, Catholicism, and magisterial Protestantism. The essential divisions to be overcome began in the eleventh and sixteenth centuries. It is amusing to see the report struggle with this European grid and attempt to apply it to the American scene. Catholics were not officially present, and the Orthodox had a role far out of proportion to their demographic presence in North America at the time. The myriad of American Protestant (is the word really helpful here?) denominations are assumed apparently to be treated under the category of classic Protestantism (e.g., Lutheran, Reformed, and Anglican).

## AMERICAN-BORN CHURCHES DIFFER FROM EUROPE

This ignores completely the ecumenical problem of the "American-born Churches"—the topic of an NCC Faith and Order consultation that I designed and chaired. The United Church of Christ has a variety of European roots, for example, but took on a distinctly dissenting cast as the church of the Puritan "Pilgrim Fathers." American Protestantism is dominated by the Methodists and Baptists. These traditions were technically born in Europe, but found their destiny, so to speak, in North America. The Black or African-American Churches are largely of the populist Baptist and Methodist type (in the nineteenth century) and more recently of the Pentecostal type (in the twentieth century). The early nineteenth century saw the emergence of various "restorationist" traditions (most notably the Disciples of Christ, and a variety of Churches of Christ, both instrumental and non-instrumental, as well as other parallel movements) that have since become global theological traditions. The Adventists (both Seventh-Day and Advent Christian) were born in the antebellum era and have become, especially the former, global Christian movements with important universities, medical centers, and theological institutions around the world. My own tradition, the Holiness Movement, was born in the same era and is now among the top ten demographically of Christian traditions around the world in the form of the Salvation Army, Church of the Nazarene, Church of God (Anderson, Indiana), and numerous other groups, including a number of indigenous Christian movements in various parts of the world. Other movements could be mentioned, most notably Pentecostalism, which by some lights, has come to be roughly a fourth of global Christians (roughly half a billion) and the dominant religious force in various parts of the "third world." We also have the ecumenical problem of the more divergent Christian traditions (e.g., the Mormon Church and the Jehovah's Witnesses) that have become global movements with American roots. These American-born churches are all now global churches shaping the third world where their dynamics are a further radicalization of the American experience and even more distant from the European experience. I am told that the four most rapidly growing religious traditions in Latin America are Pentecostalism, Seventh-Day Adventists, Mormons, and Jehovah's Witnesses—all American-born churches. If the statisticians and demographers were sophisticated enough to discern the parameters of the movement, the Holiness tradition would be seen as a fifth such force.

This diversity cannot be handled in the classic categories of European ecumenism. From the American perspective, the nineteenth century is as church-dividing as the eleventh and the sixteenth centuries. Any approach to ecumenical dialogue that starts from the tripartite analysis of Orthodox, Catholic, and Protestant is inherently and by definition "Eurocentric." The ecumenical questions raised by the diversity of American-born churches are not the questions of classic Protestantism. This is easily seen, for example, by the irrelevance of the joint declaration on justification to the Latin American situation where the central discussion is between Catholics and Pentecostals whose soteriology is closer to the Council of Trent than to Luther.

It is a difficult problem to know what to call this nineteenth-century cluster of churches. To use the term *Anabaptist* is often confusing and another reflection of an effort to force into the categories of the European experience traditions that do not fit. Half a century ago, some experimented with the term *third force* Christianity, but that has its own difficulties. This problem and that of resulting appropriate terminology should be at the center of ecumenical discussion, but they are not. It is doubtful that genuine ecumenical advance can take place without attention to these questions.

We cannot resolve these questions here, but a few comments may be in order. Is it possible to describe these movements as a single category? Probably not. I am very leery of any effort to describe American Christianity in terms of a single motif, though efforts have been made by such suggestions as "experientially oriented." Karl Barth, for example, thought American Christianity could and ought to be cultivated in terms of a pneumatological starting point, emphasizing the themes of liberty and freedom.

At the same time, it is possible to indicate some tendencies of this cluster of churches. Most have a strong restorationist motif and a consequent doctrine of "the Constantinian fall of the church." In part, this is a function of the disestablishment of religion in the United States. All denominations have had to adjust to a certain post-Constantinian cultural context, especially those national churches of European origin. The American-born churches have often embraced this motif enthusiastically and have claimed that the U.S. context provides the opportunity for a fresh start that rejects the developments of the "old world." This theme is not discussed the way it should be. I once proposed on the board of the NAAE that we discuss, during a forthcoming meeting at the Brethren in Christ institution of higher education of Messiah College, the doctrine of a "Constantinian fall of the church" as "church-dividing." My suggestion was met with blank looks (by academics and professional ecumenists!) until finally Lutheran and Catholic representatives asked whatever that might be. They were later surprised that the term was a regular feature of the dialogue at Messiah College without being given formal attention as such.

This is not just a cultural issue. It can also be analyzed theologically. By far and away, the Baptists are the most dominant form of American Protestantism, especially when one clusters together Northern and Southern Baptists, the several African-American denominations in this tradition, and various other groups. These Christians wish to be "New Testament Christians" and claim to jump over church history for immediate biblical justification of doctrine and church polity, including sacramental practice. A similar pattern is part and parcel of the Pentecostal understanding (as illustrated in Aimee Semple McPherson's famous sermon "Lost and Restored") and most other American-born churches listed above.

Methodism, the second most numerous American Protestant tradition, is an interesting case study of this question. In ecumenical circles, Methodism has often been interpreted in light of the classic tradition, especially in the work of such influential ecumenists as Albert Outler, John Deschner, and Geoffrey Wainwright. This reading has suppressed certain more radical motifs in Wesleyan thought. Wesley had a strong doctrine of a Constantinian fall, though he placed the emphasis on a decline of spirituality in the fourth century. For him, the first three centuries (or the "Ante-Nicene fathers") had a special normativity. Few have noticed that Wesley was reading, during his missionary work in Georgia, the church history of radical Pietist (and near "Anabaptist") Gottfried Arnold. Such facts justify the sort of reading that one finds in *The Radical Wesley* by Howard Snyder, who places Wesley more in the context of the left wing of the Reformation. Donald Durnbaugh similarly treated Methodism in the line of *The Believers' Church*.

These issues might be said to find focus in the question of the status of the Nicene Creed. When Wesley put together the "Sunday Service" for American Methodists, he wove together the communion service and the morning prayer service of the Anglican *Book of Common Prayer*. He, thus, had a choice of two creeds and dropped the Nicene Creed in favor of the Apostles' Creed. It would be an interesting discussion to pursue what was at stake in this decision, whether it was a product of his restorationist primitivism or his ambivalence about the fourth century.

It is a commonplace of ecumenical thought in our time that future ecumenical dialogue must take, as its starting point, the Nicene Creed. George Hunsinger makes this point in his book on *The Eucharist and Ecumenism*. But the use of this creed is almost unheard of in the American-born churches, which are often "non-creedal" and "biblicist," preferring strongly the Apostles' Creed when such is used. We need more discussion about this issue—about whether there are real theological issues at stake in this disuse of the Nicene Creed. I am inclined to think there may be and that this ecumenical consensus may be premature if we take seriously an American perspective.

In the NCC Faith and Order, I helped shape consultations and a study group on an American response to the WCC Faith and

Order study on the Apostolic Faith. We attempted to analyze theologically the American search for "apostolicity." The European context has centered on the classic views of "apostolic succession" or the preaching of "apostolic doctrine" in the case of the magisterial Reformation. I have personally experienced, and have similar reports from friends, the resistance of European ecumenists to any expansion of this discussion in terms of the complexity of the American scene, where "apostolic" fidelity is judged by different, and often behavioral, criteria. The more Anabaptist-inclined Churches judge apostolicity in terms of the renunciation of the sword in favor of a Christian pacifism. For others, the issue is church governance or structure. Some have had debates about whether there is apostolic precedence for the use of musical instruments in Christian worship. For Pentecostals, the search for apostolicity has to do with the recovery of lost charisms, often with a special emphasis on miracles of healing as the true measure of apostolicity. For the radical Oneness wing of Pentecostalism, apostolicity involves the recovery of a pre-trinitarian reading of the New Testament, emphasizing the monotheistic focus of the religion "of Abraham, Isaac, and Jacob." I fail to understand why these are not important theological questions that deserve fuller discussion and have been reassured by the reports of some European Catholic ecumenists that our work helped them better understand the diversity of American Protestantism in terms of a positive search for the "apostolic faith," rather than a process of increasing alienation from the classic tradition.

## NEXT STAGE IN ECUMENISM

If it is not already clear, I have been arguing that the "ecumenical movement" is profoundly shaped by European history in a way that has resulted in a profound "Eurocentrism" that is not adequate to the analysis of global Christianity, nor the necessary next stage of ecumenism. I have emphasized the American experience, not only because it is our own, but because, in part as a result of the missionary movements of the nineteenth century, it is, in a sense, a key that can help unlock the puzzles of global Christianity and facilitate that next stage in ecumenism.

This "Eurocentrism" is not only inadequate but also pernicious in blocking that next step. It relies on a limited range of Christian experience and blocks the emergence of new Christian voices in the modern era. I say this on the basis of a quarter of a century of work defending those voices precisely within the ecumenical movement. The great achievements of the ecumenical movement (*Baptism, Eucharist and Ministry*, for example) might even be viewed as a closing of the ranks of the ancient Churches (Catholic and Orthodox) and of part of the Reformation Churches against the rest of the Reformation and much that has happened in Christian history since. It may well be in the future that the twentieth and twenty-first centuries will rank as "church dividing" along this fissure. The task before us is to crack open the categories of this ecumenical "Eurocentrism" precisely for the sake of the future of ecumenism—of a wider, global ecumenism that takes account the whole range of Christian experience.

## FIRST CASE STUDY: ONENESS PENTECOSTALISM AND THE TRINITY

I conclude this section with two case studies of the barriers to hearing and understanding important voices that deserve to be given the space to contribute to ecumenical dialogue. The first of these is the Oneness branch of Pentecostalism—a stream of Pentecostalism almost unknown in the ecumenical world. I was fascinated, at Drew University, in the response to a Black Oneness Pentecostal student. It seemed that I was the only one on the faculty that knew how to talk to him. The Drew faculty tends to see every Black student as a potential James Cone and every Korean on a path to Minjung theology—and would probably be shocked to know that both clusters of students meet in the early mornings to pray for a protective covering as they enter classes. The second case study is intended to unfold the diversity and richness of sacramental thinking in my own tradition, the Holiness Movement. I have deliberately chosen provocative illustrations, and I fear that, for some of you, these case studies will be so offensive as to discredit much of what I have been saying. But I proceed full speed ahead.

Oneness Pentecostalism has many barriers to being heard. Most Pentecostals would prefer that you not know that a major branch of the movement rejects the classic doctrine of the Trinity, largely because such knowledge might prevent efforts to assimilate into the Evangelical movement. It has also prospered in minority communities where middle-class ecumenism is less widely practiced. I am told, however, that in some countries, it is the largest Protestant tradition (Colombia, for example, and I have heard similar comments about Mexico—and China has the large indigenous True Jesus Church). It is very influential in the African-American community—though it has perhaps the best record in the United States of bridging white and black members in the same congregation. Most Midwestern cities have a major downtown church or complex in this tradition (Indianapolis, Louisville, St. Louis, and so forth), as well as numerous smaller churches. Chicago has two major centers, a downtown complex and a megachurch in Hyde Park at the end of the elevated line. The latter grew to nearly twenty thousand members under the leadership of Bishop Arthur Brazier (died 2010), who succeeded Saul Alinsky at the head of TWO (The Woodlawn Organization, the fountainhead of the "community organizing" movement where President Obama got his start). Brazier was featured by Swiss ecumenist and missiologist Walter Hollenweger in *Pentecost between Black and White,* after a visit to the United States. Such involvement is perhaps surprisingly common in other cities where black Oneness bishops have been involved in various ecumenical (with Catholics and others) social and redevelopment projects in urban ghettos. T. D. Jakes, who appears often on television and whose books may be purchased in many airport shops, is also from this tradition. One cannot claim to reach across the racial barriers in America without attention to this tradition.

I have a particular fascination with the Asamblea Apostolica, the Mexican Church in this tradition, which has hundreds of churches centered in Mexico and California (as well as other places, including five, for example, as far afield as Chicago). This movement has spread along the lines of the migrations of the Mexican farm workers back and forth across the border—and has played a role in the farm workers movement of Cesar Chavez.

The border has required the church to be split into two denominations, one Mexican and one American. The movement is shaped by apocalypticism and tends to view this division as the product of the arrogance of Babylonian empires of the end times who dare to meddle in God's work by drawing an artificial line down the middle of the Kingdom of God. One of my favorite stories is the raiding of a church and the consequent deportation of an undocumented youth minister. The church was proud to have him back on duty by the evening service. One Mexican bishop of this church, Manuel Gaxiola-Gaxiola, was, before his death, a major ecumenist (head of the Mexican Bible Society, for example, among other involvements) and scholar (author of several books interpreting Mexican culture and religion in general as well as his own tradition). One of his protégés served as a diversity officer at Stanford University before becoming a professor of Chicano studies at Arizona State and now at Michigan. He was responsible for a National Endowment for the Humanities project on the hymnody of his church (available as a DVD). I have shared with Harvard theologian Harvey Cox the privilege of teaching in their Bible college in Mexico City, a wonderful experience.

This tradition may be traced to a 1913 split within Pentecostalism at a camp meeting in the Arroyo Seco between Los Angeles and Pasadena (a site I have visited often), when a Canadian evangelist preparing for a baptismal service puzzled over the baptismal formulas in Luke (in the name of Jesus) and Matthew (in the Trinity: Father, Son, and Holy Spirit). Someone at the camp meeting resolved this tension by appeal to the Pauline text indicating that in Christ the "fullness of the Godhead dwelt bodily." This launched a tradition that has developed a significant theology of the "name of Jesus" and the Oneness of God (see the many books of David Bernard in a predominantly white denomination in this movement). The first serious study of this movement was a consultation at Harvard, where a Oneness student appealed to the Unitarian tradition there and convinced the Divinity School to host the meeting, happy to welcome another Unitarian tradition, failing apparently to distinguish between a Unitarianism of the first person and a Unitarianism of the second person of the Trinity.

217

I have chosen this case study, in part, because the theological literature on this movement often appeals to Barth—not only because of the similar "Christological concentration" but also because of the resultant tendency toward a form of "modalism" in the doctrine of the Trinity. Oneness Pentecostalism poses a real challenge to the ecumenical movement, not only theologically (does the classic tradition have a tritheistic tendency?), but in other areas as well. What does one do with a movement that speaks in trinitarian formulae while opposing the formal doctrine? How does one deal with the "classism" (is ecumenism rooted in the middle-class world of universities and church bureaucracies?) of the ecumenical movement that ignores the churches of the farm workers and the black ghettos? How do we relate to churches rooted in part in divisions based in the non-theological factors of race and ethnicity? Why is this tradition nearly invisible to both academics and ecumenists? I have found reflection on the experience of Oneness Pentecostalism very useful in discerning the limits of standard ecumenism and breaking out of the "Eurocentric" paradigm that it usually uncritically assumes.

## SECOND CASE STUDY: HOLINESS CHURCHES AND THE SACRAMENTS

The second case study moves us closer to sacramental issues and reveals a range of important issues that get short shrift in ecumenism as it is generally practiced. The last two years of my thirty-five years of seminary faculty teaching I spent at Azusa Pacific University (APU). This university is one of the largest (about 11,000 students) and most influential of the network of the Council for Christian Colleges and Universities—many of which are now entering their second centuries of existence as the latest wave of Christian institutions of higher education outside the Christian mainstream. Azusa Pacific University is the product of the merger of three institutions: Azusa Bible College of the Holiness Quakers (major branches of the Friends, over 50 percent of those in Indiana, for example, were swept into the nineteenth-century Holiness movement); Los Angeles Pacific College of the Free Methodists (abolitionist Methodists driven out of mainline Methodism because of their advocacy of "free pews" on the basis of a highly articulated "preferential option for the poor"; founder B. T. Roberts thought that the episcopacy, for example, *might* belong to the *bene esse* of the church, but the ministry to the poor was the defining part of the *esse* of any church that claimed to follow Jesus); and Huntington Park College of the restorationist Church of God, Anderson, Indiana (combining a Campbellite [i.e., like the Disciples of Christ] ecclesiology with a Holiness soteriology). Over the years, seven different denominational traditions have supported the university. These seven differ widely in sacramental practice but find unity in a common commitment to a Wesleyan soteriology of the "second blessing" of sanctification in the Holiness tradition.

Two of these streams, the Salvation Army and the Holiness Quakers, reject sacramental practice on principle. In doing this, they seem to have a firm grip on the prophetic motif that the practice of ritual separated from justice and mercy is odious to the biblical God. The Quaker tradition is often interpreted in light of a reaction against "programmed" worship and a claim that all of life is sacramental and ought not to be localized in certain sacramental liturgies. The Salvation Army is less clear. Some have suggested pragmatic reasons for their rejection of sacraments: either its existence as a parachurch organization bending over backward to not be in competition with the established churches, or perhaps a way to finesse the problem of inviting alcoholics to a communion rail to partake of wine. Salvation Army officer David Rightmire of Asbury University has argued in *Sacraments and the Salvation Army* (a study responding to *Baptism, Eucharist and Ministry* [BEM]) for a theological rootage in the development in the nineteenth century of a "pneumatological ecclesiology" that presupposes a sort of mediation of grace in the experiential appropriation of religion. Like the Free Methodists, the Salvation Army seems to suggest that service to the poor is the defining expression of the Christian movement rather than any particular ritual practice. It is fun to trace the reaction to the Quakers and Salvationists in the WCC process leading to BEM. They are politely invited to give papers at consultations, but then rather completely ignored in the formulation of ecumenical consensus.

Three denominations practice, in effect, three sacraments. The Church of God (Anderson, Indiana), the Brethren in Christ (typologically similar to Anabaptists, but of nineteenth-century origins), and the United Missionary Church (similarly more Anabaptistic) all are committed to the practice of "footwashing," often in the context of the "love feast," sometimes a more elaborate Eucharistic meal (a real meal!) that requires reconciliation with others as a precondition of participation. These churches have a firm grip on the Johannine literature of the New Testament, which seems to be clearer in its expectation that the followers of Jesus will engage in this practice than it does that they will participate in the Eucharist. (I say this in full awareness of the "high church" exegesis of John that finds the Eucharist anticipated in the feeding of the 5,000 and the images of Christ as the "Bread of Life.") The social implications are obvious and are nicely illustrated in the logo of the Brethren in Christ, which places the bowl and towel at the foot of the cross. Again, there seems to be the implicit claim that the essential expression of the life of the church is its service to others, including those outside of the fellowship. I have yet to see a substantial ecumenical discussion of the practice of foot washing as a symbol of the missional character of the church.

Only two of the denominations (the abolitionist Wesleyan Methodists and Free Methodists) affirm, in theory, the traditional two sacraments of classic Protestantism, but what they affirm in theory they often neglect in practice. Baptism can be in any form, immersion or sprinkling, as an adult or as a child, according to the wishes of the subject or guardian (I was immersed as a teenager, ironically just as I was beginning to enter my period of doubt!), and communion is often held once a quarter. The latter reflects the Methodist history of lay ministry in which the itinerating ordained clergy convened the "quarterly conference" and presided at the table. There is a debate within Methodism about whether communion can itself be a "converting ordinance" that might not require prior baptism or church membership. There is also a debate about the centrality of communion among the "means of grace." At my denominational college, the president always asked in the first chapel of the week if we had attended to the means of grace over the weekend, by which he meant had we gone to Sunday school. I used to make fun of this in college, not only because Sunday school had never been for me a "means of grace," but also because I considered the suggestion theologically and ecclesiastically gauche. It was only much later that I understood that this position probably had its distant roots in the wider Pietist traditions that flowed through Wesley. Though he himself as an Anglican priest was a regular communicant, he recognized other "means of grace" that included small groups, Bible study, devotional personal prayer, and so on. By so doing, he set in motion trajectories in which these other pietistic practices would outrank the Eucharist in normal practice. Social questions also came to the fore as the abolitionist Methodists debated whether unrepentant slaveholders could be admitted to Communion—or even whether those who communed with slaveholders could be admitted, in a sort of second degree of separation. These debates have always seemed to me to be parallel to those in the Catholic tradition about whether divorced persons or advocates of abortion could commune, but I have always missed in ecumenical discussions attention to such ethical questions. In addition, I have often pondered the fact that I was never denied access to the Lord's table until I began to attend ecumenical meetings. Who is the real ecumenist?

My major purpose in this latter study has been to indicate some of the theological reasons that lie behind a great diversity of sacramental traditions. One might argue that this diversity is possible only because these traditions do not really believe that grace is mediated through the sacraments but through experience and other "means of grace." But I do believe the theological questions are real and ecumenical reflection is impoverished by lack of attention to some of these questions. Again, voices are suppressed, voices that need to be heard. The full range of Christian reflection on these issues needs to be present at the ecumenical table. I am more and more convinced that issues often seen as dividing along conservative/liberal lines are actually divisions along the lines of ecclesial experience and differing theologies.

# 13

# ECUMENISM, INTERFAITH RELATIONS, AND THE LAUSANNE MOVEMENT

*Don Thorsen*

"Abraham shall become a great and mighty nation,
and all the nations of the earth shall be blessed in him"
—*Genesis 18:18*

My first ministerial position in a church was to serve as the youth pastor in a Free Methodist Church in the San Joaquin Valley of California. One day, the senior pastor invited me to attend a local Christian pastors' fellowship. However, he warned me that it was the progressive, mainline fellowship in town. He preferred attending the conservative, evangelically oriented pastors' fellowship, but he was a Rotarian and the two other clergy members in the local Rotary International attended the former group. So the senior pastor of my church felt obliged to attend both pastors' fellowships. I also attended both fellowships and was surprised to discover that the two groups discussed substantively the same things—reaching out to the community by cooperating in various ministry projects, including civic events, care for the poor, and so on. The pastor fellowships had different priorities, but their beliefs, values, and practices did not appear to me to be all that different.

In subsequent years, I served in other ministerial and academic capacities and usually experienced the same phenomenon: two pastoral fellowships, at least, per town. This dichotomy, of course, does not occur merely in local towns and cities. The bifurcation between allegedly progressive, mainline churches and conservative, evangelically oriented churches—no matter how one may define those terms—seems widespread throughout the United States. No doubt, there are numerous social, cultural, political, and economic factors as well as spiritual and ecclesiastical ones for this apparent divergence within American Christianity. Some churches and denominations have done better than others in resisting the dichotomies that divide, rather than unite, Christians. But few would deny its existence within the country.

## ECUMENICAL AND INTERFAITH RELATIONS BACKGROUND

A common feeling that people express is that of "living in two worlds." For one reason or another, they find themselves trying to bridge two worlds—two perspectives, or sets of beliefs, values, and practices. My conflicted feelings come from the fact that I am an evangelical Christian who has dedicated more than a decade of time, effort, and money to the work of Christian ecumenism. The standard joke, of course, is that an "evangelical ecumenist" is an oxymoron. I have heard that joke from both evangelical friends who talk about my ecumenical work, and ecumenical friends who talk about my evangelical work. Jokes aside, however, the liminal experience of advocating simultaneously evangelical Christianity and ecumenical Christianity has, at times, been challenging. Since I come from an evangelical background, my participation in ecumenical and interfaith circles has led to other evangelicals viewing me with respect, yet caution, and sometimes vocalized suspicion. Likewise, my participation in evangelical circles has led to ecumenists viewing me with respect, yet caution, and sometimes vocalized suspicion. Déjà vu?

Personally, it has not always been easy for me to reconcile the seemingly divergent Christian trajectories with regard to the mission of God, or God's mission for Christians in the world. It is not that I have been unable—for the most part—to reconcile evangelicalism and ecumenism, but I have not always been able to articulate their complementarity in a way that won support from others. To be sure, people would agree with me "in theory," but I do not always find kindred-spirits "in practice." The zeal of fellow evangelicals seemed too narrow, unyielding, and spiritually imprudent to ecumenists; likewise, the zeal of ecumenists seemed too narrow, unyielding, and spiritually imprudent to evangelicals. The beliefs, values, and practices of evangelical Christianity and those of ecumenical Christianity seemed too divergent to synthesize in a practically applicable way.

## INVITATION TO THE THIRD LAUSANNE CONGRESS

In the summer of 2010, when I was offered an invitation to attend the Third Lausanne Congress of World Evangelization, I experienced a variety of thoughts and feelings. On the one hand, I was honored to be chosen by Azusa Pacific University, where I teach theology, to serve as one of the University's representatives in Cape Town, South Africa. On the other hand, I would have to miss the semiannual meeting of the Commission on Faith and Order, in which I have actively participated for a decade. Faith and Order represents one of the Commissions of the National Council of Churches (NCC), and leaders in the Faith and Order movement have graciously invited representatives from the Wesleyan Theological Society (WTS) and Society of Pentecostal Studies since the 1980s. I represent the WTS and am deeply grateful for the invitation, since most of the denominations that support the two aforementioned societies are not part of the NCC. In fact, it would be difficult to find much direct ecclesiastical support for my participation in Faith and Order outside the two scholarly societies, since most of the aforementioned denominations are affiliated with the National Association of Evangelicals, if they are affiliated with any ecumenically oriented organization.[1]

There was no necessary problem with attending the Lausanne Congress; however, there occurred within my mind and heart a certain irony, since so often my "two worlds"—so to speak—had been seen by others, if not me, to be in conflict. The word *conflict* may be too strong, of course. But too seldom do I find much enthusiasm from either evangelicals or ecumenists for the work and ministry of the others.

I attended the Lausanne Congress and had a wonderful experience for a number of reasons. I affirm much that went on at the Lausanne Congress. It was not a perfect event, and much of my experience in ecumenism sensitized me to problems related to some of what transpired in Cape Town. (Likewise, not all that I have experienced in ecumenical circles has been perfect, and my background in evangelicalism sensitized me to problems related to some of what transpires among ecumenists.) Attending the Lausanne Congress did little to bring closure to the conflicted feelings that I have had over my respective Christian involvements.

Further complicating matters, I began three years ago to attend the semiannual meetings of the Commission on Interfaith Relations, another one of the Commissions of the NCC. It was a natural progression, so to speak, in my interests and concerns for unity, mutual understanding, and cooperation. My earliest academic studies were in comparative Religious Studies at Stanford University, because it seemed to me, in part, that I needed to study other religions in both the intellectual as well as spiritual development of my Christianity. So, as my interests in ecumenical work increased, it seemed prudent to become more involved with interfaith relations and dialogue. But, as one can imagine, the contrast between the interreligious efforts of the Commission on Interfaith Relations can stand in even greater contrast from that of worldwide evangelism, promoted by the Lausanne Movement.[2]

Of course, my involvements with ecumenism and interfaith relations have involved far more than work with the Faith and Order and Interfaith Relations Commissions of the NCC. In addition, I am a longtime participant in the Southern California Ecumenical Council and its regional meetings of Faith and Order. I have been involved in local pastor fellowships, even when there were two fellowships in town—one oriented more toward mainline churches, and one oriented more toward evangelical Churches. Academically, I have participated as a scholar in numerous ecumenically oriented events both in the United States and internationally.

## PERSPECTIVE

*Although evangelical and ecumenical Christianity are often seen at cross purposes with one another, I consider them complementary because of the teachings of Scripture and because of my hope that evangelicals and ecumenists, who promote unity and interfaith relations, will—by the grace of God—increasingly collaborate with one another.* I do not have a grand, unifying theology that holds together diverging Christian beliefs, values, and practices. But I am constantly in the process of trying to do so, especially since I am a theologian by vocation and trade. So, I want to reflect upon the Lausanne Movement in order to talk about what I consider the complementarity of evangelical and ecumenical Christianity. In reality, there are numerous branches or streams of Christianity—and not just those of evangelicalism and ecumenism—that need to be acknowledged, affirmed, and embraced in cooperation of their witness to God in both "word and deed."

To be sure, I have often been accused of idealism, that is, of not being sufficiently aware of the realities within Christianity and of other historical, sociocultural, and political factors that work against the complementarity of which I speak. Still others may feel that I minimize their service on behalf of the mission of God. I do not want to minimize anyone or their ministries. But I grieve over enduring mistrust and lack of understanding and appreciation for the divergent branches of Christianity. So, trying to avoid the "Scylla" of idealism and "Charybdis" of realism, I want to share my perspective on some of the concerns and ministries of both the Lausanne Congress and my commitment to ecumenism and interfaith relations.

## STREAMS OF SPIRITUALITY

In the book *Streams of Living Water: Celebrating the Great Traditions of Christian Faith*,[3] Richard Foster talks about six great traditions, streams, or branches of Christianity, depending on the particular analogy you prefer. He refers to the evangelical, sacramental, contemplative, holiness, activist, and charismatic streams of Christianity. Too often, such streams have been seen in conflict, or they have led to what some people call "silos," which serve more to separate than unite their respective beliefs, values, and practices. Yet, all contribute to the gestalt of God's mission in the world, and no single stream encapsulates the whole, at least, not the whole of how Christians have ministered throughout church history. Foster advocates that the streams of Christianity, taken collectively, produce a more holistic manifestation of how God wants Christians and churches to be at work in the world.

Other Christians see more than six streams of spirituality. In other writings, I have argued for the need, at least, of two additional streams of spirituality—studious spirituality and ecumenical spirituality.[4] Of course, others could be added to these. But it seems to me that some Christians and churches have contributed to Christianity by their service in studying Scripture and other writings, and in subsequent scholarship and publications. Likewise, some Christians and churches have contributed to Christianity by their service in ecumenism and interfaith relations.

The idea of unity and diversity within churches is not new. Paul talked about it in 1 Corinthians 12:12–31, where he describes the church as the "body of Christ," having many parts. No parts of the body should consider other parts to be more important or less important, but equally important and essential to the church and its mission. Now, for most of the early years of my life, I thought of Paul's analogy only in terms of the local church, or possibly within my denomination—the Free Methodist Church. Different people within local churches positively contributed their diverse gifts and talents; likewise, different churches within the denomination positively contributed their diverse gifts and talents. It was not until later in life that I began to see how the diversity of denominations and churches around the world, not affiliated with my church or country, positively contributed their diverse gifts and talents to the ecumenical church—the catholic, universal church of Jesus Christ. Thus, 1 Corinthians 12:12–31 represented a powerful analogy for how evangelical and ecumenical Christians complement, rather than conflict, with one another.

I do not understand why, at least in theory, there should be any necessary conflict between the emphases, or "spiritual streams," characteristic of evangelical, ecumenical, and other Christian traditions. But in practice, things do not always work out so well. When Edinburgh 2010 occurred, suspicion and disregard among evangelicals arose; likewise, in my opinion, when Cape Town 2010 occurred, suspicion and disregard among ecumenists arose. One can write off some of the divisiveness due to ignorance; some of it occurs due to hurt and misery that happened as the result of particular church beliefs and practices. Indeed, it would take far too long to recount all the ways that Christians have been unloving and unjustly hurtful toward one another, as well as to adherents of other faiths or religions. Without doubt, some of the ill will may be attributed to sin—a theological assessment not always welcome in Christian communities.

## THIRD LAUSANNE CONGRESS OF WORLD EVANGELIZATION

The Third Lausanne Congress of World Evangelization brought together more than 4,000 representatives from 198 countries around the world. They met for eight days in Cape Town and discussed, strategized, and encouraged worldwide evangelism. The plenary events (including Bible studies, sermons, addresses, reports, and worship events) were translated into eight different languages, and simulcast electronically to thousands of locations throughout the world. Plenary participants came from fourteen different continents and subcontinent areas of the world.

The Lausanne Congress tried to be more inclusive than the two previous meetings in Lausanne, Switzerland (1974) and Manila, Philippines (1989). Representatives, who attended by invitation, included pastors, evangelists, missionaries, academics, and laity, who all support evangelism. Allocations of invitations were used to encourage a larger number of women and younger Christians (under 40 years of age) to participate as well as representatives from as many countries as possible. Likewise, limits were placed on the number of Western Christians who could attend, for example, from the United States. Churches and denominations were represented widely from around the world, but the Lausanne Movement is not denominationally sponsored. Instead it reflects a loose organization of parachurch organizations,[5] academic institutions,[6] and Christian media[7] from around the world. The hodgepodge that makes up the Lausanne Movement explains, in part, why it took twenty-one years for a third Congress to occur. The plan is that future Congresses will take place every ten years.

The Lausanne Congress could be called ecumenical in the sense that it promotes cooperation in evangelistic ministry by as many Christians, at as many times and places, as possible. Willem Visser't Hooft, for example, who was the first Secretary General of the World Council of Churches, distinguished between three types of ecumenism: church-centered (visible unity), doctrine-centered (theological unity), and cooperation-centered (ministerial unity).[8] The Lausanne Movement has exemplified the last two types of ecumenism: doctrine-centered and cooperation-centered. The Lausanne Covenant was the first ecumenical statement written in 1974, which has become one of the most widely revered confessions, at least, among worldwide evangelical Christians. The Manila Manifesto (1989), coupled with the Cape Town Covenant (2011), represent theological and ethical elaborations, reflective of the Lausanne Covenant.

Of course, one could argue that the Lausanne Movement—and other evangelistically oriented Christian organizations—represent some of the greatest challenges to ecumenism. The Lausanne Movement cooperates with the World Evangelical Alliance (WEA), which is the largest ecumenical gathering of evangelical Christians worldwide. Likewise, the Lausanne Movement is supported by the National Association of Evangelicals (NAE) in the United States. The WEA and NAE are variously considered counterpoints, at best, to the World Council of Churches and the National Council of Churches. It extends beyond the scope of this discussion to assess the dynamics of the relationship between the aforementioned organizational bodies, even if each—ironically—describes themselves as ecumenical. Herein exists, once again, a contributing factor to the conflicted feelings I experience with regard to my ecumenical interests. There are, of course, additional ironies that exist among Christians worldwide, which add to the dilemma.

## WHAT ARE DIFFERENCES?

The primary goals of the Lausanne Movement and the National Council of Churches are different. One emphasizes evangelization more, and the other emphasizes ecumenism more. But adherents of the Lausanne Movement would not, by and large, deny the need for ecumenism, nor would adherents of the NCC, by and large, deny the need for evangelization. Certainly, there would be differences in concerns, methods, and emphases in their respective ministries, but they would not outright deny them. Of course, each organization would want to promote their particular calling with regard to the mission of God in the world, and they would want to reserve the right to define key terms the way that they want. But on paper, that is, "in theory," there do not seem to me to be irreconcilable differences.

If one looks at the documents representing the Lausanne Movement, one will find repeated expressions of concern over the types of evangelistic proclamation that do injustice to the Gospel of Jesus Christ as well as to others. Sometimes people make a distinction between "evangelism" and "proselytism." Evangelism (or evangelization) is considered the appropriate way to share the Gospel in word and deed, which is lovingly respectful and non-manipulative toward others. In contrast, proselytism is considered the inappropriate (or sinful) way to share the Gospel, which is unjustly disrespectful and manipulative toward others.[9]

The Manila Manifesto, which represents a theological and ethical elaboration of the Lausanne Covenant, explicitly talks about the various needs to be lovingly respectful of others, collectively as well as individually. For example, it talks about three issues of concern that arose over the Lausanne Movement's call to world evangelization. First was the concern by countries that Christian evangelism would lead to the political overthrow of their leaders; apparently this was a concern most often expressed by Communist countries. Second was the concern about methods of evangelism that were unjust, misleading, and exploitive. Third was the concern that the aforementioned methods of evangelism infringed upon the ability of people to respond freely to the Gospel. In response to these concerns, the Manila Manifesto says:

First, Christians are loyal citizens, who seek the welfare of their nation. They pray for its leaders, and pay their taxes. Of course, those who have confessed Jesus as Lord cannot also call other authorities Lord, and if commanded to do so, or to do anything which God forbids, must disobey. But they are conscientious citizens. They also contribute to their country's well-being by the stability of their marriages and their homes, their honesty in business, their hard work and their voluntary activity in the service of the handicapped and needy. Just governments have nothing to fear from Christians.

Secondly, Christians renounce unworthy methods of evangelism. Though the nature of our faith requires us to share the gospel with others, our practice is to make an open and honest statement of it, which leaves the hearers entirely free to make up their own minds about it. We wish to be sensitive to those of other faiths, and we reject any approach that seeks to force conversion on them.

Thirdly, Christians earnestly desire freedom of religion for all people, not just freedom for Christianity. In predominantly Christian countries, Christians are at the forefront of those who demand freedom for religious minorities. In predominantly non-Christian countries, therefore, Christians are asking for themselves no more than they demand for others in similar circumstances. The freedom to "profess, practice and propagate" religion, as defined in the Universal Declaration of Human Rights, could and should surely be a reciprocally granted right.[10]

Certainly there may be (and has been) debate over what constitutes civil disobedience, unjust evangelistic methods, and the manipulation of others. The debates have not been settled, and I do not intend to settle them now. But the stated concerns of the Lausanne Movement do not, in my opinion, inherently conflict with those expressed by the National Council of Churches.

Other theological differences between the Lausanne Movement and the National Council of Churches could be discussed, but I will focus only on one. It has to do with whether the NCC supports evangelization and the proclamation of the good news of Jesus Christ. A great documentary example, in my opinion, is the Mission Statement of the Commission on Faith and Order. It says: "To call the churches to the goal of visible unity in one faith and in one eucharistic fellowship expressed in worship and common life in Christ, and to advance toward that unity that the world may believe."[11] The last phrase says, "that the world may believe."[12] Although the priorities and methods differ, the overall message points to a similar goal—that the world may believe. Again, one can debate the definition of terms and the extent to which parts of the mission of God are (or should be) prioritized. Although there exist undeniable differences in practice, the documentary evidence suggests that the Lausanne Movement and NCC are complementary, if Paul's analogy of the church as the body of Jesus Christ has any power of persuasion.

## THE LAUSANNE MOVEMENT AND INTERFAITH RELATIONS

I feel encouraged about the possibilities of Christian rapprochement between the work of the Lausanne Movement and that of ecumenists, for example, in the Commission on Faith and Order. Admittedly, the respective works of the Lausanne Movement and the Commission on Interfaith Relations is more complex and, thus, more difficult to reconcile. Part of the dilemma, in my opinion, is that there is not agreement among either evangelicals or ecumenists—with whom I am familiar—with regard to how Christians ought to view people of other religions or faiths.

Having attended the Third Lausanne Congress, I know that many with whom I spoke are eminently aware of the need for Christians to be just as well as loving when it comes to evangelization. I also know that there were differences in opinion about the degree to which Christians should engage in dialogue for the sake of mutual understanding and cooperation, rather than for the goal of conversion. The documents of the Lausanne Movement try to communicate care and fairness toward others, without evangelistic agenda. But there is no guarantee that such practices reflect the beliefs and values of all who attended. To be sure, some representatives at the Lausanne Congress opposed dialogue, lest it interfere with evangelization. Moreover, there exist numerous personal and cultural agendas that go far beyond published statements by the Lausanne Movement. After all, the leadership and documents of the Lausanne Movement are entirely voluntary; they have no control over individuals or organizations affiliated with them. The leadership and documents further acknowledge that many representatives at the Lausanne Congress come from churches and denominations affiliated with the World Council of Churches and National Council of Churches, so there is no overt competition between the aforementioned ecumenical organizations.

With regard to how Christians view those of other faiths or religions, there is not always agreement among representatives of the World Council of Churches and National Council of Churches. One way to illustrate these differences can be found in the book by Paul Knitter entitled *Introducing Theologies of Religions*. Knitter develops four models with regard to how Christians view people of other faiths or religions. They are as follows:

1. *Replacement Model* ("Only One True Religion"): "In the final analysis, Christianity is meant to replace all other religions....In the end—or, as soon as possible—God wants there to be only one religion, God's religion: Christianity. If the other religions have any value at all, it is only a provisional value."

2. *Fulfillment Model* ("The One Fulfills the Many"): "The model for a Christian theology of religions that we explore in this part represents a move from seeing Christianity as the 'replacement' to the 'fulfillment' of other religions.... They believe that other religions are of value, that God is to be found in them, that Christians need to dialogue with them and not just preach to them."

3. *Mutuality Model* ("Many True Religions Called to Dialogue"): "[T]he statement that Christianity is not the only true religion is 'good news'....If the Fulfillment Model usually landed more heavily on the side of Jesus' particularity, in this Mutuality Model the greater weight will fall on the side of God's universal love and presence in other religions."

4. *Acceptance Model* ("Many True Religions: So Be It"): "What we are calling the Acceptance Model thinks it can do a better job at this balancing act....It does so not by holding up the superiority of any one religion, nor by searching for that common something that makes them all valid, but by accepting the real diversity of all faiths."[13]

The majority of Christians in church history follow the first model—the Replacement Model. This is true of most evangelically oriented Christian traditions. Nowadays, it may not always be considered the most politically correct way to view people from other faiths or religions, but it is thought to do justice to biblical teachings, if not also the greater part of historic Christianity.

Some Christians may actually feel threatened by the other models listed above. It is like the proverbial slippery-slope argument: Once you allow for some diversity or pluralistic view of truth among religions of the world, then how can you prevent yourself from sliding into a type of relativism, which sacrifices Jesus' claim to represent "the way, and the truth, and the life" (John 14:6)? This fear is especially pronounced in a world progressively thought of as postmodern, wherein longstanding views of the legitimation of truth are challenged.

Despite the criticism of exclusiveness and intolerance, evangelical Christians need not feel alone about the fact that, largely speaking, they reflect the Replacement Model. Indeed, Knitter argues that even the World Council of Churches affirms this model in its official statements.[14] Although the WCC affirms interfaith dialogue, it does not stray far from historic Christianity. Knitter says:

> Conversations between the Gospel and other religious paths may find points of similarity, but ultimately any similarities would give way to a more fundamental dissimilarity, or what was called discontinuity. Replacement, understood generally as total replacement, has the final word.[15]

In some WCC documents, members seem to be pushing beyond the borders of the Replacement Model to a hybrid of other models above. Far more might say so in person. But nothing official has been changed, according to Knitter. The WCC still affirms the Replacement Model in its official documents.

Even from the perspective of the Replacement Model, increased dialogue, understanding, appreciation, support, and collaboration is achievable, especially in issues of mutual concern (e.g., ending poverty, advocacy for social ethics). Indeed, it is desirable in an increasingly small, yet inextricably connected, world. For example, some evangelically oriented Christians advocate a Partial Replacement Model of interfaith relations. Clark Pinnock, for one, advocates a more inclusive view of the relationship between Jesus and other religions. He emphasizes the person and work of the Holy Spirit as universally present and active in the lives of everyone, Christian and non-Christian. Pinnock goes so far as to say that "God's boundless mercy is a primary truth that cannot be compromised."[16] Thus, Christians must "recognize that God can save outside of the visible boundaries of Christianity."[17]

Not everyone involved with ecumenism and interfaith relations would agree with Knitter's interpretation of official documents by the World Council of Churches and National Council of Churches. Even if Knitter is correct, then they would say that they disagree with the WCC and NCC. In fact, Knitter considers the Replacement Model inadequate for his understanding of Christianity, and in other books argues for a more progressive model.[18] As of now, it is debatable with regard to what the consensus is among Christians around the world. Until noteworthy changes occur in documentation by the WCC and NCC, there is no irreconcilable difference between their beliefs and those stated by the Lausanne Movement with regard to how Christians view people of other faiths or religions.

## EXCLUSIVISM, PLURALISM, AND INCLUSIVISM

Far easier categories with which to think about the relationship between Christians and other faiths or religions are those of exclusivism, pluralism, and inclusivism. Basically speaking, exclusivism reflects the Replacement Model, arguing that no one is saved who does not name the name of Jesus, so to speak (John 14:6; Rom

10:9–17). Second, pluralism is the view that all religions are equally valid, which represents a variation of universalism or universal salvation (1 Cor 15:22; 2 Pet 3:9). It is debatable, of course, whether pluralism represents the Fulfillment Model, Mutuality Model, Acceptance Model, or all of the above. Third, inclusivism is generally understood to mean that people may be saved without explicitly referring to Jesus or the church. Now, this may mean that their salvation is still guaranteed by the atonement of Jesus, but not necessarily. Inclusivism may simply mean any position in between exclusivism and pluralism, which may comprise quite a range of theological viewpoints. Thus, inclusivism provides a great deal of liberty and, perhaps, elusiveness (mystery, paradox, or dialectic), in relating with people of other faiths or religions.

Several verses in the Bible suggest that people may be saved who never heard of Jesus, lived before the time of Jesus, or heard but did not understand the Gospel message of salvation. Paul talks about those who are not given the law; he says that their conscience will either accuse or excuse them from judgment (Rom 2:13–15). God does not want any to perish; God will not condemn people just because they were born at the wrong place or time (1 Tim 2:4; Rev 22:2). It may be that God will, at some time, present the Gospel to all people, even if it occurs after the present life, just as Jesus was reported to have made proclamation to those who had died during the time of Noah (1 Pet 3:18–19).

Historically, prominent Christians and Christian traditions have argued for the possibility that people may be saved in unexpected ways. For example, the Westminster Confession makes a distinction between ordinary and extraordinary means of salvation. Thomas Oden references the Westminster Confession, which "cautiously stated that there is no ordinary possibility of salvation outside the church (XXV.2), leaving extraordinary means to God."[19] Stephen Merrill concurs: "No Orthodox can maintain that all outside the Church are damned. As a personal problem, the answer of the question must be left in the hands of Him 'who desireth not the death of a sinner' but wills 'that all men be saved.'"[20]

In my experience of ecumenical and interfaith relations, people prefer to use the language of exclusivism, pluralism, and inclusivism. Indeed, I prefer to use them as well; they seem simpler and less theologically problematic than Knitter's models. But Knitter challenges us to go deeper into our understanding of the precise relationship between Christians (and Christianity) and those of other faiths or religions. It may be that the categories of exclusivism, pluralism, and inclusivism are more serviceable—practically as well as conceptually—for Christians in general, and for advocates of ecumenism and interfaith relations in particular. But Knitter reminds us that, regardless of apparent differences, there continue to be striking similarities among the majority Christian groups in the world, regardless of whether their ministerial priorities favor interfaith dialogue or evangelism.

## BLESSING THE NATIONS

How do I view people of other faiths or religions, or how do I—as an evangelical—reconcile my evangelicalism with my concern for interfaith relations as well as for ecumenism? I do not have a systematic theology that works out all the biblical, historical, and conceptual kinks. Be that as it may, let me share the trajectory on which I am headed, and the starting points that are of help to me. Although I may not have yet perfected the theory per se, there is method to my belief—so to speak—that evangelism along with ecumenism and interfaith relations are complementary, rather than woefully incompatible.

Let me begin by talking about the stated tasks of the Commission on Interfaith Relations, which seem to me to be imperative affirmations for Christians and churches. They are:

In partnership with NCC member communions, the Interfaith Relations Commission will

- articulate a Christian theology for Interfaith Relations

- provide educational materials to churches

- train church members in interfaith relational skills

- create ecumenical opportunities for relations with communities of other religious traditions[21]

The stated outcomes for these tasks include

- seeking peace with justice
- fighting poverty
- encouraging the proper stewardship of planet Earth[22]

It is difficult to imagine any Christian or church disagreeing with these outcomes, though in actuality some do. Even at the Lausanne Congress, there was debate over a number of theological issues—the aforementioned outcomes notwithstanding. Other issues at the Lausanne Congress included whether there should be more (or fewer) women in public positions of leadership, whether plenary addresses should be in the speaker's primary language (rather than English), whether issues of social justice should become more (or less) a concern of the Lausanne Movement, and so on. The Lausanne Congress was not without debate, as one would expect among any Christians, at least, historically speaking. Also debated was the degree to which Christians should engage in dialogue with people from other faiths or religions, without necessarily being for the goal of conversion. To be sure, there were differences of opinion. Consensus was not reached. But representatives were free to dialogue, and I expect that such issues will continue to be debated in the future.

I expect further that debate about issues related to interfaith relations, dialogue with people from other faiths or religions, evangelism, and other issues will continue to be debated by members of the Lausanne Movement as well as by those affiliated with the World Council of Churches and National Council of Churches. Most theological and ethical issues of import, historically speaking, have taken centuries to resolve, if ever. Thus, it seems presumptuous of Christians today to expect immediate resolutions to questions and concerns that exist. But progress can be made.

I find the concept of "blessing the nations" a helpful biblical reference—a heuristic (or interpretive) tool—for advocating why Christians should be concerned about interfaith relations, and in particular, interfaith dialogue, without the goal of conversion. The concept of "blessing" goes back to Abraham. God promised to make a great nation through the offspring of Abraham (Gen 12:2). Thereafter, God told Abraham that he and his progeny—physical and spiritual—would be a blessing to everyone: "I will bless those who bless you, and the one who curses you I will curse; and in you all the families of the earth shall be blessed" (Gen 12:3). Abraham was, not only to be a father of one nation, but of many nations: "I will make you exceedingly fruitful; and I will make nations of you, and kings shall come from you" (Gen 17:6; cf. 17:4–5). Of course, one of those nations presumably arises due to the progeny of Ishmael (Gen 17:20), but it includes much more. Through Abraham, "all the nations of the earth shall be blessed" (Gen 18:18). Moreover, by Abraham's "offspring shall all the nations of the earth gain blessing for themselves, because you [Abraham] have obeyed my voice" (Gen 22:18).

Of course, there is more than one way to interpret the aforementioned passages in the Book of Genesis. In what ways might the nations be blessed? Rob Barrett, for example, discusses three rabbinic interpretations of Abrahamic blessing: Some place more emphasis on the role of God; others place more emphasis on how nations ought to emulate Abraham; still others emphasize the need to convert the nations.[23] The apostle Paul continues the theme of blessing nations when he speaks of Abraham in the context of law and faith:

> Just as Abraham "believed God, and it was reckoned to him as righteousness," so, you see, those who believe are the descendants of Abraham. And the scripture, foreseeing that God would justify the Gentiles by faith, declared the gospel beforehand to Abraham, saying, "All the Gentiles shall be blessed in you." For this reason, those who believe are blessed with Abraham who believed. (Gal 3:6–9)

Of course, Paul considered Jesus the "offspring" of Abraham through whom the culmination of God's blessings would occur (Gal 3:16). The apostle Peter echoes this theme in his preaching. Speaking in Solomon's Portico, Peter said, "You Israelites...You are the descendents of the prophets and of the covenant that God gave to your ancestors, saying to Abraham, 'And in your descendants all the families of the earth shall be blessed.' When God raised up his servant, he sent him first to you, to bless you by turning each of you from your wicked ways" (Acts 3:12, 25–26). Although the blessing begins with the Israelites, they extend to all nations, that is, to all families of the earth.

Barrett takes a rather narrow approach to understanding the concept of blessing the nations. Although he says that the first thing Christians must keep in mind is that they are to "live obediently," Barrett argues that Christians should also "serve God by presenting him [Jesus] to all the nations as the one true God."[24] However, other interpreters of these Abrahamic passages conceive of the theme of blessing the nations more broadly. For example, David Smith considers it a call to be more understanding and embracing of those who are culturally different;[25] some organizations exist to embody an "Abrahamic alliance," which "is a movement of faithful Jews, Christians and Muslims who are deeply committed to loving the God of our father Abraham with all our heart, soul, mind, and strength, and loving our neighbor as ourselves."[26] Still others consider the blessing of nations a call to interfaith relations and dialogue. On behalf of the VI Plenary Assembly of the Catholic Biblical Federation, Adel Theodore Khoury wrote an article entitled "Abraham—A Blessing for All Nations according to the Jewish, Christian and Islamic Traditions." He sees great potential in looking to Abraham as the starting point for interreligious dialogue, at least, amongst Judaism, Christianity, and Islam. Khoury says:

> Membership in the posterity of Abraham can foster an open encounter between the faithful of the three Abrahamic religions. By relating to his faith and to his obedience to the commands of God, even amidst trials and tribulations, one can find in him a common point of reference which embraces all men of goodwill, open to faith and disposed to embrace the good. This attitude is capable of broadening the horizons of believers so as to make room for all human beings and all peoples and to make them witnesses of the blessing God granted to Abraham and that he entrusted to him for all the nations of the earth.
>
> Rather than being an object of dispute and wrangling between the three faiths that claim him, Abraham can become the initiator and the guarantor of a serious dialogue

between them and of a fruitful cooperation for the good of all humanity.

For we live today in a world which, in the context of pervasive globalization, is no longer and can no longer be the world that some individuals can confiscate for their profit at the expense of others. Our present is the present of all of us together, and our future is the future of all of us together. We must finally stop treating one other like adversaries; we must succeed in making ourselves partners of one another; and we must strive to create between us an atmosphere of trust that will render us capable of becoming—if God wills it—one another's friends. This will lead us to practice a universal solidarity with each other and all of us together with respect to all human beings, the solidarity of all with respect to all.[27]

The potential for dialogue among people from different faiths or religions may (and will) extend far beyond those of Judaism, Christianity, and Islam. The blessing may extend to all types of peoples and nations, faiths, and religions. Admittedly, some Christians interpret the blessing of nations as a call to evangelism, but not all do. Certainly, if Christians believe that they are called to be a blessing to nations, such blessings would most likely include evangelism. But being a blessing to others might include a great deal more. It may also include helping others with their physical, social, political, economic, and other needs. Such care and advocacy would not exclude their spiritual wellbeing, nor would it narrowly focus on it.

Would evangelism and missions continue to occur? Yes. Might dialogue occur, and not just for the sake of evangelism? Yes. How? Blessing the nations may include both dialogue and evangelism. In fact, one may expect both to occur. Not every dialogue about one's basic beliefs, values, and practices need to be for the sake of evangelism. Likewise, dialoguing cannot help but include some statements about the Gospel of Jesus Christ and of conversion, since they are inextricably bound up with Scripture and church history. In true dialogue, people do not share only polite chitchat that does not extend to the depths of their most cherished beliefs and values. Eventually, Christians would want to know what constitutes conversion in other faiths or religious traditions; they would want to listen sincerely to the cases made for alternative religiosity. If true dialogue occurs, then Christians would also be expected to share what they believe about sin, repentance, faith, baptism, and other aspects related to salvation. It is unreasonable to expect that authentic dialogue would preclude any discussion of conversion or comparable religious experiences.

## MAKE DISCIPLES OF ALL NATIONS

Interestingly (ironically?), "blessing" or care for the nations figures centrally in the so-called Great Commission in Matthew 28:16–20. In other writings, I define evangelical Christians as "People of the Great Commission," and how making a connection between "blessing the nations" and "making disciples" is crucial, at least, to evangelical Christians.[28] Technically, it is not to individual people to whom Christians are sent to minister; it is to nations. They are to "go" to "all nations," "make disciples," "baptizing," and "teaching them to obey everything that I [Jesus] have commanded you" (Matt 28:19–20). Although Christians in general and evangelical Christians in particular tend to interpret this latter passage as a charge to evangelize, the precise wording of evangelization does not appear. It is assumed that, if disciples are to be made, then there needs to be converts. Fair enough. But far more emphasis is placed upon making disciples, than upon evangelism and missions. In addition, more emphasis is placed upon nations than individuals. Could it be that the Great Commission can be viewed as a supplement to blessing the nations?

I believe that there are times for everything, as the Book of Ecclesiastes suggests ( 3:1–8). There are times to evangelize and do missions, and there are times for dialogue. The two ministries can complement one another. Indeed, those who are zealous for evangelism and missions can also be seen as complementary to those who are zealous for dialogue. Zeal in itself does not offend those who are not Christians. Would we not expect those from other religious traditions to have their zealots? Thus, zeal in itself is not the problem; it is how people express that zeal. None of the aforementioned groups of Christians intend to offend or act unjustly toward anyone; instead, they try to do what is loving.

As a rationale for embracing other nations, Christians appeal to the logic of "loving one's neighbor as oneself" (Mark 12:28–31). It is a tried and true argument for almost any kind of outcome.[29] But it is not as precise a biblical starting point for relating Christianly toward those who are not Christians, or are indeed adherents to other faiths and religions. Certainly, loving one's neighbor as oneself reinforces the concept of blessing the nations. In fact, I would argue that much of what Scripture says reinforces how Christians are to influence far more than individuals spiritually. They are to influence nations as well and also people's physical, emotional, and social well-being. Do these considerations help us at all to understand with greater appreciation and application of Jesus' repeated references to the reign of God—the "kingdom of God?"

## CONCLUSION

The work of ecumenism and interfaith relations need not be seen as contradictory or in opposition to the work of evangelism, reflective of the Lausanne Movement. Surely their respective beliefs, values, and practices seem to exist, at times, at cross purposes. But each stream or branch of God's mission in the world may be seen as complementary, reflective of the unity and diversity represented in Paul's analogy of the church (universal) as the body of Jesus Christ (1 Cor 12:12–31).

Even the distinctive work of interfaith relations need not be seen as contradictory or in opposition to the work of evangelism. If there is to be openness and honesty at the deepest levels of interreligious dialogue, then there needs to occur times when sharing occurs without the goal of evangelism. Likewise, if there is to be genuine openness and honesty, then there also needs to occur times when sharing includes the presentation of respective views of salvation, enlightenment, or self-actualization, even when said with great earnestness and zeal.

If Christians believe that the nations are blessed through Abraham and the God of Abraham, then the blessings need to include more than spiritual blessings. Scripture talks about spiritual blessings, but it also talks about a great deal more. In order for the *whole* Gospel of Christianity to meet the *whole* needs of the *whole* world, then there needs to be a greater understanding, appreciation, and implementation of the complementarity of the works of evangelism, ecumenism, interfaith relations, and other dimensions of the Gospel of Jesus Christ. Tendencies to narrow or reduce the Gospel to particular concerns and ministries, regardless of their cruciality to the Gospel, distort the totality of God's mission for Christians and churches in the world. Focusing on the wholeness of God's mission and the ministries of Christians and churches will help them to complement and cooperate with one another so that "all the nations of the earth shall be blessed" (Gen 18:18).

## NOTES

1. There are exceptions, the most notable being participants in the Wesleyan Theological Society who are members of the United Methodist Church and of the Church of God (centered in Anderson, Indiana). Both of these denominations are members of the National Council of Churches, and they send denominational representatives to serve in the Commission on Faith and Order.

2. I do not make a distinction between the words *evangelization* and *evangelism*. The Lausanne Movement uses the word *evangelization,* which is broadly used by Christians and churches around the world. Some dislike the word *evangelism* because they have an aversion to any "-ism," considering it contrary to biblical, historic Christianity.

3. Richard Foster, *Streams of Living Water: Celebrating the Great Traditions of Christian Faith* (San Francisco: HarperSanFrancisco, 1998).

4. Don Thorsen, *An Exploration of Christian Theology* (Peabody, MA: Hendrickson, 2008), 304–6, 312.

5. Notable Christian organizations include the World Evangelical Alliance, National Association of Evangelicals, InterVarsity, and numerous evangelistic and missions organizations, such as the Billy Graham Crusade. Billy Graham was one of the founders of the initial Lausanne Congress, as was John Stott, who was affiliated with InterVarsity.

6. Fuller Theological Seminary, which is the largest seminary in the world, was one of more visible academic institutions at the Lausanne Congress due, in part, to its School of World Missions.

7. The magazine *Christianity Today*, whose founding editor was Billy Graham, helped to plan and sponsor the first Lausanne Congress. It and other worldwide Christian media organizations continued their support and coverage in Cape Town.

8. See Willem Adolph Visser't Hooft, quoted by Colin W. Williams, *John Wesley's Theology Today* (New York: Abingdon, 1960), 10. The actual typology Visser't Hooft set forth included church-centered, Erasmian, and Pietist type ecumenism.

9. The discussion of evangelization and proselytism is complex, and its complexity depends upon how terms are defined. For further information about the topic, see "The Challenge of Proselytism and the Calling to Common Witness," Joint Working Group between the World Council of Churches and the Roman Catholic Church, World Council of Churches Web site, 25 September 1995, available at http://www.oikoumene.org/resources/documents/wcc-commissions/joint-working-group-between-the-roman-catholic-church-and-the-wcc/challenge-of-proselytism.html (accessed July 16, 2012).

10. "Manila Manifesto," Lausanne Movement, 1989, available at http://www.lausanne.org/en/documents/manila-manifesto.html (accessed July 16, 2012).

11. "Mission Statement," Commission on Faith and Order, National Council of Churches, available at http://www.ncccusa.org/unity/missionfo.html (accessed July 16, 2012).

12. I know that there are differences of opinion among those in the NCC with regard to how the Mission Statement should be interpreted. Most with whom I have spoken affirm that the work of Faith and Order as well as the NCC includes proclamation of the Gospel of Jesus Christ. However, others have argued that the fruit of "visible unity" is that "that the world may believe," but properly speaking, the work of both Faith and Order and the NCC is visible unity.

13. Paul F. Knitter, *Introducing Theologies of Religions* (Maryknoll, NY: Orbis Books, 2002), 19, 63, 109, 173.

14. By implication, Knitter identifies the National Council of Churches with the Replacement Model.

15. Knitter, *Introducing Theologies*, 43.

16. Clark Pinnock, *A Wideness in God's Mercy: The Finality of Jesus Christ in a World of Religions* (Grand Rapids: Zondervan, 1992), quoted by Knitter, *Introducing Theologies*, 47.

17. Ibid.

18. For example, see Paul F. Knitter, *One Earth Many Religions: Multifaith Dialogue and Global Responsibility* (Maryknoll, NY: Orbis Books, 1995); and *Without Buddha I Could Not Be a Christian* (London: Oneworld Publications, 2009).

19. Thomas C. Oden, *Life in the Spirit, Systematic Theology: Volume Three* (New York: HarperSanFrancisco, 1992), 328.

20. Stephen Merrill, quoted by Oden, *Life in the Spirit*, 328.

21. "Mission Statement," Interfaith Relations Commission Handbook, National Council of Churches, September 2005, available at http://www.ncccusa.org/pdfs/IRChandbook2008.pdf (accessed July 16, 2012).

22. Ibid.

23. Rob Barrett, "Abraham and the Blessing of the Nations: Jewish and Christian Interpretations," 2–8, in coffeewithbarretts.com, 3 July 2001, available at http://coffeewithbarretts.com/writings/AbrahamBlessingNations.pdf (accessed July 16, 2012).

24. Ibid., 8.

25. David I. Smith, "How Not to Bless the Nations," *Perspectives: A Journal of Reformed Thought,* December 2005, available at http://www.rca.org/page.aspx?pid=3059 (accessed July 16, 2012).

26. Abrahamic Alliance International Web site, Who We Are, available at http://www.abrahamicalliance.org/about/ (accessed July 16, 2012).

27. Adel Theodore Khoury, "Abraham - A Blessing for All Nations according to the Jewish, Christian and Islamic Traditions," Catholic Biblical Federation, 4 September 2002, available at http://www.c-b-f.org/start.php?CONTID=05_02_05_03_01_00&LANG=en (accessed July 16, 2012).

28. See Steve Wilkens and Don Thorsen, *Everything You Know about Evangelicals Is Wrong (Well, Almost Everything): An Insider's Look at Myths and Realities* (Grand Rapids: Baker, 2010), 198.

29. John Fletcher comes to mind in his book *Situation Ethics*. Although Fletcher has, at times, been caricatured, many think that his Christian ethical theory allows far too much human subjectivity in ethical decision making.

# 14

# CHRISTIAN SCIENCE CHRISTIANS' HEALING PRACTICE

## A Contribution to Christian Pilgrimage

*Shirley Paulson*

In an ecumenical setting, Christians define their pilgrimage in a variety of ways, but the power that draws them together is the agreement that Christ's salvific work is the destination. Whether their pilgrimage takes place in an annual *via crucis,* a private communion with God, a trip to visit the Shrine of Our Lady of Guadalupe, or singing a congregational hymn, Christians are engaged in the work of salvation.[1] Those who are conscious of their pilgrimage as such also readily admit that the journey itself provides opportunity for moral and spiritual significance. I would like to propose that the practice of Christian healing is an overlooked, but important form of pilgrimage. Properly understood, it is a transformative aspect of Christian pilgrimage. It involves a change of heart, a deeper relationship with God, and more spiritual thought; physical change is merely an outward manifestation of the spiritual transformation.

I have noticed that those who heal in Christ's name, not only encounter the presence of the Holy Spirit, but also, through their healing works, draw closer to others who experience the same Spirit. Healing was never intended to be a source of denominational or theological competition, because it is a purely spiritual activity that patterns the work of the master. It is a direct means for participating in the history of salvation, because each healing experience involves a genuine touch of Christ in the individual's life.

Successful healers are lifted and strengthened by the Holy Spirit, and they are usually quick to acknowledge the power of redemption or blessing beyond their personal abilities or knowledge. Although the followers of Jesus throughout the past two millennia have scattered into different regions and followed different paths for their ministry, their ability to heal originated in the teachings of Jesus and the power of the Holy Spirit.

Current denominational perspectives on Christian healing are jewels to be exposed to the light and celebrated, not because they stand in solitary light, but because they indicate the multifaceted aspects of Christ's presence in the human condition. Michael Kinnamon, Secretary General of the National Council of Churches, argues that "a denominational name is a wonderful adjective but an idolatrous noun." Explaining further, he claims "one should not be a Methodist. You are Methodist Christians. One is not a Presbyterian. You are Presbyterian Christians...Insofar as they are vital aspects of renewal absorbed into the whole of the church, they are glorious parts of the tradition and I celebrate them."[2] In order to support my claim that Christian healing is an important aspect of pilgrimage, wherein we come together in Christ, I will describe in fuller detail my own healing experience from the perspective of a "Christian Science Christian."

As understood by Mary Baker Eddy, the founder of the Christian Science denomination, healing was never intended as a unique secret belonging to a small sect. Rather, she thought of it as a rediscovery of the early Christian practice, accomplishing its purpose in the same way it did for the first Christians. It was a gift to humanity, as are all genuine elements of Christianity, such as the forgiveness of sin and the preaching of the good news. Therefore, the Christian Science Christians' healing practice today is not only a distinct contribution to everyone on pilgrimage toward Christ, but it bestows practical blessings for the world.

This particular form of Christian healing unites with all other Christian practices, insofar as Jesus Christ is called upon as our savior. It supports the Christian commitment to relieve oppression and suffering. It bears practical witness to the in-breaking action of the goodness of God. And its approach to questions of theodicy has the potential to break theological logjams. All these claims can be illustrated with glimpses at my own healing experiences.[3]

## THEODICY

When I was a teenager, a rather serious infection shot up through my leg from a blistered toe. I called upon a Christian Science practitioner. (Now perhaps I might call him a "Christian Science Christian practitioner!") He gently spoke to me of the spiritual order of God's kingdom, helping me recall some spiritual ideals we had discussed together before that moment of need. For instance, "perfect Love"—or God—was right there with me, he reminded me, casting out all my fear. The unquestionable consistency of God's goodness and power assured me that God wanted me to be safe and was able to comfort me.

The accidental mishap that inflamed the blister on my foot was not enough to undermine God's authority and capacity to care for me. I began to feel at peace quickly, and then a moment of deep gratitude came over me. As I listened to this man's calm voice, I began humbly to admit God's "ways [were] higher than [my] ways" (Isa 55:9).[4] It made sense to me that God, the creator of the universe, would know more than people knew. Our human minds could theorize and formulate opinions, but only the God that created us would know what is certain truth about us. The God who organizes the order of numbers, who inspires a baby to smile, and who never fails to love, was more important to me than the problem with my leg. I became very close to God's tender love and mentally moved away from the trouble.

Within a few moments, we finished the conversation and I went into the living room to tell my mother about it. In that short time, the pain had completely lifted, and the discoloration was fully removed. There never was another symptom related to the infection.

The simple, rather childlike trust I had in the goodness of God during that brief phone conversation raises natural questions concerning God's relationship with human suffering. Had God caused the suffering? Where was God when I got hurt? Does God permit pain and danger? Is God capricious, helping some but not others? And, on a larger scale, is God helpless in the face of a holocaust or tsunami? These questions lead to the basic problem of theodicy: how is the goodness of God vindicated in view of the existence of evil, large or small?

In a 1987 article, "Theodicy After Auschwitz and the Reality of God," Stephen Gottschalk addressed the question squarely. He refutes a common assumption of both classic theodicy and its critique in process theology, namely that God and evil coexist.

> [They both] presume that the experience of evil is just what it appears to be: an unchallenged reality against which other realities are to be measured. Yet is the same factual quality, a quality of unmistakable authenticity and concreteness, attributed to humanity's experience of God?
>
> ...Paradoxically, the usual statement of the problem of theodicy implicitly assumes that there can be no God-experience, or that it can be dismissed as so "subjective" that it is extraneous to any theological discussion. Accordingly, the empirical reality of evil is held to be indubitable but that of God questionable. On the other hand, when an individual does have an intense God-experience, the problem of evil begins to recede as a stumbling block to faith.[5]

Gottschalk effectively redefines the problem of theodicy by calling into question the basis on which we make sense of two irreconcilable realities. The Bible is full of instances in which God's infinite goodness and omnipotent grace are proclaimed and celebrated. The Bible also records the suffering of humanity in vivid detail. On the one hand, a dualistic view, adopting the existence of both God and evil in the same sense of the term, results in a loss of divine sovereignty and goodness. On the other hand, as Gottschalk points out, Mary Baker Eddy's "rigorous Augustinian and Puritan defense of God's absolute sovereignty and goodness...refuses to ascribe evil in any form to a God who is wholly good."[6]

Eddy's response to theodicy, then, is that God, who is both infinite good and wholly omnipotent, is incapable of producing evil. "It would be contrary to our highest ideas of God," she writes, "to suppose Him capable of first arranging law and causation so as to bring about certain evil results, and then punishing the helpless victims of His volition for doing what they could not avoid doing."[7]

Another significant aspect of Gottschalk's critique on modern notions of theodicy is the role of human experience. When I suffered pain from an infection, one could say my "reality" included a no-God experience. I was conscious of fear, of pain, of material laws, and God was far from my thought. But the prayer roused me to an intense and present God-experience. I was close to God; I dropped my preoccupation with the material drama; I trusted God; I felt loved by God. Gottschalk's description is apt: "when an individual does have an intense God-experience, the problem of evil begins to recede as a stumbling block to faith."[8] Not only did I lose my fear and my sense of trouble, but I also had no further sense of suffering. There was no infection in my mind or body.

## JESUS CHRIST, OUR SAVIOR

Another experience illustrates in more detail the actual saving action of Christ during a healing process. I developed a severe lung condition with prolonged, persistent coughing spells, and put myself in voluntary quarantine at home. I prayed, as was my custom, but the condition worsened. Within a few weeks, I had become bedridden and then shortly after, I was nearly incapacitated. My husband, who had always supported my prayers for healing, became alarmed. After work one evening, when he found me dangerously ill, he asked to take me to the hospital. I resisted, because my experiences in healing have inspired more confidence in Christ, my savior, than in doctors who do not know my soul. But the Christian Science practitioner who was praying for me this time inquired whether I had asked God about this decision. I had not.

So I prayed for guidance but was surprised with the response I heard: "Do you love your husband?" The question startled me, as it made me realize how I had been excluding him from my prayers, distancing myself from him. I was appalled at my uncaring and unloving attitude, and I repented fervently. I yearned to do everything in my power to love him, so I decided for his sake that I would go to the hospital in the morning. It never occurred to me to expect healing in the hospital, because I believed the situation would ultimately only be resolved through Christ, my only real savior. No doctor would be able to discern my spiritual concerns, but I did want to find some means for consoling my husband. From that moment forward, my prayer shifted my focus from self-centered concerns to a renewed desire to love better. God's presence was very clear to me throughout the night, and by early morning, I realized the pain was receding. I regained enough strength to walk downstairs, and I was ready to eat a normal breakfast. Before we could even leave for the hospital in the morning, the entire illness had drained away. I spent the day fixing up our home and making it a place of welcome for my husband.

What had my savior done? On the basis of the previous discussion on theodicy, one might be tempted to hastily conclude no savior would be needed in a theology claiming only the reality of good. On the contrary, the need for a savior becomes most apparent when the contrast between painful suffering and the desired consciousness of God's all-ness is acute. When it is easier to doubt God's presence than to dismiss the intensity of suffering, we *need* to be saved. When we are unable to discern and cherish the infinitude of God's goodness through our mortal weaknesses, we are utterly dependent on the power of the savior to awaken and guide us to the light. The lesson from theodicy, then, is to welcome the savior's action affirming the constancy of God's goodness. Even when we feel enveloped in darkness, the work of the savior is to bring us to God's absolute goodness.

Mary Baker Eddy uses an analogy with the earth and the sun to illustrate the human need to change perspective. "The earth's diurnal rotation is invisible to the physical eye," she writes, "and the sun seems to move from east to west, instead of the earth from west to east. Until rebuked by clearer views of the everlasting facts, this false testimony of the eye deluded the judgment and induced false conclusions."[9] From our position of standing on the earth, observing the sun, we perceive a distorted relationship between earth and sun. If we could position ourselves to observe the earth from the point of view of the sun, we would discern the correct relationship, that is, the earth revolving around the sun. Unable to view it properly on our own senses, we need the assistance of astronomy to understand the correct relationship between earth and sun.

In like manner, as we suffering humans attempt to know God from our finite point of view, we perceive a distorted relationship between God and us. That is, we tend either to make God in our own image and likeness—vengeful, weak, or fickle—or else we cannot help seeing ourselves as grossly distorted images of a good God. If there were some way to reverse our points of view, and observe ourselves from God's infinite perspective, it would be apparent that God sees us as God made us, in God's image and likeness. God, who is not weak, sinning, sick, or dead, beholds the image as sinless, healthy and whole, as in Genesis, where God "saw everything that he had made, and indeed, it was very good" (1:31).

As in the astronomical example, we are unable to properly view God's creation (or the *real* relationship) with our own senses, and we need the assistance of the savior to do so. This savior moves our flawed, finite perceptions to the opposite perspective of infinite God. Eddy spoke of this movement of thought as the work of Christ—or God's word—speaking to human consciousness, enabling it to behold and experience the good and health created by God.

During the evening of my healing, I remember the moment I surrendered to the guidance of Christ. I was ready to let go of my self-absorption, my willfulness, and my concerns for my own body. It was an influence beyond myself, because until that time, I had not even taken into consideration the fears and struggles of my husband. Now I wanted to love above all else, and this is the indication that Christ is present. Like moving from earth to the sun's perspective to discern the right relationship between these two bodies, I responded to the call to move from my earthly (self) perspective to the consciousness of divine love. I cried tears of repentance and eagerly abandoned my self-absorption, even before I saw the assurance of God's will and power to bless the whole universe. The "God-experience" had become more real to me than the absence of God. At that moment, I was well.

# NEITHER GNOSTICISM NOR MARTYRDOM

Christian Science Christian healing bears practical witness to the in-breaking action of the goodness of God. Prayer draws us into awareness of that presence, and it discerns the evidence that "the Word [indeed] became flesh" (John 1:14).[10] It is celebrated, not only for its compassionate release from human suffering, but also for its affirmation of the scriptural promise in Luke, "...nor will they say, 'Look, here it is!' or 'There it is!' For, in fact, the kingdom of God is among you" (17:21). The earlier discussion on theodicy highlights the theological foundation for healing based on God who is an absolute sovereignty, wholly good, and including no evil. It includes no attempt to justify two irreconcilable truths: God and *not*-God. Or, as Gottschalk summarized it:

> Jesus brought the new reality of the Kingdom into the midst of present experience, obviating the very question of theodicy by refusing to concede the existence of a realm in which God's active supremacy did not demand to be acknowledged. That he contested the grounds of *present* experience for the Kingdom of God is evident in his own statement of the meaning of his healing works: "If I by the finger of God cast out demons, then the Kingdom of God is come unto you."[11]

However, claiming the existence of a spiritual reality contradicting a sensually perceived world can evoke images of Gnostic heresy.[12] Some important distinctions should be noted. Whereas Irenaeus and other church fathers claimed that Gnostics hated the body and sought release from the material world in order to dwell in an aeon far from the place where mortals dwelt, a Christian Science perspective welcomes the presence of Christ in our present human condition. Humans are comforted, and bodies are healed as Jesus healed them; bodies are neither disdained nor discarded.

Another significant distinction is the Christian Scientists' acknowledged need for a savior. If Gnostics claimed that bodies and earth only *seemed* to exist while they were privileged to dwell in the spiritual realm, they would have no occasion for a savior to save them from that which does not exist. A Christian Science perspective includes the necessity of a savior until every last vestige of opposition to God's sovereignty is destroyed. The struggle for salvation does not negate the present reality of God's omnipotence and goodness; it merely indicates the human need for help, for a savior who saves from the limitations of human consciousness.

Human participation in salvation is not an easy task. As Jesus said, "If any want to become my followers, let them deny themselves and take up their cross and follow me" (Mark 8:34). According to Christian Science teachings, taking up the cross involves such difficult tasks as rebuking self-righteousness, pride, fear, greed, and everything else that would separate us from the pure love of God. But these impediments to Godlikeness are worth the effort to denounce, because cross-bearing is strengthening.

When cases of healing are not progressing properly, both the healer and patient naturally strive to take up their cross and follow even more faithfully the life of Christ. Christian Science Christians are like all other Christians when they seek the savior: at times, we all feel the grace of God leading us through the troubled waters; at other times, we are bitterly disappointed in our mortal failings.

Despite my years of spiritual progress and multiple healings for myself and others, I struggled a few years ago with a worsening case of eczema that did not yield to prayers. I was well aware that there are many healings of eczema through Christian Science treatment documented in the Christian Science magazines, but I was facing the stubbornness of my own condition. I had lost mobility and was no longer able to fulfill my family obligations.

While students of Christian Science, in general, do not choose to consult a doctor, there are no church rules on such matters. In this situation, I ultimately decided to meet with a doctor and comply with his prescription, primarily in order to be a support to my family. My decision represents neither an ecclesial nor theological mandate but rather an honest assessment of my current spiritual strength. Other Christian Scientists might well have made a different choice based on a variety of spiritual perspectives. In the account of Jesus' disciples asking Jesus why they were unable to heal a case that he successfully healed, Jesus replied that their faith was "too little" (Greek: *oligopistia*) (Matt 17:20).[13] A Christian Science perspective on this incident is that Jesus did not condemn his disciples;

but as in other instances, he encouraged their growing understanding of his teachings and his spiritual practice.

Regardless of my present capacity to discern and obey the spiritual laws of God, I am certain that I will ultimately conform to them. Troubled human experiences invite a deeper experience with God's love, and I welcome the lessons learned, even if they are interrupted with setbacks. God is with us through every valley experience.

Another factor in my decision was my consideration of some of the disturbing issues I find in conventional medicine. The never-ending promises of material theories tend to manipulate those who trust them, to the point of spiraling dependency on another god. Also, the inequity with which medicine favors the wealthiest people in the world is inconsistent with God's abundant love for all. Fundamentally, the greatest problem with medicine is that research and analysis of matter never serves to improve one's relationship with God.

And yet, I also contemplated the early martyrs and considered how far I was willing to go in sacrificing temporal comfort in my pursuit of knowing and following God. An extreme position of opposing something that can provide temporary assistance is not always wisdom. God's healing presence is marked by gentleness, not cruelty. As when the ancient persecution lifted, I too was willing to wait for the time of greater strength. I considered the more difficult decisions confronting the early Christian martyrs. Was it better to abandon their families and win the glories of heavenly promises? Or should they hold their Christian loyalty privately in their hearts (thus avoiding inevitable death) in order to remain useful to their families? I decided on the temporary cooperation with a "lesser god" in order to better serve others. In that decision, I was grateful for the support from the doctor, but I also reaffirmed my loyalty to God.

Keeping all these theological perspectives in mind, the overriding guidance for my decision came from the commandments of Jesus—to love God with my whole heart and to love my neighbor as myself (Mark 12:33). My condition had made increasing demands on my family, and the physician was confident that his treatment would enable me to return to normalcy quickly.[14] It appeared to be the most loving decision for my family's sake. But I wondered if this kind of assistance in medicine would temper my obedience to the first commandment—loving God with my whole being. Would I allow it to become a distraction from my growth God-ward? Only in my private communing with God could I attest to my fidelity, and I am satisfied that I have been able to continue to progress with my spiritual healing works since that time.

## THE CHRISTIAN COMMITMENT TO RELIEVE OPPRESSION AND SUFFERING

The motives for healing one's own body cannot be selfish ones. About nine years ago, I began to feel symptoms of arthritis in my knee and finger joints. The difficulties increased very gradually, so I paid little attention to it at first. Finally, it became clear that this kind of disease would only worsen if left alone, and I needed to confront it immediately and thoroughly. As I began to pray, it dawned on me that my situation was not a private one. Many people suffer from arthritis, and it is a kind of illness that symbolizes oppression, pain, and endless suffering. It represents helplessness and hopelessness. I thought of how frequently I have praised God for sending the Messiah who promised to "let the oppressed go free" (Luke 4:18).[15]

Now it occurred to me that if I truly believed there was a power that could overthrow helplessness and oppression for humanity, I would need to fully accept it for myself. Believing in its truth required more than a theoretical agreement; I knew it would require Christian transformation within me. Again, I called upon my savior to help—not to give me the pleasures of material comfort—but to help me discern the power of Christ healing oppression for humanity. Oppression in any form, including disease, was subject to the authority of Christ.

One of the first issues that came to light in my prayer was the humble realization that an infinite God loves everyone equally and unconditionally. Oppression appears to privilege some and depress others. But this simple thought of God's universal love validated my plea against medical prognoses. For example, one of the basic assumptions regarding arthritis is that some people have weaker cartilage than others. But if God does not favor some over others, and if the "image and likeness of God" does not include superiority and inferiority, then I had a right to God's loving power as much as anyone else. I was convicted with this divine love, realizing how much more loved I was than I had ever considered. A severe repentance swept through me, to the extent that I longed to undo the minor acts of oppression toward others I had unwittingly indulged in. Fully occupied for the next couple of weeks with the desire to bring justice wherever possible, I unknowingly distanced myself from the struggle with pain in my joints.

Then one morning when I awakened, I discovered almost no discomfort. Within a few days, all my knuckles returned to normal size; all pain vanished completely. I have not experienced any similar sensations since that time. The threat of permanent pain and decline has been replaced with a permanent awareness and desire to support the equality of all humanity. It became even clearer to me that my own struggle had not been a private battle, but one bringing me in solidarity with the rest of the world standing in need of redemption.

## PRAYERS FOR OTHERS

Further confirmation for me that Christian prayer is not designed for selfish gain is the scriptural verse from 1 John: "Beloved, since God loved us so much, we also ought to love one another" (4:11). It persuades me that the knowledge of being loved by God inspires action on my part, to love others as I have been loved. Every encounter with God is a call to do likewise for my fellow human beings. My healing of arthritis is a continual call for me to pray for the lifting of oppression in any form—disease, poverty, injustice, violence, patriarchy, or victimization. Suffering, anywhere in the world, is a call for prayer. Mary Baker Eddy writes of prayer and what it should accomplish:

> The test of all prayer lies in the answer to these questions: Do we love our neighbor better because of this asking? Do we

pursue the old selfishness, satisfied with having prayed for something better, though we give no evidence of the sincerity of our requests by living consistently with our prayer? If selfishness has given place to kindness, we shall regard our neighbor unselfishly, and bless them that curse us; but we shall never meet this great duty simply by asking that it may be done. There is a cross to be taken up before we can enjoy the fruition of our hope and faith.[16]

For this reason, a Christian Scientist Christian generally considers his or her prayer as the greatest gift to give humanity. It requires taking up one's cross, and it requires faithful persistence until harmony is restored. Several years ago, I had stepped into a Christian Science Reading Room, located in the middle of my hometown, to make a purchase. A very disheveled man came in just after me and asked the attendant for enough money to catch the train. She explained the policy that she was unable to give money and expressed her regret. I stepped outside with the man as he left, and told him I would be happy to pray for him if he wanted me to. This was a bitter cold winter day, and he showed me the holes in his shoes and worn out gloves. He said he had no money and nowhere to go, but I told him I trusted God to be his Father and Mother and would care for him immediately.

When I drove home and began to pray, I began doubting my prayers. At that moment, he had no money; it would be impossible for him to earn an instantaneous income, and he was clearly uneducated and too tired to work. There were serious socioeconomic issues involved in his immediate need. I drove back to town, to find him and offer him the money he needed. But I could not find him. Then, I knew I had to pray earnestly enough that I could trust and believe in his immediate God-given care; I was unable to dismiss him with a few dollars from my pocket!

I started with gratitude to God for being present, for guiding and caring for all, and for providing this man with everything he needed. I was sorely tempted to retreat back to my own disbelief, more convinced of his lack and impossible situation than God's ability to care for him. I battled my disbelief, complacency, and doubt in my prayer's efficacy. Again, I repented of my little faith, and struggled to thank God more persistently for being present in this man's life.

I persevered with my prayer for several weeks, turning my doubt to gratitude for God's care for him every time I thought of him.

About six months later, I was working in the same Reading Room, when I noticed a man who passed by the window and abruptly turned around to come inside. He was standing tall, cleaned up, beaming, and exclaimed, "Ain't you the lady that believed in me that day last winter?! I came back to give you the dollar you gave me. I've got a job now, and...." I was stunned to see him, and as he finished his story, I kept wondering about the dollar. I know I had not given it to him, because I doubt I would have prayed so vigorously! But what he said about my believing in him was true.

Most of the world is unaware of my prayer, and the world is still in great need. Yet, I believe prayer is the most powerful act of good I am able to do for humanity. I think my experience with prayer is more efficacious than any other human activity I can perform. I also believe prayer for our "neighbors" anywhere in the world is the Christian's calling to follow in the steps of our master, Jesus Christ.

While prayer is generally the Christian Science Christian's first line of defense for humanity, the Christian Science Church is devoted to the betterment of humanity in practical ways. Its publishing of *The Christian Science Monitor* is an example of its commitment to the understanding of the human condition everywhere in the world. Established by Mary Baker Eddy as a means for thinkers of the world to remain fully engaged in the needs of humanity, it has inspired acts of generosity and kindness to troubled areas in the world. Additionally, sometimes branch churches organize charitable activities; often individuals respond in their own ways. But the foundation of activity is almost always a prayer for healing.

## CONCLUSION

It is in this commitment to love God and to love our neighbor that Christian Science Christians unite with other Christians. Whether they support medical research or turn away from medical models, most Christians would likely agree with the ELCA Statement on Health Care: "When we limit illness to disease and health care to cure, we miss the deeper dimensions of healing through restoration to God."[17] When healing draws us closer to God, this is the foundation for unity. It reminds us Christ has called us on pilgrimage, and we are journeying forward.

The ultimate ecumenical model for Christians is the day of the Pentecost, when the Holy Spirit swept through the community, drawing together people from distant lands. They spoke the native languages of Europe, Asia, and Africa, and yet, they understood each other in their mother tongues. It is of special interest that the subject of their intensely animated discussion was about "God's deeds of power" (Acts 2:11). Whether these deeds were the healing of the sick, stilling storms, or the resurrection of Jesus, clearly the excitement of the conversation was the evidence of God's power made known on earth. And the Holy Spirit brought them together to share the good news.

The sign of true pilgrimage is the evidence that the Holy Spirit is still stirring the hearts of Christians. Where there is animated talk about "God's deeds of power," we can hear each other clearly in our God-given native tongues—love, humility, honesty, and pure hearts. When healing results from the stirring of the Holy Spirit in this way, we recognize we are engaged in true spiritual pilgrimage. If there has been a kind of "ecumenical travel fatigue"[18] among Christians, the spirituality required for healing is a welcome remedy. It provides visible evidence that Christ is among us, and it rouses us to testify and encourage each other in our journeys.

# FREQUENTLY ASKED QUESTIONS ABOUT CHRISTIAN SCIENCE

1. What is a Christian Science practitioner, and how is one recognized?

   A Christian Science practitioner who is formally recognized by The Mother Church (The First Church of Christ, Scientist) is permitted to advertise in the official *Christian Science Journal*. The public practice of Christian Science involves specific treatment for a patient who requests it. Metaphysical healing requires an educated and developed spiritual sense of the presence and power of Christ, by which one treats the mental causes of disease and human troubles.

2. Why is the church called Church of Christ—comma—Scientist?

The first name for her church was "Church of Christ." Of course, there were other churches named "Church of Christ," so she changed the name to Church of Christ (Scientist). Eventually a comma took the place of the parentheses. There isn't any known explanation for Mary Baker Eddy's choice of the use of the comma. The term *Scientist* is used as an adjective, conveying what kind of Church of Christ it is. Another example of this use is the "Church of Christ, Instrumental" to distinguish it from the Church of Christ that doesn't believe in using musical instruments. In the case of the Christian Science Church, the term *Scientist* shows that this Church of Christ sees Christianity as Science and Jesus Christ as a Scientist.

3. What is your expectation about health and healing?

Jesus Christ is the master and model for Christian Science healers. According to the Gospels, the motive for his healing works was compassion. He rebuked the cause of suffering, and gave thanks to God for the power of healing. Mary Baker Eddy writes in *Science and Health with Key to the Scriptures* (37), "It is possible,—yea, the duty and privilege of every child, man, and woman,—to follow in some degree the example of the Master by the demonstration of Truth and Life, of health and holiness." She considered the universal capability for healing (ourselves and others) was due to the ordered laws and scientific method she discovered in Jesus' works.

4. What is your attitude toward death?

Jesus is again the model for Christian Science practice. There is no record of his encouragement for anyone to die or consider life to be finished. Rather, he raised three people from death: Jairus' young daughter, the widow's son from Nain, and his friend Lazarus. While there have been relatively few instances of Christian Science treatment raising the dead, or near-dead, the goal in Christian Science is to gain the spiritual maturity and understanding requisite to follow Jesus' example. Christian Science does not regard death as a necessity for spiritual growth, any more than sickness or sin are. Jesus taught at least two individuals how to find eternal life even while on earth: a rich man who had to sell his goods and a lawyer who learned how to love his neighbor. Therefore, the attitude toward death is to resist it as "the last enemy to be destroyed" (1 Cor 15:26).

5. What is sin, and how do you deal with it?

Sin is the notion of being separated from God. It is an inevitable state for all mortals, because whatever is born of the flesh, and not of the Spirit, exists apart from God. It is manifested in everything unlike good, God, such as anger, lust, dishonesty, selfishness, revenge, and so forth. Christ is the redeemer, because Christ is the power that enables us to be reborn of Spirit. Atonement is a complex theological issue; but in Christian Science it means that Jesus' experience on the cross is proof that God is the ultimate victor, and that sin cannot keep us forever separated from God. That knowledge inspires an individual's honest recognition of sin along with a desire for repentance so severe that the belief in sin is destroyed.

6. What is heaven, and what is hell?

The New Testament use of the term *hell* includes both Hades and Gehenna. Hades was understood as a place one goes temporarily after being buried, and where the soul is separated from the body. Christian Science regards Jesus' parable of the rich man and Lazarus (Luke 16:19–31) as an indication of a kind of soul-searching process of probation after death. Jesus used the other term, *Gehenna,* when he warned that anyone who insults or gets angry with a brother or sister would be in danger of hell fire. This indicates, in Christian Science, that whatever sin separates us from God will be totally and eternally destroyed. The experience of hell, therefore, is self-imposed agony and the effects of sin. It feels like suffering of all sorts, but it is destroyed by Christ, our redeemer.

The Bible conveys two meanings for "heaven" as well. The Hebrew scriptures indicate a heavenly dome that separates earthly things from the things of God. This concept in Christian Science explains the line of demarcation between truth and error. The New Testament "heaven" infers the reign of God, as in "It [heaven] is the throne of God" (Matt 5:34), and "an angel of the Lord, descending from heaven, came and rolled back the stone and sat on it" (Matt 28:2). Christian Science emphasizes Jesus' teaching from the Lord's Prayer that God's will be done on earth as in heaven, thereby enabling us to discern a sense of heaven's harmony here and now.

## NOTES

1. John T. Ford cites a number of examples of contemporary reenactments of Jesus' passion as evidence that "We as Christians are participants in the history of salvation, even though the crucifixion happened nearly two millennia ago." "Unity and Mission: A Pilgrimage of Accompaniment," *Journal of Ecumenical Studies* 45, no. 2 (Spring 2010): 189. My claim in this article is that Christian healing is another form of such participation.

2. Michael Kinnamon, "Where Christians Reflect, Connect, and Learn," Faith and Leadership (Interview, May 25, 2010), available at http://faithandleadership.com/multimedia/michael-kinnamon-denominations-are-wonderful-adjectives-idolatrous-nouns (accessed May 7, 2012).

3. Christian Science Christian healing is highly individual, because it takes place within the consciousness of the individual who experiences it. It is applied theology, wherein the improved

understanding of God and our relationship with God bring about the favorable bodily results. Therefore, an analysis of healing stories illustrates the interconnectedness between anecdotal evidence and theological frameworks.

4. The entire verse reads: "For as the heavens are higher than the earth, so are my ways higher than your ways and my thoughts and your thoughts."

5. Stephen Gottschalk, "Theodicy After Auschwitz and the Reality of God," *Union Seminary Quarterly Review* 41, nos. 3–4 (1987): 79.

6. Ibid., 84.

7. Mary Baker Eddy, *Science and Health with Key to the Scriptures* (Boston, MA: The First Church of Christ, Scientist, 1875, republished 1994), 230.

8. Gottschalk, "Theodicy After Auschwitz," 79.

9. Eddy, *Science and Health,* 121.

10. The full quote from John 1:14 reads: "And the Word became flesh and lived among us, and we have seen his glory, the glory as of a father's only son, full of grace and truth." Mary Baker Eddy comments on the first portion of that passage (quoting the King James Version): "'The Word was made flesh.' Divine Truth must be known by its effects on the body as well as on the mind, before the Science of being can be demonstrated. Hence its embodiment in the incarnate Jesus,—that life-link forming the connection through which the real reaches the unreal, Soul rebukes sense, and Truth destroys error" (*Science and Health,* 350).

11. Gottschalk, "Theodicy After Auschwitz," 88.

12. As the over-generalized term *Gnostic* covers such a broad spectrum of ancient writings, there is no singular definition that could cover all aspects of it. When I refer to "Gnosticism," I use it in its historically devised sense—referring to the perceived heresies that contradicted Christian orthodoxy.

13. See Matthew 17:14–20.

14. While I believed there was a possibility that the prescribed ointment would bring physical relief, I do not think of medicine as God's means of healing. Mary Baker Eddy explains in *Science and Health with Key to the Scriptures,* "It is plain that God does not employ drugs or hygiene, nor provide them for human use; else

Jesus would have recommended and employed them in his heal-ing....Sometimes the human mind uses one error to medicine [sic] another. Driven to choose between two difficulties, the human mind takes the lesser to relieve the greater" (143). In this case, I thought of the medical prescription as a temporary, or lesser, sup-port while I continued my prayer for a more spiritual understand-ing of God.

15. This phrase is part of Jesus' self-identification with the full scriptural promise that "The Spirit of the Lord is upon me, because he has anointed me to bring good news to the poor. He has sent me to proclaim release to the captives and recovery of sight to the blind, to let the oppressed go free."

16. Eddy, *Science and Health,* 9.

17. *Caring for Health: Our Shared Endeavor,* Evangelical Lutheran Church in America Social Statement, 2003, available at http://www.elca.org/What-We-Believe/Social-Issues/Social-Statements/Health-and-Healthcare.aspx (accessed May 7, 2012).

18. I borrow this phrase from John T. Ford. He claims "The lack of an 'ecumenical spirituality' seems to have been a basic lacuna that has resulted in a kind of ecumenical travel fatigue." "Unity and Mission: A Pilgrimage of Accompaniment," *Journal of Ecumenical Studies* 45, no. 2 (Spring 2010): 192.

# 15

# ASIAN AMERICAN EQUIPPING SYMPOSIUM

## A Space of Intersection across Ethnicity, Generation, and Gender

*Young Lee Hertig*

In his essay "A Pilgrimage of Accompaniment," John T. Ford describes Christians on a pilgrimage accompanied by Christ and with *fellow* believers as companions.[1] Considering the fact that the etymology of "companion" in Latin means breaking bread together (com-"with" + panis-"bread"), the sacramental meaning of companionship is embedded. Exploring the interrelated dynamics of unity and mission, Ford describes a tight sense of belongingness in community and companionship in spite of a road that is difficult and a terrain that is unpredictable. A pilgrimage is always difficult—for some more than others.

## THEOLOGICAL EXCLUSION

The question of Asian American space and context began to arise when I first enrolled in a seminary in St. Paul, Minnesota, in January 1981. The question that welled up within me was, "Why was the Asian American Christian experience excluded from the theological curriculum?" With every class delving into European theology, I wondered if there was even an American theology, let alone an Asian American theology. Clearly, the entire theological menu was of European taste, cooked by European-American chefs with their choice ingredients.

Similarly, Charlene Jin Lee, a respondent to Jonathan Tran's keynote address at the inaugural Asian American Equipping Symposium (AAES), described the theological exclusion of people of color with a topographic analysis of theological table and seating arrangements. Jin Lee pondered: Who is present at the table and who is not? "Many seats have been taken up and warmed for a long time—for centuries, in fact—by the same people," and, thus, the owners of the theological table "have established a lingo, a way of thinking, a way of being that is unfamiliar to us," but we "sit quietly" and must remind ourselves that "they" are "not the owners of theology." She called forth humility and grace in reassessing the seating arrangements at the theological table in the effort to construct theologies.[2]

At the table, somehow, non-Europeans like me were to remain guests forever—more spectators than participants, more random bystanders than real pilgrims. Unsettled about being a passive observer-learner as a seminarian, I decided to learn more about the dynamics of the Gospel and culture. I began reading books written by Fuller missiology faculty, and, for the first time, I found some affirmation regarding my questions. Paul G. Hiebert's books and teachings accompanied me in my pursuit of unpacking intergenerational conflict within immigrant churches; frequently these conflicts stemmed from conflicting world views. From this point on, I devoured multidisciplinary missiology that integrated theology, culture, and psychology, which Fuller Seminary uniquely offered.

More than three decades later, Asian American seminarians still confront the same questions and issues![3] Asian American consciousness has not yet entered into the theological palace despite the fact that Asian Americans represent the largest constituency among minority student populations in all major seminaries. Nonetheless, the majority of the seminary classes continue to take students back to European theologies, in spite of the evident globalization of Christianity in general and of the American church in particular.

Consequently like a tree without roots, seminarians and seminary graduates experience a theological and cultural dissonance that makes it difficult for them to cope with the conflicting winds that blow in cross-cultural and intergenerational ministry today. The result is a silent exodus and high attrition rate among American-born Asian leaders who are very much needed for the health of the body of Christ.

# THE SILENT EXODUS OF ASIAN AMERICAN PASTORAL LEADERS

## Deculturalized Seminary Curriculum

Emmanuel Katogole captures the importance of stories and identity formation. He posits, "Stories not only shape how we view reality but also how we respond to life and indeed the very sort of persons we become."[4]

Likewise, pastoral leadership formation in seminaries, when excluding ethnic groups' stories, misses a crucial educational component related to identity formation. From theological leadership formation perspective, the casualty of curricular exclusion of minority groups' stories is, indeed, costly and results in the silent exodus from ministry.

The seminary's deculturalized curriculum inadequately prepares young Asian American pastors for ministering in church contexts, which intertwines ethnicity, generation, and gender. They experience identity confusion at three levels—personal, cultural, and theological. Without tools to engage in contextualized clergy formation, seminarians and pastors try to pound "a square peg into a round hole." Caught between the deculturalized seminary education and the culture-specific church context, seminarians, in general, feel "out of tune" in both contexts.

As a result of dual dislocation, Asian American seminarians develop a *neither/nor* rather than a *both/and* identity, which contributes to high attrition rates. In contrast, the task of navigating complex ministry situations demands a convergent leader, who, like an orchestra conductor, synthesizes all the different sounds of theological/cultural instruments into a harmonious composition. The few leaders who show signs of resiliency, however, tend to lack an Emotional Quotient (EQ) and, thus, people skills. Regretfully, like a gerbil on a continual revolving track, each new generation seems to be on a perpetual pioneering track due to generational disconnection.

Theological and cultural dissonances result in fragile, not resilient, leaders who opt out and exit rather than persist when confronted with the inevitable challenges of ministry. What is missing in this chronic vicious cycle is access to the wisdom and accompaniment of pastoral leaders seasoned in ministry contexts.

## Vacuum of Mentorship in Churches

According to extensive research conducted by Charles R. Foster, Lisa E. Dahill, Lawrence A. Goleman, and Barbara Wang Tolentino in their book *Educating Clergy*,[5] theological education, unlike other professional schools, often lacks apprenticeship. The local church should provide space for seminarian apprenticeships.

Regretfully, both the rhythm of immigrant church ministry and the linguistic and cultural gap make it impossible to accompany the next generation of leaders: they are left alone or at best isolated on the pilgrimage.

One of the most pervasive church dividing issues in Asian American Churches involves the clashing generational divide, often without mediators in sight. Consequently, many young adults have left their parents' churches, burned out by lack of nurture.

Intramurally, church pastors of the first-generation immigrant church do not mentor the younger generation of English-speaking pastors due to a number of reasons: (1) the busy schedule of the immigrant church; (2) the linguistic differences between the first and second generation pastors: they really do not speak each other's language; (3) worldview differences: the two generations do not see either the world or the church in the same way.

In spite of the intergenerationally embedded structure under one roof, social divisions remain strong. Since most ministerial formation is done in seminaries, the deculturalized seminary curriculum also contributes to a massive silent exodus and a high attrition rate among Asian American pastoral leaders. At risk in the foreseeable future are empty church buildings with no succeeding generations to continue the first generation's hard work and commitment.

## De-genderized Seminary Curriculum

Although the feminist movement has empowered many women faculty, gender equality still remains to be seen both in theological institutions and in churches. Although the presence of female faculty in seminaries provides women's leadership role models, nevertheless, it does not necessarily translate into a gender inclusive curriculum. According to recently released data by the Association of Theological Schools, gender balance in both student enrollment and faculty composition still lags. The total number of male Master of Divinity students in 2010 was 23,017 and the total female Master of Divinity students 9,763. The total number of Asian male Master of Divinity students was 1,635 (7.1 percent) and Asian female Master of Divinity students 408 (4.2 percent). Whereas the total Asian Master of Divinity students, without counting doctoral students, amounts to 6.2 percent, the total percentage of Asian faculty remains at 3.2 percent.[6]

Rarely do female clergy have access to the more influential church pulpits either in immigrant congregations or in English-speaking congregations. For these reasons, AAES was launched to provide a space where pan-Asian American leaders could come together across the boundaries of ethnicity, generation, and gender.

The inaugural Equipping Symposium kicked off on November 2–3, 2009, at Fuller Theological Seminary. The vision of gathering Asian American Christian leaders, one of the most scattered groups in existence in the seminary, crystallized at this time. As an African American pastor once said: "When you don't have teeth to chew, gum it." In implementing our vision, we relied on daily divine whispers and riding along the whimsical wind of the Spirit.

# THE ROOMINESS OF GOD AND A SPACE OF ACCOMPANIMENT

The keynote speaker of the inaugural conference of AAES, Dr. Jonathan Tran, Assistant Professor of Christian Ethics at Baylor University, framed his lectures on the past and the future of churches with a "both-and" paradigm, not an "either-or" paradigm.

It was an appropriate approach in light of the multifaceted theme of "bridging": theologies between the churches, the past with the future, and diverse intra-ethnic groups. Elaborating on the theological hook "God is roomy," Tran attempted to expand horizons that can contain intergenerational clashes, ethnic memories, and beyond.

As depicted in the Psalms and Isaiah, God is, indeed, roomy. Yet, at a human level, when stretching our horizons, we are in need of tangible accompaniment with flesh and bone. The Israelites were accompanied by God and their leaders—Moses and Joshua—during their journey in the wilderness. Likewise, immigration is a pilgrimage and the journey involves uprootedness and, thus, throws one into a precarious space that begs for God who accompanies the body of Christ that offers belongingness. Being stretched beyond one's imagination in this journey, God's provision anchors the people of God, and the immigrant church provides a sense of familial belonging.

## CREATING A SPACE OF ACCOMPANIMENT FOR ASIAN AMERICANS

God stressed repeatedly the significance of telling succeeding generations the power and wonders of God's praiseworthy deeds (Ps 78:4). The American-born generations are deprived of their parents' stories due to the generational separation both at home and in immigrant churches in general; the children of immigrants all too often do not know and so do not understand their parents' culture. In addition, the churches focus on the biblical stories without enough roominess for familial and ecclesial stories, while the seminary curriculum centers on Europeanized stories without enough roominess for non-European stories. As Joanne D. Birdwhistell succinctly put it, the storyteller shapes "people's actions, ideas, and values, and identities in all sorts of significant ways."[7] In their educational journeys, Asian Americans have been faithful listeners of stories shaped by the dominant group. Consequently, many remain confused—their theological and personal identity uncertain and confused.

Hence, AAES was created as a space to invoke and tell silenced stories of Asian American Christianity by Asian Americans across generations, ethnicities, and gender. Furthermore, AAES offers a space of accompaniment and learning from Asian American leaders. We believe that when Christian leaders are rooted in both their cultural and theological identities, they can withstand the conflicting winds inevitably encountered in ministry and so become resilient. The inaugural AAES forged multiple partnerships between the churches and Fuller Theological Seminary. The AAES became ecumenical in composition, representing diverse seminaries in Southern California, and local churches with diverse denominational representations and nondenominational churches alike.

## FOOD AS A SOURCE OF HEALING AND BELONGING

Many women pioneers, feeling as if they have parachuted from nowhere to a neverland, find themselves deprived of resources to negotiate life's challenges, let alone to be guides in future directions. As Jin Lee put it, we have been "floating somewhere between belonging and exclusion."[8] We have also faced gender and racial barriers from both our own ethnic churches and from mainstream Christian institutions. In preparing for the inaugural AAES, the primary barrier I experienced was the inaccessibility of pulpits in Asian American churches for women regardless of languages spoken. Fortunately, we found an alternative space to hold a prayer banquet and mobilized the community through cooking. [9] Where there is rice, people gather and share our common symbolic identity. A Korean American female panelist, Miyoung Yoon Hammer, shared: "I have never attended a Korean church that did not serve potluck at the end of every service. During potluck, people are at once physically and emotionally fed and church life comes alive."[10]

In sharing meals, the church becomes a source of "healing" and "belonging," according to Yoon Hammer. When women leave the immigrant church, they sorely miss the ethnic food and table fellowship. Spiritual formation takes place during table fellowship.

Table fellowship becomes sacramental and formative. In addition, Asian American Christianity's table fellowship with an abundant fusion of food symbolizes both ethnicity and sacrament. Just as Jesus often was seen going to and from or at meals, people of color connect deeply through table fellowship. Undoubtedly food symbolizes the richness of ethnicities and so a sense of belonging, laying the groundwork for spiritual growth and *communitas*, which Victor Turner describes as breaking in through the surface of marginality, creating a bonded people "in their wholeness wholly attending."[11]

Even when a person leaves an ethnic church for a mainstream congregation in search of a gender-inclusive ministry, it is the lunch after church that is greatly missed. Now that Jin Lee chose gender equality over ethnicity, she "coerces" her husband to go and grab *soon doo boo* (spicy tofu soup) after serving at a Caucasian congregation.

Eating spicy tofu soup at a restaurant leaves out the "bread fellows"—the immigrant church. However, remaining in the immigrant church for ethnic belongingness leaves out gender equality. Nevertheless, satisfying appetites for both ethnic food and gender equality in immigrant churches seems to be a remote reality. Therefore, women leaders like Charlene Jin Lee and Miyoung Yoon Hammer settle for something piecemeal while seeking different companions who fully embrace gender equality. Hence, a symbolic belongingness lingers through yearning for ethnic foods that cannot be eradicated from their souls. Hopefully, they may find companions (com+panis) along their journey of departing from the immigrant church and to the mainstream body of Christ.

# CONCLUSION

What does unity and mission look like among Asian American ethnic Christians who are mostly Evangelical? What key ingredients can one find in Asian American Christian practice that may contribute to the mission of unity in regard to issues that divide the church? Ford's description of "Christians as pilgrims accompanied by Christ and companions along the way"[12] depicts the ecumenical movement's "diverse dimensions" and "perspectives" that allow different Asian American ethnicities to join in table fellowship while simultaneously contributing the richness of their cultural traditions.

The AAES, as a space of pan-Asian American accompaniment, exudes the spirit of ecumenism and unity as we tell our diverse stories around the table we rearranged. At this intersecting space, our culture and ethnicities are no longer excluded. Many panelists at the AAES conference used food literally and metaphorically in describing ethnic churches.[13] As we share the fusion of Pan-Asian and American foods, both the physical and spiritual, indeed, we are nourished and enriched by our common ancestry. In this space, Asian American women no longer need to choose piecemeal treatment of gender equality over ethnicity but may sit at the table as equal companions—*bread fellows*.

Queen Esther hosted a series of banquets under the guidance of her cousin Mordecai, and her companions were King Xerxes and his officials. What would the theological formation process look like if we were to have our Mordecai who unlocked Queen Esther's imagination? The theological formation *of* churches, *by* churches, *with* churches waits to be unleashed, thereby, curtailing perpetual pioneering and, thus, the silent exodus of our pastoral leaders. In fact, we will be able to enter into the theological palace, not merely as decorative beauty contestants, but as theological patriots and truly companions on the pilgrimage of mission and unity.

As Katongole put it, "Who we are and who we are capable of becoming, depends very much on the stories we tell, the stories we listen to, and the stories we live."[14] Indeed, the partnership between the Institute for the Study of Asian American Christianity (ISAAC) and Fuller Theological Seminary has been resourceful and fruitful in generating Asian American Christian stories. President Richard J. Mouw's accompaniment throughout the journey of AAES, along with Asian American participation, has kept the dream alive.

## NOTES

1. John T. Ford, "Unity and Mission: A Pilgrimage of Accompaniment," *Journal of Ecumenical Studies* 45, no. 2 (Spring 2010): 12.

2. Charlene Jin Lee, "Response #2, Response to Jonathan Tran," *SANACS Journal: Society of Asian North American Christian Studies: The Asian American Equipping Symposium Edition* 2 (2010): 64.

3. A three-hour-long listening session among Korean American seminarians in 2005 on Fuller Theological Seminary's campus revealed that they were raising exactly the same questions as in the mid 1980s. The listening session was documented and circulated to Fuller's administrators prior to launching AAES.

4. Emmanuel Katongole, *The Sacrifice of Africa: A Political Theology for Africa* (Grand Rapids, Michigan: Wm B. Eerdmans Publishing Co., 2011), 2.

5. Charles R. Foster and others, *Educating Clergy: Teaching Practices and Pastoral Imagination* (San Francisco: Jossey-Bass, 2006).

6. ATS Data Table 2010–2011:2-Enrollment, Table 2.12–A Head Count Enrollment, by Race or Ethnic Groups, Degree, and Gender, 2010 in *The ATS News in Brief*, April 2011, available at http://www.ats.edu/Resources/PublicationsPresentations/Documents/AnnualDataTables/2010-11AnnualDataTables.pdf (accessed July 16, 2012).

7. Joanne D. Birdwhistell, "Ecological Questions for Daoist Thought: Contemporary Issues and Ancient Texts," in *Daoism and Ecology: Ways Within a Cosmic Landscape*, ed. N.J. Girardot, James Miller, and Liu Xiaogan (Cambridge, MA: Harvard University Press, 2001), 25.

8. Jin Lee, "Response #2," 63.

9. Our meeting space, formerly known as "Mama's Pasadena," now is changed to "Chef's Center" as a job creation initiative in Pasadena, California, under the Episcopal Diocese of Los Angeles.

10. Miyoung Yoon Hammer is an Associate Professor of School of Psychology at Fuller Theological Seminary. She was one of the respondents during the inaugural Asian American Equipping Symposium on November 2, 2009. "Response #1, Response to Jonathan Tran," *SANACS Journal: Society of Asian North American Christian Studies: The Asian American Equipping Symposium Edition* 2 (2010): 58.

11. Victor W. Turner, *The Ritual Process: Structure and Anti-Structure* (Chicago: Aldine Publishing Company, 1969), 128.

12. Ford, "Unity and Mission."

13. See Ken Fong's extended metaphor of food to describe his church and his leadership at Evergreen Baptist Church, Los Angeles. "Response #4, Response to Jonathan Tran," *SANACS Journal: Society of Asian North American Christian Studies: The Asian American Equipping Symposium Edition* 2 (2010): 78–79.

14. Katongole, *The Sacrifice of Africa*, 2.

# 16

# TRANSFORMING A NATION THROUGH MISSION

## A Case Study on the Church in Albania

*Anton C. Vrame*

The whole of the church's life should be a "laboratory of the resurrection."[1] Through this lens, the work of the missionary church can become transformational or transfigured, not just for personal lives, but also for a society as a common journey of faith. The work of the Orthodox Church of Albania, under the leadership of His Beatitude Archbishop Anastasios Yannoulatos, provides evidence for such an assessment. This case study will focus on the work that has been done by just one church in the country and demonstrate how missionary work can transform a nation.

In the aftermath of World War II, Albania became a Communist nation, ruled by Enver Hoxha. From its initial alliances with the Soviet Union, until 1960, and with the People's Republic of China, until 1978, Albania eventually isolated itself from virtually all contact with other nations (much like North Korea today). Following the death of Hoxha in 1985, the Communist government attempted to liberalize the society, which led instead to economic collapse and social unrest. In 1992, the Communist government was voted out of power, and parliamentary democracy was established. While much progress has been made in a short period of time, Albania remains the poorest nation in Europe.

The Christian population traces its origins to the first century CE, especially in the city of Durrës (ancient Dyrrachium). Today, while estimates vary, Albania is 70 percent Muslim (Sunni and Bektashi), 20 percent Orthodox Christian, and 10 percent Roman Catholic. Government policy during the Communist era steadily eroded religious life until 1967, when Albania was declared an atheist nation. At that point, all forms of religion were made illegal, with houses of worship destroyed or repurposed into "cultural centers." Believers could be arrested and imprisoned for simple acts of faith.

Describing the era of persecution, Elizabeta Xhokaxhi said:

> We suffered a lot when the churches were closed, but I kept all my icons. I put them in wardrobes and other hiding places. There was a house in Tirana where a woman had icons. They found out and came for them…. Then she made the sign of the cross on herself. "I am the icon of the cross. Take me." But they decided she was crazy, and so she wasn't arrested.[2]

As the Communist government was collapsing, Christian missionaries entered the country to see what remained of their communities. Orthodox Christian missionaries, who had worked previously with Archbishop Anastasios, entered the country in 1991, led by the archbishop (then the Acting Archbishop of East Africa). In July, 1992, the Ecumenical Patriarchate of Constantinople restored the institutional church, and Anastasios was enthroned as archbishop of the Orthodox Autocephalous Church of Albania. As the archbishop stated, "In fact, I was not so much accepting a throne—that sounds rather comfortable!—but embracing the cross."[3]

The situation in Albania challenges our assumptions about the nature of "missionary work." In the classic Orthodox Christian understanding, beginning with the examples of Byzantine saints Cyril and Methodius in the ninth century, down to the work of the missionaries in Russian Alaska in the eighteenth and nineteenth centuries, missionary work involves traveling to non-Christian places or lands, establishing a physical presence of some kind, and beginning to bear witness to the Gospel in order to attract new followers of Christianity. Assuming it is successful, the mission expands throughout the place, spreading Christianity and establishing a church. The missionaries develop various institutions and the necessary means for their sustenance, from written literary languages to schools and other philanthropic institutions, as well as houses of worship.

In the case of Albania, missionaries entered a country that had a Christian population and a church that had existed for centuries, but because of the government it had been all but destroyed. The missionary work was to resurrect a possibly deceased church. The challenge facing Archbishop Anastasios and the missionary community was for a minority religious community to act as a positive agent in a society that had been devastated by the paranoid rule of the Communist regime, even as it rebuilt the Orthodox Church and its ecclesiastical life after nearly forty years of active and violent persecution.

Because Anastasios was a Greek citizen, members of the Albanian government were also suspicious of his intentions and his connections to the Greek government, which historically had seen southern Albania as a Greek territory. Early in his ministry, in 1994, "A law was almost passed that would have forced any non-Albanian religious leader to leave the country."[4] As Anastasios has stated, "The fact that I was Greek, not Albanian, was a daily theme in hostile press articles, speeches in Parliament and television reports. The message was very simple: If you are a Greek, you must be a spy."[5] Not helping matters was the initial push by some persons outside Albania to send Greek bishops to assist Anastasios and create a synod of bishops. After considerable negotiation, in 1998, two bishops of Albanian citizenship and ethnicity were elected for the synod of bishops, as well as one Greek. In addition, some in the Albanian émigré community, especially those living in the United States for generations, also raised concerns about Anastasios's presence. They had worked very consciously to create an Albanian identity distinct from a Greek identity, including within the church. For example, there are two ecclesiastical jurisdictions of Albanian Orthodox in North America: a three-parish jurisdiction associated with the Ecumenical Patriarchate of Constantinople, and a thirteen-parish Albanian Archdiocese of the Orthodox Church in America.

Throughout, Anastasios has been committed to walking with the people of Albania: He has learned Albanian and become an Albanian citizen; he has ordained Albanians as bishops and priests; and his staff is filled with Albanians. Missionaries, who are usually from the United States and Greece, live alongside Albanians, often sharing apartments with them, always learning the language and living as ordinary Albanian citizens, as they go about their ecclesiastical work.

In about sixteen years, the Orthodox Autocephalous Church of Albania has experienced a resurrection, which has been a significant aspect in the transformation of Albanian society. Finding only ruins of Orthodox Christian structures, missionaries have worked to restore its buildings, organizations, and life—in most cases starting from scratch. There remained only twenty-two Orthodox clergy, mostly elderly and infirm, of the 440 before World War II. In addition, since Albania is the poorest nation in Europe, the church has also worked to develop programs in the area of education, health care, development and relief, culture and environmental preservation, and restoration.[6] The church has taken back or purchased property not only to build houses of worship, open a seminary, and develop church-based programs, but also to create and operate schools and after-school programs for children and to offer professional training for adults in business management, accounting, computers, and laboratory work.

The church operates "after-school programs" in which children of all religious backgrounds are being tutored, play games, and engage in other enrichment activities, such as music. The church operates a medical center in Tirana and a mobile dental clinic for the smaller cities. The archbishop has stated that the widow of Enver Hoxha has been a patient in the medical clinic. All of these programs are open to anyone in the country, regardless of their religious affiliation.

During the financial collapse caused by nationwide pyramid (Ponzi) schemes in 1996–97, the church stepped in to assist those brought to poverty. During the Kosovo war (1998–99), the church organized a relief program, worked in the refugee camps, and assisted the mostly Muslim refugees. Anastasios temporarily closed the seminary in Durrës and sent the students to work with the refugees and alongside other Christian aid programs. Anastasios "recalled how some of the seminary students were initially afraid, worried that some of the refugees might be hostile to Orthodox Christians, even if they were there to help." One student asked him,

"But will the cross I am wearing provoke some?" The archbishop replied "that it was enough to wear the cross in his heart."[7] A year after the war, the Orthodox Church still maintained a camp for Kosovar refugees, until 2001.[8] Today, the church operates programs for Muslim youth in Kosovo.

The church has collaborated with universities in Tirana and in Greece to initiate an environmental protection program that trains postgraduate students and develops programs to protect rivers and forests and solid-waste management.

Through its "missionary work," the Orthodox Autocephalous Church of Albania has become a significant agent for reconstruction and infrastructure development, which has benefited the entire nation. The church-operated social services in education and health care also benefit the entire population. In both cases, the goal is serving the population, whether or not anyone accepts Christianity or joins the church. In fact, Anastasios seems unconcerned about this issue. His goal is to serve and build the nation.

Archbishop Anastasios said:

> When we build or restore a church or monastery, often we also have to rebuild the road. I was once asked what gift I would like; I think they meant an icon. I said, "I would like a bulldozer." They were surprised! "But what can you do with a bulldozer?" "We can build roads in the remote areas so that we make more humane the life of our people."[9]

Under the initial guidance of a bishop with a missionary vision, building roads and repairing buildings has provided the place for the people of Albania to journey together to rebuild the infrastructure and restore confidence in their nation. As Anastasios said, "We are journeying towards the kingdom of God together."[10]

Supporting this development work has taken millions of dollars. The archbishop calls himself an "international beggar," seeking out funds from around the world. He and the reports on his work are quite open about the ecumenical and interfaith nature of the church's missionary work in Albania. Anastasios said, "I am everyone's Archbishop. For us each person is a brother or sister. The church is not just for itself. It is for all the people."[11]

The work of the Orthodox Autocephalous Church in Albania has transformed the lives of those it serves. That work has also transformed the lives of people who serve. One would expect people who have lived under such conditions to be angry with their lot. Instead, through the work of the last fifteen years, the converse seems to be the case. Raimonda Shqeva's attitude seems typical:

> It is sometimes hard to learn not to hate, not to attack. You can convert only with love. We must be careful of each other and never use force. If someone cannot hear us, then let us pray for that person. We each go at our own speed....Our Archbishop has taught us that each person is an icon of God. We must not judge others! We must help anyone in need, no matter what.[12]

# NOTES

1. Olivier Clément, *The Roots of Christian Mysticism* (New York: New City Press, 1995). Clément attributes the phrase to Romanian theologian Dumitru Staniloae.

2. Jim Forest, *The Resurrection of the Church in Albania: Voices of Orthodox Christians* (Geneva: WCC Publications, 2002), 39.

3. Ibid., 106.

4. Ibid., 107.

5. Ibid.

6. For details about the work in Albania, see Lynette Hoppe, *Resurrection: The Orthodox Autocephalous Church of Albania, 1991–2003* (Tirana: Ngjalla Publishers, 2004).

7. Forest, *Resurrection of the Church*, 122–23.

8. Hoppe, *Resurrection*, 26–27.

9. Forest, *Resurrection of the Church*, 111.

10. Ibid., 108.

11. Ibid., 113.

12. Ibid., 84.

# BIBLICAL REFLECTIONS

# 17

# THE FIFTH STATION OF THE WAY OF THE CROSS

## "Simon of Cyrene Helps Jesus Carry His Cross"

*John T. Ford*

## INTRODUCTION

On Friday, March 20, 2009, in conjunction with its semiannual meeting, the members of the Faith and Order Commission of the National Council of Churches participated in "the Way of the Cross" at the Shrine of Saint Mary of Regla, Patroness of Little Havana, a Western Rite Antiochean Orthodox and Apostolic Church (1920 S.W. Sixth St., Miami, FL 33135), which was founded in 1982. After the service, the members of the working group on "Unity in Mission" discussed "the Way of the Cross" both as a religious experience and as a paradigm for our ecumenical pilgrimage. In line with that discussion, the following reflections on the "fifth station" combine bible study, historical/theological analysis, artistic representations, and spiritual meditations that hopefully could be adapted for both personal devotions and ecumenical prayer services.

In their accounts of the painful journey of Jesus to Calvary, the three Synoptic Gospels mention that a bystander was conscripted to help carry the cross of Jesus.[1] The Gospel according to Mark succinctly describes this event:

> After mocking him, they stripped him of the purple cloak and put his own clothes on him. Then they led him out to crucify

him. They compelled a passer-by, who was coming in from the country, to carry his cross; it was Simon of Cyrene, the father of Alexander and Rufus. (15:20–21)

In a centuries-old devotional tradition, this Gospel scene is reenacted as the "fifth station" of the *via crucis*—"the way of the cross"—a ceremonial procession that commemorates the final steps of Jesus carrying his cross to his crucifixion on Golgotha: Jesus winding his way through the streets of Jerusalem, following the *via dolorosa*, which may be variously translated: "the Way of Sorrows" or "the Route of Suffering" or "the Road of Pain."[2]

For Christians, following the Stations of the Cross is not merely a matter of historical reenactment—a poignant reminder of the death march of Jesus—but an opportunity for prayerful reflection on the sacrifical sufferings of Jesus, who was and is the source of our salvation. Succinctly stated, the purpose of the stations is not only representation, but "re-presentation"—making present again—the passion of the Christ in the minds and hearts of Christians today.

In Europe, the practice of placing Stations of the Cross in churches dates back to medieval times, but the practice of retracing the steps of Jesus during the last days of his life goes back at least to the fourth century.[3] Although the stations along the *via dolorosa* are conveniently marked for pilgrims in modern Jerusalem, the precise route that Jesus followed to Calvary has long been disputed. Similarly, the number of commemorative stations has varied; the current number of fourteen dates from the eighteenth century.[4]

Ordinarily placed inside churches but sometimes erected outside in gardens or courtyards, the fourteen stations—which range from simple wooden crosses to elaborate life-sized or even larger figures—begin with the condemnation of Jesus by Pilate and conclude with the burial of the body of Jesus in the sepulchre.[5] Nine of the stations represent events recorded in the Gospels; the other five are based on centuries-old traditions.[6]

The Stations of the Cross have long been a subject of religious art. Artists have usually designed a complete set of stations, but some artists have focused on a particular station, especially the crucifixion. A variation on individual Stations of the Cross can be seen in Scenes from the Passion of Christ by Hans Memling (ca. 1433–94), who incorporated a number of events—including the Last Supper, the carrying of the cross, the crucifixion, the burial and the resurrection—into the same painting;[7] in the lower right-hand part of the painting, Simon can be seen helping the fallen Jesus carry a "T-shaped" cross. As is typical in Renaissance religious art, the donors are depicted in the picture—in this case as praying at opposite sides in the lower corners of the painting; symbolically, the donors, like all Christians, are called to be witnesses of the passion and resurrection of Christ.[8]

Since the fifth station—Simon of Cyrene helps Jesus carry his cross—is a biblically based station, it is an appropriate topic for "bible study" in the dual sense of a topic for historical/theological analysis and as a scriptural event providing spiritual reflection.

## HISTORICAL/THEOLOGICAL ANALYSIS

Although "carrying the cross" is central to the narrative about the journey of Jesus to Calvary, artists and scholars sometimes differ in their descriptions of this event. On the one hand, artists frequently depict Jesus as carrying an entire cross—consisting of two attached pieces of wood: the *stipes* (the upright or vertical beam) joined with the *patibulum* (the horizontal beam). On the other hand, many scholars think that Jesus only carried the *patibulum* and that the *stipes* was already in place at Golgotha—"the place of the skull" (Matt 27:33; Mark 15:22), the site for executions, which was then outside the walls of Jerusalem.

Artistically, of course, it is easier to depict Jesus carrying a whole cross and, then, positioning Simon as assisting Jesus in shouldering it or taking over the task completely. In fact, it would seem difficult to carry an entire cross weighing a couple hundred pounds any distance; even carrying a *patibulum*, which could weigh fifty pounds or more, would have tested the strength of a tortured victim; in addition, there is evidence that the *stipes* was left in place at execution sites, both for convenience in carrying out future death sentences and as a warning to potential malefactors.[9]

During the journey of Jesus to Calvary, Simon was forcibly recruited by the Roman executioners, who had the legal prerogative of drafting people to aid as needed for work details and similar projects. The soldiers presumably did not want the condemned to die en route: they would not have been carrying out the execution as ordered, nor would they have had the entertainment of seeing the humiliation, suffering, and death of their prisoner. Public executions in the Roman world were not only symbolic reminders of imperial authority and presumably deterrents for would-be criminals, but also spectacles for entertaining the populace.[10]

When it seemed that Jesus might die en route, the Roman soldiers, looking over the people in the crowd, apparently spotted a man who seemed athletic enough to help carry the cross. Or perhaps his clothing indicated that he was a visitor to Jerusalem and so not likely to protest. Or perhaps Simon was chosen because he may have shown distaste for the cruelty of the execution or sympathy for Jesus. Accidentally or providentially, the person chosen to help Jesus carry the cross was a person named Simon of Cyrene.

The name "Simon"—which means "Hearkening" or "Listening"—was a name typical of the time. Simon, of course, was also the original name of the apostle Peter, who a few hours earlier had denied that he even knew Jesus and seemingly did not join the execution procession to Calvary.[11] Ironically, the person who was conscripted to help Jesus carry his cross had the same name as the leading apostle, who had followed Jesus from Galilee to Jerusalem, but then failed to follow him on his final journey: one Simon "hearkened"—albeit against his will, the other Simon chose not to do so.

The "hearkening Simon" came from Cyrene, an ancient city near the modern city of Bengasi in Libya (North Africa). At that time, Cyrene had a large Jewish community—descendants of Judean Jews who had settled there during the reign of Ptolemy Soter (323–285 BC). The Cyrenian Jews had a synagogue in Jerusalem, which served pilgrims who came for the celebration of Jewish feasts. It is unclear whether Simon was a pilgrim from the Diaspora, who had come to Jerusalem to celebrate the feast of the Passover or whether he was a native of Cyrene, who had become a resident of Palestine and "was coming in from the country" (Mark

15:21) and chanced to enter Jerusalem at the very time that Jesus was being led out to be crucified.

Beginning with the fifth station, Simon presumably helped carry the cross until Jesus arrived at Calvary, but what occurred subsequently was not recorded: Did Simon watch while Jesus was stripped of his garments (tenth station) prior to being nailed to the cross (eleventh station)? Or did Simon prudently disappear before Jesus' crucifixion (twelfth station), death (thirteenth station), and burial (fourteenth station)?

Although some have linked Simon with the "men of Cyrene" who preached the Gospel to the Greeks (Acts 11:20), Simon, after his singular act of coerced charity, disappeared from the New Testament; however, he subsequently appeared in Gnostic literature.[12] According to extra-biblical tradition, Simon eventually became Bishop of Bosra (Arabia) and was martyred for being a Christian. The inclusion of the names of Simon's sons, Rufus and Alexander, in the Gospel of Mark suggests that they were well known in the early Christian community; according to tradition, Rufus and Alexander became Christian missionaries. It is also possible that the Rufus mentioned by Paul in Romans (16:13) was the son of Simon of Cyrene. In 1941, an ossuary, dating prior to AD 70 (the year of the destruction of Jerusalem) and inscribed in Greek—"Alexander Son of Simon"—was discovered in the Kidron Valley in a burial cave that once belonged to Cyrenian Jews; however, one cannot be certain that this inscription refers to the Simon and Alexander of Mark's Gospel.

## MODERN DEPICTIONS

Although historical data about Simon of Cyrene are meagre and while he is almost completely absent from the Christian liturgical tradition, his role in aiding Jesus carrying his cross continues to appeal to modern media and contemporary artists.

In films depicting the life of Jesus, Simon is a prominent figure, even though the actors who have played the role of Simon have had notably different backgrounds: in the silent film *The King of Kings* (1927), Simon was played by William Boyd; in *King of Kings*

(1961), Rafael Luis Calvo portrayed Simon; in *The Greatest Story Ever Told* (1965), Simon was played by Sidney Poitier; in *The Passion of the Christ* (2004), Jarreth J. Merz portrayed Simon. One might speculate about the significance of such casting in attempting to relate the scriptural Simon to contemporary interpretations of Scripture.

Similarly, in the world of modern religious music, Ray Boltz's song "Watch the Lamb" (1986) provides a vignette of Simon and his two sons on "Good Friday." When his sons question him about what they will see, Simon advises them: "Dear children, watch the lamb." Simon also cautions his sons that there will be a crowd in Jerusalem that day to celebrate the Passover. On reaching Jerusalem, Simon senses that something is amiss; instead of joyful worshipers, there is an angry crowd crying out for the crucifixion of Jesus. When Simon and his sons attempt to leave the scene, they cannot get away; they are forced to take part in a distasteful drama. Simon's sons wonder why these three men are being put to death. One of the men pleads for mercy; another, violent and arrogant, screams at the crowd. The third man—Jesus—badly beaten with a crown of thorns on his head and blood pouring from his body, falls to the ground. As the crowd yells, a Roman soldier grabs Simon's arm and commands: "You, carry His cross." Simon tries to resist, but the soldier reaches for his sword. Simon then shoulders the cross of Jesus and continues down the street with the blood of Jesus streaming down Simon's cheek. Arriving at Golgotha—the place of execution—Jesus is nailed to the cross, yet, with love in his eyes, prays: "Father, forgive them" and then dies. The drama of the death of Jesus is not over for Simon. What explanation can he offer to his weeping sons? The most that Simon can do is to embrace his sons and face the cross: "Dear children, watch the lamb."[13]

Both in Scripture and in artistic depictions, the fifth station represents a unique event—a *kairos*—that has inspired Christians to "Take up [your] cross and follow Me" (Mark 8:34). The example of Simon has been the inspiration for the "Cyrenian movement," originating in the United Kingdom and the Republic of Ireland, whose guiding principle of "sharing the burden" is used to explain its approach in providing services to homeless and other disadvantaged groups in society.

## MEDITATIONS

Christians making the Stations of the Cross usually pause at each station for a period of meditation or spiritual reflection; there are numerous texts for such meditations, which are usually accompanied by traditional prayers and hymns. The following meditation on the fifth station was written by John Henry Newman (1801–90):

> Jesus could bear His Cross alone, did He so will; but He permits Simon to help Him, in order to remind us that we must take part in His sufferings, and have a fellowship in His work. His merit is infinite, yet He condescends to let His people add their merit to it. The sanctity of the Blessed Virgin, the blood of the Martyrs, the prayers and penances of the Saints, the good deeds of all the faithful take part in that work which, nevertheless, is perfect without them. He saves us by His blood, but it is through and with ourselves that He saves us. Dear Lord, teach us to suffer with Thee, make it pleasant to us to suffer for Thy sake, and sanctify all our sufferings by the merits of Thy own.[14]

Pope John Paul II also wrote a set of meditations on the Stations of the Cross; he commented on the fifth station:

> In a Lenten hymn we hear the words: "Under the weight of the Cross Jesus welcomes the Cyrenean." These words allow us to discern a total change of perspective: the divine Condemned One is someone who, in a certain sense, *"makes a gift" of his Cross*. Was it not he who said: "He who does not take up his cross and follow me is not worthy of me" (*Mt* 10:38)? Simon receives a gift. *He has become "worthy"* of it. What the crowd might see as an offence to his dignity has, from the perspective of redemption, given him a new dignity. In a unique way, the Son of God has made him a sharer in his work of salvation. Is Simon aware of this?
>
> The evangelist Mark identifies Simon of Cyrene as the "father of Alexander and Rufus" (15:21). If the sons of Simon of Cyrene were known to the first Christian community, it can be presumed that Simon too, while carrying the Cross, came to believe in Christ. From being forced, he freely

accepted, as though deeply touched by the words: "Whoever does not carry his cross with me is not worthy of me." By his carrying of the Cross, *Simon was brought to the knowledge of the gospel of the Cross*. Since then, this gospel has spoken to many, countless Cyreneans, called in the course of history to carry the cross with Jesus. [15]

Pope John Paul concluded his meditation with the following prayer:

> O Christ, you gave to Simon of Cyrene
> the dignity of carrying your Cross.
> Welcome us too under its weight,
> welcome all men and women
> and grant to everyone the gift of readiness to serve.
> Do not permit that we should turn away from those
> who are crushed by the cross of illness
> loneliness, hunger or injustice.
> As we carry each other's burdens,
> help us to become witnesses to the gospel of the Cross and
> witnesses to you,
> who live and reign for ever and ever. *Amen.*

## SPIRITUALITY

However important the biblical background to the Stations of the Cross, however detailed the historical data, however profound the theological analysis, however numerous the modern interpretations, however spiritually insightful the meditations, perhaps the final word about the Stations of the Cross should be that of participants:

> After a Good Friday procession in which thousands accompanied an enactment of Jesus carrying his cross through San Antonio's downtown streets, parishioner and journalist Victor Landa stated: "Every step down the Via Dolorosa is an affirmation of our past, an understanding of our present, and a courageous entrance into our future."[16]

## NOTES

1. Both parallel passages (Matt 27:32; Luke 23:26) mention Simon of Cyrene; however, only Mark describes him as "the father of Alexander and Rufus." In contrast, the Gospel of John (19:17) not only does not mention Simon, but emphasizes that Jesus carried the cross himself.

2. The "Way of the Cross" provides Christians with the opportunity not only of remembering the "passion of Christ" but also of "re-presenting"—making present again—that event in their own lives. Thus, the "Way of the Cross" is not merely a memorial drama, but also an experiential meditation: a prayer in action.

3. For example, Egeria (Aetheria), a Spanish (Gallic) woman wrote a detailed account (*Itinerarium Egeriae* or *Peregrinatio Aetheriae*) of her pilgrimage to Jerusalem (ca. 381–384). Further information and links to translations are available at http://home.infionline.net/~ddisse/egeria.html (accessed July 17, 2012).

4. In 1731, Pope Clement XII fixed the number at 14; however, a fifteenth station, commemorating the resurrection of Jesus, is sometimes added.

5. The fourteen stations are as follows: (1) Jesus is condemned to death; (2) Jesus takes up his cross; (3) Jesus falls the first time; (4) Jesus meets his mother; (5) Simon of Cyrene helps Jesus carry the cross; (6) Veronica wipes the face of Jesus; (7) Jesus falls the second time; (8) Jesus meets the daughters of Jerusalem; (9) Jesus falls the third time; (10) Jesus is stripped of his garments; (11) Jesus is nailed to the cross; (12) Jesus dies on the cross; (13) the body of Jesus is taken down from the cross; (14) the body of Jesus is laid in the tomb.

6. The stations representing the three "falls" of Jesus (3, 7, 9), the meeting of Jesus with his mother (4), and Veronica's wiping of his face (6) are not found in the Gospel accounts of the passion of Jesus.

7. A copy of Memling's painting (1470–1, Galleria Sabauda, Turin) is available at http://www.artbible.info/art/large/351.html (accessed July 17, 2012).

8. The donors have been identified, respectively, as Tommaso Portinari, a Florentine banker in Bruges (lower left-hand side) and

his wife Maria Baroncelli (lower right-hand side) on the basis of their resemblance to portraits of the couple painted by Memling, available at http://www.wga.hu/frames-e.html?/html/m/memling/1early2/04passi.html (accessed July 17, 2012).

9. The way that the *patibulum* was attached to the *stipes* is a further question: most depictions of the crucifixion of Jesus show the *patibulum* a couple feet below the top of the *stipes*, thereby, leaving room for the proclamation ("Jesus of Nazareth: King of the Jews"); however, Roman executions often placed the *patibulum* on top of the *stipes*, thereby, giving the cross a "T-shape."

10. For example, see the description of the executions in the Roman Coliseum available at http://www.roman-colosseum.info/colosseum/roman-executions-at-the-colosseum.htm (accessed July 17, 2012).

11. For Peter's denial, see the Gospel of John 18:15–27; John 19:25–27 does not list Peter as being present at the crucifixion.

12. According to the Gnostic *Second Treatise of the Great Seth*, Simon, not Jesus, was the one who suffered and died on the cross; a translation of this treatise is available at http://www.gnosis.org/naghamm/2seth.html (accessed July 17, 2012).

13. Ray Boltz, "Watch the Lamb," 1986. The lyrics are available at http://www.uulyrics.com/music/ray-boltz/song-watch-the-lamb/ (accessed July 17, 2012).

14. John Henry Newman, "Fifth Station," *Stations of the Cross* (Oxford: Family Publications, 2009); this meditation is preceded by a traditional invocation ("We adore thee, O Christ, and we bless thee") and response ("Because by thy Holy Cross thou hast redeemed the world"), and followed by the recitation of the Our Father, Hail Mary, Glory Be, and the versicle: "Have mercy on us, O Lord." In the Family Publication of Newman's *Stations,* each station is accompanied by the reproduction of an appropriate painting and a (translated) verse from the thirteenth-century hymn *Stabat Mater Dolorosa* ("The Sorrowful Mother stood"), a hymn that is traditionally sung by groups making the Stations. The Latin text and English translation of the *Stabat Mater Dolorosa* is available at http://www.stabatmater.info/english.html (accessed July 17, 2012). Newman's "Short Meditation on the Stations of the Cross," which was originally written about 1860 and then used a second time in

1885, was published in his *Meditations and Devotions*, 155–69, and is available at http://www.newmanreader.org/works/meditations/meditations5.html#stations (accessed July 17, 2012).

15.  The text of the Stations of the Cross by Pope John Paul II is available at http://www.vatican.va/holy_father/john_paul_ii/speeches/documents/hf_jp-ii_spe_20000421_via-crucis_en.html (accessed July 17, 2012).

16.  Timothy Matovina, *Guadalupe and Her Faithful: Latino Catholics in San Antonio, from Colonial Origins to the Present* (Baltimore: The Johns Hopkins University Press, 2005), 146.

**18**

# BIBLE STUDY: HOW DID JESUS DEFINE HIS MINISTRY?

A Study of Matthew 28:16–20 and Luke 4:16–21

*Don Thorsen*

## INTRODUCTION

How did Jesus define his ministry? Certainly, Jesus undertook the ministry of the Messiah (or Christ, "the anointed one"), whereby through his life, death, and resurrection, people may be reconciled with God (John 3:16). Similarly, Christians have been given "the ministry of reconciliation" (2 Cor 5:18). But, according to the words of Jesus: How did he define his ministry?

Jesus said many things about his ministry, and Christians throughout church history have tried to summarize what he said. However, Christians and churches have not always agreed with regard to the nature and role model of Jesus' ministry. Some have defined his ministry evangelically, emphasizing evangelism and missions. Others have defined it more in terms of apostolicity, sacraments, liturgy, preaching, biblical study and its application, holiness, discipleship, spiritual disciplines, social activism, spiritual gifts, ecumenism, and so on.

Most Christians would not want to limit Jesus' ministry to any of the particular manifestations of it in historic churches. Of course, diversity in and of itself is not necessarily inappropriate, since the apostle Paul talked about the church as a body consisting of many interdependent parts—eyes, ears, mouths, hands, and feet (1 Cor 12:4–31). Just as local churches consist of members of diverse gifts and talents, the church universal consists of churches and denominations of diverse gifts and talents.

Throughout church history, Christians wondered about the particular mission to which they believed God called them—the *missio Dei* (Latin, mission of God). As already mentioned, there has not been unanimity among Christians and churches with regard to what the mission of God is or should be for them. A common biblical passage to which they have looked is Matt 28:16–20, the so-called Great Commission. It emphasizes going, making disciples, baptizing, teaching, and remembering. This final exhortation by Jesus to the disciples influenced the extraordinary growth of Christianity in the first century as well as subsequent centuries. But does the Great Commission sufficiently define Jesus' ministry and does it specify the mission of God for Christians and churches today?

## HOLISTIC MISSION OF GOD

*Although the Great Commission represents an essential part of the mission of God, it does not define the totality of Jesus' ministry and it does not exhaust the ministries to which God calls Christians and churches today because the Bible presents a more holistic mission of God than can be encapsulated in a single passage.* Certainly, a number of Bible verses or passages could be chosen to highlight the breadth and depth of God's concerns for humanity. For example, a key passage can be found in Luke 4:16–21, which recounts a story that began at the beginning of Jesus' ministry. In fact, it can be argued that a ministry is usually defined at the beginning of its implementation, rather than at the end. The Great Commission may represent a final priority that Jesus emphatically did not want his disciples to neglect. But Luke 4:16–21 announces and defines Jesus' ministry as poignantly as Matthew 28:16–20, portraying the holistic dimensions of God's mission for Christians and churches to the world.

So let us study the two passages: Matthew 28:16–20 (Great Commission) and Luke 4:16–21, which I will call—for the lack of a better term—Jesus' First Sermon. The two passages are complementary, rather than contradictory. A study of both helps to develop the breadth and depth of Jesus' ministry, which has profound implications for how we as Christians and churches go about the mission of God today.

## Great Commission—Matthew 28:16–20

> Now the eleven disciples went to Galilee, to the mountain to which Jesus had directed them. When they saw him, they worshipped him; but some doubted. And Jesus came and said to them, "All authority in heaven and on earth has been given to me. Go therefore and make disciples of all nations, baptizing them in the name of the Father and of the Son and of the Holy Spirit, and teaching them to obey everything that I have commanded you. And remember, I am with you always, to the end of the age."

The last words Jesus tells his disciples in the Gospel of Matthew are known as the Great Commission. The fact that Jesus said these words only to the eleven disciples has not prevented Christians and churches from applying them as relevant to all believers (v. 16). The Great Commission speaks of the disciples' worship of Jesus—a clear reference to his divinity (v. 17). It speaks of lingering doubt; even the miracle of the resurrection does not eradicate the ongoing need for faith (v. 17). The Great Commission also speaks of authority—"all authority in heaven and on earth" (v. 18). Jesus' reference to his surpassing authority was to be remembered as much as anything else in encouraging the disciples on the brink of leaving them.

Then the well-known exhortations occur: Go! Make disciples! Baptize! Teach! Remember! For some Christians, these exhortations serve as the sum total of their understanding of the mission of God today. Certainly they have been influential in how many Christians and churches go about ministry. In both "word and deed," the Great Commission has been put into practice recurrently throughout church history.

All Christians and churches have affirmed the Great Commission, but not all have made it the centerpiece in their understanding and implementation of the mission of God. It is not a matter of acceptance but of priority.[1] Although the Great Commission is often used as a plea to evangelize, no explicit mention of evangelism or evangelization is mentioned. It talks about going, making disciples, baptizing, teaching, and remembering, which envisions a more comprehensive mission than just evangelism. Of course, it is difficult to make disciples without engaging in evangelism of some sort. So, Christians need to come back to the passage over and over again in order rightly to interpret, embody, and live out the Great Commission.

Affirmation of the Great Commission does not preclude other biblical beliefs, values, and practices. Indeed, no single verse (or set of verses) should be thought of as the sum of the Gospel. Any prioritizing of Scripture (or "canon within the canon") can lead to distortion. So wisdom, prudence, justice, and courage (the cardinal virtues) need to be used as well as faith, hope, and love (the theological virtues) in rightly divining the nature and extent to which Christians and churches implement the Great Commission in both word and deed.

"Going" emphasizes that the Gospel of Jesus Christ is for "all nations," both Gentiles (non-Jews) as well as Jews (v. 19). The inclusiveness of the Great Commission reminds us of one of the marks of the church found in the Nicene Creed. The marks describe the church as one, holy, catholic, and apostolic. Catholicity reminds us of how the Gospel is for all people, regardless of their race, ethnicity, culture, gender, language, or nationality.

"Making disciples" involves more than making converts (v. 19). It has as much or more to do with the nurturing and mentoring of believers, similar to the way Jesus gathered disciples and trained them. Regardless of one's *theory* (or theological understanding of the Great Commission), in *practice* Christians and churches place far more emphasis on discipleship than upon evangelism. Even the most evangelistically oriented churches spend more time, talents, and money dedicated to nurturing and mentoring believers than in making converts.

"Baptizing' incorporates believers into the church—the body of true believers (v. 19). Jesus was baptized, and he commanded his disciples to be baptized as well. Throughout church history, Christians have had different understandings of the nature and obliga-

301

tion of baptism. Some consider it a sacrament, ordained by Jesus, which serves as a means of grace by which people are cleansed of sins and made children of God as well as vouchsafed for heaven. Others consider it a sacrament, but more a symbolic act or ordinance than a means of grace. Still others do not require baptism, considering all of life sacramental, which makes it unnecessary (and perhaps misleading) to uplift baptismal practices above other religious practices. Despite differences, Christians and churches historically have considered their understanding and implementation of baptism crucial to their mission. The crucial nature of baptism becomes all the more important given Jesus' command to perform it "in the name of the Father and of the Son and of the Holy Spirit" (v. 19). The liturgical reference solemnizes both the ritual of baptism and the trinitarian reference to God.

"Teaching" refers to, among other things, Jesus' teaching of the Gospel (v. 20). Of course, Jesus' teachings include far more, which both the disciples and other followers thereafter benefited from immeasurably. His teachings are not just to be taught and heard; they are to be obeyed. Jesus' teachings include things he "commanded" them. Grace, mercy, and forgiveness are key components of the Gospel, but they do not preclude Jesus' expectation that his disciples—all his followers—act obediently (orthopraxis) as well as believe and worship rightly (orthodoxy). To these so-called "orthos," one could add others: right heart (orthokardia); right affections (orthoaffectus); right passions (orthopathy); right community (orthocommunitas); right society (orthosocietas); and so on. Jesus' Gospel was holistic; it applied to all areas of life and not just to right beliefs, or even right actions. We sometimes truncate the Gospel with our categorizations that restrict, rather than liberate, the fullness of it.

Finally, "remembering" pertains to all of the above, so to speak (v. 20). In particular, we are to remember that Jesus is with us always. We're never alone; we're never without our savior, lord, and friend. Biblical commentators point out that Jesus refers to the prophecy in Isaiah, quoted in Matthew 1:23, which refers to Jesus as "Emmanuel," meaning "God with us."[2] We are to be encouraged because we do not live and act on our own power and abilities. It is God who graciously works in and through us, through the presence and power of the Holy Spirit, enabling us to be and minister on behalf of God's mission today.

## First Sermon—Luke 4:16–21

> When he came to Nazareth, where he had been brought up, he went to the synagogue on the sabbath day, as was his custom. He stood up to read, and the scroll of the prophet Isaiah was given to him. He unrolled the scroll and found the place where it was written:
>
> > "The Spirit of the Lord is upon me,
> > because he has anointed me
> > to bring good news to the poor.
> > He has sent me to proclaim release to the captives
> > and recovery of sight to the blind,
> > to let the oppressed go free,
> > to proclaim the year of the Lord's favour."
>
> And he rolled up the scroll, gave it back to the attendant, and sat down. The eyes of all in the synagogue were fixed on him. Then he began to say to them, "Today this scripture has been fulfilled in your hearing."

The Gospel of Luke says that Jesus had begun a preaching and teaching ministry in synagogues throughout Galilee, and that he had been praised for it (Luke 4:14–15). Although I refer to this passage as representing Jesus' First Sermon, he does not preach so much as he is asked to read from Scripture and comment upon it.

Jesus came to speak in Nazareth, where he had been brought up (v. 16). Indeed, it was his custom of regularly attending synagogue, being faithful to Jewish Sabbath observances (v. 16). He was given the scroll of the prophet Isaiah, since scrolls were kept in special places in synagogues. Jesus unrolled the scroll, turned to Isaiah 61, and read to the congregation, which no doubt included those who knew him, perhaps from childhood (v. 17). The readings, as found in the Lukan passage, actually represent a paraphrase or conflation of several passages: Isaiah 61:1, 58:6, and 61:2 (vv. 18–19).[3] Perhaps Luke summarized the readings of Isaiah and Jesus' comments upon them; perhaps Luke gives his own construal of the subject matter.

After the Scripture reading, Jesus rolled up the scroll, gave it back to an attendant, and sat down (v. 20). According to Luke, everyone's eyes were intently focused on Jesus. Then Jesus said, "Today this scripture has been fulfilled in your hearing" (v. 21). It is not easy to interpret, at first glance, what Jesus meant by the fulfillment of Isaiah's words. Are the words to be taken prophetically, and Jesus fulfilled the prophecy? Do Isaiah's words, more specifically, serve as a prophecy about him being the messiah? Or, do the words represent a longstanding prophetic mission to proclaim God's words to the poor, care for their needs—both physical and spiritual—and, finally, to proclaim the jubilee release from slavery and other socioeconomic obligations? In exactly what way did Jesus consider the words of Isaiah to be fulfilled?

Regardless of how one interprets the prophetic nature of the Isaiah passage, Jesus considered it representative of his mission— of his ministry. So, in order to gain more insight into the nature of that mission and ministry, we need to study the meaning of Isaiah's words and consider their application both in the life and service of Jesus as well as in their meaning for Christians and churches today.

The Isaiah passage begins with the words, "The Spirit of the Lord is upon me, because he has anointed me" (v. 18). These words may or may not be taken literally. That is, the prophetic nature of Isaiah does not need to be understood as being historically predictive. Instead, they may be understood symbolically or representative of "forth-telling" the words of God, rather than fulfillment of a "fore-telling" of them. Prophecy includes both forth-telling and fore-telling. So Jesus' statement of their fulfillment may be more of a description of God's mission and ministry in general, rather than his revelation as the messiah. Certainly, Luke considered Jesus to be the Messiah—someone with whom the Holy Spirit was present, and who empowered Jesus (Luke 4:1, 14). Jesus' anointing may have been a special revelation of the Messiah, but the reference more likely has to do with anyone who fulfills the divinely-inspired exhortations of Isaiah.

For what does Isaiah say the Spirit anoints: "to bring good news to the poor" (v. 18). The first part of this exhortation has to do with bringing good news—the Gospel (Greek, *euangelion*). Interestingly, this emphasis on bringing (or witnessing) places more emphasis on traditional understandings of proclamation of the Gospel than what is found in the Great Commission. Regardless of whether one thinks that the bringing of the good news should occur more in "word" or "deed," the exhortation to do it is undeniable. In a sense, both Christians and churches cannot help but witness to or proclaim Jesus in all that they say and do. Perhaps a more important question has to do with the kind of witness or proclamation they bring to others.

The second part of Jesus' opening exhortation is more intriguing, perplexing, and perhaps challenging. The passage says "to bring good news to the poor" (vs. 18). Why the poor? Is the Gospel only for the poor? Even a cursory survey of the New Testament demonstrates that this is not the case; the Gospel is for everyone! Be that as it may, there seems to be an undeniable concern—if not priority—given to the poor. Theologically, some Christians have talked about Jesus as embodying a "preferential option for the poor." Certainly, Jesus seems concerned to minister to those who are impoverished in so many ways—spiritually, physically, financially, socially, and so on. Again, even a cursory survey of the New Testament demonstrates that Jesus repeatedly went out of his way to heal, cast out demons, care for the poor, and generally minister to the holistic needs of people. In a sense, all people are impoverished in one way or another. But Jesus wanted to be sure that the most impoverished not be overlooked with regard to bringing the good news—in its entirety—to people.

Subsequent to the exhortation to bring good news to the poor, the Isaiah passage continues by talking about proclaiming "release to the captives," "recovery of sight to the blind," and letting "the oppressed go free" (v. 18). Are these physical, tangible ways of ministering to people of equal value as the proclamation dimensions of bringing the good news? After all, Christians and churches often seem to place more emphasis upon the spiritual, intangible dimensions of the Bible. But the Isaiah passage does not seem to distinguish between the value of the spiritual and physical dimensions people experience; likewise, it does not seem to distinguish between the kinds of challenges they experience. Thus, ministry needs to include care for all the ways people are impoverished, and this study of Jesus' ministry includes care for people's physical well-being in addition to their spiritual well-being.

The Isaiah passage ends with a reference to proclamation of "the year of the Lord's favor," an allusion to Old Testament references to the year of jubilee (v. 19). Jubilee refers to Holiness Code regulations in the Book of Leviticus that returned land and freed indentured slaves, among other practices, after seven cycles of sabbaticals (seven years), equaling approximately forty-nine years. The practice of jubilee represented a liberating and equalizing practice among Jews, which especially aided those who had become impoverished, one way or another, over the previous decades. Jubilee primarily applied to social, political, and economic redemption, but it was analogous to the redemption God freely gave to Israel, to those who believe in God for their atonement.

In sum, Jesus had no problem saying that his ministry embodied the words of Isaiah. He came to proclaim, and to do so especially on behalf of the poor. He came to proclaim release, provide recovery of sight to the blind, let the oppressed go free, and proclaim the year of the Lord's favor. His ministry was not limited to the spiritual realm; his ministry was inextricably bound up with caring for all the needs of people. It was a holistic ministry that cared for every dimension of impoverishment people experienced.

## COMPLEMENTARITY OF SCRIPTURE AND UNITY IN MISSION

Do these two passages of Scripture conflict with one another, or are they complementary? Certainly, the passages have been understood and applied differently in church history. They have also been used, at times, to divide Christians and churches rather than unite them. But more Christians and churches have viewed the passages as complementary to one another. Both contain important principles and guidelines from Jesus. We would do well to understand and apply both passages in ways that contribute to effective efforts in ministry and ecumenical relations.

Of course, one could ask whether Scripture contradicts Scripture. To be sure, Scripture is vast and contains a variety of perspectives, which has left some Christians and churches confused, if not conflicted. But the two passages of Scripture studied are not in conflict; they do not present two Gospels, which are mutually exclusive. On the contrary, they provide balance and stimulation for communicating the reconciling, healing, just, holistic Gospel of Jesus—a wholeness impossible to encapsulate in any single word, passage, action, or event in the Bible. The Great Commission and First Sermon together produce a whole greater than the sum of the discrete parts contained in each passage.

The Great Commission emphasizes the going and making of disciples more than Jesus' First Sermon. But the First Sermon emphasizes more explicitly the bringing of good news. It is ironic that the latter scriptural passage emphasizes "bringing" and "proclaiming" more than the Great Commission, though Christians and churches have not generally looked to Jesus' First Sermon for promoting evangelism and missions. Both passages emphasize the need to go beyond the immediate, cultural, racial, ethnic, tribal, linguistic, and national confines of people. Both passages emphasize the need to obey all the teachings, beliefs, and values of Jesus.

Each biblical passage has its own unique contributions to make in understanding and applying Jesus' ministry. Each has a slightly different emphasis, but each reinforces and expands upon the other. Indeed, more than the two portions of Scripture are needed for meeting the multitudinous needs of people and of the world today. The Bible, in general, and the New Testament, in particular, contains numerous statements about the holistic nature and extent of involvements to which God calls Christians and churches. No two passages are sufficient. Be that as it may, the Great Commission and First Sermon embody two of the most influential summations of Jesus' ministry—summations that have been integral to historic Christian and church self-understanding and to their respective ministries.

On the one hand, the Great Commission emphasizes the importance of discipleship and mentoring believers, one-on-one and in small accountability groups. It emphasizes the rites, rituals, and liturgical practices of historic churches. The Great Commission also emphasizes the need to remember that Jesus is with us, giving us authority, and empowering all that we think, say, and do.

On the other hand, the First Sermon emphasizes the special place that caring for the poor—in all its manifestations, physically and socially as well as spiritually—God intends for Christians and churches. It emphasizes how we ought to minister to the variety of ways that people are impoverished—those who are physically challenged; those who are held captive, personally or institutionally; and those who are oppressed—which involves advocacy ministries as well as compassion ministries. The First Sermon also emphasizes the concept of jubilee and the liberating of people and groups of people from the social, political, and economic binds that perpetuate the causes of their impoverishment.

Too often, Christians and churches have used these biblical passages in ways that divide Christians. For example, evangelically oriented Christians have promoted evangelism and missions at the expense of caring for the poor and oppressed. Likewise, other Christians and churches have promoted social justice at the expense of making disciples of all nations. Rather than work cooperatively and ecumenically, the Great Commission and First Sermon have been used to distract, divide, and discourage the holistic ministry of Jesus. But the aforementioned emphases are not mutually exclusive. If we look at the two biblical passages as complementary, rather than in conflict, then Christians and churches will probably have more balanced and effective ministries. It will also help them to become more understanding and supportive of one another, which—after all—contributes to the unity we seek.

## CONCLUSION: WHAT THEN SHOULD WE DO?

The Great Commission and Jesus' First Sermon serve as complementary guides for Christian and church ministries today. They reinforce and augment each other, creating a more holistic understanding of Jesus' ministry and the kind of ministries to which he calls us to implement today. The two biblical passages do not exhaust the ways in which we may demonstrate our love for God and for others, but they provide a profound starting point for how Christians and churches ought to minister. It is a starting point to which we may beneficially return again and again in order to reassess, reenvision, and reapply Jesus' beliefs and values for people and the world today.

A complementary view of the Great Commission and First Sermon contribute to the unity of Christians and churches as well as their unity in mission. Commitment to mission—to the *missio Dei*—helps to unite us. Integrating definitions of ministry, which minimally include the Great Commission and First Sermon, contribute to Christian service in ways that are both biblical and holistic. It also contributes to fulfilling more effectively the ideal of ministry exemplified in the person and work of Jesus Christ.

Finally, the Gospel of Luke records questions people asked John the Baptist after he called them to repentance. They asked, "What then should we do?" (Luke 3:10; cf. 3:12, 14). To each, John gave different answers, based upon the particularities of who they were and what they did in life, but his exhortations united rather than divided them. The same could be said in response to the complementarity of the Great Commission and Jesus' First Sermon: Do both! Integrate rather than disconnect their exhortations to minister. Do not limit the Gospel and ministry of Jesus; instead recognize and implement their holistic relevance for the variety of needs of people and society today. Be unified in ministry, and be unified one with another. May a broadened understanding of the nature and extent of Jesus' ministry contribute to God's mission for Christians and churches.

## NOTES

1. In talking about the Great Commission, I draw upon my work with Steve Wilkens, entitled *Everything You Know about Evangelicals Is Wrong (Well, Almost Everything): An Insider's Look at Myths and Realities* (Grand Rapids: BakerBooks, 2010), 198–201.

2. *The New Oxford Annotated Bible*, An Ecumenical Study Bible, ed. Michael D. Coogan and others, 3rd ed. (New Revised Standard Version with the Apocrypha; Oxford, New York: Oxford University Press, 2001), Matthew 28:20, n. 20 [55 New Testament].

3. *The New Oxford Annotated Bible*, Luke 4:18–19, n. 18–19 [103 New Testament].

# 19

# GOSPEL AND EMPIRE
## A Bible Study

*Dale E. Luffman*

Now after John was arrested, Jesus came to Galilee,
proclaiming the good news of God, and saying, "the time is
fulfilled, and the kingdom of God has come near; repent,
and believe in the good news."

—*Mark 1:14–15*

## TEXT AND CONTEXT

There has been a noticeable increase in conversations among Christians of late regarding the significance of empire. Certainly, a number of factors have contributed to the increased conversation and dialogue. An extended decade-long war in Afghanistan, reports of state-sanctioned torture, the unique and uncontested position of the United States as the dominant military, economic, and political power in the world, together with increased economic difficulties at home and abroad have fueled the conversation for an increasing number of Christians. As calls for peace are ignored, frustration grows. Talk concerning the growing divide between those possessing great wealth and those who are not able to make ends meet in simply providing basic necessities for living is on the rise, and many are led to ask the question, "How is the Christian to understand the relationship of the Gospel to one's life and witness in the presence of empire?"

The presence of empire and its pervasive influence that it exercises on Christian communities of every age and era and in every place, first of all, needs to acknowledged and confessed. How might

311

Christians be helped to discern, not only the seductive powers exercised by empire, but also the claim of the Gospel for an alternative orientation? Is it possible for the Christian community to express itself faithfully in a time of fear, realistically facing with genuine Christian hope problems associated with the presence of empire? To these questions, and to the subject of Gospel and empire, we now turn.

Deeply embedded in popular Christian belief is what might be called "Christian privatism." This orientation would essentially describe a commitment to approaching texts of Scripture with an overriding concern for answers to personal issues. This orientation would also pursue a quest for personal holiness as well as existential happiness. Unfortunately, this reading can become a very personal affair, frequently expressing itself in the pursuit of a "personal savior" or the desire for some kind of self-fulfillment. Such a pursuit often results in a domestication of the Gospel witness that regards Jesus, not so much as the Lord of the world, but as Lord of one's heart. In this kind of privatism, it is the heart into which Jesus is invited to dwell and to have dominion. Refuge is often sought here.

In an increasingly uncertain world, one that is abounding in conflict, the seeking for refuge in personal self-fulfillment is quite understandable. Such seeking can, however, and frequently does lead to a Christianity of self-absorption. It places the witness of the good news primarily in the private sphere, frequently muting the witness of the Gospel in the larger world of society, culture, and the church. Often, this view of a privatized Gospel is co-opted by the forces of empire.

"Christianity can hardly be understood apart from empire," writes Joerg Rieger. "The Roman Empire was the context of the earliest beginnings of Christianity, and most of the subsequent major developments of Christian theology and the church are located somewhere in the force fields of empire as well."[1]

Often these connections are either taken for granted or simply overlooked. Christianity cannot escape empire inasmuch as the influence of empire, those massive concentrations of economic, military, and cultural power, all permeate aspects of human life. In many ways, empire acts like a force field, extending its influence and co-opting rival alternatives. Because this is so, Daniel L.

Migliore counsels that "Christian faith must approach every human culture with a critical eye."[2]

# HISTORICAL AND THEOLOGICAL ANALYSIS

The Gospel of Mark was originally composed to speak clearly to the followers of Jesus. Mark's Gospel was written to help early Christians, who as imperial subjects, needed to learn some very hard lessons about their world and about themselves as a disciple community residing in the world of empire.

Recall that the first books of the Old Testament were brought together in a canonical form in Judah's Babylonian captivity. This project formed the first part of what we have come to know as the Hebrew Bible. This captive community formed Scripture so that it could ultimately form their unique community. With a similar impulse, Mark writes of an authentic way of following Jesus. Just as the emerging texts of the Old Testament provided a counter-narrative to the Babylonian culture and its religious traditions, Mark comes to the aid of the early disciple community. He creates a Gospel with the intent of helping the community of Jesus' followers to discern the seductive power of empire while at the same time asserting the counter-claim of the way of Jesus understood through discipleship. Some have considered the first Gospel to be written as a manifesto of sorts: a proclamation of radical discipleship in the world. This unique Gospel seems to question what has become the prevailing practice of Christians whose study of the Bible has become preoccupied with private and heavenly matters, while the world becomes impaled on the imperial cross of violence and subjugation.

Mark, the oldest of the canonical Gospels, likely originated amid the developing conflicts of the Roman-Jewish War of 66–70 CE. The work has a prevailing sense of urgency—this work takes empire very seriously. One of the questions that seems to be asked by Mark's readers is this: "What are we to do when the Romans reach Jerusalem with their armies?" This is a question born of crisis. Jerusalem is under threat. The counsel of Mark's Jesus is that they are to flee to the mountains: "But when you see the desolating sacrilege set up where it ought not to be (let the reader understand), then those in Judea must flee to the mountains" (Mark 13:14). This language recalls the Book of Daniel (9:27; 11:31; 12:11) and its testimony regarding God's judgment on imperial occupation in the temple in Jerusalem. The disciples of Jesus to whom Mark writes would readily understand that what is meant is that the presence of the Roman eagle brought by an invading army is a symbolic expression of a consuming imperial power and authority, subjugating both the temple and the people. As an empire casts its influence and might over the land, resulting in sacrilege and destruction, Mark's Jesus proclaims, "All will be thrown down" (13:2). The disciples become aware that they have no future with Jerusalem; they should, therefore, head for the hills!

In Mark's Gospel, Jesus systematically confronts agents of empire and their destructive causes. Jesus does this while simultaneously articulating an alternative community of discipleship—a community that can see, hear, and understand. Tension between these two forces, of empire and discipleship, pervade this Gospel narrative.

Both Babylon and Rome stand as symbols of worldly empire in the biblical narrative. Mark's Gospel honestly recognizes that religious traditions, beliefs, and practices are often inescapably intertwined with the discourses as well as the institutions of empire. The disciples frequently just do not get it! They do not understand. Their lack of comprehension exposes the human tendency to fail to distinguish between the claim of the Gospel and the claims of empire.

Traditions, beliefs, and practices often unintentionally reinforce and legitimize domination as in the case of Peter's response to Jesus when asked, "Who do people say that I am?" (Mark 8:27). In doing so, religions themselves possess the potential of sustaining the soul of empire even though the values of empire are at odds with the sentiments of religious traditions. Popular Christian privatism is often a vehicle that naively becomes a supportive agent of empire.

Mark is an ideological narrative of sorts. It is a manifesto of an early Christian discipleship community. In Mark, the Gospel narrative enters the war of myths that dominate the social order and challenges the structures of power. Only by laying open the potential religious ties to empire, are persons of faith able to see the possible ways by which the Gospel provides potential alternatives to the domination and violence of empire. In this first Gospel, this inclination is confessed, and disciples are given an alternative to pursue.

Note the first verse in the Gospel of Mark. A confrontation is announced: "The beginning of the good news of Jesus Christ, the Son of God" (Mark1:1). Here an echo of Isaiah is heard: "How beautiful upon the mountains are the feet of the messenger who announces peace, who brings good news, who announces salvation, who says to Zion, 'Your God reigns'" (Isaiah 52:7). This opening is intended as a prelude to the rest of the book especially Mark 1:14–15, verses that announce the nearness of God's reign through God's representative. The opening is intended to invite the followers of Jesus to make those necessary adjustments so that they might become disciples of God's in-breaking kingdom, and not become subjects of the prevailing order of things dominated by the forces of empire.

At the time of Mark's writing, it was common for the imperial representatives to "bring good news." The Gospel of Caesar was *Pax Romana*, the peace of Rome. This peace was initiated and sanctioned by force and was sustained by the gods. It embodied the reign of the emperor/empire. Mark begins his straightforward narrative audaciously announcing the "beginning" of a counter-narrative, a counter-gospel. Mark heralds one whom he claims to be both "Messiah" and "son of God." A new reign is proclaimed! Mark provocatively begins his faithful narrative by announcing a new divinely authorized sovereign: Jesus. He is the beloved (Mark 1:11). For the disciples of Mark's community, the message would be blatantly clear. Jesus, being God's beloved, is absolutely essential to the disciple's capacity to proclaim and live in a radically new way. The disciples are no longer to be subject only to the prevailing imperial ethos and the power and dominion of the empire. A new distinctive claim has been made.

The arrival of the reign of God demonstrated in Mark's "good news" brings to the attention of the first-century readers the hopes of Second Temple Jews present at the time, but also all the ways in which these hopes had been compromised by the collaboration of the Jewish elite with the Roman empire. In the Book of Mark, Jesus' call to "repent" is an invitation to discern and perceive life differently. Through the eyes of Mark's Gospel, the disciple is called to perceive life from the perspective of God's in-breaking, and not from the communication of imperial propaganda.

Mark's Jesus challenges the disciples to recognize that the Gospel radically opposes the religion of the empire and its agenda, even if that empire confesses "in God we trust." The Gospel challenges disciples to consider carefully what one has been raised to understand and on what one places one's hopes. It might be said that the task of the church in every age is to liberate the church in its teaching and preaching from the false theologies of its age and free it to proclaim that "the kingdom of God has come near" (Mark 1:15).

Key to the disciples understanding is the counter-claim of the Son of Man or the Human One. Even though Jesus' mission may elicit memories of Davidic kingship, Mark's Jesus goes out of his way to suggest a more fruitful and faithful alternative. Instead of an understanding of an empire-like Davidic kingdom, Jesus is represented as offering a counter-story. "The Son of Man must undergo great suffering, and be rejected" (Mark 8:31). Even though Peter protests, Jesus insists that it is his version of the story that is to be listened to (see Mark 1:11). The path of Isaiah's suffering servant and not the Davidic warrior king is the Jesus-attested story that is to be followed by the disciples in the community for which Mark writes. The course that Jesus has taken, and the course commended by Mark's Jesus, is one of radical discipleship: "If any want to become my followers, let them deny themselves and take up their cross and follow me" (Mark 8:34).

Jesus instructs those who would follow him that, although they are inclined to be power hungry and self-serving disciples living in the midst of a power hungry and self-serving culture, they must reject outright the ways of empire that defines things as they are. They must adopt new eyes for seeing, and new ears for hearing and understanding.

Perhaps one of the central purposes of Mark's Gospel is this: to undermine the authority of those who benefit from the convoluted allegiances of empire and religion. It appears that Mark's criticism, though it is framed in a specific historical context, is addressed to every culture and every political system. In Mark's Jesus, the conspiracy between empire and religion (symbolized by the temple) is exposed. It is to be replaced by a gathered community of discipleship that is faithful in its pursuit of God's in-breaking reign. That we miss this in our reading of Mark and the New Testament is evidence of the power of empire and its pervasive influence that it exercises on Christian communities of every era and in every place. How eagerly we embrace the way of empire, and how quick we are to do so in the name of Jesus.

## HANGING NEW PICTURES IN OUR MIND'S GALLERIES

Fred B. Craddock has often said that it is the task of the preacher to assist the hearer of the sermon to hang new pictures in the gallery of the mind. Good preachers do this. Mark, the Gospel writer, is a good preacher!

Let Mark create some new pictures in the gallery of your mind. Carefully and thoughtfully read and reflect on the following passages from the Gospel of Mark. After reading each one of them silently, read each one of them out loud. Hear what is being said. Pause and contemplate what you read and hear. Linger in the texts. Read the questions to the right of the passage, allowing the question(s) to stimulate your contemplation. Pray following the reading and contemplation of each passage.

| | |
|---|---|
| Mark 1:14–15 | How is it that the reign of God is seeking to come near at this time, in this place? How does this understanding speak to the influence of empire in your life? |
| Mark 13:14 | From what might you need to flee? |
| Mark 13:1–2 | What is it that you see being thrown down? What will fill the void? |

Mark 8:15    What is the measure of influence that the "good news" brings to your life? What is brought to the community of faith? What counter-narrative to empire might you pursue?

Mark 8:27–38    Who is Jesus, for me (for us!), today? What real difference does it make when "the time is fulfilled, and the kingdom of God has come near" (Mark 1:15)? How does our confession offer an authentic prophetic witness?

## NOTES

1. Joerg Rieger, "Christian Theology and Empires," in *Empire and the Christian Tradition: New Readings of Classical Theologians*, ed. Kwok Pui-lan, Don H. Compier, and Joerg Rieger, (Minneapolis: Fortress Press, 2007), 1.

2. Daniel L. Migliore, *The Power of God and the Gods of Power* (Louisville: Westminster John Knox Press, 2008), 23.

# 20

# ECCLESIAL IDENTITIES AND ECUMENICAL APPROACHES

*John T. Ford*

The origins of the ecumenical movement go back to the World Missionary Conference at Edinburgh, Scotland, in 1910.[1] After the conference, two different ecumenical approaches took shape: "Faith and Order," which has sought visible unity on the basis of doctrinal agreement and institutional compatibility, and "Life and Work," which has sought to manifest Christian unity through cooperative projects.[2] Although these two international ecumenical movements united in 1948 to form the World Council of Churches, their two different approaches to visible church unity are still operative today: Faith and Order ecumenists seek visible unity on the basis of interchurch covenants grounded on doctrinal agreement and mutual reconciliation of ministry; Life and Work ecumenists seek to achieve a visible and united Christian witness through cooperation on a wide variety of social projects.

The centennial of the Edinburgh Conference prompted many ecumenists to ask: "What is the future of the ecumenical movement?"[3] Some ecumenists have lamented the onset of "an ecumenical winter" characterized by a fundamental lack of interest in ecumenism among numerous Christians and even marked resistance to ecumenism on the part of some Christians, due in part to resurgent denominationalism.[4] Paralleling this disinterest is the evident absence of effective ways of implementing ecumenical agreements at all levels of church life: for example, even those churches that have entered into ecumenical covenants with other churches at the national or international level do not always implement such covenants at the local level. Similarly, local ecumenical initiatives may not be replicated elsewhere and so have little effect regionally or nationally.

If ecumenists need to do a better job in implementing ecumenical agreements at every level of church life, it also seems important to recognize that the ecclesial identity or denominational preference—the "church choice"—of Christians is an important and often unnoticed factor in the ecumenical attitudes and involvement of American Christians.[5]

## ECCLESIAL IDENTITIES

In American Christianity at the beginning of the twenty-first century, one can recognize three distinctive ecclesial identities related to three basically different understandings of the church. First are those Christians whose beliefs and practices are influenced primarily by theological traditions and liturgical ceremonies predating the Age of the Enlightenment that began in the seventeenth century; for want of a better term, this group can be called "recapitulative." A second ecclesial identity group consists of Christians whose doctrines and devotions are basically influenced by theological perspectives and spiritual practices influenced by the Enlightenment; this second group can be termed "reformulative." A third identity group, which began emerging during the latter part of the twentieth century, distances itself from both Enlightenment theologies and traditional liturgies on the one hand and searches for new ways of being Christian on the other; this group can be described as "reinvigorative."

These three terms—recapitulative, reformulative, reinvigorative—are intended to be descriptive, not exclusive.[6] Although these ecclesial identities usually correlate with forms of worship, doctrinal beliefs, and pastoral ministries, the same person may be recapitulative in personal preferences about liturgy, reformulative in the case of doctrine, and reinvigorative in the exercise of pastoral ministry; in other words, the same person may prefer liturgies that derive from the patristic era, may be on the "cutting edge" of current theology, and may be personally committed to social outreach. Accordingly, while these three identities may correlate to some extent with denominational affiliation, most denominations and many local churches have people who identify themselves with more than one group.

First of all, these three groups are often differentiated by the different ways in which they understand Christian history. Christians of a recapitulative mentality tend to see the past as *a perennial norm* for the present; although acknowledging that the doctrines of the past need to be restated in modern terminology and church practices need to be updated for the present, recapitulative Christians consider the historical essentials basically mandatory and unchangeable. In contrast, Christians of a reformulative mindset tend to understand Christian history as a *paradigm* for the present; Christian doctrine and worship periodically need to be remodeled to fit contemporary worldviews; elements of the past that no longer speak to people in the present need to be reverently discarded and replaced with expressions of belief and worship more suitable for the present. Christians whose attitude is reinvigorative understand Christian history as providing *parallels* for the present, but feel that if Christianity is to be relevant today, then the doctrine and life of the church today must be completely reinterpreted and restructured, not simply refurbished.

These three different ecclesial identities surface in a variety of ways. Frequently, one or other of these groups is predominant within a particular denomination or a specific local church. Some churches characterize—and so seemingly self-identify—themselves in such terms as "traditional" or "mainline" or "contemporary." Nonetheless, to some extent, all three groups are found within the major denominations and, sometimes, in the same local church; for example, one suburban church advertises itself as "A Congregation in the Reformed Tradition with a Multicultural Style of Worship and a Person-oriented Ministry"—recognizing and apparently attempting to satisfy two or three different ecclesial identity groups simultaneously.

How well a congregation can meet the varied and sometimes divergent theological/liturgical/ministerial expectations of three different groups at a single Sunday service is obviously challenging. On the one hand, an attempt to blend three different liturgical styles into the same worship service may be a bit dissonant and leave everyone feeling somewhat dissatisfied; on the other hand, opting for a single ecclesial/liturgical/ministerial identity may result in the eventual estrangement of the other two groups and their departure for more congenial congregations.[7]

Another way local congregations attempt to respond to these three different ecclesial identities is by scheduling multiple options for worship each Sunday. Some Roman Catholic parishes, for instance, schedule a "Latin Mass" for more traditionally oriented parishioners (Masses using the liturgy of Vatican II as the main menu) and a "youth Mass" geared toward the mentality of young people. Although some parishioners may alternate among these three types of liturgy, most people opt for one type regularly if not exclusively. Accordingly, three different groups are using the same building for liturgy, but they may rarely, if ever, worship together or even interact with one another: ecclesial identities may create distinct congregations using the same church facilities.

Sometimes these three different ecclesial identities are evident in church architecture and furnishings. On the one hand are churches that have had no major renovation since the time when they were built decades ago; their ecclesial/liturgical ethos, like their architecture, continues to be the same. On the other hand are Gothic and colonial churches whose interiors have been completely renovated in a modern style—sometimes with incongruous results—as one disaffected church member complained: "gargoyles and guitars don't go well together." A third example is provided by some churches built in suburbia in the second half of the twentieth century—churches that were quite innovative in design—sometimes to the extent that they seem more like theaters than houses of worship, at least to the more conventionally minded.[8]

While Sunday worship is obviously one place where these three different ecclesial/liturgical identities surface, they are also apparent in other areas of congregational life. While many churches model their social ministry on the parable of the "Good Samaritan" (Luke 10:25–37), they may do so in distinctively different ways. For example, Christians of a recapitulative bent seem most comfortable in raising funds and donating equipment to organizations aiding needy people; recapitulative Christians typically respond generously to "mission appeals" from missionaries working among the disadvantaged, both at home and abroad. In contrast, reformulative Christians may feel that being a "Good Samaritan" really requires direct involvement by ministering one-on-one to persons in need: reformulative Christians often want to staff a soup kitchen, build a habitat for the homeless, or partner with a "mission church" at home or abroad—sending members to and receiving members from the partner church.

Christians of a reinvigorative mindset, however, may envision their role of "Good Samaritan" as a call to change specific structures: the fact that a man on the Jericho road was robbed indicates the lack of effective security for travelers; accordingly, reinvigorative Christians may decide that giving money to the victim and helping with his rehabilitation, although obviously important, are basically insufficient: what is really needed is better security— accordingly a church-related group might campaign for improved police protection, advocate educational programs for prisoners, establish half-way houses, and so on.

Perhaps the most salient indicator of the presence of these three ecclesial preferences in contemporary American society is the fact that many people no longer attend the nearest church of their denomination; rather, they search for a church whose worship service, ministerial practice, and social outreach resonate with their ecclesial preferences, regardless of denomination. If these three different identity groups have distinctly different attitudes about liturgy, church design, and social programs, do they also have quite different expectations about ecumenism?

# RECAPITULATIVE ECCLESIAL IDENTITY

Recapitulative-minded Christians, at least implicitly, often idealize a specific form of pre-Enlightenment Christianity that they consider the best example, and even the normative way, of how Christians should live the Gospel today. As an example of recapitulative Christianity, one thinks of the Amish, who have replicated both a worship style and a lifestyle characteristic of the seventeenth century. Other recapitulative Christians, while opting for a modern lifestyle, retain a centuries-old liturgical style; for example, many

Eastern Christians celebrate the divine liturgy of St. John Chrysostom that dates back to the fifth century. Similarly, a Quaker meeting may follow the same basic format as it did in the seventeenth century, while simultaneously expecting the promptings of the Spirit to address twenty-first-century issues; likewise, some Roman Catholics prefer to attend a Tridentine Mass, even though they do not understand liturgical Latin. In a constantly changing world, recapitulative Christianity provides a haven of stability, a harbor of security, but most of all, a sense of the sacred.

The list of various forms of recapitulative Christianity could go on at length, since most Christian communions have an "ideal era" at some point in their history when their basic doctrines were formulated and their forms of worship were established. Nonetheless, the way that such an "ideal time" is celebrated varies widely. Reformulative-minded Christians may simply memorialize that ideal time as a treasured historical moment, while Christians of a reinvigorative mentality may idealize the present as the locus of developing revelation. Recapitulative Christians, in contrast, try to preserve and observe that ideal time to the fullest extent possible. Thus, the ideal time was not only a special event in the past; it is revered as a spiritual treasure in the present. To outside observers—especially those with a modern or postmodern mentality—traditional liturgies may seem sociological curiosities or antiquarian anomalies; to recapitulative Christians, however, these practices have two major values that continue to provide spiritual nourishment for older members, while, simultaneously, perhaps surprisingly, attracting young people.

First of all, traditional liturgies often provide a sense of the sacred that sometimes seems absent in other forms of worship. The liturgies of the Eastern Churches, for example, provide an experience of transcendence that carries worshipers beyond the present limitations of time and space; similarly, the inspirational words and dynamic music of Wesleyan hymnody lift the hearts and souls of worshippers beyond the cares and concerns of the present to the eternal God; likewise, the eloquent silence of a Quaker meeting allows the Spirit to speak quietly and compellingly in an otherwise noisy world; the simple majesty of Gregorian chant makes worshipers aware of the *mysterium tremendum*,

324

and so forth. Not only do lifelong churchgoers value such services, young people—often bored with apparently routine worship or dissatisfied with seemingly superficial adolescent services—may find traditional liturgies particularly appealing as profoundly enriching spiritual experiences.

Second, traditional services provide a sense of stability and continuity. For older people, such forms of worship may serve as a link with a spiritual past that otherwise seems to have vanished from the modern world. For younger people, who feel rootless in today's highly mobile society, traditional liturgies may provide, not only a sense of spiritual security and certitude of convictions in a world where the multiplicity of religious options seems both confusing and endless, but also a sense of community and continuity in a technological society, where change is rampant and where relationships are tenuous and transitory. Traditional services have the potential to make the transcendent accessible in the all-too-problematic present.

How do recapitulative Christians view ecumenism? Insofar as they have found a spiritual home both in terms of certitude in faith and stability in practice, ecumenism may not be a high priority. Since recapitulative Christians already have a spiritual home, why should they change what is a treasured part of their lives? This is not to say that they are unwilling to have others attend their worship; in fact, they usually want others to find the spiritual enlightenment and ethical guidance that they have found in their church. Nor are recapitulative Christians—with some exceptions—hostile to ecumenism; in fact, many are quite willing to participate in cooperative ecumenical projects. But recapitulative Christians frequently see little purpose in attempting to bring Christians together in terms of worship and ministry, particularly if ecumenism involves changing their traditional style of worship or modifying their fundamental beliefs.

Nonetheless, most recapitulative Christians are usually willing to participate in Life and Work–type projects, provided that these projects accord with their own beliefs and practices; simultaneously, they usually resist any involvement in projects that run counter to their conscience.[9] The ecumenical commitment of recapitulative Christians, then, may be both specific and partial—whole-hearted cooperation on some projects, yet, deliberate avoidance of projects that run counter to their principles. In addition, while recapitulative Christians often welcome others to their eucharistic celebrations, they may be unwilling to share their Eucharist—since shared belief is deemed necessary for eucharistic sharing. Finally, recapitulative Christians may find "ecumenical services" somewhat prosaic, even superficial, lacking the spiritual depth that they find in their own cherished liturgical celebrations.[10]

In sum, while recapitulative Christians are not usually anti-ecumenical, their practice of ecumenism may be decidedly selective in terms of liturgical sharing, doctrinal agreement, and cooperative projects. Ecumenically speaking, recapitulative Christians tend to be fairly comfortable with a "Life and Work" approach that allows them to choose the projects on which to cooperate and avoid those that are incompatible with their convictions. At heart, recapitulative Christians may see little need to modify their ecclesial identity because it has provided them with deep spiritual satisfaction. Nonetheless—and perhaps surprisingly—there are many recapitulative Christians, including church leaders and theologians, who are deeply committed to the ecumenical movement; they are grateful for the "gifts" that other Christians bring to the ecumenical table; however, ecumenists from recapitulative churches may be "exceptions to the rule": they sometimes find very limited ecumenical interest and involvement among their co-religionists.[11]

## REFORMULATIVE ECCLESIAL IDENTITY

For many Christians today, denominational identity is definitely not as important as it was a half-century ago. In recent decades, for example, many ministers have studied at theological schools sponsored by denominations other than their own. In fact, many people, including some ministers, have little hesitancy about moving from one denomination to another in the course of their spiritual journey. In part, such mobility reflects a complementarity of theology, ministry, and liturgy: even though their respective histories, denominational traditions, and ecclesiastical polities are quite different, many Protestant Churches share a commonality in doctrine, a compatibility in ecclesiastical structures, and a congeniality in forms of worship.[12]

There are, of course, many issues dividing churches today: some issues, such as abortion, homosexuality, political advocacy, social activism, and immigration policy are church dividing not only between but within denominations. In spite of such divisive issues, many members of mainline American Churches are convinced that there is already an underlying invisible unity existing among Christians; their question is how can and should this invisible unity be visibly manifested?

Some ecumenists feel that the route to visible unity is that of corporate church union; in fact, some American Churches, such as, the United Church of Christ, the United Methodist Church, the Presbyterian Church (USA), and the Evangelical Lutheran Church in America are the products of unions of previously independent denominations. Such united churches are living testimony that the effort to unite churches is really a viable ecumenical possibility. Other ecumenists, in contrast, seek to achieve greater visible unity without sacrificing their cherished denominational traditions. For example, the reorientation of the proposed "Church of Christ Uniting" to its present format of "Churches Uniting in Christ" seems indicative of the desire to attain visible unity, while simultaneously preserving denominational identity.[13]

Another recent and surprisingly successful effort toward visible unity has been achieved under the leadership of the Evangelical Lutheran Church in America, which has entered into full communion agreements with the Episcopal Church (1999),[14] the United Methodist Church (2009),[15] the Moravian Church (1999),[16] and three churches of the Reformed tradition (1997): the Presbyterian Church,[17] the United Church of Christ,[18] and the Reformed Church in America.[19] These agreements allow Lutherans to receive communion at the other covenanting churches and vice versa; they also provide for the recognition and reconciliation of the ministries of the covenanting churches. In effect, visible unity is acknowledged and advanced, while denominational identity is preserved.

Such ecumenical agreements seem problematic as well as paradigmatic, however. One evident problem is that some churches that are in full communion with the Evangelical Lutheran Church seem reluctant about entering into communion with each other; how this "third party ecumenism" will work out in practice remains to be seen. Nonetheless, these "third party" agreements may well prove paradigmatic for the future: churches that have difficulty in achieving fellowship with each other because of theological disagreements, ecclesiastical differences, and historical conflicts may be able to achieve virtual ecumenical fellowship through a third party church as an intermediary.[20]

Although there are comparable examples of church unions in other countries,[21] the effort to achieve unity via agreement seems characteristically American: Americans often prefer to proceed contractually, with all basic provisions stipulated in advance, while allowing for future development. Such an approach has the merit of assuring all participants that their major concerns have been addressed in the covenanting document, without precluding the possibility of further development and future growth. Like any legal contract, such covenants cannot envision all future contingencies, but they can spell out ecclesial guidelines that promise that future developments will sustain denominational continuity by protecting doctrinal principles, maintaining ecclesiastical structures, and preserving liturgical practices—all without foreclosing future creativity.[22]

Parenthetically, such a contractual approach also seems basically compatible with Roman Catholicism. Although its current Code of Canon Law does not establish detailed canonical procedures for the union of other churches with the Roman Catholic Church, two recent events—the reconciliation of a traditionalist group[23] and the approval of an Anglican Rite[24]—suggest that current Vatican approaches to visible church union are open to a process of facilitating full communion agreements that allow uniting churches to maintain treasured aspects of their traditional liturgy, ecclesiastical structures, and liturgical practices, when entering into visible organic union.

In any case, many mainline Protestant Christians acknowledge the existence of an underlying invisible unity, evidenced by a commonality of doctrine, structure, and practice. Indeed, this commonality has been the basis for decades of ecumenical dialogues that have resolved many issues that were once considered to be insurmountably church dividing. Moreover, both the Enlightenment legacy and the Anglo-Saxon legal tradition seem to make the recognition of visible union via covenanting agreement a congenial approach for many American Christians. In effect, Christians of a reformulative mentality seem amenable to achieving visible unity through the comparative approach of Faith and Order:[25] Where do we agree? Where do we disagree? How can these disagreements be resolved so that visible unity can be achieved? Although the negotiations to achieve agreement have frequently been time consuming, this approach has proved to be ecumenically fruitful in achieving several church unions, as well as in negotiating a number of recent communion agreements.

## ECUMENISM IN THE CHANGING AMERICAN CHURCH

In the past half-century, the religious landscape in the United States has been dramatically changing due to two quite different phenomena: immigration and innovation. First of all, recent immigration has included large numbers of Christians from other countries, as well as numerous immigrants who belong to other religious traditions.[26] Many Christian immigrants are still in the process of assimilating ecclesially, as well as linguistically, culturally, politically, and socially.[27] In some cases, Christian immigrants who belonged to a church in their own country that has no counterpart in the United States have created a new denomination. In many cases, however, Christian immigrants who are members of churches that are affiliated with international communions have joined their American counterparts—though usually as a separate language group sharing the facilities of an American Church.

From an ecumenical perspective, immigrant Christians sometimes import polemical attitudes from their home countries and so may be surprised at the irenic ecumenical atmosphere that generally prevails in the United States. Insofar as immigration has been changing the religious profile of the United States, it is evident that new types of ecumenical outreach are urgently needed.[28] What is not so evident, however, are the varied ecclesial identities of immi-

grant Christians: in some instances, their attitude seems characteristically recapitulative—they want to recreate the traditional Christianity of their native country. In other cases, immigrant Christians
seem to blend various types of reformulative Christianity into
uniquely new patterns; simultaneously, some immigrant Christians
who have sacrificed the past for a better future seem attracted to
revitalized forms of Christian community. What remains to be seen
is what ecclesial identities immigrants will choose in the future.

## REINVIGORATIVE ECCLESIAL IDENTITY

A second significant change in the American Christian population is evident from the fact that many traditional and mainline
churches have been experiencing declining numbers.[29] Seniors are
the majority of members in many congregations, which now have
only a smattering of members middle age and younger—prompting more than one minister to ask: "Where have all the young people gone?" The first—and disheartening—response to this question
is that a significant percentage of young people have simply opted
out of any formal religious affiliation: a recent survey of American
religious preferences indicated that "no religion" is now in third
place.[30] Whether this is a temporary phenomenon that will change
as young Americans grow older or a permanent exodus remains to
be seen.

In any case, the diminished number and even absence of
young people in many traditional and mainline churches may be
linked to religious agnosticism or scientific secularism: as far as
many young people are concerned, God is no longer needed in
today's world. In other cases, this lack of any specific religious preference may stem from an overabundance of religious options—
there are so many religious opportunities available that some young
people decide to experiment with a variety of religions on a casual
basis, without ever committing themselves to any particular religion
or church. For many young people, religion is only one option
among many attractions competing for attention in their lives.

Another factor influencing young people seems rooted in
philosophical postmodernism, which simultaneously rejects the sci-

entism of the Enlightenment on the one hand and existentialism's "turn to the subject" on the other. Among other results of this new genre of personalism is the emergence of people who style themselves as "spiritual but not religious": people who are interested in preternatural phenomena, such as angels, or practice meditative exercises, such as yoga, but have little or no interest in becoming members of any institutionalized Christian community. Such people may be professedly spiritual, yet generically anti-institutional: religion is a private affair, not a communal endeavor, much less a church commitment.

Still another group of young adults is constituted by "seekers" whose antecedents are often Christian, but who are estranged from mainline Christian Churches for a variety of reasons—sometimes because they find traditional Christian doctrines incredible, or mainline worship services unrewarding, or church-sponsored activities irrelevant, and so forth. For some "seekers," the ultimate religious question is not, "What is true?" but "How will religion help me?" For such people, religion is not so much a matter of doctrinal teachings as of spiritually uplifting events, not so much a matter of denominational affiliation as of humanitarian service. An obvious corollary to such attitudes, as far as ecumenism is concerned, is that there is little interest in the doctrinal and ecclesiological questions that are customarily discussed by Faith and Order.

The cumulative effects of pluralism, relativism, and postmodernism seem to have affected large numbers of young people who do not feel at home in any traditional or mainline denomination, yet who still, somewhat surprisingly, want to belong to a Christian community. Their search has spawned a wide variety of contemporary ecclesial movements. One of the most successful responses to the desire for an innovative Christianity is the emergence of megachurches—some of which are denominationally affiliated, although their denominational affiliation may be downplayed, while others are independent. Megachurches usually provide a comprehensive menu of ministries for their members—ranging from worship services to day care, from sports activities to summer camps, from teen groups to marriage preparation, from senior citizen services to grief counseling, and others.[31] In fact, megachurches sometimes seem like religious shopping malls, where any and all of a person's spiritual needs, along with many self-developmental needs, can be conveniently met under one roof.

Still another product of the "seeker generation" is the "emerging church," whose participants believe that their decentralized, yet developing, movement transcends such "modernist" labels as "conservative" and "liberal," and seek to live their Christian faith in an admittedly "postmodern" society by creating a conversation that will result in forms of Christian worship, evangelism, and community suitable to twenty-first-century America.[32] Similar to the "emerging church" in its reaction against the doctrines of the Enlightenment and the structures of traditional and mainline churches is the "missional church." Searching to form a postmodern Christian community, the missional church has been described as "a body of people sent on a mission who gather in community for worship, encouragement, and teaching from the Word that supplements what they are feeding themselves throughout the week."[33]

## A NEW ECUMENICAL PROCESS?

In the United States at the beginning of the twenty-first century, there is then a wide variety of "new profile" Christians, ranging from immigrants and seekers to emerging and missional church proponents. How do these quite different groups view ecumenism? Does ecumenism have anything to say to them?

The first generation of immigrant Christians may have minimal interest in ecumenism; their time is consumed with the survival-related mechanisms of establishing themselves in this country—economically, culturally, socially, politically. Spiritually, they may tend to replicate the Christian practices that they experienced in their countries of origin; their imported religious practices and worship provide them with an island of stability in the turbulent waters of a new and problematic world.[34] Even if the American denominations with which many immigrants are affiliated are ecumenically oriented, comparatively few immigrant Christians seem to have time for, much less interest in, ecumenical endeavors. If ecumenism is not on the radar screens of most immigrants, however, there are some encouraging indications that the children of immigrants are developing ecumenical initiatives.[35]

In similar ways, but for quite different reasons, postmodern American Christians seem to have minimal interest in ecumenism. Insofar as megachurches are nondenominational, their leaders and members may see little need for formal involvement in ecumenical discussions. On the one hand, leaders of megachurches apparently feel that they are already preaching and teaching in an ecumenical way, or at least in a trans-denominational or post-denominational way; in any case, people coming from many different denominations have found a spiritual home in megachurches. On the other hand, megachurches often have a wide range of ministries that parallel Life and Work–type projects; in fact, some megachurches have resources to support social projects well beyond what many ecumenical organizations can afford to offer.

In analogous ways, insofar as emergent and missional churches owe their existence to dissatisfaction with the doctrine, worship, and projects of traditional and mainline churches, as well as to a desire to create new and vital forms of Christian life and worship, it is hardly surprising that such churches have shown little interest in Faith and Order–type theological discussions, though they might be interested in Life and Work–type cooperative projects if they were invited to participate. In sum, "new profile" Christians—whether immigrant, seeking, emerging, missional, or postmodern—to date have been minimally attracted to the forms of ecumenism characteristic of Faith and Order. Would these "new profile" Christians be interested and become involved in a new approach to ecumenism?

## UNITY IN MISSION

As previously mentioned, for the past century, there have been two contrasting and sometimes competing approaches to ecumenism: Faith and Order and Life and Work. The contrast between these two movements has often been summarized in the axiom: "doctrine divides; service unites." Like most axioms, this one can be deceptive. The theological work of Faith and Order has fostered considerable ecumenical understanding and produced ecumenical agreements that have backgrounded covenants for church unions as well as full communion. Nonetheless, Faith and Order has labored under an inherent deficiency. While Faith and Order methodology has been adept at discovering where churches agree and disagree and in discerning whether such disagreements are fundamentally church dividing or not, the process has often remained on a theological level. There are hefty tomes of ecumenical consensus statements shelved in theological libraries;[36] unfortunately, few of these statements have made much of an impact on the actual life of the churches.[37] Stated succinctly, a basic weakness in the accomplishments of Faith and Order is that ecumenical agreements are often not implemented through ecclesial actions.[38]

Similarly, the ecumenical cooperation fostered by Life and Work has often brought churches together for Good Samaritan projects that otherwise would be beyond the resources of any single church. Nonetheless, such ecumenical projects have sometimes run aground because of basic disagreements about issues as varied as abortion, suicide, and euthanasia; marriage, divorce, and homosexuality; war and peace; public funding and immigration; human rights and political involvement.[39] Stated succinctly, a basic weakness in Life and Work methodology is that cooperative activity does not necessarily lead to either doctrinal agreement or ecclesial reconciliation. Obviously, the two movements need each other: Faith and Order agreements need to be practically implemented at every level of church life; Life and Work projects need to have a theological basis.[40]

Accordingly, both movements would seemingly benefit from an expanded methodology that emphasizes "mission" as a vital component of the search for "unity." In a sense, the relationship between "unity" and "mission" is a retrieval and reintegration of one of the original components of the ecumenical movement. While much of American ecumenism has focused on resolving questions posed by Faith and Order and participating in projects sponsored by Life and Work, comparatively, little attention has been paid to the third ecumenical stream that flowed from the Edinburgh Missionary Conference of 1910: the International Missionary Council.[41] This lack of attention may be due in part to the fact that many

American Christians still think of "mission" in terms of sending American missionaries overseas, even though the United States is currently experiencing a type of "reverse mission": in recent years, many American Churches have been receiving new members and also new ministers from other parts of the world.

On the one hand, many immigrant groups invite clergy from their home country to minister in the United States. On the other hand, some American Churches, faced with a clergy shortage, are recruiting ministers from other countries to serve in the United States.[42] In addition to transnational churches providing "missionaries to the United States" to serve American Churches, megachurches, emerging churches, and missional churches dissatisfied with the present state of American Christianity have recognized the need for new types of mission in this country in response to secularism and materialism.

These varied missionary endeavors suggest that American ecumenism needs to recapture the sense of mission that was the essential dynamic that launched the ecumenical movement a century ago. Recognizing the need to incorporate a "mission" dimension into ecumenical efforts, the "Unity in Mission" working group of the Faith and Order Commission of the National Council of Churches formulated the new ecumenical approach that is presented and discussed in this volume.[43] As its basic vision, "Unity in Mission" employs the biblically based theme of pilgrimage, which has traditionally been used to describe the Christian life in general and the ecumenical movement in particular.

Not only is this pilgrimage theme biblical, it has the advantage of resonating well with all three ecclesial identities. First, recapitulative Christians often envision life as an eschatological journey from the sinfulness of this world to the sanctity of the next; in particular, insofar as the celebration of the divine liturgy is a mystical moment in which Christians are touched by transcendence, the whole Christian life should be envisioned as a pilgrimage toward the celebration of the eternal liturgy within the Trinity.

Second, the pilgrimage theme also resonates with reformulative Christians who envision the ecumenical journey toward the visible unity of the church as a process of living and working together as a prelude and prerequisite to resolving doctrinal disputes and reconciling ministerial differences. If members of main-line churches have sometimes been disappointed that the ecumenical pilgrimage has progressed too slowly, they should be encouraged that some communion covenants have been ratified and that some church unions have been finalized. During the twentieth century, the ecumenical pilgrimage may have been slow paced, but overall the progress has been significant.

Third, the pilgrimage theme obviously resonates with the migration experience of immigrant Christians, who are seeking a better life—not only economically, socially, and politically, but also spiritually and, hopefully, ecumenically. In addition, the pilgrimage theme of "Unity in Mission" should also be attractive to postmodern Christians, who are dissatisfied with both traditional and mainline churches and are seeking new ways of being Christian. Insofar as postmodern Christians are seekers, they are implicitly pilgrims. Accordingly, the pilgrimage theme proposed by "Unity in Mission" seems basically compatible with both immigrant and postmodern seekers.[44]

For these groups, another appealing aspect of "Unity in Mission" should be that this approach is intentionally participatory. On the one hand, a characteristic quest of immigrants is their desire to participate actively in their church as well as in their new homeland. On the other hand, an important ethos of Christian seekers is their desire to participate in a Christian community that addresses the problems of the world. Another dimension that should be appealing to both groups is that mission-oriented dialogue begins with questions, not answers. Both immigrant and seeker Christians are actively trying to answer basic questions about the nature of Christian belief and its place in the modern world. As an ecumenical approach, "Unity in Mission" provides both groups with a new opportunity for seeking answers together. Last but not least, the pilgrimage approach of "Unity and Mission" seems to accord both with the desire of immigrants for a new homeland and with the penchant of seekers for a dynamic development of the church's preaching of the Gospel in the contemporary world.

Accordingly, the pilgrimage approach of "Unity in Mission" has a double potential. On the one hand, while respecting the healthy tension between "Faith and Order" and "Life and Work," "Unity in Mission" proposes a new ecumenical approach that benefits from the best features of both these ecumenical approaches: the commitment of Faith and Order to resolving doctrinal differences and reconciling ministerial structures as well as the dedication of Life and Work to evangelize through cooperative responses to human needs. Simultaneously, the pilgrimage approach of "Unity in Mission" should resonate, albeit in different ways, with the different ecclesial identities of contemporary American Christians, whether they are traditional or mainline, immigrants or seekers, emerging or missional—whether their ecclesial identity is recapitulative, reformulative, reinvigorative—or a combination thereof. Pilgrimage is possible, indeed essential, for all Christians.

As with all ecumenical endeavors, the crucial challenge is to communicate this invitation to all Christians in such a way that they will join the ecumenical pilgrimage proposed by "Unity in Mission." Although the terminology is new—and new terminology is necessary to meet the new American reality of the twenty-first century—the challenge is basically biblical: an ecumenical rephrasing of the "Great Commission": "Go, therefore, and make disciples of all nations, baptizing them in the name of the Father and of the Son and of the Holy Spirit, and teaching them to obey everything that I have commanded you. And remember, I am with you always, to the end of the age" (Matt 28:19–20).

## NOTES

1. See the classic history of W. A. Visser t' Hooft, *The Genesis and Formation of the World Council of Churches* (Geneva: World Council of Churches, 1982).

2. The French term *Foi et Constitution* seems clearer in indicating that "Faith and Order" refers to "doctrine and church structure"—the way that the church is "ordered" or organized: congregational, connectional, episcopal, etc.

3. Information on the 2010 Conference is available at http://www.edinburgh2010.org/ (accessed July 14, 2012).

4. See Ola Tjørhom, "An 'Ecumenical Winter'? Challenges in Contemporary Catholic Ecumenism," *Heythrop Journal* 49, no. 5 (September 2008): 841–59.

5. Ecumenists have not been particularly attentive to the correlation between the ecumenical attitudes of the proverbial people in the pews and their denominational affiliation and ecclesial identities.

6. This unusual terminology has been deliberately chosen in order to avoid the presuppositions and connotations associated with a variety of other more familiar terms.

7. As reported by Amy Sullivan, "Fully 44% of Americans have changed faiths at least once" ("Church-Shopping: Why Americans Change Faiths," *Time* [28 April 2009], available at http://www.time.com/time/nation/article/0,8599,1894361,00.html [accessed July 14, 2012]).

8. See, for example, the illustrated commentary on different styles of church architecture by Marilyn Chiat, *North American Churches: From Chapels to Cathedrals* (Lincolnwood, IL: Publications International, 2004).

9. This approach to ecumenical cooperation was enunciated by the Third World Conference on Faith and Order, which met at Lund, Sweden, in 1952: "Should not our churches ask themselves whether they are showing sufficient eagerness to enter into conversation with other churches, and whether they should not act together in all matters except those in which deep differences of conviction compel them to act separately?" available at http://ecumenism.net/archive/encounter.htm, #3 (accessed July 14, 2012).

10. For example, Roman Catholics who participate at ecumenical services often want to attend Mass as well, since it is an essential part of being Catholic, even though the ecumenical service may be personally enriching.

11. See, for example, the concerns expressed about the slow pace of "ecumenical reception" expressed by the contributors to *Receptive Ecumenism and the Call to Catholic Learning: Exploring a Way for Contemporary Ecumenism,* ed. Paul D. Murray and Luca Badini-Confalonieri (New York: Oxford University Press, 2008).

12. See, for example, the extensive doctrinal agreement—with the exception of the much-debated chapter (7) on ministry—achieved by the Consultation on Church Union, in *The COCU Consensus*, rev. ed., ed. Gerald F. Moede (Princeton: Consultation on Church Union, 1985; revised edition, 1989).

13. For information about Churches Uniting in Christ, see: http://www.cuicinfo.org/; also see John T. Ford, "COCU Pilgrimage Ends, CUIC Pilgrimage Begins," *Ecumenical Trends* 31, no. 4 (April 2002): 7–10.

14. Information on the full communion agreement between the ELCA and the Episcopal Church is available at http://www. elca.org/Who-We-Are/Our-Three-Expressions/Churchwide-Organization/Office-of-the-Presiding-Bishop/Ecumenical-and-Inter-Religious-Relations/Full-Communion-Partners/The-Episcopal-Church.aspx (accessed July 14, 2012).

15. Information on the full communion agreement between the ELCA and the United Methodist Church is available at http://www. elca.org/Who-We-Are/Our-Three-Expressions/Churchwide-Organization/Office-of-the-Presiding-Bishop/Ecumenical-and-Inter-Religious-Relations/Full-Communion-Partners/United-Methodist-Church.aspx (accessed July 14, 2012).

16. Information on the full communion agreement between the ELCA and the Moravian Church is available at http://www. elca.org/Who-We-Are/Our-Three-Expressions/Churchwide-Organization/Office-of-the-Presiding-Bishop/Ecumenical-and-Inter-Religious-Relations/Full-Communion-Partners/The-Moravian-Church.aspx (accessed July 14, 2012).

17. Information on the full communion agreement between the ELCA and the Presbyterian Church (USA) is available at http:// www.elca.org/Who-We-Are/Our-Three-Expressions/Churchwide-Organization/Office-of-the-Presiding-Bishop/Ecumenical-and-Inter-Religious-Relations/Full-Communion-Partners/Presbyterian-Church-USA.aspx (accessed July 14, 2012).

18. Information on the full communion agreement between the ELCA and the United Church of Christ is available at http:// www.elca.org/Who-We-Are/Our-Three-Expressions/Churchwide-Organization/Office-of-the-Presiding-Bishop/Ecumenical-and-Inter-Religious-Relations/Full-Communion-Partners/United-Church-of-Christ.aspx (accessed July 14, 2012).

19. Information on the full communion agreement between the ELCA and the Reformed Church in America is available at http:// www.elca.org/Who-We-Are/Our-Three-Expressions/Churchwide-Organization/Office-of-the-Presiding-Bishop/Ecumenical-and-

Inter-Religious-Relations/Full-Communion-Partners/Reformed-Church-in-America.aspx (accessed July 14, 2012).

20. For a perceptive discussion of the problems and potential inherent in this "new portrait of visible unity," see Michael Root, "Once More on the Unity We Seek: Testing Ecumenical Models," in *The Unity We Have and the Unity We Seek: Ecumenical Prospects for the Third Millenium*, ed. Jeremy Morris and Nicholas Sagovsky (London: T & T Clark, 2003), 167–77.

21. Among the best-known examples are the United Church of Canada (1925), the Church of South India (1947), and the Church of North India (1970); in contrast, the proposal by the Consultation on Church Union for a "Church of Christ Uniting" (1970) was not accepted by the participating churches.

22. See John Henry Newman, *An Essay on the Development of Christian Doctrine* for a discussion of the "notes" of authentic doctrinal development, available at http://www.newmanreader.org/works/development/index.html (accessed July 14, 2012).

23. For information about the lifting of the excommunication of the Bishops of the Society of St. Pius X (popularly known as "Lefebvrists"), see https://www.zenit.org/article-24938?l=english (accessed July 14, 2012).

24. An English translation of *Anglicanorum Coetibus* is available at http://www.vatican.va/holy_father/benedict_xvi/apost_constitutions/documents/hf_ben-xvi_apc_20091104_anglicanorum-coetibus_en.html (accessed July 14, 2012).

25. The Faith and Order movement has sought to achieve doctrinal consensus and the reconciliation of ministries as a means for attaining visible unity among Christians; see "A Brief History of Faith and Order," in National Council of Churches of Christ in the USA, *Faith and Order Commission Handbook*, 3–11, available at www.ncccusa.org/pdfs/FaithAndOrderHandbook.pdf (accessed July 16, 2012).

26. The CIA World Fact Book estimates the religious affiliation of the U.S. population as follows: Protestant 51.3%, Roman Catholic 23.9%, Mormon 1.7%, other Christian 1.6%, Jewish 1.7%, Buddhist 0.7%, Muslim 0.6%, other or unspecified 2.5%, unaffiliated 12.1%, none 4% (2007 est.), available at https://www.cia.gov/

library/publications/the-world-factbook/geos/us.html (accessed July 14, 2012).

27. See, for example, the thought-provoking analysis of Jacques Audinet, *The Human Face of Globalization: From Multicultural to Mestizaje*, trans. Frances Dal Chele (Lanham-Boulder-New York-Toronto-Oxford: Rowman & Littlefield, 2004); the translation is very readable, but sometimes more paraphrase than exact equivalent.

28. See John T. Ford, "Hispanic Ecumenical Dialogue: Progress and Potential: A Review of *Building Bridges, Doing Justice*," *Ecumenical Trends* 39, no. 11 (December 2010): 4–8, 15, 164–8, 175.

29. See the American Religious Identification Survey, as reported in *USA Today*: while the decrease in membership affects churches nationwide, there are regional differences; for example, the number of Roman Catholics is decreasing in the "rust belt" but increasing in the "sun belt" due to the influx of retirees and immigrants, available at http://www.usatoday.com/news/religion/2009-03-09-american-religion-ARIS_N.htm (accessed July 14, 2012).

30. According to the American Religious Identification Survey (ibid.), the number in the category "no religion" now outranks every religious group except Catholics and Baptists.

31. See, for example, the variety of programs offered by Willow Creek Community Church, available at http://www.willowcreek.org/ (accessed July 14, 2012).

32. See, for example, Scot McKnight, "Five Streams of the Emerging Church," *Christianity Today* 51, no. 2 (February 2007) describes the emerging church as prophetic, post-modern, praxis-oriented, post-evangelical and political, available at http://www.christianitytoday.com/ct/2007/February/11.35.html (accessed July 14, 2012).

33. Friend of Missional, available at http://www.friendof missional.org/ (accessed July 14, 2012). Also see: Alan J. Roxburgh and M. Scott Boren, *Introducing the Missional Church: What It Is, Why It Matters, How to Become One* (Grand Rapids, MI: Baker Books, 2009); Alan J. Roxburgh, *Missional Map-Making: Skills for Leading in Times of Transition* (San Francisco: Jossey-Bass, 2010).

34. Architectural replicas of the homeland religion can be seen in suburban Washington along New Hampshire Avenue, where there are, not only Christian churches built in Asian and

Byzantine styles, but also places of worship that are Arabic, Buddhist, Hindu, etc.

35. See John T. Ford, "Hispanic Ecumenism: New Findings and Possibilities," *Ecumenical Trends* 31, no. 10 (November 2002): 1–5 (145–9).

36. Among the many compilations of ecumenical documents, the following are particularly useful: *Growth in Agreement: Reports and Agreed Statements of Ecumenical Conversations on a World Level,* ed. Harding Meyer and Lukas Vischer (New York: Paulist Press; Geneva: World Council of Churches, 1984); *Growth in Agreement II: Reports and Agreed Statements of Ecumenical Conversations on a World Level, 1982-1998,* ed. Jeffrey Gros, Harding Meyer, William G. Rusch (Geneva: WCC Publications; Grand Rapids, MI: Eerdmans, 2000); *Growth in Agreement III: International Dialogue Texts and Agreed Statements, 1998-2005,* ed. Jeffrey Gros, Thomas F. Best, Lorelei F. Fuchs (Geneva: WCC Publications; Grand Rapids, MI: Eerdmans, 2007); *Growing Consensus: Church Dialogues in the United States 1962 to 1991,* ed. Joseph A. Burgess and Jeffrey Gros (New York: Paulist Press, 1995); *Growing Consensus II: Church Dialogues in the United States 1992 to 2004,* ed. Lydia Veliko and Jeffrey Gros (Washington, DC: U.S. Conference of Catholic Bishops, 2005); *Building Unity: Ecumenical Dialogue with Roman Catholic Participation*, ed. Joseph A. Burgess and Jeffrey Gros (New York: Paulist Press, 1998); *Deepening Communion: International Ecumenical Documents with Roman Catholic Participation*, ed. William G. Rusch and Jeffrey Gros (Washington, DC: U.S. Catholic Conference, 1998).

37. One notable exception to this lack of attention is *Baptism, Eucharist and Ministry* (Faith and Order Commission, World Council of Churches, 1982), available at http://www.oikoumene.org/en/resources/documents/wcc-commissions/faith-and-order-commission/i-unity-the-church-and-its-mission/baptism-eucharist-and-ministry-faith-and-order-paper-no-111-the-lima-text.html (accessed July 14, 2012); the so-called "Lima Text" has over a million references on Google.

38. See Michael Root, "Ecumenism," in *The Blackwell Companion to Catholicism*, ed. Frederick Christian Bauerschmidt and Trent Pomplum (Oxford: Blackwell, 2006), 432–47, at 443; and

John T. Ford, "Oberlin 2007: The Need for an Expanded Methodology?" *Ecumenical Trends* 36, no. 8 (September 2007): 5–8, 15.

39. For a comprehensive treatment, see Michael Root, "Ethics in Ecumenical Dialogues: A Survey and Analysis," *Journal of Ecumenical Studies* 45, no. 3 (Summer 2010): 357–75.

40. As Justo González, *Mañana: Christian Theology from a Hispanic Perspective* (Nashville, TN: Abingdon, 1990), 74, has emphasized: "there can be no division between life and work on the one hand and faith and order on the other, for as we work and live out the gospel we gain new insights into the meaning of our faith and the proper order for the church."

41. Information about the International Missionary Council is available at http://www.oikoumene.org/en/who-are-we/organization-structure/consultative-bodies/world-mission-and-evangelism/history.html (accessed July 14, 2012).

42. For example, in its 2012 survey of Roman Catholic ordinands to the priesthood, the Center for Applied Research in the Apostolate of Georgetown University reported: "Almost three in ten ordinands were born outside the United States with the largest numbers coming from Viet Nam, Colombia, Mexico, Poland, and the Philippines" from "The Class of 2012: Survey of Ordinands to the Priesthood," p. 6, available at http://www.usccb.org/beliefs-and-teachings/vocations/ordination-class/upload/Ordination-Class-of-2012-Report-FINAL.pdf (accessed July 19, 2012).

43. Six essays with an introduction, written about "Unity in Mission" by members of the Faith and Order Study Group have been published in *Journal of Ecumenical Studies* 45, no. 2 (Spring 2010): 178–248.

44. Presumably, neither immigrant Christians nor Christian seekers would have difficulty joining the ecumenical pilgrimage in terms of the basic "Statement of Faith" proposed by such ecumenical bodies as the National Council of Churches: *"The National Council of Churches is a community of Christian communions, which, in response to the gospel as revealed in the Scriptures, confess Jesus Christ, the incarnate Word of God, as Savior and Lord"*; available at http://www.ncccusa.org/about/about_ncc.html#Statement%20of%20Faith (accessed July 14, 2012).

# CONTRIBUTORS

**S. Wesley Ariarajah** (Methodist Minister from Sri Lanka) is currently Professor of Ecumenical Theology in the Drew University School of Theology, Madison, New Jersey. Before joining Drew in September 1997, he served the World Council of Churches for sixteen years as Director of the Interfaith Dialogue Program and as Deputy Secretary.

**Mitzi J. Budde** (Evangelical Lutheran Church in America) is Head Librarian and Professor at Virginia Theological Seminary, Alexandria, Virginia.

**Susan E. Davies** (United Church of Christ) is Jonathan Fisher Professor Emerita, Bangor Theological Seminary.

**Donald W. Dayton** (Wesleyan Church) is a retired theology professor who has been active in the ecumenical movement (global and national) for over a quarter of a century.

**Ernest Falardeau, SSS** (Roman Catholic) is a Blessed Sacrament Father and Senior Associate at St. Jean Baptiste Catholic Church, New York, New York.

**John T. Ford** (Roman Catholic Church) is Professor of Theology and Religious Studies at The Catholic University of America, Washington, DC.

**Young Lee Hertig** (Presbyterian Church, USA) is Executive Director of ISAAC (Institute for the Study of Asian American Christianity) and teaches at Azusa Pacific University and Fuller Theological Seminary.

**Michael Kinnamon** (Disciples of Christ) is Spehar-Halligan Visiting Professor of Ecumenical Collaboration in Interreligious Dialogue at the School of Theology and Ministry, Seattle University, Seattle, Washington, and was General Secretary of the NCC (2008–2011).

**Antonios Kireopoulos** (Greek Orthodox) is Associate General Secretary for Faith & Order and Interfaith Relations at the National Council of the Churches of Christ in the USA.

**Dale E. Luffman** (Community of Christ) is Ecumenical and Interfaith Officer for Community of Christ and Instructor in Practical Theology for Community of Christ Seminary, Independence, Missouri.

**Matthew D. Lundberg** (Christian Reformed Church in North America) is Associate Professor of Theology in the Department of Religion at Calvin College in Grand Rapids, Michigan.

**Kevin Park** (Presbyterian Church [PC(USA)]) is an Associate for Theology in the Office of Theology and Worship in the General Assembly Mission Council of PC(USA).

**Shirley Paulson** (Church of Christ, Scientist) is Head of Ecumenical Affairs of the Church of Christ, Scientist, Boston, Massachusetts.

**Don Thorsen** (Independent) is Professor of Theology in the Graduate School of Theology at Azusa Pacific University.

**Anton C. Vrame** (Greek Orthodox) is Director of the Department of Religious Education of the Greek Orthodox Archdiocese of America, Brookline, Massachusetts.

# No More
# Broken
# Places

*Finding Wholeness in God*

# OTHER BOOKS BY CAROLYN RATHBUN SUTTON:

*Journey to Joy*
*Eye-openers*

To order, call 1-800-765-6955.
Visit us at www.reviewandherald.com for information on other
Review and Herald products.

# NO MORE BROKEN PLACES

*Finding Wholeness in God*

# CAROLYN RATHBUN SUTTON

REVIEW AND HERALD® PUBLISHING ASSOCIATION
HAGERSTOWN, MD 21740

The author assumes full responsibility for the accuracy of all facts and
quotations as cited in this book.

Scripture quotations marked NASB are from the *New American Standard Bible,* ©
The Lockman Foundation 1960, 1962, 1963, 1968, 1971, 1972, 1973, 1975, 1977.

Texts credited to NIV are from the *Holy Bible, New International Version.* Copyright © 1973,
1978, 1984, International Bible Society. Used by permission of Zondervan Bible Publishers.

Texts credited to NKJV are from The New King James Version. Copyright © 1979, 1980,
1982 by Thomas Nelson, Inc. Used by permission. All rights reserved.

This book was
Edited by Andy Nash
Copyedited by Delma Miller and James Cavil
Designed by Emily Harding
Electronic makeup by Shirley M. Bolivar
Cover Photo by Tony Stone Images
Typeset: 11/14 Bembo

PRINTED IN U.S.A.

05  04  03  02  01          5  4  3  2  1

**R&H Cataloging Service**
Sutton, Carolyn Rathbun, 1944-
    No more broken places: finding wholeness in God's will.

    1. Christian life.   2. Nehemiah.   3. Bible. O.T. Nehemiah.   I. Title.

                        248

ISBN 0-8280-1500-7

# FOR THREE OF GOD'S FRIENDS—

*Joanie Carle*

*Nadine Proctor*

*Suzan Williams—*

*who not only helped light my path*

*through a foggy place*

*but also handed me bricks*

*for repairing the brokenness.*

*Things change, but God—and real friends—don't.*

*Thank you!*

# CONTENTS

*Section Three*
## TALL ON THE WALL

*Epilogue*

*The path is here, somewhere*

*among the brambles, but I am*

*blind and cannot*

*see the way.*

*And so I take*

*each step with utmost care*

*and pray*

*that I will miss the rocks,*

*the thorns, the potholes . . .*★

---------------

★*From Phydella Hogan, "The Path,"* Matchsticks *(Fayetteville, Ark.:* *Lost Creek Press, 1992), p. 24.*

# *Preface*

# ALONE IN THE FOG

*"We are toss'd and driv'n on the restless sea of time;*
*Solemn storms and howling tempests oft eclipse the*
*bright sunshine."*
**—Alfred B. Smith**

"No way!" I exclaimed to the dashboard of my '91 Ford Escort.
"Have we really come this far?" In December's predawn darkness I'd
chanced to glance down at the odometer just as it registered
99,993 miles.

Wow! Only seven miles to go before I hit the big 100,000! The tires
of my little white car continued racing me down southern Oregon's
Interstate 5 toward an early-morning dental appointment. My mind
retro-scanned the past six years with its four vertical and horizontal
transcontinental trips. How this little car and I had bonded! Mentally I
tried listing all the states we'd been in and the scores of students we'd
ferried on lengthy field trips. Feeling a sudden sense of exhilaration and
triumph, I quickly lost myself in comfortable contemplation of completed travels.

## The Crash

Then, without warning, I crashed right into it—a dense wall of
heavy, black fog. Instinctively I tapped the brake pedal. The resulting
skid atop the highway surface carried me into a knotted-stomach state
of nerves.

Oh no! Black ice! I suddenly realized that not even one of my successful trips in this car could help me see the broken white lines that I so

desperately needed to see. Not one warm memory of travels past could dissipate the present fog long enough for me to locate a simple off-ramp sign. I might be only three and a half miles short of completing the 100,000 mark . . . but the proud mileage meter left me clueless as to where the next 50 yards of this trip would take me.

Just then a noisy, unidentifiable vehicle passed and pulled its bulk confidently into my lane. Its taillights barely penetrated the blackness. Yet seeing light—any kind of light—gave me a small degree of comfort. The ghostly lamps ahead pulled to the right, but my gut instinct told me to go straight.

*What do I do?* I wondered desperately. In a split second I chose to follow the hazy orange taillights of the mystery vehicle. A half minute later the driver braked. In the fog-diffused beam from a red stoplight, I could tell we were at an intersection.

When the fog above me turned an eerie green, I made a left-hand turn onto what I hoped was Barnett Road. Cautiously I made my way from one intersection to another. Other skidding cars and patches of near-blackness between intersections caused frequent disorientation to sweep over me. Almost too late I recognized the main turnoff to the medical complex. Over-reactive braking sent my little Ford into a slow 180-degree spin, stopping just short of the curb.

I calmed my nerves, restarted the engine, and drove down the long driveway. Soon hazy beams of light streaming through my dentist's office windows illumined an icy parking spot just outside the front door. Heaving a great sigh, I shut off the engine. The odometer had just regis-tered 100,000.

Dr. Ritacca looked incredulous as I walked through his front door. "With the conditions so treacherous out there, how did you ever make this early appointment on time?"

I tried to get the trembly out of my voice. "Well, I just went from one dim light to the next and hoped I wouldn't lose my way in the darkness between intersections."

## Foggy Patches

We all encounter patches of fog from time to time in life's travels. We arrive at dark intersections of perplexity, pain, doubt, or fear, not knowing which direction to turn. Though we can clearly "see" the past—even some dazzling mini-miracles God may have worked on our behalf—we still have trouble discerning which direction to take in the *present* fog.

A recent experience has led me to believe that we can begin discerning God's will for a specific foggy place in our lives when, with His help, we start making appropriate choices in the general areas for which He's already revealed His will in the Bible. When I started trying to make only God-honoring choices at each intersection, God eventually led me to a well-lighted place at the end of a particular journey I was on.

I believe He will do the same for you—whether you've just run into a thick fogbank or whether you've been wandering around in the dark for a long, long time.

Through David God tells us, "I will instruct thee and teach thee in the way which thou shalt go: I will guide thee with mine eye" (Ps. 32:8). That's not just a pretty thought—it's a promise!

*Section One*

# UP THROUGH THE FOG

*"Even the night shall be light about me. . . .*
*The darkness and the light are both alike to thee."*
**Ps. 139:11, 12**

Are you in a "foggy place" right now, without a clue as to where to take your next step? Your fog may be not knowing how to deal with an unpredictable teenager, or how to carry on in spite of a crushing brokenness. Or your fog may be chronic . . . as you try to "maintain" in a world gone mad.

My foggy place involved a potential midlife love story. It involved two men, actually. Between the first man and me swirled a fog of confusion. In the last section of this book I'll tell you much more about his pivotal role in this love story.

The other man was much, much older. Yet my unexpected encounter with him (details in Sections One and Two) turned my world upside down—for the better! It was he who provided me with specifics on how to find the light I needed.

I pray that you too will find new perspectives from his wise example—perspectives that will take the guesswork out of your future decision-making, perspectives that will help you discern the taillights of God's will.

# What a Guy!

*(Based on Nehemiah 1:1-3)*

*"We . . . desire that ye might be filled with the knowledge of his will in all wisdom and spiritual understanding."*
**—Colossians 1:9**

Not long ago I found myself in an emotional fog-out. This fog-out was preceded by a divorce, then followed by more than a half decade of "singlehood." During this period God had proved Himself to be a faithful partner and guide. I'd assumed, therefore, it was going to be "just the two of us" all the way to the kingdom. And that was that!

## Impending Marriage Proposal?

Then I slowly began realizing that a certain prayer partner, a kindly gentleman who lived 3,000 miles away from me, had become a closer friend than I'd ever intended. (He's the younger man in my love story.) I also began realizing that despite my stated commitment to eternal singlehood, I might soon be the unlikely recipient of a marriage proposal. The thought sent me into a state of near panic.

The very nature of my fears told me that there was brokenness in my heart that still needed repair, personal issues that needed resolution. How could I possibly decipher God's will from deep inside my own emotional turmoil? Praying—and stewing—about my situation for a number of months, I finally decided on a game plan.

My plan was to focus morning devotions on selected Bible characters who'd encountered foggy patches in their lives. I'd see how they'd negotiated treacherous traveling conditions to end up in the well-lighted center of their heavenly Father's will.

## Strange Encounters of the Biblical Kind

Energized by my new plan, I made a list of Bible characters to research: Esther, Isaiah, Moses, Daniel. But on just the second day I accidentally bumped into the most unlikely character to advise me with my dilemma. He almost jumped off the pages of Scripture and into my life. And what a helpful guy he turned out to be!

Who was he exactly?

Well, an answer about him on the TV show *Jeopardy!* would go something like this: "This individual was one of the most significant people to 'happen' between Daniel-in-the-lions'-den and Jesus-in-the-manger."

The question, of course: "Who was Nehemiah?" (That's the older man in my story.)

Nehemiah. Strong, yet sensitive. Solitary, yet social. Tough, yet tender. Aware of the big picture, yet attentive to detail.

## The Broken Wall

I first "met" Nehemiah[1] in my personal devotions one early snowy January morning. He—like me—was at a fog-blurred crossroads.

A trusted steward (though also a Jewish exile) in the palace of the Persian king Artaxerxes, Nehemiah had just received gut-wrenching news from his brother. The city's wall—the protective defense about the restored Temple and its people—still lay largely in ruins. Just as bad, the exiles who had returned—the remnant—were "in great distress and reproach" (Neh. 1:1-3, NASB). Until the wall could be rebuilt, Nehemiah knew that both the Temple's and his people's survival were in danger.

## Nehemiah's Foggy Place . . . and Mine

Worried about Jerusalem's vulnerability inside its broken wall, Nehemiah wanted to know if he, personally, was to do anything about it.

*Boing!* When I read about Nehemiah's dilemma, a resonating alarm went off inside my head. Like Nehemiah, I too longed for "knowledge of His will" (Col. 1:9, NASB) in the midst of my own anxiety, confusion, and lingering brokenness. I needed a strong wall about my "temple"—my personhood with its spiritual, emotional, and social components. With keenest interest then, I began to study this man, hoping—through his life—to find answers to my own questions.

Let me tell you: By the time this circa-400 B.C. man finished Jerusalem's wall, neither the wall nor I was ever the same again! Not only did Nehemiah supply me answers; he also threw in a great deal of hope and comfort. Is it any wonder, then, that the Hebrew translation of Nehemiah's name means "Comfort of Yahweh"?

## The Nehemiah Album

In order for you to know Nehemiah better, I have endeavored to craft Section One of this book into a "photo album." I hope the Nehemiah Album will serve as a reminder of God's promise: "I will . . . teach you in the way which you should go" (Ps. 32:8, NASB). May this album reassure us that He wants us to "understand" what the will of the Lord is" (Eph. 5:17), as He has already prepared a unique path for our feet (Eph. 2:10).

As you turn the pages of the Nehemiah Album, you will see that when we make choices according to God's general (already-revealed) will, God eventually supplies details about His specific will for our lives (see Is. 30:21).

Although Nehemiah was a hard worker, this book is not about the importance of works. Rather, it's about the importance of choices.

Many crossroads at which Nehemiah found himself are the very same ones at which we so often stand. So hold on to your handbag, buckle on your tool belt, and prepare to rise above the rubble! In record time Nehemiah's choices can have you back on your feet and walking on the wall, straight toward the center of God's will . . . for every area of your life.

# AT THE EGO ALTAR

## RECOGNIZE A HIGHER AUTHORITY, PART 1

**(Based on Nehemiah 1:2-5)**

*"Before we can pray, 'Thy Kingdom come,'*
*we must be willing to pray, 'My kingdom go.'"*
—*Alan Redpath*[2]

*"For it is God which worketh in you both to will*
*and to do of his good pleasure"*
—*Philippians 2:13*

*Blam!* The icy metal chair on the ski lift slammed into my rib cage as another skier, seeming to come out of nowhere, attempted to lunge onto the chair beside me.

*Ouch!* I groaned quietly as a sharp pain stabbed between my third and fourth ribs. The young orange-jacketed man waved his poles about wildly, while two lift operators pushed him securely into the chair. Then he dropped both poles onto the snow beneath us.

"We'll send your poles up on the next chair!" yelled one operator. The next thing I knew, my chairmate had suctioned a quivering hand to my right wrist.

*Oh, great!* I thought. *I'm 50 feet above the ground and stuck with a maniac for the next 10 minutes.*

"Excuse me," I said, delicately trying to extricate my arm from his viselike grasp. "I've found that it works better if one holds on to the side of the chair closest to one." Forcing a cheerful-sounding voice, I continued, "See how I'm holding on to *my* side of the chair? Now why don't you try holding on to *your* side?"

Suddenly the young man seemed to sense how dependent he looked, clinging to my sleeve. "Oh, yeah," he blurted. "I can do that."

## Ski Bum

"So how long have you been skiing?" I asked, attempting to ignore the stabbing in my side every time I inhaled the frosty air.

"Never tried before," he answered, bravado flooding his voice. "This will be my first run. Gotta cousin waitin' for me at the top. Tried to get onto his chair a couple before this one, but I fell off."

I believed it.

"But this is an intermediate to *advanced* run," I cautioned.

"I know, but I can do anything I put my mind to. Always have. You might say I'm a real sports jock." He started listing the sports at which he excelled. The recital of his athletic prowess plus the bone-chilling air seemed to stretch the last seven minutes of the ride into 30. As we neared the top, my seatmate suddenly asked, "So how do you get off one of these things?"

"Very quickly," I answered with unfeigned sincerity. After all, that was certainly *my* plan.

"Oh, *I* can do that!" he assured me.

The bumping, scrambling noises made by his body and skis as they scraped down the icy exit ramp behind me quickly faded into the distance. I skied to the base of the run and then got back onto the same lift. Halfway back up, I saw my previous seatmate sliding down the mountain on his back, cheered on by his reckless cousin.

Forty-five minutes later I approached another lift, where I overheard two operators talking about a "crazy guy who can't ski." It seems this person had boarded the chair against their orders. Now they'd alerted ski patrol at the top of the mountain.

Disembarking at the top of the lift a few minutes later, I noticed three members of the ski patrol subduing an individual in a familiar orange ski jacket. The authorities were strapping him—against his vigorous protests—into a toboggan for mandatory downhill transport. Until the throbbing snowmobile engine fired up and drowned him out, the skier's cries pierced the frosty air: "But I *can* ski! I really can! I'm a-a-a-a-a-awssom-m-me!"

Obviously the ski bum had never read Dwight L. Moody's advice:

"Be humble or you'll stumble."[3]

## Humble Official

How different in attitude was this egotistical ski bum from Nehemiah, the young courtesan in the Persian court. Nehemiah had many reasons to be proud, if not egotistical. Singled out for his abilities, his courtly appearance, his trustworthiness, he alone had become a confidant of Artaxerxes, the Persian king.

When Nehemiah's brother brought distressing news that "the wall of Jerusalem . . . is broken down" (Neh. 1:3), Nehemiah could have chosen to think, *Oh well—too bad for the remnant who chose to go back to that dumpy little capital. What does a broken wall have to do with me now that I'm financially secure and highly favored here at the palace?*

Or Nehemiah, professionally and physically comfortable, could have chosen to assume a *que sera sera* attitude. He could have decided to "live above" the dilemma of the beleaguered remnant in Jerusalem, letting them—under the leadership of the weary old scribe Ezra—fend for themselves.

And again, Nehemiah could have viewed the plight of his Hebrew brethren much as I viewed the plight of the ski bum. The children of Israel, like the skier wannabe, had risked near-annihilation by ignoring a higher Authority. God hadn't abandoned them; they'd abandoned Him by choosing to live in national idolatry outside the rules and safety regulations of God's "ski resort." Therefore, God had allowed the Persian "ski patrol" to escort these recalcitrant, idolatrous rebels off His "slopes." Good riddance!

## First Snapshot

Nehemiah's first thought, however, upon hearing the plight of his countrymen, was not for his nation's honor—or even his own. It was for God's.

Our first snapshot of Nehemiah shows him in anguish as he "sat down and wept, and mourned certain days, and fasted" (verse 4) after hearing the distressing news. In deep humility and sorrow Nehemiah wept tears of recognition that his nation—at an international level—had disrespected both God's name and His authority.

Like an acquaintance who starts keeping her distance if she feels rejected, God had withdrawn Himself, leaving Israel to the consequences of its own choices.

## Getting Personal

May I ask a personal question? Have you ever wept over having dishonored your Creator and driven His presence away? I have. And what a lonely grief it is to recognize you have no one to blame but yourself. In times like these, guilt threatens to crush out any vestiges of the spiritual life. Yet all is not lost, because of . . . who God is.

Familiar with the sacred writings (as his subsequent prayer would reveal), Nehemiah knew that in His great heart of love, God has a special place for those who humbly recognize who He is.

"Thou hast heard the desire of the humble," wrote the psalmist. "Thou wilt prepare their heart, thou wilt cause thine ear to hear" (Ps. 10:17).

Prepare their heart for what?

The following verse answers that question: "To judge the fatherless and the oppressed, that the man of the earth may no more oppress" (verse 18). God will prepare the hearts of the humble . . . to share in His authority through loving service to others.

In addition, God will "cause" the ear of the humble to "hear" His will for their lives. In other words, He intends for our lives to have meaning to others. "And your ears will hear a word behind you, 'This is the way, walk in it'" (Isa. 30:21, NASB). God intends to show us His will for our lives. No matter what we've been or who we are, these promises offer us continual hope because of who . . . God is.

This snapshot of Nehemiah reminds us that the pursuit of God's will starts when we choose to acknowledge His authority over every area of our life. We must begin with an honest answer to this question: In relationship to God's altar, where is my ego?

## Your Turn . . .

In relationship to God's altar, where is *your* ego?

# A RACE DOWN "THE FACE"

## RECOGNIZE A HIGHER AUTHORITY, PART 2

**(Based on Nehemiah 1:6-11)**

*"Shew me thy ways, O Lord; teach me thy paths."*
— **Ps. 25:4**

The wannabe skier in the previous chapter wasn't the only memorable face on the slopes that day.

I was at Dodge Ridge as a weekly teacher-chaperone with about 100 students from my school. On ski day each week we teachers took turns "patrolling" the various runs to make sure our students were skiing safely.

At the base of the bunny slope I spotted a small navy-blue mound floundering in the snow amid a tangle of short skis and poles.

"Don't worry," chirped a little voice from the depths of the very damp bundle. A small, perspiring face emerged from beneath a snow-salted knit cap. A big smile lit up his 7-year-old face.

"I'm falling down a lot today, but that's OK, because the ski instructor taught us how to get up."

Quickly searching for an encouraging word, I said, "I sure like the way you just get right up again and keep trying, Toby."

"Thank you," he said brightly.

I went up the chairlift with him. On the way back down he fell repeatedly. But Toby would always struggle to his feet, gasp for air, and say something like "The ski instructor told me to keep the tips together" or "The ski instructor said to bend my knees." Once, as we rode up the chairlift, he confided, "The ski instructor said that if I practice everything he says to, I won't fall down very much. The ski instructor sure knows a lot."

Even after I left the vicinity of Chair One, Toby's plucky attitude, teachable spirit, and faith in the unsurpassing knowledge of the ski instructor carried me through the rest of the day.

The following week, true to the ski instructor's word, Toby hardly fell at all.

## Week Three

"Teacher, want to see something the ski instructor taught me?" asked a familiar voice as I disembarked on the summit of Chair Three, which led to "The Face"—a notoriously steep, mogul-studded run.

It was Toby. "Follow me!" he called over his shoulder.

"Toby, wait! I don't think you're ready for this yet. The Face has a lot of moguls!"

"I know," he beamed, "but the ski instructor taught us how to do 'em."

By now we'd skied too far down the slope to climb back up for descent down an easier run. Pausing in front of Toby, I planted my poles and planned a strategy. The 60-plus moguls rose, tall and imposing. Focusing on the task before me, I decided to zig-zag slowly around the icy giants the best I could, choosing the easiest path possible for my plucky little companion.

"Toby," I instructed, "we must go very, *very* slowly because—"

Before I could explain my plan, Toby began chanting, "Tips together, bend my knees, here I go! Tips together, bend my knees, here I go!"

*Whoosh!* He swept past me and down . . . The Face.

"Wait!" I cried out. "Aren't you going to follow—"

I watched in fearful amazement as, tips together and knees bent, he went straight over the *top* of the nearest mogul. Then his short body dropped completely out of sight on the other side.

"Dear God," I'd just started praying when Toby's navy-blue knit cap popped into view as he mounted the next mogul. With a shout of exhilaration he disappeared again.

I pushed over the edge of the first drop-off in hot pursuit. Up and down the moguls he bobbed, miniature poles tucked into his armpits, tiny skis in a perfect wedge. Then he—and everyone else—suddenly disappeared from view as a monstrous mogul came out of nowhere, leveling *me* with a body slam.

Three falls later I shamefacedly joined Toby at the bottom of The Face.

"I saw you fall," he informed me cheerfully before adding, "but I liked how you just got right up again and kept trying."

"Thank you, Toby," I murmured, shaking powdery snow from the inside of my sunglasses.

"Teacher, next time you might try bending your knees a little bit more."

My return smile was a bit forced. "I'm so proud of you, Toby! I can't believe the progress you've made in just three weeks."

"I couldn't have—unless I did what the ski instructor taught me." The first grader was radiant. "Hey," he called to a passing student, "I just beat the principal's wife down The Face!"

And he had done just that—because of a simple choice: to recognize the authority of his ski instructor.

## Skiing on God's Authority

During His temptation in the wilderness, God's Son was able to keep standing only because it was on His Father's authority. Throughout His ministry Christ continually admitted that, as a human being, "I can of mine own self do nothing" (John 5:30).

Likewise, Nehemiah admitted that without God's instruction in his life, he would never be able to ski, much less keep standing. Life for him would keep being the same old routine of hopelessness. In these words, he recognized God's authority and his own willingness to become teachable: "Let thine ear now be attentive, and thine eyes open, that thou mayest hear the prayer of thy *servant*" (Neh. 1:6).

How would God respond to Nehemiah's admission? And how will He respond to yours and mine when we acknowledge His authority over every facet of our lives, allowing our hearts to become teachable?

## The Most Caring Authority

As a schoolteacher I sometimes experienced the defiance of a student who would not recognize my authority in the classroom. One year Mickey defied his parents, me, and other faculty members. Our principal invited the local youth pastor, whom Mickey admired, to sit in on a last-ditch conference with the rebellious ninth grader and his mother.

I was near tears the whole time. Mickey had so much potential, was so brilliant, so capable of being a valuable student leader. Yet there he sat, smug in his own authority. Through his arrogance and anger he couldn't even begin to see how much we loved him and were pulling out all the stops to "save" him for our school. Again and again we told him we forgave him, offering him another chance if only he would promise to make different choices in the future.

"I am who I am!" he kept insisting. "I'm not gonna change!"

Finally the youth pastor spoke up. "Mickey," he said, "you have been defying the authority of those who love you and want to take care of you. First you bucked your parents' guidelines. After that, your teachers'. Then it was the principal's authority. For the moment you're choosing to remain in defiance of them all."

"So?" retorted Mickey.

"So . . . soon you'll be a card-carrying member of mainstream society. But you will still have laws and rules to deal with and people in authority trying to keep you safe and happy. If you buck them, however, they have the right to put you in prison."

"Guess that's about it then," retorted Mickey in a cocky tone.

The pastor thought for a moment and then answered. "You're right. That's about it. For if you buck civil authority, the only One left to defy will be God. And, Mickey, if you resist His authority—and His help—then there's no one left to care about you."

## "But I Don't . . ."

"But," you might say, "*I don't set myself up as being a higher authority than God.*"

I'm tempted to think that too . . . when I'm forgetting the countless times through the years that I've been critical, gossipy, or judgmental. The times, I've compared myself to others, and entertained thoughts or feelings of pride. The times I've blundered through decisions without first asking for and knowing God's will.

Because of my own painful recollections, I can relate to Nehemiah's remembering the countless times he'd defied God's authority. I can relate to his feelings of failure, to his frantic plea for God's listening ear, to his desire to become God's "servant" (see verse 11).

What was God's response to Nehemiah when he chose to replace his own "authority" with God's? To *share* His authority with Nehemiah!

Just as amazing, God has promised to do the same for those of us who overcome the habit of being our own authorities. "To him that overcometh," says Christ, "will I grant to sit with me in my throne, even as I also overcame, and am set down with my Father in his throne" (Rev. 3:21). As Nehemiah asked for God's ear, God asks for ours: "He that hath an ear, let him hear what the Spirit saith . . ." (verse 22).

Imagine that! The choice to recognize the Creator's right to ultimate authority in our lives will eventually result in the privilege of sharing this authority!

Nehemiah shows me, a sinner, that no matter how many times I fall, I have the freedom to get up and keep trying. My Instructor—because of who He is—will patiently keep pointing my ski tips in the right direction. He will continue to help me bend my knees to absorb sin's buffeting.

Best of all, my ultimate caring Authority will keep guiding me—despite life's imposing moguls—right into His will.

## Dear Father . . .

Like that wannabe skier, we so often—and so arrogantly—bluster our way through life's daily decisions. Yet we have neither the skills to maneuver treacherous slopes nor the wisdom to choose the best trail.

Lord, help us to internalize the fact that we are *not* the highest authority of our lives. You are.

Give us the willingness to lay our egos—with all their self-sufficiency and unmerited pride—upon Your altar. Give us a teachable spirit. Then teach us the way.

Thank You for being who You are—our Creator, our Redeemer, our Highest Authority, and . . . our Friend.

In Jesus' name, we pray.

Amen.

# LOOKING FOR THE LAMB

*LOOK FOR GOD*

*silly sheep, we*
*bleating about*
*in self-importance*
*as if*
*the responsibility*
*were all ours*

*not remembering*
*it was*
*the Shepherd*
*Who found*
*the lost lamb—*
*and not*
*the other way*
*around*

*and yet . . .*
*the Shepherd*
*showers*
*bonus blessings*
*on sheep*
*who choose*
*to seek*[4]

**—Carolyn Rathbun Sutton**


"How was your first day of school?" I asked little Matthew, waiting for his ride on the school's front steps.

"It wasn't good at all!"

"Why?" I asked.

"I had a bad day," he pouted. "Your day would've been bad too if you couldn't have been with *your* dad."

Soon after I learned that Matthew's parents had separated the previous summer. After that, I made certain to return Matthew's "Hi" whenever he greeted me.

By Christmas vacation he had developed the habit of looking for me at lunch. Often he would sneak up from behind and give me a chokehold hug around the neck.

One day, after his chokehold greeting, he stood silently beside my chair while the students around us carried on an animated conversation. Then he tapped me on the shoulder.

"There's just one thing I don't understand about *us*," he said solemnly.

Having not a clue as to what he was about to say, I asked, "What is it?"

"How come," he answered, his blue eyes big, "it's always *me* looking for you? Why don't *you* ever come looking for me? It makes me sad when I'm the *only* one doing the looking."

"Oh, Matthew," I said, "from now on, I promise to look for you every day."

The next day, before sitting down with my older students to eat, I consciously looked for Matthew and spotted him at a far table in a group of rowdy little classmates. Just as I started walking in his direction, he looked up, saw me, and began to wave. Then he caught himself and quickly lowered his head. But I could see him peering out from under his long eyelashes as I approached. The closer I got, the lower he dropped his head. But the big smile on his face revealed his delight that I had come looking for him.

When I got close enough, I called out, "Matthew! Matthew! There you are! I've been looking everywhere for you!"

Dropping his soggy sandwich on the table with a thud, Matthew jumped out of his chair and threw his arms about my waist.

"You were looking for *me* this time!" he shouted joyfully. "You were looking for *me!*"

Then he backed away as a playful expression came over his face. "You were looking for me—but *I* let you find me."

## Balanced Friendship

Nehemiah understood enough about God's character to know God delights in humankind's responding to His love. Like that lonely first grader, God must sometimes become a bit weary of having to always look for me.

The Bible contains a story about a good Shepherd who went looking for a lost lamb. The only thing the lamb had to do was to agree to go home with the Shepherd. The only way that little lamb could "look for" the Shepherd was to allow itself to be picked up and carried.

Something happened to my friendship with Matthew when I started taking the time to look for him. He began opening up to me—about the kinds of little cars he played with, about the TV shows he watched with his dad. Later on he talked about missing the mother who didn't live with him anymore and how afraid he was—when flying alone to visit her—that the airplane "might fall into the water or the mountain."

When I take time to look for God—not just during my early-morning devotional time, but throughout the entire day—He opens up to me as well. In countless ways He shows how much He cares about me and about what I'm doing.

Like Matthew, Nehemiah was keenly feeling Israel's—and his—pain from an imbalanced relationship with God.

*We asked for this mess we're in,* Nehemiah could have reasoned—and stopped there. *After all, Israel hasn't "looked" for God in decades.*

Yet Nehemiah was familiar enough with the ancient writings—and their revelation of God's character—to know he would find God once he started seriously "looking" for Him, once he opened his heart to God's Spirit. Years before, Jeremiah had written, "You will seek Me and find Me, when you search for Me with all your heart" (Jer. 29:13, NASB).

God knew that Israel's only hope in a hopeless situation was to respond once again to His love. Nehemiah also realized that Israel's friendship with God would go nowhere unless the nation agreed to be carried back into the fold.

## Second Snapshot

Our second snapshot in the Nehemiah Album shows him still down on his knees. First he acknowledged a higher Authority, and now he is looking for God. This portrait of Nehemiah encourages me to use worries and concerns, praises and people who cross my mind, as *reasons* to respond to God's drawing. It encourages me—in the words of that old spiritual—to "call Him up and tell Him what you want."

Usually, in the pursuit of balance for a friendship that has gotten lopsided, the other friend in the mix more than welcomes one's efforts to respond. God is such a friend.

When we open up to God, He opens up to us. He's told us how this works in James 4:8. "Draw nigh to God, and he will draw nigh to you." After all, God gives us the same assurance that little Matthew gave me the first day I looked for him: "I will be found by you" (Jer. 29:14, NASB).

# BAD HARE DAY

## SUBMIT TO GOD'S AUTHORITY, PART 1

**(Based on Nehemiah 1:4)**

*"I have been driven many times to my knees by the overwhelming conviction that I had nowhere else to go. My own wisdom, and that of all about me, seemed insufficient for the day."*
**—Abraham Lincoln**[5]

*"To be poor in spirit is to know in our heart of hearts that we really need God."*
**—Doug Webster**[6]

*"Humble yourselves in the sight of the Lord, and he shall lift you up."*
**—James 4:10**

An African hare gave me the clearest example I've ever witnessed of what Nehemiah did next in his pursuit of God's will.

Brer Rabbit, along with Snow White, had come to live with us at the request of our 7-year-old son (who also named the brown and white rabbits, respectively). My first reaction to his request as we stood looking at the row of caged rabbits (at a Rwandan university experimental produce/livestock farm) had been " I don't think so."

My private reasoning went something like *Who in her right mind would want a couple rabbits as pets? I mean, a* couple *rabbits would be fine. But you know how rabbits are—two today . . . 22 tomorrow.*

Yet after quietly discussing the matter with my husband behind the cages, we decided to grant our son's request. We hoped our child's assuming the care of two rabbits would provide him some excellent training in taking responsibility.

Kent was beside himself with joy and spent most of his time in the backyard hugging and kissing the two hares. His father and I had constructed—with chicken wire and wooden slats from our missionary packing crates—a passable rabbit hutch. How our family enjoyed sitting out on the back lawn in the late afternoon watching our newly acquired critters hopping about and nibbling on the local version of crabgrass!

Inevitably, bunny babies came and went. Snow White settled happily into her parental role, as did Brer Rabbit—for a time.

## The Great Escape

Then one day it happened.

"Mom!" screamed a panicked Kent. "Brer Rabbit's running away!" Schadrach, the gardener who'd witnessed the "prison break," was right behind him.

It seems that when Kent opened the door of the hutch for some postlunch bonding time with his bunnies, Brer Rabbit made a run for it. Kent's father was already back at school teaching his first afternoon class.

Schadrach took charge. "Tugende!" ["Let's go!"] he ordered. What a sight we must have been: I, hoisting up my long African-print skirt in order to run better; Kent, tears drying on his cheeks as his chubby legs tried to match the stride of the nimble Schadrach who was trying to keep Brer Rabbit in his sights.

We intermittently hollered out phrases of three different languages in an attempt to communicate such concepts as "There—in the neighbors' garden!" and "Watch out for the low-hanging stalk of bananas!"

Our basic running formation was as follows: Brer Rabbit in the lead by a few heads (the large cabbages in all missionary gardens tended to distract him), then Schadrach, then me, with Kent quickly gaining.

I marveled at the little hare's apparent stamina and energy, at his desperate courage in an attempt to elude three pursuers.

Schadrach skillfully maneuvered the rabbit back up onto the road, then ran around some bushes and blocked him. The terrified hare turned toward Kent and me. I very much expected Kent's little rabbit to leap out of our path in yet another dizzying direction. But he didn't.

Instead, he suddenly gave me a crash course in Submission 101.

## I Give Up!

Stopping dead-still in the center of the dirt road, Brer Rabbit looked frantically at Schadrach and then back at us. Making a strange little leaping motion, he came down hard—and flat. His heaving tummy literally hit the dust, causing multiple diaphanous mini-clouds to swirl up above his furry prostrated form. The rabbit's long brown ears and front legs stretched out before him on the road. His elongated hind legs extended far behind the white puff of a tail.

Then, with nose in the dirt, Brer Rabbit emitted a frail, pitiful cry, the only sound I would ever hear him make.

Alarmed, I asked Schadrach in broken Kinyarwanda, "Is he dead?"

"No," the man chuckled. "He's *submitting*. He knows he can't run away anymore." With that, Schadrach confidently walked up to the limp, trembling bunny, picked him up by the ears, and placed him tenderly in Kent's arms.

In the following years I had several more opportunities to observe Brer Rabbit's submission habit. The little creature seemed content and safe in the backyard for weeks on end. Then he would suddenly bolt out into the danger-filled world. He'd dodge rabbit-eating locals and nearby neighborhood watchdogs before running himself half dead. Only when he allowed himself to be "captured" was Brer Rabbit completely safe from life-threatening dangers.

## Brer Israel

How closely Israel's behavior, in Nehemiah's time, resembled that of Brer Rabbit's! Nehemiah clearly saw the mortal danger in which his countrymen had placed themselves by repeatedly "fleeing" from God into the dangerous world of idolatry.

As Kent wanted simply to provide his rabbit with happiness and safety, so God—ever so much more—wanted the same for Israel, the apple of his eye (Zech. 2:8). And He wants the same for us. After all, God "set His affection to love" us (Deut. 10:15, NASB).

The bad news about Jerusalem's broken wall—brought to Nehemiah by his brother—reinforced the Hebrew cupbearer's intense desire that the God-Israel relationship once again be restored. Nehemiah understood that only in wholehearted submission would Israel find the peace, security, and happiness they so desperately desired (see Deut. 10:12, 13). He knew Israel had exhausted themselves running from God.

Brer Rabbit's habit of submission reminds me that when I find myself raising clouds of dust from racing to and fro, I can stop, throw myself down wherever I am, and plaintively call out, "I give up!" (Frankly, I get exhausted when I run in circles. Don't you?)

And when we throw ourselves in the middle of the road, God won't leave us lying there. Because He is a loving Authority He will tenderly pick us up and carry us back to safety. As my friend Kemba Esmond put it, God will meet our needs "when we come to the end of ourselves."[7]

# WHY SCOOTER'S MISSING OUT
## SUBMIT TO GOD'S AUTHORITY, PART 2

**(Based on Nehemiah 1:4)**

*"Those who have a hungry heart and broken spirit
are the favorites of God."*
**—Helmut Thielicke**[8]

*"First, give yourself to God.
You may be sure He'll look after what is His."*
**—Anonymous**[9]

What, exactly, is submission? And what does it have to do with learning God's will for a situation in my personal life? The first question my dictionary can answer. The second question God's Word will answer (later in this chapter).

My dictionary describes *submission* in terms such as "yielding, "surrendering," "resignation," "obedience," and "meekness."[10]

Those terms certainly don't describe Israel's attitude (circa Nehemiah) toward God.

On a more personal—and disturbing—note, those dictionary terms don't describe what my attitude toward God has often been. And they certainly don't describe Scooter's attitude toward me!

## Scooter and Jammer

Recently I exchanged 12 used CDs for two baby pygmy goats. Though not related, they look like twins. Yet their behaviors are as different as night and day.

Jammer chooses to jam his nose into my outstretched grain-filled hand for a snack. He chooses to dance along at my heels when we go for walks. He chooses to lie back passively in my arms while his hooves are being trimmed. When I say "Jammer, give me a kiss!" he presses his moist little nose against my chin expecting a molasses-grain treat.

Jammer is submissive, yet well adjusted—and very, very happy. His trusting state of mind manifests itself in energetic midair gymnastics and joyful bleating whenever a family member approaches the goat pen.

Scooter, on the other hand, literally scoots off when someone approaches. The gray hair down the center of his back stands rigid. He's nearly impossible to catch and hold when it's hoof-trimming or vaccination time. He absolutely refuses to submit to human authority.

While Jammer gratefully leans into a back rub, Scooter stands at a safe distance. Warily but wistfully he listens to Jammer "talk" to his human guardians. Poor Scooter! By his own unhappy choices, he's missing out on a much better quality of life.

In a state of nonsubmission we, like Scooter, just don't know what we're missing. Jesus said, "Come unto me, . . . and I will give you rest" (Matt. 11:28). In not submitting to God, we forfeit the peace He wants to give us.

## Some *Hows* of Submission

Perhaps Nehemiah's desire to submit to God's authority has encouraged you to reexamine your present attitude toward God. Perhaps you'd like to "relax" more in the arms of God. But how does one go about doing this?

I've found two specific scriptural *hows*. They remind me of two unique, yet common, life experiences: being born and taking a first step.

*1. Relax in the Birth Canal*

The first how I find in words Jesus spoke to Nicodemus. "Marvel not that I said unto thee, Ye must be born again" (John 3:7).

I imagine you don't recall putting a whole lot of effort into your own birth. You can't remember asking yourself, *H'mm, should I go feet first or arms first or head first? Hey, if I go head first—I'll be able to see where I'm going!*

No, neither you nor I put any effort into our birth process. We had neither the courage, the strength, the heart, nor the brains to make any of it happen. If we *could* have communicated, it would have been more along the lines of "Hey, Mom and Doc! If I'm to be . . . it's up to thee!"

Similarly, we start the submission-to-God process by giving up, in various ways, our run from God and simply collapsing at His feet—just as we are. "If my people . . . shall humble themselves, and pray, and seek my face, and turn from their wicked ways; then will I hear from heaven, and will forgive their sin, and will heal their land" (2 Chron. 7:14).

Just as we had neither courage, strength, heart, nor brains enough to help out with our own physical births, we lack those same qualities regarding our spiritual births. Yet, with our permission, God can spiritually "birth" us. He supplies the courage by taking away our "spirit of fear." He gives us "power, . . . love, and . . . a sound mind" (2 Tim. 1:7) to replace our deficiency of strength, heart, and brains. In short, He fills us with His Holy Spirit (see Acts 13:52).

*2. Put Your Best Foot Forward*

With God's Spirit now controlling us, Paul tells us how to continue the submission process. "Present your bodies a living sacrifice," he writes, and "be ye transformed by the renewing of your mind" (Rom. 12:1, 2). *Wait a minute, Paul,* I thought upon first reading this text, *are you saying that this* how *requires an effort on my part?*

His answer would have to be yes. Here's a simple explanation why.

Although my parents doted over me when I was a soft-pink, wrinkly, colicky baby, they still longed for another day. That day came when I was 10 months old—when my mind and body coordination decided to cooperate . . . in the form of a first step.

In the first *how* of the submission process we say, "God, I'm open to being 'born,' but I leave it up to You to 'deliver' me and fill me with Your power." In the second *how* we tell our heavenly Parent, "I choose, with Your support, to put one foot in front of the other and start walking."

This glorious walk in submission begins anew—and continues—with each choice we make (see 1 Cor. 6:19, 20, Rom. 6:13; and Rom. 8:9).

The "fruits" of our choice to submit will be evident in our interactions with others (see 1 Peter 2:13-3:12).

## Payoffs a-Plenty!

Jammer's payoffs from his choice to submit are similar to—but a mere shadow of—the temporal payoffs we receive from submitting our bodies, minds, and wills to God. Here, in brief, are only six of them.

*Payoff 1:* Jammer enjoys *companionship* with me. With this companionship come my guidance and protection. Likewise, with God, we enjoy companionship with God through His indwelling Holy Spirit (see Eph. 3:16-20) when we submit to Him.

*Payoff 2:* Jammer knows he's a *member of the family* and makes himself right at home whether it's down at the barn or up on our front porch. He confidently asks for treats, climbs into our laps, and "talks" to us. By submitting ourselves to God's authority, we too become members of His family (see Rom. 8:14-17).

*Payoff 3:* Jammer has *perfect peace*—fearing neither a diesel-spewing tractor nor a hungry red-tailed hawk flying overhead—when he's with me. God also gives me perfect peace (see Phil. 4:6, 7) when I submit to Him.

*Payoff 4:* Jammer has *protection* when he's with me. Everything about Jammer's body language shows he's confident that I stand between him and danger. Likewise, submission to God brings us both spiritual and physical protection. In fact, submission to God takes us out of the immediate clutches of the devil. "Submit yourselves therefore to God. Resist the devil, and he will flee from you" (James 4:7). For God strengthens the submissive heart to resist the seductive attractions of pride, display, self-gratification, and spiritual apathy.

*Payoff 5:* With me Jammer will *always know where to go.* I lead him well away from the nearby coyote den in the woods. I lead him on a gravel path, which will keep his growing hooves naturally trimmed. To the submissive, meek, gentle-spirited follower, God promises to show the way. "The meek will he guide in judgment: and the meek will he teach his way" (Ps. 25:9).

*Payoff 6:* Finally, I take pride in *showcasing* Jammer because he brings so much joy to whoever makes his acquaintance. When company wants to see the goats, Jammer is the one I enjoy "exalting." His sweet spirit and playful antics absolutely delight the guests. Likewise, God has promised to "exalt" those who submit to Him. "Humble yourselves therefore under the mighty hand of God, that he may exalt you in due time" (1 Peter 5:6).

When hot-tempered John and boisterous Peter finally submitted their hearts to God, He exalted them. Even the highly educated members of the Sanhedrin shook their heads as they "observed the confidence of Peter and John, and understood that they were uneducated and untrained men, they were marveling, and began to recognize them as having been with Jesus" (Acts 4:13, NASB).

## It's Your Choice

Who wouldn't like companionship with God, membership in His family, perfect peace, big-time help in resisting the devil, specific guidance for the details of our lives, and a little more respect? All this is available to those making the choice to submit to God.

As if all these weren't enough, God has one final, eternal blessing for the submissive. "He will beautify the meek with salvation" (Ps. 149:4). With nothing to lose and everything to gain, may our constant prayer be:

*As comes to me cloud or sun,*
*Father! Thy will, not mine, be done.*[11]

# Oops!

## *Realign One's Soul, Part 1*

**(Based on Nehemiah 1:5-11)**

*"Confession is good for the soul."*
**—Grandmother**

*"Most of our troubles stem from too much time on our hands
and not enough on our knees."* [12]

He was the *last* child I expected to pray.

Brandon, a foster child I'd never met before, had taxed my nerves from the minute he'd entered the children's Bible study class. In and out (mostly *out*) of his chair, grabbing things from other children, interrupting the stories and class discussion—he had me reprimanding him almost continually.

I can't count the times I had to say:

"Sweetheart, it's time to listen now—not talk."

"No, that mandolin is *not* a toy—please put it back in the case."

"No, nature center activities stop during lessontime."

"I'm sorry, you can't have another turn until *all* the other children have had *theirs*. I need you to sit down!"

In spite of the fact he was nearly driving me up a wall, he broke my heart. Years spent as a schoolteacher helped me understand that Brandon had a severe attention deficit problem. I sensed he wanted to please me but just couldn't make his nervous body obey his nobler impulses. Once when I moved away from him to help another child, he looked over at me sadly and blurted out, "But I want you to sit next to *me*."

## Unexpected Offer

One Sabbath morning, with a sigh of relief, I brought the Bible class to an end.

"Who would like to offer closing prayer?" I asked, glancing meaningfully in the direction of the prim Abbie.

Neither she nor any of the other perfectly behaved children responded.

"I want to! Can I, please? Huh?" Brandon exploded from his seat waving his arm in the air.

"Sure, Brandon," I answered, masking my shock. "Girls and boys, let's bow our heads." Obediently the children bowed their heads—all but Brandon, that is. Instead he dropped clumsily to his knees, squeezed his eyes shut, tightly folded together his wiggly fingers, and forced the resulting double fist into his chin.

"Dear Jesus," he began, "dear Jesus, uh, uh—oh, dear Jesus—oops! Help. Oops! Help!" At this point I opened my eyes to see Brandon, scarlet with embarrassment, directing his frantic plea for help at *me* instead of at heaven.

My heart melted. Instantly I was down on my knees beside him. At first he painstakingly attempted to repeat my every word. Then he just sighed in comfortable resignation as I finished the prayer for him. Loudly echoing my "Amen," Brandon looked up at me, holding still just long enough to flash me a dazzling smile of appreciation.

## Next Snapshot, Please . . .

Let me point out the next snapshot in my Nehemiah Album. Here he is, in his chamber, down on his knees.

"No," you protest, "you've already shown me this photo of Nehemiah—several times over, in fact."

Ah! So you're starting to see a pattern here? So did I. In the original outline for this book I allotted one chapter for Nehemiah's prayer. But every time I tried pushing impatiently ahead in the story, he was still down on his knees.

These nearly identical snapshots remind me of a certain picture of

Christ. You know the one—that old classic of Him on His knees, His hands clasped, His pleading gaze directed toward heaven. And all this in a lonely corner of Gethsemane. Jesus well knew that the power of prayer alone would equip Him to complete the job His Father had sent Him to do.

Likewise, Nehemiah was a man of preaction prayer. The Bible documents that Nehemiah spent a whopping four months (roughly 120 days; see Neh. 1:1; 2:1) in prayer before completing a 52-day job (see Neh. 6:15). That's 43 percent more time *praying* about God's broader will . . . than actually *accomplishing* God's specific will—once God revealed it to him. What a resounding reminder of the role prayer must play in our lives if God is going to accomplish His will in and through us.

Martin Luther once said, "I have so much to do today that I shall spend the first three hours in prayer."[13]

So what was Nehemiah talking to God about for such a long time? The same things we need to talk to God about in order to experience a soul realignment.

In a nutshell, Nehemiah, like little Brandon in my children's Bible class, was exclaiming, "Oops!" before crying out, "Help!"

# SHOWDOWN AT THE CHIROPRACTOR'S

## REALIGN ONE'S SOUL, PART 2

**(Based on Nehemiah 1:5-11)**

*"Let the wicked forsake his way, and the unrighteous man his thoughts: and let him return unto the Lord, and he will have mercy upon him; and to our God, for he will abundantly pardon."*
**—Isaiah 55:7**

*"Prayer is a powerful thing, for God has bound and tied Himself thereto."*
**—Martin Luther**[14]

In a recent interview on National Public Radio, a book reviewer stated that on one Internet Web site, more than 4,000 religious/spiritual/devotional book titles were available.

"Why is there suddenly so much interest in spiritual reading?" asked the interviewer.

"Because," the reviewer responded, "people are suddenly expecting new things to take place at the arrival of the new millennium. They want a better understanding of spiritual things and harmony of soul with whatever's out there in the universe."

People *are* searching for ways to experience a soul "realignment" with "whatever's out there in the universe." Many are attempting to re-align their souls at New Age centers such as Archangel Michael's Soul Therapy for Personal and Planetary Healing in Shasta City, California. Others are "trying on" Eastern philosophies, while millions consult astrologers and psychics. (*Vogue* magazine now even has its own psychic to which readers can send their questions.) Meanwhile, a book of ancient

Jewish traditions is the latest religious fad reading among Hollywood entertainment professionals.

## Nehemiah's Soul Realignment

Two components made up Nehemiah's continuing soul realignment: a Scripture-based knowledge of God's character and a commitment to personal prayer. These two components set the stage for the most significant "Oops!" prayer he would ever offer.

After receiving his brother's disturbing news about Jerusalem's broken wall, Nehemiah went to his knees. What happened there was pivotal to his discovering God's specific will not only for his life but also for thousands of his countrymen.

Let's look briefly at the five R's that comprise Nehemiah's powerful, life-changing prayer.

## R 1: Recognition

The first R we've already discussed in chapters 1 and 2. Nehemiah *recognizes God's authority.* "O Lord God of heaven, the great and terrible God," his prayer begins (Neh. 1:5).

Notice that Nehemiah isn't intimidated by God's greatness, for he has heard the timeless tales of God's faithfulness. Scripture has made him familiar with who God is. With confidence Nehemiah calls on a God "that keepeth covenant." He opens his heart to a God whose authority is based on kindness and whose "mercy" is legendary.

Nehemiah ends this respectful salutation by acknowledging that God's obligation (based on an earlier covenant) to bestow goodness is only to those who have chosen to lay their egos on His altar. For they are those who "love him and observe his commandments" (verse 5).

## R 2: Realignment

After a prayerful recognition of who God is, Nehemiah desires a *readjustment of his character.* Have you had an adjustment recently? I have. The ache generally begins on the left side of my neck, next to the spinal column. If I don't see my chiropractor within a couple days, I can pretty much count on a tight burning across my midback about 10 inches below my now-stiff neck. Sometime within the next two weeks I will most certainly wake up with painful jabs extending from my left hip down to my knee. All of the above are caused by subluxations (neurological disruptions from my vertebrae being out of their natural alignment).

How do I get rid of this intense discomfort? By getting an adjustment from Dr. Kellim, my trusty chiropractor. The longer I wait to see him, however, the longer it takes for the symptoms to diminish and for my body to heal.

I wish I were the perfect patient, but when I go in for an out-of-whack alignment, I often feel as if it's showdown at the OK Corral.

Dr. Kellim, both feet planted firmly on the floor, faces me. Looking me dead in the eye after surveying my open medical chart, he firmly (but kindly) asks, "And what activities have you been doing that might have contributed to this most recent misalignment?"

Then it's true confession time. "Well," I once had to admit, "I tried to help dig a little drainage ditch for a couple hours, uh, swinging a pickax." Another time I confessed, "I went snowmobiling." (I left out the part about the nasty little spill on the icy washboard surface.)

Admitting my unhealthful choices to the doctor is not easy—especially since he's been so faithful giving me sound help and advice to the contrary. But (thank goodness!) as long as I'm in a state of submission on his adjustment table, my doctor is always willing to realign my spine.

Nehemiah went to the divine Chiropractor for a character adjustment. What made the realignment of his soul possible?

Confession did. Confession of specific sins. "We have dealt very corruptly against thee" (verse 7), Nehemiah shamefacedly admits. We have traded praise for pride, relationship for rebellion, true worship for willful idolatry, saintliness for sinfulness.

Nehemiah reminds me that what visits to my chiropractor do for subluxations of the spine, confession does for subluxations of the soul. Chiropractic realignment restores healthy communication between my brain and my nerves. Heavenly realignment restores healthy communication between my soul and my God.

## R 3: Recollection

The third R in Nehemiah's prayer is *recalling God's promises*. When I was about 4, Daddy set safety ground rules for a new game I called "catch me." I'd stand on a chair or garden wall while he stood a few feet away. When he was sure I'd be safe, he'd nod and say, "OK."

Then I'd scream, "Catch me!"

"I will!" he'd promise. Fearlessly and giddily, I'd leap into his outstretched arms. The only time I hesitated to leap was the first time. After that I knew I could trust his promise to catch me whenever I took a "leap of faith."

Nehemiah's prayer recalls God's promises to "catch" Israel as long as they'd choose to jump into His outstretched arms. Nehemiah's prayerful recollections included words such as "remember" (verse 8) and "yet will I gather" and "bring them [Israel] unto the place that I have chosen to set my name there" (verse 9).

Especially in times of crisis we need to look over our shoulder to those times when God's strong arm brought us through tough situations. Times when we could count on God to "catch" us. Nehemiah knew that God's previous actions and promises from the past were His potential actions and eternal promises for the present as well as the future. We can have the same assurance. For God has promised, "My covenant will I not break, nor alter the thing that is gone out of my lips" (Ps. 89:34).

## R 4: Renewal

In the fourth R of Nehemiah's prayer, the young man *renews his commitment* to the human-divine relationship. Israel, Nehemiah confides to God, would henceforth "desire to fear [honor, worship, reverence] thy name" (Neh. 1: 11).

In this renewed personal commitment Nehemiah assures God he has more than just confession of sin in mind. He also has repentance in mind.

Most of us have claimed the promise "If we confess our sins, he is faithful and just to forgive us our sins" (1 John 1:9). But without a committed resolve to repent of our sins—and then abandon them—our confession is worthless.[15]

In one short verse, Isaiah tells us how to renew a commitment to God. "Let the wicked *forsake* his way, and the unrighteous man his thoughts: and let him *return* unto the Lord, and he will have mercy upon him; and to our God, for he will abundantly pardon" (Isa. 55:7). If we don't make a moral choice to "return" to God, renewal is impossible.

One of my wonderful storytelling uncles recalled an example of a nonrenewal confession at a Kansas church service during his boyhood years. He told it something like this:

"I remember once two ol' German boys during a Bible discussion at church. Something was said during the service, and the one guy got into it with the ol' boy sitting behind him.

"Then the one behind grabs a hymnal, stands up, and *whack!* down on the head it comes. Of course, everybody reacts and says, 'We can't have this going on in the church. Everybody needs to love one another. You need to apologize!'

"So the one in back stands up and says, 'Please forgive me, brother. I done wrong to hit you.' Then he adds real quick, 'But remember—I *did* hit you a good one!'"

As with confession, we can't repent on our own. Christ takes the responsibility to "give repentance to Israel, and forgiveness of sins" (Acts 5:31).

Renewal involves the *abandonment* of known sin and the return to behavior and thought choices that glorify God.

## R 5: Requests

Nehemiah ends the soul realignment process by *requesting God's blessings.* Three of them, to be exact.

The first blessing Nehemiah requests is *God's undivided attention.* "Let now thine ear be attentive to the prayer of thy servant" (Neh. 1: 11). Many friends enrich my life. The ones to whom I am closest, however, are those who listen to me as much as I listen to them. Like me— and you—Nehemiah had an emotional need to be heard.

Boldly now Nehemiah asks for the second blessing: *success.* "Prosper, I pray thee, thy servant" (verse 11). After all, hadn't Jeremiah written nearly 200 years earlier that, regarding Israel, God had "plans for welfare and not for calamity" to give Israel "a future and a hope" (Jer. 29:11, NASB)?

The third blessing for which Nehemiah prays is an indication from God on how he is to proceed. Since Nehemiah's greatest obstacle to becoming involved in the rebuilding of Jerusalem's wall will be his boss, the king, he specifically requests mercy from the king (Neh. 1: 11).

## For Us, Too

There we have it—Nehemiah's soul-aligning *Oops!* prayer in five simple components: *recognition* of God's authority, *realignment* through confession and repentance, *recollection* of God's promises, *renewal* of commitment to God, and a specific *request* for His blessings.

By the way, God's blessings of (a) a listening ear, (b) success in personal endeavors, and (c) indications of how we are to proceed in life's details are ours as much as they were Nehemiah's—if we are willing to undergo a soul realignment.

Shall we make an appointment with the heavenly Chiropractor right now?

# Praying Nehemiah's Prayer

*Realign One's Soul, Part 3*

Let Nehemiah lead you through a soul-realignment prayer.

Dear Father,

*[Recognition of God's authority over one's life]*

I acknowledge that You alone are all-knowing and all-loving and all-wise. You, my Creator, remain faithful to every word You speak and every promise You make. Therefore, I worship You as the ultimate authority in my life.

*[Realignment through confession]*

I also acknowledge any responsibility for the broken wall in my life. I want to confess the self-sufficiency, self-pity, and pride with which I have diverged from my covenant with You. Specifically, I admit that I have not given You authority over the area(s) of _____ in my life. I confess the times my choices have hurt not only myself but also others. Help me to make things right with them.

But most of all, I confess the times my choices have hurt You. I resolve, by Your grace, to abandon these sins once and for all. I praise You and thank You for Your precious forgiveness of which I am so undeserving but which I now still gratefully accept.

*[Recalling God's promises]*

Thank You for Your track record of faithfulness to me. Thank You for the Bible promises through which You've let me know Your outstretched arms are always extended to "catch" me when I step out in faith. Just now I would like to recall Your promise in _____ (Bible text/s). I claim it (them) for the current foggy place(s) in my life.

*[Renewing one's commitment to God]*

Lord, I want the "desire to fear thy name." I want my heart open for Your cleansing, healing Spirit to flood through the gaping holes in my broken wall. I want to trust You alone to listen to my soul's burdens. I need You to show me—in Your time—how to wisely and appropriately deal with them. In all these areas I renew my commitment to cooperate with You.

*[Requesting God's blessings]*

Finally, because You are patiently fashioning me into Your child, Your willing servant, and Your trustworthy friend, prosper me and grant me mercy—especially regarding _____.

All these things I pray in the name of Your Son, who so fervently prayed for me [see John 17:20].

Amen.

# FLYNG AIR COCKROACH

*WAIT PERSEVERINGLY ON GOD, PART 1*

*(Based on Nehemiah 2:1–3)*

*"By perseverance the snail reached the ark."*
—*Charles Spurgeon*[16]

*"Rest in the Lord, and wait patiently for him."*
—*Psalm 37:7*

The last statement in Nehemiah's prayer provides us with a valuable prayer principle: As you wait for God's clues to the resolution of your specific request, pray from within your present context as well as for those within that context.

Nehemiah prayed, "Grant [me] mercy in the sight of this man [Artaxerxes, the Persian king]." Nehemiah then explains why he made this request of God: "For I was the king's cupbearer" (Neh. 1:11).

Nehemiah might have assumed his present "context" (the Persian palace with its affluent king) had nothing to do with resolving the burden on his heart: to see poverty-riddled Jerusalem's broken wall restored. Yet what a false assumption that would have been! Looking back on my own life, I too am amazed at how prayerfully surrendering an apparently infertile "context " is just one more helpful way station on the road to God's revealed will.

## High and Dry in Ethiopia

Almost since a toddler, I'd prayed, "Dear God, help me be a missionary when I grow up."

Then one day, there I was—17,000 feet above a parched Ethiopian desert with sharp gusts of wind tossing the tiny African aircraft back and forth. We passengers were sicker than dogs. (The memory of that flight still makes my stomach churn.) The cabin air inside the double-prop plane was sweltering. Air turbulence prohibited the two-person flight crew from serving drinks to relieve our burning throats.

Newlyweds of just a year and brand-new missionaries, my husband and I were suffering from jet lag and wearing the same clothes for the third day in a row. Obviously we hadn't felt exactly fresh when we'd boarded our flight in Mombasa.

During a muggy two-day stopover there, we were disappointed to learn that neither our personal effects nor our car had yet arrived on the African continent. With no car we'd have to use the remainder of our quickly dwindling traveler's checks for airline tickets. Now we were "puddle-jumping" (though it was much too dry for puddles) on short flights from Mombasa . . . to Addis Ababa . . . to a sandy runway some-where in Ethiopia . . . to Kampala, Uganda, en route to our final Congolese mission station destination.

My tongue cleaved to the roof of my mouth as I tried not to groan audibly. An acrid, fetid stench wafted through the cabin, confirming what my ears had already told me. Several fellow passengers (mostly Peace Corps volunteers and indigenous people en route to the hinter-lands) were *not* keeping down their salted peanuts and ham sandwiches. And I wasn't feeling so good myself.

With only the tightly cinched seat belt keeping my head from hitting either the ceiling or the person across the narrow aisle, I thought, *Things just can't get any worse!*

## Crummy Context

Then they got worse—for that's when I first saw the cockroach. It was crawling along the lower of two rails composing the open luggage rack above. And it was *huge.* I would have screamed except I was almost to the point of losing *my* peanuts too. Mesmerized by its horror—movie qualities, I watched Mr. Cockroach advance from above the head of my husband. From there it moved directly above a European woman sitting in the window seat directly ahead of us.

Our plane suddenly hit an air pocket. Small pieces of luggage flew up to the ceiling, then dropped back down. Several people emitted cries of alarm while an elderly man toward the front of the craft retched loudly.

Either a piece of moving luggage bumped the cockroach or it simply lost its grip. For the next thing I knew, the obnoxious bug was facing the nearest window and hanging only by its two front legs. Back and forth it swung, long feelers waving desperately about. Then the plane lurched abruptly to the right. Like a graceful trapeze artist, the cockroach released its hold on the thin metal bar and did two quick forward flips before plummeting directly into the woman's lap below.

Only her seat belt kept the hysterical passenger from exiting her seat and landing on the African desert before the rest of us did. Her deafening screams and thrashing arms and legs were soon imitated by the passenger seated next to her—and then by the passenger on the other side of the aisle. The insect itself frantically and quickly scurried out of sight.

A half hour later the reality of my "context" hit me right between the eyes.

During a brief refueling stopover at an airstrip whose "terminal" was a glorified lean-to, I dropped my dizzy and perspiration-soaked self down on a mound of parched earth. As the African sun dehydrated me, I fought tears and thought, *I want my mommy! Whatever made me think I might be cut out to be a missionary?*

For years I'd prayed for this. Now here I was. *Oh, dear God, what have I done?* All I could do now was let the blistering wind dry my tears, and then reboard the plane with the other green-tinted passengers.

## Anachronistic Contexts

The Bible speaks often of anachronistic—or out-of-place—contexts. For example, before becoming the wife of David, Israel's future king (see 1 Sam. 25:39), Abigail suffered through the earlier context of being married to a surly drunkard (verses 3, 36).

Vice pharaoh Joseph's *preparatory* context was prison.

Four-star general Gideon's *premilitary victory* context was to watch his army of 32,000 (see Judges 6 and 7) melt to 300.

In his *earlier traumatic* context Daniel was subjected to the humiliation of becoming a eunuch (see Dan. 1:7) before becoming prime minister to a number of monarchs.

In her *initial* contexts Esther was orphaned and destined for a heathen king's harem (see Esther 2:7, 3, 4) before becoming queen of Persia.

Notice that none of these individuals ran ahead of God. Abraham, Jacob, and Moses, on the other hand, all got into serious trouble when they didn't wait for God to first reveal His will.

Jeannette Johnson posits what disastrous results might have resulted had people of God in the past not *waited* for His detailed instruction. "Consider," she says, "some of [God's] great acts. Instructions for building the ark, for conquering Jericho, for crossing the Red Sea—all were step-by-step directions. Had Noah designed the ark, it may have sunk. Joshua's parade plans may have invited an enemy attack. Moses' foray into the Red Sea may have turned into a session of free swimming lessons."

I like Jeannette's personal application: "When God gives a goal, He also outlines each step necessary to reach it—a road map. Planning ahead with God is right . . . [but] expecting a risk-free road map shows lack of faith in God.

"God can use you if by faith you receive step-by-step instructions from Him. Don't be the man or woman, the boy or girl, who says, 'Oh, I know what God wants me to do. Now I'll just figure out how to do it.' That's like trying to draw your own road map." [17]

## Back to Africa

My flight on "Air Cockroach" was certainly evidence that I would not have a "risk-free road map" experience in the mission field. But it was a valuable introductory lesson to my nine-year course entitled Beginning Missionary 101. That Ethiopian cockroach provided me with much needed practice in perseverance—and waiting on God—under duress. Throughout the succeeding nine years in Africa, cockroach encounters and multiple waits helped strengthen my courage and bolster my faith.

As time passed, I began to understand these unpleasant waiting experiences were necessary for my own character construction and absolutely essential before God could use me in subsequent ministry projects—projects that never even entered my head the day Mr. Cockroach and I were bouncing through the East African clouds.

## Nehemiah's Context, Mine, and Yours

This chapter's snapshot from the Nehemiah Album shows him four months after the day he first knelt before God with the burden of Jerusalem's broken wall on his heart. We see Nehemiah bearing a silver goblet on a jewel-studded tray.

As he approaches the monarch's table, the purple and gilded palace uniform hides neither his heavy heart nor his fear of the king's displeasure. The eyes of the king's young cupbearer are red from weeping, his face gaunt from fasting. His gait is forced; his countenance sorrowful (see Neh. 2:2).

It's in this pose the snapshot was taken. And there he stands within his palace context—vulnerable, willing, and—waiting.

> *Sit still, my daughter! Just sit calmly still!*
> *Nor deem these days—these waiting days—as ill!*
> *The One who loves thee best, who plans thy way,*
> *Hath not forgotten thy great need today!*
> *And, if He waits, 'tis sure He waits to prove*
> *To thee, His tender child, His heart's deep love.*
>
> *Sit still, my daughter! Just sit calmly still!*
> *Thou longest much to know thy dear Lord's will!*
> *While anxious thoughts would almost steal their way*
> *Corrodingly within, because of His delay—*
> *Persuade thyself in simple faith to rest*
> *That He, who knows and loves, will do the best.*[18]

# A PARTIAL SYLLABUS FOR . . . WAITING 101
## WAIT PERSEVERINGLY ON GOD, PART 2

**(Based on Nehemiah 2:1–3)**

*"God makes a promise—faith believes it, hope anticipates it, patience quietly awaits it."* [19]

*"Patience is often bitter, but its fruit is sweet."* [20]

I haven't forgotten about the love story I promised, at the beginning of this book, to share with you. But plot development in real-life stories often takes time. It did in mine.

I remember that spring afternoon as I sat among tall, waving grass on a levee slope. The water before me was alive with thousands of ducks bobbing up and down in search of supper. Migrating white pelicans floated overhead.

Divorce had thrown my social options wide open. And, yes, I was desperately lonely. Yet I'd seen so many others in my situation make unwise, impulsive, and hurtful decisions. I reached into the backpack on the grass beside me and pulled out my writing tablet and pen. With the saline breeze persistently tugging at my paper and whipping the hair about my face, I penned the following commitment to God . . . to wait on Him.

## Patience

*Patience is a lonely friend*
*Whose company is dull,*
*A solitary voice within*
*To hold one back where fools rush in.*

*Patience is a useful friend*
*(She comes from God above)*
*To draw the line when one can't see*
*One's certain vulnerability.*

*Yet in God's presence I abide—*
*With Patience on the other side.*
*Flanked by their gentle company,*
*I'm sheltered in our group of three.*

*No doubt, I'll be the last to know*
*If four is how our group should grow—*
*First God and Patience must agree,*
*Then He'll tell her, and she'll tell me.*

*So single-minded until then,*
*With loneliness I shall contend*
*For Patience is . . .*
*A lonely friend.*

## Nehemiah's Syllabus

Nearly every college professor I had seemed to delight in providing his or her students with a thick, imposing syllabus. The syllabus contained an outline of content to be studied—and mastered—during the semester.

The syllabi I found the most helpful also contained "thought questions" to ponder while working my way through the semester's material.

What follows is a brief list of "thought questions" Nehemiah's example leads us to consider. They could prove very helpful during patient waits on God regarding "broken wall" situations in our lives. These thought questions also help focus our prayers.

## Nehemiah's Thought Questions for Waiting 101

*1. What is your immediate context?*

Is it the drudgery of housework? Is it the rat race at an office or in a classroom? Is it a pain in your heart or an anxiety inside your head?

Persian Palace Food 'n' Beverage may have been Nehemiah's context, but it was also his connecting point with God. Like Nehemiah, we too can make our context . . . our prayer chapel.

*2. Is there a "King Artaxerxes" in your context?*

For which significant individual(s) in your context can you offer special prayers? (Remember that Nehemiah's example strongly suggests we should pray for them. And Job 42:8, 12-15 reminds us that Job's miserably ill fortunes began to change for the better after he started praying for the three disparaging visitors in his immediate context.)

*3. How can I know my prayer requests are within God's will?*

How can we avoid asking "amiss," as James 4:3 puts it? This final question brings us to a deeper level in the pursuit of God's will. It brings us face-to-face with His . . . measuring rod.

# FOR THE BIRDS!

## "MEASURE" PRAYER REQUESTS, PART 1

**(Based on Nehemiah 2:1-4)**

*"O Lord, thank You for all You've done, and keep up the good work."*
**—A child's prayer**

*"The most promising method of prayer is to allow oneself to be guided by the word of the Scriptures, to pray on the basis of a word of Scripture. In this way we shall not become the victims of our own emptiness."*
**—Dietrich Bonhoeffer**[21]


"Here, birdie; here, birdie," I called quietly to a group of blackbirds splashing in a post-rain-shower puddle. "Come fly to my hand and be my pets." Then I held very still—and waited for God to act. I knew it would take Him only one second of heavenly magic to get me at least one bird.

Grandma Sherrig had just read me a story about an immediate-answer-to-prayer situation before telling me to "go play" while she headed kitchenward to make a blueberry pie.

Still sitting on the couch, I'd thought and thought about that story. It had made the prayer procedure seem so magical, so simple, so . . . cause-and-effect: Ask, give God a minute to get His act together, and then . . . *boom!* He gives you whatever you asked for.

For some time I'd been really wanting some birds of my own. *Yes,* I decided, *if it worked for that little boy in the story, it'll work for me.* Slipping to my knees, I specifically asked God for birds as pets and then grabbed my winter jacket. Now I was in the backyard to collect on my prayer request.

My moving closer to the birds startled them. They fluttered up and then landed at a more distant puddle. As I approached their new location, they left the second puddle and came back to the first one.

I went back into the house for a banana with which to entice them. That didn't work either. Next I came out with a jar lid filled with water, since I was sure the puddle water would be much too muddy for them to drink. No go.

I tried sweet-talking them. I even tried tweeting and chirping sounds. In desperation I tried silence. In short, I did everything I could think of to put me in line with my prayer request.

Evidently I was so bothersome to the birds they soon flew away to find another playground.

Grandma was rolling out a piecrust when I came into the kitchen crying.

"What would you do if you *had* birds?" Grandma asked, drying my tears.

"I'd give them peanut butter sandwiches, dress them in doll clothes, and keep them warm in a shoe box on the oven door," I told her.

Grandma's laugh hurt me. She gently explained, "The birdies would have died if they were your pets because you don't know how to keep them alive. Maybe God knew it would be better to keep the birdies safe than for you to have them as pets."

These new ideas were challenging my childish theology. I had to agree that I didn't want to be the cause of any bird obituaries. I certainly hadn't looked at the big picture—especially the fact that I didn't know how to care for birds in captivity.

Then Grandma suggested something that really blew me away. "Maybe—just maybe—asking for wild birds as pets was something you shouldn't even have prayed for."

## Exposed!

Was Nehemiah's long wait on God because he, like me, had been praying for the wrong things? Let's have a closer look at how Nehemiah used God's "measuring rod" to evaluate his prayer requests.

First, Nehemiah had been asking for reconciliation between God and himself, as well as for Israel. Nothing wrong with that. God, too, had wanted a close relationship with His people (see Deut. 28). In fact, this divine desire is scattered through the earlier sacred writings as a "measuring rod" for prayer requests.

Nehemiah had also asked for mercy in the eyes of the king. Earlier writings, especially the Proverbs, abound with admonition—as well as suggestions—about being at peace with those around us. So that request qualified by God's measuring rod as well.

But Nehemiah had also been praying for something else. The first few verses of Nehemiah 2 describe the scenario for the exposure of Nehemiah's secret prayer. It happened like this.

King Artaxerxes observed to Nehemiah one morning, "You look as if you lost your last friend [or something close to it; see Neh. 2:2]."

Nehemiah briefly explained about Jerusalem's broken wall (verse 3). Then King Artaxerxes took Nehemiah by surprise with this question: "So how can I help?" (see verse 4).

Nehemiah's answer—after a quick silent prayer—revealed the specific request he'd been making of God for the past four months: "Send me to Jerusalem so that I can rebuild the wall."

Whoa! Wait a minute! Praying for Israel's reconciliation with God is one thing. But praying for an all-expense-paid trip to the Holy Land is quite another. Such a request even borders on the presumptuous, does it not?

With that type of boldness Nehemiah risked not only knocking off Artaxerxes' kingly socks, but also getting himself knocked right into a dungeon—or worse. Did Nehemiah have a right to make such a request? And even more, did he have the right before God to pray such a prayer?

The king's amazing reaction to Nehemiah's astounding request we'll look at soon enough. But first, let's establish the fact that simply praying for what we want is "for the birds." Yet we never have to pray in ignorance, for God's measuring rod—the Bible—provides clear guidelines by which we can "measure" our prayer requests.

# WEDNESDAY AFTERNOON BIRD WOMAN
## "MEASURE" PRAYER REQUESTS, PART 2

*(Based on Nehemiah 2:1-5)*

*Advertisement in a small-town newspaper:*
*"Read your Bible to know what people ought to do.*
*Read this paper to know what they actually do."* [22]

*"For as the heavens are higher than the earth,*
*so are my ways higher than your ways,*
*and my thoughts than your thoughts."*
**—Isaiah 55:9**

*"I delight to do thy will."*
**—King David in Psalm 40:8**

Previously I mentioned that this whole Nehemiah encounter started when I was searching to know God's *specific* will for my eventual choice concerning a friendship in my life. In the meantime God's "measuring rod"—the Bible—had provided me with much information concerning His general will for my life.

For example, I knew that God wants my life choices to bring honor to His name (1 Cor. 10:31). He wants me to be a stepping-stone (Rom. 14:13) and a loving example (1 Tim. 4:12). He wants me to be ready when He comes the second time (Luke 12:40). And so on.

While seeking biblical counsel for a possible upcoming marriage proposal-response decision, I was also becoming aware of some primary guidelines by which to "measure" my desires and concerns. I also believe these basic guidelines apply to any dilemma.

Let's look at five of them, which I tailor-worded to my own situation. You can tailor-word them to yours. Here's what I asked myself: If I chose to say "Yes" to a possible marriage proposal . . .

1. Would this decision bring *glory to God?* (In my case, would marriage to my gentleman friend be a marriage that would honor God? See 1 Corinthians 10:31.)

2. Would my choice be *spiritually edifying?* (Would a marriage draw us closer to God, or would we be stumbling blocks to each other? See 1 Corinthians 10:23.)

3. Would being married help or hinder my *personal readiness for Christ's return?* (Would I get so caught up in the relationship that my spiritual concerns would become secondary? After all, Paul issues a warning about this in 1 Corinthians 7:32-35.)

4. Would my choice be something to which *those who truly care for me—my family, praying friends, and local church leaders—could give their blessings?* (Consult Proverbs 15:22 and Hebrews 13:17.)

5. Would it be *an accurate witness to others* observing me and my choices? (See Proverbs 14:5 and John 5:31, 32.) [23]

## Back to Nehemiah

In the previous chapter I posed this question: Was Nehemiah's specific prayer request for a trip to Jerusalem presumptuous? In the context of his prayer in Nehemiah 1, I would have to say no.

First, Nehemiah hadn't been *telling* God to send him to Jerusalem; he'd been telling God he was *willing* to go. Then he'd obviously been asking God His opinion on the matter.

Nehemiah's specific request was within the framework of (1) persevering long-term prayer and fasting, (2) recognizing God's authority, (3) confession and the expressed resolve to abandon former sins, and (4) gratitude and trust that God is merciful, faithful, and just.

During these months of Nehemiah's prayer and fasting, don't you suspect that God was molding Nehemiah's will to match His own? Don't you suspect that He was strengthening the holy purpose He had instilled in the heart of the king's cupbearer?

Nehemiah's motives for this prayer request were (1) that the glory of

God be lifted up before the heathen nations and (2) that the broken-wall relationship between God and His chosen—but wayward—people be rebuilt. Also important was Nehemiah's willingness to wait and work within God's timetable.

## Back to the Birds—Within God's Timetable

Remember my immature prayer request nearly 50 years ago that wild birds fly into my hands to become pets? After hearing my grandmother's perspectives, I was at peace with God's negative response.

However, last spring one of the supervisors at an animal rehabilitation center, where I volunteer a half day each week, approached me.

"Would you be interested," she wanted to know, "in being trained to care for 60-plus orphaned and injured baby birds that have been dropped off here?" My mind flashed back to my childhood prayer.

With a smile my supervisor couldn't have begun to understand, I answered, "Yeah; sounds like fun."

As Wednesday Afternoon Bird Woman, I now hand-feed gruel from "bottle" syringes to baby swallows. I make sure a small, judiciously placed heater keeps the nursery air adequately warm. I clean tiny cages, fluffing fresh pine needles under my "pets," and occasionally exercise an injured wing.

But the best part about being Bird Woman is going out to the aviary where juvenile birds are learning to fly and eat birdseed and mealworms (though I still take along a large syringe-bottle for the "toddlers").

Ear-shattering chirps and wing-fluttering anticipation greet me when I walk through the double screen doors with fresh food and water. Noisy young starlings, blue jays, robins, crows, pigeons, and sparrows light on my head, shoulders, back, and arms. For an instant I stand in awe of all this feathered craziness of which I am the momentary center.

For 50 years God gave me the opportunity to grow in wisdom and submission. From inside the aviary I marvel at this new point of divine contact.

## Caught in Time

This brings us back to the Nehemiah Album. Again, our snapshot shows no action on Nehemiah's part. He stands before the king, having at last exposed the desire of his heart. His cards are all on the table. He is at the mercy (or wrath) of the most powerful monarch on earth. The king stares at Nehemiah in disbelief: This Hebrew slave wants to leave a palace and be a nobody back in Jerusalem!

Four long months of prayer and fasting. Four long months of preparation. But for what? The king's cupbearer doesn't have a clue what's about to happen. (As far as that goes, neither do we. Like Nehemiah, we may be on the verge of leaving the skillet for the fire.)

Yet even at this point in the story, Nehemiah has shown us this: When we commit to a *prayerful* present uncertainty, God will open our hearts to receive the patience we need to wait on heaven's timetable. He will give us the wisdom to understand His broader will, the discernment to know when to make a move, and the courage to take the first step.

# GETTING THE SCOOP

## DO ONE'S HOMEWORK

**(Based on Nehemiah 2:1-8)**

*"Failure to prepare is preparing to fail."*
**—John Wooden**[24]

*"The preparations of the heart . . . [are] from the Lord."*
**—Proverbs 16:1**

*"And your ears will hear a word behind you, 'This is the way, walk in it,' whenever you turn to the right or to the left."*
**—Isaiah 30:21, NASB**

Have you ever heard a sad story that went something like this?

"I'd *never* have married him—not if I'd known he was going to dump me after I'd worked my fingers to the bone getting him through grad school. I should have seen some warning signs, but I just couldn't get past my feelings for him at the time. I just *assumed* things'd work out."

Or a story that sounded like this: "I've had nothing but problems since coming here! At the time of the move I really *felt* that God wanted me to relocate to get away from my past. But maybe I was the one who wanted to get away. I'm afraid the move might not have been God's will after all."

Sad stories, indeed, told to me by a couple of acquaintances. Most of us have a sad story or two we could tell, as well. Stories of times when we didn't "get the scoop" on a person or a situation before we acted. Instead we substituted our *feelings* or *assumptions* for tangible, spiritual evidence of God's guidance in our lives.

If he hadn't been so cautious, Nehemiah would have been in danger of doing the same thing concerning Jerusalem's broken wall. The events about to occur in his life with lightning speed might have sent Nehemiah into a frenzy of high-pitched excitement had he not been well-grounded, on his two knees, for the past four months.

## Between a Rock and a Hard . . . King

When King Artaxerxes demanded to know why Nehemiah looked so sad (see Neh. 2:2), the young man in one fearful sentence quickly explained about Jerusalem's wasted wall (see verse 3).

"How can I help?" the king unexpectedly asks. In a nano-second, Nehemiah shoots a silent prayer heavenward (see verse 4) and is instantly ready with his reply: "Please give me permission to go to Jerusalem and build the wall (see verse 5).

Had Nehemiah not been hard at work "getting the scoop," he might have blown a once-in-a-lifetime opportunity, and Israel would have suffered even more. But Nehemiah is ready—mentally and spiritually. At this critical moment the young Hebrew is in no danger of basing his decisions on *feelings* or *assumptions*.

You and I can avoid the danger and aftermath of emotion-based decisions if we faithfully do our temporal and spiritual homework as Nehemiah did. You see, by carefully questioning his brother, Nehemiah knew very well what Jerusalem's needs were. By carefully inquiring about God's will, the young cupbearer had also learned what his task—and his needs—would be.

## Independent Workaholic Women, Take Note!

Nehemiah knew when it was time to ask for help—specific help. Are you one who takes great pride in being able to "do it all" by yourself? Do you like others to perceive you as "superwoman"? (Been there—done that!) When was the last time you acknowledged that you needed help? When was the last time you asked someone to help you? (Hint: Think back to the last time you felt life's stress was letting up a little bit because you asked for help.)

Even Jesus asked others for assistance. He asked the Samaritan woman at the well for a drink of water. He requested that His disciples procure a "rental donkey" for His triumphal entry into Jerusalem. If Jesus Himself modeled human interdependency, why is it so hard for some of us to ask for a little help now and then?

Nehemiah asks for specific help, detailed help. "Beams for the gates of the fortress which is by the temple, for the wall of the city" and also "for the house to which I will go" (Neh. 2:8, NASB). Though Nehemiah is making plans to take care of others, he was also making plans to *provide for his own needs* as well. His present homework would make things easier for his future walk on the wall.

Are you, like Nehemiah, taking care of yourself? In the midst of your daily rush to care for those about you, what provisions are you making for your own physical, emotional, and spiritual well-being? Remember that both Moses and Jesus gave us permission to do this: "You shall love your neighbor as *yourself*" (Lev. 19:18, NASB; Matt. 22:39, NASB).

Without batting an eye, the king now asks how long his cupbearer wants to be gone. With the queen as witness, the king and the cupbearer agree upon Nehemiah's departure and arrival itinerary (see verse 6). The king also agrees to send letters to the governors through whose lands Nehemiah must pass.

His homework in Persia completed, Nehemiah does one last characteristic thing before hitting the interstate to Jerusalem. He credits all this sudden good fortune to "the good hand of my God upon me" (verse 8).

When we, under God's guidance, do our homework and take care of ourselves as well as others, we can surely anticipate that "the good hand" of our God will be upon us.

## Dear Father,

Thank You for the privilege of "instant" prayer. Open my eyes to building "resources" within my own context. Give me the courage to ask for appropriate help.

Lord, though You told me to anticipate opposition in this world, help me to remember also that You told me to "be of good cheer; I have overcome the world" (John 16:33).

Thank You for family and friends who love me.
In the name of Jesus, my master builder,
Amen.

# Don't Tell the Neighbors Everything You Know!

## *Proceed With Prudence*

*(Based on Nehemiah 2:9-16)*

*"Caution is a good risk to take."* [25]

*"Don't pick on your sister when she's holding a baseball bat."*
**—Author Unknown**

*"She [a prudent woman] openeth her mouth with wisdom; and in her tongue is the law of kindness."*
**—Proverbs 31:26**

Blah-blah-blah-blah! At the age of 4½ I assumed the world loved hearing me talk. Our poor neighbor was trying to wash his car, but I kept getting in his way.

"So my birthday's in October, and my baby brother's is in July," I continued. "My mommy and daddy are gone every day to school, and Grandma is here alone with us. She makes butterscotch pudding for dessert. Just Pat—he's the dog—is here when we go to church. Sometimes we don't even lock our doors."

"Carolyn!" my father's voice boomed out of nowhere. "Come here!" The neighbor man probably heaved a great sigh of relief. Walking me around the corner of our house, Daddy squatted down to my level and fixed his piercing black eyes on my face.

"Don't tell the neighbors *everything* you know!"

At first his reprimand hurt me. But life has since taught me what prudent advice that was.

Even Jesus didn't tell the neighbors everything He knew. He was prudent in dispensing information. "I have yet many things to say unto you," He told His disciples, "but ye cannot bear them now" (John 16:12).

## Caution in the Capital

Nehemiah's father must have given him the same bit of advice my father gave me. He, with all the authority the Persian king had given him, had finally arrived in Jerusalem. Huge plans and a million details were swirling through his mind. Yet Nehemiah didn't breathe even one word about his plans to "the neighbors": "Neither told I any man what my God had put in my heart to do at Jerusalem" (Neh. 2: 12).

Even before Nehemiah set foot back in Jerusalem, opponents had begun coming out of the woodwork (see verse 10). They were already making plans to attack Nehemiah emotionally, physically, and spiritually (see verses 19, 20). So Nehemiah, with a few trusted advisers, simply and quietly saddled up his horse for an after-dark, clandestine fact-finding mission along the broken wall of the city.

Why was Nehemiah cautious? I can think of two reasons.

## I Can't Believe I Told Him!

First, the unwise (even private) dissemination of information could lead to public embarrassment or even a sabotaging of God's plans to rebuild the wall.

"Cherie's getting married to Bryant!" a close friend, Janie, confided to me one March afternoon my senior year of college. "But it's a secret, so don't tell anyone! 'Cuz they're not going to announce it until after spring break!"

I fully intended to keep this secret to myself. But just before spring break I was having a rare chance to lunch and visit off-campus with my brother. As the meal progressed we shared about the latest love interests in our lives. Then various friends' names came up—including Bryant's. Bryant was my brother's best friend. It felt so delicious to know something my brother didn't!

Suddenly I decided to tease—and then trust—my brother with the secret. His eyes growing wide with amazement was well worth my sharing it—at the moment, anyway. But trouble brewed on the horizon.

My friend Janie returned from spring break in a state of agitation. "Did you tell your brother about Cherie and Bryant's engagement?"

"Yes," I shamefacedly admitted. "But he promised not to say anything."

"Well, he didn't—except to Bryant's mother at a party they were having for their friends!"

"No way," I groaned. "I can't believe I told him!"

Janie continued. "And then she went right to Bryant and asked him if it were true and why he hadn't told his parents—"

I grew sick to my stomach as Janie's agitated voice continued relating the story.

"Then Bryant went to *Cherie* and confronted her about betraying their special secret, and she had to admit that she'd told me. OK, so then she's all upset at me and calls *me*. I could have just died, because of course I had to admit that I told you. Now their plans for a surprise announcement at a surprise engagement party are all messed up!"

"I'm soooo sorry," I whimpered.

"Know what?" she continued, evidently not hearing me. "I told my father about the whole thing. I told him I wasn't that upset with you. It's that *dumb brother* of yours that just couldn't keep a secret!"

"What did your dad say to that?" I asked, a bit relieved to be off the hook.

"Well," a little smile finally played about her lips before she broke into laughter. Dad said, 'It sounds to me like *three* dumb people couldn't keep a secret!"

Janie's dad saw things all too clearly.

Because Nehemiah was jealous for the plans God had for Jerusalem's wall, he kept his mouth shut. At that point he didn't know whom he could trust—either inside or outside the walls.

By involving too many—even well-meaning—people too quickly, Nehemiah would have risked embarrassment to the cause of God. He wanted to make the surprise announcement to just the right people at just the right time.

## Griz and Cat

Another possible reason for Nehemiah's prudence after unexpectedly arriving in Jerusalem was that he didn't want unnecessary trouble from within his own ranks.

A Montana grizzly bear, hit by a train, helped me better understand Nehemiah's prudence. I encountered Griz at Wildlife Images, a Grants Pass, Oregon, wildlife rehabilitation center, where he'd been transported after his severe injuries.[26]

One evening, when Griz was voraciously ingesting the contents of his "bear bucket" supper, Wildlife Images founder Dave Siddon saw a skinny yellow kitten creep toward the bear. Holding his breath, Dave braced himself to witness the sudden death of the furry feline.

When the kitten had almost reached the bucket, Griz withdrew his giant head and stared at the newcomer. Unexpectedly he nosed a small chunk of meat toward the starving kitten, which began devouring it.

This kind gesture was the beginning of the unheard-of bear-cat friendship. Because Cat (as the staff named it) was wild, it never allowed a human being near it. Yet it lived peacefully inside Griz's compound for years, daily sharing the bruin's bucket meals and curling up inside its huge front paws for naps and protection. (Once the two friends even shared their meal with a mother skunk and her kittens, who then waddled back off into the surrounding woods.)

As long as Cat stayed inside the enclosure of the protective grizzly, it was safe from coyotes, mountain lions, and man. Under those conditions, the only possible threat to its life was something from within—like a disease.

The time would come for Nehemiah to spring the announcement concerning his mission to Jerusalem's broken wall. But the premature dissemination of information to all but a few trusted advisers could have set him up for sabotage from within. Like Cat's movement within the safety of Griz's compound, Nehemiah's prudence within God's "compound" protected his mission from unnecessary danger.

## Prudent Example

Nehemiah's example shows us how to proceed with prudence on two fronts.

First, his example suggests that as long as we are searching out God's will on a matter (by prayer, Bible study, and the counsel of a few trustworthy people in our lives), we are under no obligation to make our private business public domain.

Caving in to the pressure of prying girlfriends, a college coed once revealed that she thought her long-term boyfriend was planning to propose to her the following Saturday night. What a shock it was to her—and to everyone she'd told—when he broke up with her instead! It seems he'd heard about his supposed plans from someone the girl had told. What public embarrassment could have been avoided!

Second, Nehemiah's example of prudence reminds us not to push beyond the privacy boundaries that someone else—under God's guidance—has set up. If we respected each other's right to privacy, what gossip, rumors, and misunderstandings would be avoided! What damage to God's work would never occur! While on this earth, Jesus went out of His way to caution people against speaking or acting imprudently.

If we, like Nehemiah, make the choice to proceed with prudence, God—in His own timing—will show us when it's time, publicly, to act on the obvious.

# YOUR PLACE ON THE WALL

## ACT ON THE OBVIOUS

**(Based on Nehemiah 2:17–3:32)**

*Children commenting on the obvious:*
*"The general direction of the Alps is straight up."*
*"Never smart off to a teacher whose eyes and ears are twitching."*
*"Beware of cafeteria food when it looks like it's moving."*
**—Author Unknown**

*"You can't get much done by starting tomorrow."*
**—Author Unknown**

*"If you have a talent, use it in every which way possible.*
*Don't hoard it. Don't dole it out like a miser. Spend it lavishly—*
*like a millionaire intent on going broke."*
**—Brendan Francis**

*R-r-r-r-i-i-i-ip!*

"Oh, no!" I cried, quickly standing up.

"What's wrong?" asked Janet, another first-time camper still bending over to touch her toes during early-morning exercises.

"I ripped out the seat of my pants when I bent over."

"So go put on another pair," she counseled, stating the obvious.

Mom had packed all my camp clothes—including the seven pairs of lightweight cotton "peddle-pushers" she'd just made—in bags, each marked for a day of the week. Now I faced a dilemma: I couldn't put on the "Tuesday" pants because it was only Monday. So I put on the brand-new, stiff "emergency jeans" as Mom called them.

But on Tuesday morning when the girls' director yelled "Everybody, touch your toes—no exceptions!" I, in my Tuesday pants, bent over again. This time both Janet and I heard the dreaded *r-r-i-i-i-ip!* Again, I put on the emergency jeans, which were even stiffer after a day of dusty hiking trails and horseback-riding. By the end of the day their roughness had chapped the skin of my legs.

Shivering outside in the frigid mountain air waiting for exercises to begin on Wednesday, 10-year-old Janet gave my 8-year-old self some very mature advice: "If you don't want to ruin your Wednesday pants," she said matter-of-factly, "then just *don't bend over!*"

Nehemiah, like Janet, was someone who could spot the obvious and then act on it.

## Nehemiah in Action

Jerusalem's wall needed restoration? Then fine, he would rebuild it.

Inside the city, he called a special assembly of the leaders. Because he'd done his homework, he was able to accurately portray Jerusalem's distress. Because he'd kept a discreet ear close to the international grapevine, Nehemiah could describe Jerusalem's standing among neighboring nations as a "reproach" (Neh. 2:17). Because of his fasting and answered prayers, he could prove to his countrymen that "the hand of my God" (verse 18) had opened the way for Jerusalem's broken wall to be rebuilt.

Nehemiah's proof of Heaven's favor on their behalf filled the Hebrews with courage. They "strengthened their hands for this good work," and the people were roused to "rise up and build" (verse 18).

In a great swell of excitement and hope, the people—by families and by professions—stepped forward to receive their work assignments. Even the opposition's rumblings of future stormy attacks (see verses 19, 20) could not dampen their newly energized ardor for God's cause.

Among those Nehemiah inspired was Gladys.

Who was Gladys? Gladys was a diminutive, single missionary woman in China during the earlier part of this century. From her study of Nehemiah, she had learned to act on the obvious. So when nearly 100 Chinese war orphans needed to flee before invading Japanese forces,

Gladys acted on the obvious. With no food, money, or protection against Japanese ground patrol or dive bombers . . . sick from fever, typhus, pneumonia, and suffering from malnutrition . . . Gladys acted on the obvious.[27]

Born in 1902, shy, uneducated Gladys Aylward seemed destined to work as a housemaid in England for the rest of her life. Yet a powerful appeal in a local church about desperate needs in China stirred in her a desire to serve God in this foreign land.

England's China Inland Mission preparatory school, however, discharged her after only three months for being "too old to learn a foreign language." Yet through a series of providences and incredible sacrifices, Gladys arrived in China. She always knew she would "if God wills it for me."[28]

At her mission, the Inn of the Eight Happinesses, her ministry of love and selflessness soon endeared her to the hearts of the surrounding people, including the mandarin, who asked her to be his district's foot inspector (verifying that parents were no longer binding the feet of their baby daughters). Eventually the mandarin himself became one of her converts.

## Enemy Invasion

When the Japanese invaded China in 1937, Gladys's life changed forever. Now her ministry included the establishment of orphanages for the war's most pitiful victims, the children.

The fact that her name was quickly rising to the top of the enemy's "most wanted" list didn't stop Gladys from acting on the obvious. Seventy 4- to 8-year-olds, seven older boys, and 20 older girls (including a slave girl being groomed for the mandarin's harem until Gladys intervened) needed to be smuggled out of this dangerous part of China. There was no one to help them. Except Gladys—who acted on the obvious.

During the trip Gladys felt that God directly intervened in providing food and ferries for river crossings—and strength for traversing mountains. (The normally traveled paths the weary children could not use because of enemy soldiers patrolling them.)

At one point the whole group—collapsing from pain, deprivation, and fatigue—broke down and wept inconsolably. Then Gladys prayed and rallied them, and they continued on their way.

Upon their arrival at the orphanage at Fufeng, Gladys threw herself into a round of war-needs activities for the next few months. Eventually she again collapsed from exhaustion. When she regained consciousness in a strange hospital, she could recall nothing of the past year.

Regaining a measure of strength, Gladys spent the remainder of her life working on behalf of Christian missions in China. In 1970 a doctor ordered Gladys to bed, saying that she was suffering from the flu—and exhaustion.

Gladys began realizing she was on her deathbed, and her mind drifted to Nehemiah. Nehemiah, the servant, had always been her special Bible hero. It seemed that she too had restored a few walls, built a few gates. She too had resisted intimidation.

"O God, 'spare me according to the greatness of thy mercy,' " prayed Gladys, quoting Nehemiah. Before going to her rest, she repeated the final words of Nehemiah: "Remember me, O my God, for good." [29]

Alan Burgess, in his tribute to this woman who always acted on the obvious, wrote that she lifted hearts because of her courage and "passionate belief that through God you can move those mountains which block out a view of the sun." [30]

## Your Place on the Wall

We turn to our last snapshot in the Nehemiah Album (which covers only Persia to Jerusalem). In it is captured the first few minutes of the newly started reconstruction work on Jerusalem's broken wall.

High above the bustle on an unbroken section of wall stands Nehemiah. Oblivious to the panoramic view before him, he holds in one hand a partially unrolled blueprint scroll. With the other hand he gestures toward a huge pile of rubble below. A dozen or so shovel-carrying men—and several more pushing the Hebrew version of wheelbarrows—are headed in the direction to which Nehemiah is pointing.

Around Nehemiah, at various heights on the great broken wall, are what appear to be family groups working together (see Neh. 3), equipped with buckets, trowels and—wait a minute! Look at the upper corner of this snapshot. Is that a group of women working together? (See verse 12.)

Yes, it is! The daughters of Israel had their work to do as well in the cause of God, but that shouldn't surprise you. After all, He had a place for Gladys, and He has a place for you!

## Your Place on the Wall

*Fishgate, armory, tower, and stair—*
*Connecting walls in need of repair*
*Past prison and fountain, horsegate and pools.*
*Farmer, guard, ruler—each took up his tools.*

*Priests, apothecaries, goldsmiths—all*
*Set out that day to build a wall.*
*Regretful for their God defied,*
*"Now let's rise up and build!" they cried.*

*Though hearing the enemy's threat and scoff,*
*E'en daughters of Israel could not be put off.*
*Each had her place on the wall to rebuild,*
*Each trusted God for His strength to be filled.*

*Oh, daughter of Israel, God's will is His call;*
*Take heart, for He'll show you* your *place on the wall.*
*Mothers, teachers—whatever you do—*
*The good hand of Jesus is resting on* you!

**—Carolyn Rathbun Sutton**

---

[1] According to the *New American Standard Bible* (Study Edition, p. 544), the book of Nehemiah coincides with the reign of the Persian king Artaxerxes I (464-423 B.C.), quite probably Queen Esther's stepson. Some Bible scholars wonder if she was possibly instrumental in Nehemiah's being appointed to this prestigious and trusted position in the Persian court.

[2] Quoted. in *The Complete Book of Practical Proverbs and Wacky Wit*, Vernon McLellan, comp. (Wheaton, Ill.: Tyndale House Pub., Inc., 1996), p. 198.

[3] In *Practical Proverbs*.

[4] See the promise for seekers of God in Hebrews 11:6.

[5] In *The Complete Book of Practical Proverbs and Wacky Wit*, p. 192.

[6] Doug Webster, *The Easy Yoke* (Colorado Springs: NavPress, 1995), p. 56.

[7] Kemba Esmond, in *From the Heart,* ed. Rose Otis (Hagerstown, Md.: Review and Herald Pub. Assn., 1997), p. 196.

[8] Helmut Thielicke, *The Silence of God* (Grand Rapids: William B. Eerdmans Pub. Co., 1962), p. 17.

[9] From *The Complete Book of Practical Proverbs and Wacky Wit,* p. 88.

[10] David B. Gurainik, editor in chief, *Webster's New World Dictionary,* 2nd College ed. (New York: World Pub. Co., 1968), p. 1418.

[11] Sarah Flower Adams (1805-1848). "He Sendeth Sun, He Sendeth Showers," *The Quotable Woman,* ed. Elaine Partnow (Los Angeles: Pinnacle Books, 1977), p. 25.

[12] From *The Complete Book of Practical Proverbs and Wacky Wit,* p. 225.

[13] Quoted in *Prayer Powerpoints,* Randall D. Roth, comp. (Wheaton, Ill.: Victor Books, 1995), p. 23.

[14] Quoted in *Prayer Powerpoints,* p. 36.

[15] Further scriptural references concerning principles of confession, repentance, and victory include 1 John 5:1-10 and 1 Peter 1:2-8; 1 Cor. 15:57.

[16] In *The Complete Book of Practical Proverbs and Wacky Wit,* p. 184.

[17] Jeannette Johnson, from a May 1996 sermon preached at Bellevue, Washington.

[18] J. Danson Smith, quoted in *Streams in the Desert,* ed. Mrs. Charles E. Cowman (Uhrichsville, Ohio: Barbour Pub. Inc., 1965), entry for February 5.

[19] E. C. McKenzie, *14,000 Quips and Quotes* (Grand Rapids: Baker Book House, 1980), p. 383.

[20] *Ibid.,* p. 384.

[21] Quoted in *Prayer Powerpoints,* p. 171.

[22] E. C. McKenzie. *14,000 Quips and Quotes* (Grand Rapids: Baker Book House, 1980), p. 43.

[23] You may find the following resources helpful for a more in-depth study regarding the Biblical measuring rod discussed in this chapter: James Cecy, "Biblical Decision Making or How to Determine God's Will," Women's Counseling Training Seminar (audiocassettes and workbook) (Fresno, Calif.: Jaron Ministries International, Inc., 1994); Ron Halvorsen, *Prayer Warriors,* (Fallbrook, Calif.: Hart Research Center, 1995).

[24] Quoted in *The Complete Book of Practical Proverbs and Wacky Wit,* p. 194

[25] E. C. McKenzie, *14,000 Quips and Quotes,* p. 64.

[26] From Kristin von Kreisler. *The Compassion of Animals.* (Rocklin CA: Prima Publishing, 1997), pp. 228-231.

[27] Sam Wellman, *Gladys Aylward,* (Uhrichsville, Ohio: Barbour Pub., Inc., 1998), p. 192.

[28] *Ibid.,* p. 23.

[29] *Ibid.,* p. 202.

[30] Quoted in Robert B. Pamplin, Jr., *One Who Believed, True Stories of Faith* (Newberg, Oreg. [ P.O. Box 88, Dundee, OR 97115]: 1993), p. 94.

*Section Two*

# STAYING BROKEN IS NOT AN OPTION

Have you, like me, ever been in Nehemiah's shoes? At one point or another, have you made a conscious decision to regroup, refocus, and rebuild a broken wall in your life? Of course you have. Then *kablam!* An enemy snuck up and blindsided you, right? An enemy such as hurt, anger, worry, discouragement, negative thinking, or fear.

Several of these very enemies were in the process of throwing me from my partially restored wall when Nehemiah valiantly came to my rescue. How? By showing me through his example that these attacks—which he also suffered—were providing me with opportunities for making powerful new choices.

OK, so I'd finished reading the first four chapters of Nehemiah. At this point he was on the wall working his way higher and higher above the fog in the valley below. Yet *I* still didn't have enough light to get out of my foggy place. I still didn't know what I should do about a potential marriage proposal, should it come. So . . . I kept on reading.

And am I glad I did! The next few chapters of Nehemiah contained precise strategies for dealing with the very same "enemy attacks," temptations, and issues I was facing in my own life—and which you face in yours.

In a nutshell, Nehemiah's primary responses to these attacks eventually not only gave me unmistakable instruction for finding God's will in my own quandary, but also provided me with key choices I can always make for dealing with any foggy situation I will meet this side of the grave.

I pray his example will do the same for you.

# HEADING FOR THE HOSPITAL

*UNLOAD THE HURT ON JESUS*

**(Based on Nehemiah 4:1-6)**

*"Hi. I am probably home. I'm just avoiding someone I don't like.
Leave me a message, and if I don't call back, it's you."*
**—answering machine message**

*"All of us know from experience how burning and hurtful angry, careless,
or bitter words can be. . . . Words of . . . anger shot at us when we are
tired . . . or vulnerable can leave burn scars only God can heal."*
**—Ron Halvorsen**[1]

*Kafoom!* The explosion ripped through the moonless African night
and shook our house. In horror, we watched the roof lift off the campus
fuel storage shed across the little dirt road. Pieces of rafter flew through
the swirling red-orange columns of flame shooting up toward the bending eucalyptus trees.

Hundreds of miles from the nearest fire department, my husband, 3-
year-old son, and I huddled against the far wall of our living room
should our own front windows blow out during the continuous explo-
sions. Finally, brick-penetrating heat drove us from the living room and
sent us scurrying—by flashlight—to the huge pot of drinking water in
the kitchen at the back of the house.

A missionary colleague, wanting to evaluate the school's fuel supply,
had entered the storage shed, and held a kerosene lantern above a gasoline
barrel whose small lid he'd just twisted off. While he strained to see the
level of fuel in the large container, his lantern's flame suddenly ignited the
accumulating fumes from the gasoline. Fortunately, he escaped that pri-

mary explosion with only second degree burns to his face and neck.

Until the early-morning hours, containers of various fuels continued exploding. One type burned more slowly than another, others erupted immediately into hot flames. The containers of butane gas, however, didn't explode until the heat was so intense the metal was about to melt. Then the stopper blew off, and a spectacular white flame shot 30 yards into the sky.

It really didn't matter when or how the fuel ignited or exploded throughout that terrifying night. For in the end, all fuel types had played their devastating roles in the total demise of the wooden shed and the charred, once-stately eucalyptus trees. All fuel types had burned themselves out until nothing remained for the flames to consume—though the resulting rubble of twisted metal and ash on the remaining concrete slab stayed red-hot for days.

## Fiery Attack

Nehemiah's first enemy attack came in the form of fire. No, it wasn't arson, although Nehemiah's attackers would certainly have been labeled "arsonists" by New Testament writer James. Rather, Nehemiah's archenemies, Sanballat and Tobiah, launched this initial attack by shooting off their fiery tongues (see James 3:5, 6).

Who were these two guys who felt so justified in catapulting themselves into Nehemiah's face? To make a long story short, Sanballat appears to have been the governor of Samaria (see Neh. 4:1, 2), which means he had a large army at his disposal. That made him Nehemiah's worst enemy to the immediate north (see verse 2).

Tobiah, on the other hand, was probably of Hebrew descent with shirttail relatives in Jerusalem. (We can now better understand why Nehemiah was so careful not to discuss his reconstruction plans with just anybody.) Tobiah had joined forces with the Ammonites, a comparatively large Transjordan territory to the northeast and east of Jerusalem (see verse 3). Virtually surrounded by a confederation of enemies, Nehemiah was at great risk before he even started on his project.[2]

Nehemiah's enemies met and began plotting his downfall. First, Sanballat became "furious and very angry and mocked the Jews" (verse

1, NASB). He referred to the Hebrews as "feeble Jews" and sarcastically asked if they thought they'd be able to "revive the stones from the dusty rubble" (verse 2, NASB).

Next Tobiah hopped up to the podium and jestingly asserted that Nehemiah's builders were doing such a slipshod job that "if a fox should jump on it, he would break their stone wall down!" (verse 3, NASB). That cheap shot probably brought a huge reaction of jeers, raucous cheers, and disdainful laughter.

How hurtful it feels to be ridiculed! We all know how careless words can demoralize the "builders" whether that builder is a child working on a school project or a fellow church member working on a new ministry or a nameless stranger who has shown up in church wearing her best— faded jeans and a soiled jacket. Words of criticism or gossip can destroy both projects and people.

Max Lucado states that "there is nothing more painful than words meant to hurt. That's why James called the tongue a fire. Its burns are every bit as destructive and disastrous as those of a blowtorch."[3]

Word of the public derision soon reached Jerusalem, and the enemy arrows threatened to hit home. Would these verbal attacks soon be followed by a military attack? the people probably wondered with growing unease.

At this critical point in the earliest days of the building project, Nehemiah had a quick choice to make: How would he handle this hurtful attack?

Nehemiah decided to take the hurt to the hospital—as Jo Jo did.

## Away From the Doghouse

Jo Jo, a Labrador retriever, was trotting one afternoon down a Kentucky road minding his own business.[4] The sleek canine never was really sure what hit him. Perhaps he strayed out too far into the road. Perhaps the person operating the oncoming vehicle was driving under the influence. All Jo Jo knew was that when he heard the screech of grinding brakes, he immediately felt a tremendous impact that sent him flying through the air.

Landing in a heap, Jo Jo heard the vehicle rush off down the road. The retriever tried to raise his head, but every effort brought him immense pain.

In the midst of his misery and full-body hurts, Jo Jo's doggy brain foggily recalled a warm place that smelled of friendly humans. After many attempts, Jo Jo finally lifted his head and then struggled to his feet.

Incredibly, Jo Jo dragged himself for one mile down the road. One mile to the place he had seen in the depths of his mind.

An animal hospital!

Virtually on his last bruised leg, Jo Jo "checked" himself in. Soon the vet and his staff were hard at work patching up the wounded pup.

Why did Jo Jo go automatically to the veterinary hospital? Because that's where his master boarded him while away on trips. There Jo Jo had previously received food, good care, and a whole lot of love.

As automatically as Jo Jo headed for the hospital when he was hurt, Nehemiah headed for God. He recalled that "the good hand of my God [was] upon me" (Neh. 2:8) and it was to that good hand that he imme-diately went to hide his hurt. "Hear, O our God," he exclaimed, "how we are despised!" (Neh. 4: 4, NASB). Next, in an honest explosion of his feelings, Nehemiah asked God to take care of the problem, though he revealed his human nature by giving God a few pointed suggestions for how to deal with his enemies. Nehemiah explained why he hoped God would go after Sanballat and Tobiah: "They have demoralized the builders" (v. 5, NASB).

After leaving the heavenly hospital, Nehemiah went one other place—back up on the wall to work. He chose not to let his enemies' angry attacks drain his emotional energies or distract his physical energies from the task God had given him to do.

Had Nehemiah allowed his countrymen to fret or brood over what they had just heard, "fumes" in their emotional "fuel supply" might have accumulated and later been ignited causing widespread national destruc-tion once again.

## Harbored Hurts?

What about you? Are you carrying a load of harbored hurts? Prudent, empathetic friends, a trusted pastor, family members, or a pro-fessional counselor can often help us deal with hurt before it turns into anger. Yet hurts cannot be fully unloaded until we do with ours what

Nehemiah did with his—take them to Jesus.

Corrie ten Boom so beautifully encourages us to take advantage of this privilege: "As a camel kneels before his master to have him remove his burden at the end of the day, so kneel each night and let the Master take your burden."[5]

# DON'T EVEN GO THERE!

## DEAL WITH ANGER ON A DAILY BASIS

**(Based on Nehemiah 4:1–6)**

*"A closed mouth gathers no feet."*
**—Author Unknown**

*"Be angry, and yet do not sin; do not let the sun go down on your anger."*
**—Ephesians 4:26, NASB**

"Look at the little princess in a church dress!" taunted Sandra.

"You mean the little baby! Betcha can't jump over this," teased Connie, her brunette pigtails flying as she sailed through the air.

In the days before refuse trucks picked up trash, the six families living on our lane dumped lawn clippings and household trash into the neighborhood garbage pit on the adjoining vacant lot. Every two weeks or so, one of the neighborhood fathers would set the trash ablaze, reducing it to a layer of grimy ashes.

Though I was scrubbed, shampooed, and dressed in a clean pink dress for Friday evening worship and supper, the voices of neighborhood children drew me into the backyard. They were daring each other to jump over the garbage pit—and they were doing it.

No 4-year-old likes to be called a baby. And Connie had glided so effortlessly over the hole. Maybe that pit wasn't as wide as it had looked the afternoon Daddy had showed it to me and warned me to stay away from it.

Watching the excited children take turns sailing through the air, I suddenly found myself near the edge of the pit. I wrinkled my nose at the sight of the used bandages and moldy cantaloupe rinds lying beside the blackened banana peels.

"What about it, baby? Afraid to try?" Harold sneered.

"I think the little princess in the church dress could do it," cooed Connie in an uncharacteristically sweet voice. Her sudden smile encouraged me.

"Nah, she's a baby."

That did it! Taking a giant step backward, I ran toward the pit and jumped as hard as I could. The next thing I knew, my short legs were burrowing through decomposing garbage into two feet of black, powdery ashes.

Their mocking . . . then my anger. Oh, if only I had dealt with my anger as Nehemiah dealt with his. The other children might still have taunted me as "the little princess." But at least I would have been a *clean* little princess.

## Painful Lessons From the Kitchen Stove

My kitchen stove has taught me three ways not to handle anger.

First, it's taught me not to be a hot-oiler. Once, when making popcorn the old-fashioned way, I let the oil overheat in the pan. Smelling smoke, I reached for the handle of the pan just as its contents ignited and hot oil exploded all over my hands and forearms.

Hot-oilers are individuals who "heat up" fast and then explode in damaging ways. You might recall Moses, who in a fit of anger slew an Egyptian, setting back God's plans 40 years to liberate the enslaved Hebrews.

We've all known hot-oilers. Mrs. Y, an elderly missionary woman I once casually knew, was evidently one. While doing her weekly shopping one Friday at an open-air African market near her home, she caught a young man snatching the wallet from the unlatched straw shopping bag dangling from her shoulder. As he darted off through the masses of people, Mrs. Y started screaming, "Thief! Thief! Get 'im!" Bystanders immediately grabbed the young man and held him while someone went for a police officer. But that wasn't enough for hot-oiler Mrs. Y.

Swinging her heavily laden shopping bag, she rushed at the thief, relentlessly clobbering his head and shoulders. Needless to say, her uncontrolled reaction hurt the thief as well as the cause of God.

That old familiar proverb reminds us that "he who is slow to anger is better than the mighty" (Prov. 16:32, NASB). At times Christ expressed anger, but never in ungodly ways. His anger He always *directed at the sin,* not the sinner.

While some people are hot-oilers, my stove also reminds me that others are slow-burners. I've ruined a number of colorful aluminum burner covers by not remembering I've turned on the underneath burner to a low but steady heat. Slow-burners don't explode. They do a slow, destructive burn. They brood over hurts of the past, continue to feel victimized, and put forth little effort to deal with their pain and anger.

Slow-burners do their damage quietly. And often it's done before anyone is aware of it. Delilah was a slow-burner. She disguised her anger over Samson's treatment of the Philistines. Letting it quietly simmer, she worked a slow, subtle revenge on Samson until he was damaged beyond human repair.

Again, let's look at Jesus. Unlike slow-burners, He always exercised His anger *in love:* love for His children or love for His Father's cause. When casting money changers out of the Temple, He declared, "It is written, My house shall be called the house of prayer; but ye have made it a den of thieves" (Matt. 21:13).

Finally, my stove has taught me that if I choose to handle my anger as a hidden-gasser, it could become the most destructive anger of all. If I accidentally turn on a gas burner but neglect to ignite the fumes, the gas buildup will begin filling up the kitchen. Explosion-caused eyebrow singes on a number of occasions remind me of the hidden-gasser danger. Others less fortunate than I have lost their lives.

Peter's explosion at the serving maid in the Temple courtyard before Christ's crucifixion (see Matt. 26:69-74) is a good example of someone who let irritations build up to the explosion point. Unlike Peter, Christ always expressed His anger *in a controlled manner.*

Attention, hot-oilers, slow-burners, and hidden-gassers! (That's most of us.) Because we risk destroying ourselves—and others—by these varied forms of anger, we all have one common need. That's the need *to forgive.* To forgive whoever has caused the hurts we have allowed to become anger.

After Job cried out his pain to God, God told him how to handle his feelings: by praying for those hurting him and causing his anger. When Job did this, God unexpectedly moved: "And the Lord restored the fortunes of Job when he prayed for his friends" (Job 42:10, NASB).

Have you noticed that the longer forgiveness is put off, the harder it is to proffer?

## How Nehemiah Stayed Out of Trouble

Nehemiah dealt with incipient anger immediately and decisively by not doing several things most of us *do* when we feel our emotional temperatures rising.

First, Nehemiah *did not initiate the ill will*. Sanballat and Tobiah were the ones "stirring up the pot," not Nehemiah. He had chosen, in Paul's words, to "pursue peace" (Heb. 12:14, NASB).

Second, Nehemiah *did not participate in the argument*. Although we're acquainted enough with Nehemiah to know he could speak up when necessary, he apparently saw no point in responding to his harassers this time. Christ made a similar decision before Pilate (see Matt. 27:14). Of this incident, Peter recalls, "And while being reviled, He did not revile in return; while suffering, He uttered no threats, but kept entrusting Himself to Him who judges righteously" (1 Peter 2:23, NASB).

How many marriages would be stronger and more loving if spouses could learn to "abandon the quarrel before it breaks out" (Prov. 17:14, NASB). This *doesn't* mean we should avoid working out important issues. This simply means that some things just aren't worth fighting over.

Proverbs 22:24 counsels us not to "associate with a man given to anger (NASB)." How much trouble many of us would avoid if we resisted the temptation to respond to someone's peevishness with a clever, classic putdown! Nehemiah, to use a current idiom, didn't "even go there."

Finally, Nehemiah *stayed out of other people's business*. Whatever Sanballat and Tobiah were—or weren't—doing, Nehemiah left them alone . . . and in the hands of God.

We can avoid much trouble by minding our own business and taking necessary precautions. After hearing about the Mrs. Y marketplace incident, I always carried my handbag securely jammed into my armpit with the shoulder strap wound over my head and opposite shoulder. And

I'd smile to myself when I'd see a "thief type" leaning under some tin-roof overhang nudge a potential colleague—and nod in my direction. Often from them I'd hear the grudging observation, *"Uy'umugor'azi gufata neza!"* (Loose translation: "That woman really knows how to hang on to a handbag!")

For nine years I passed by literally hundreds of potential marketplace thieves—without even one incident. Why? Because I wasn't inviting trouble in the first place.

## Super Suggestion

One of the best suggestions I ever heard for getting a peaceful night's sleep came from a pastor. After turning to Ephesians 4:26, he read, " 'Do not let the sun go down on your anger,'" (NASB). Then he added, "Even if you have to stay up until the wee small hours of the morning—set things right before you go to bed for the night."

He obviously knew that hostility and anger and "an unforgiving spirit are acids which destroy our capacity to worship and pray."[6]

How long has it been since you had a good night's rest? What festering hurt-turned-anger can you give to God? What incident, with God's help, would it be a great relief to put to rest? Whom do you need to forgive or reforgive?

Ask God to help you make Nehemiah's choice: to deal with your anger today before the sun sets yet another time.

# SIDE DISHES FOR THE ENTRÉE

## BE WATCHFUL

**(Based on Nehemiah 4:6-9)**

*"Prayer should never be an excuse for inaction.*
*Nehemiah prayed,*
*but he also set watches for protection—*
*he used common sense."*
**—Corrie ten Boom**[7]

*"But watch thou in all things."*
**—Paul, in 2 Timothy 4:5**

"Hurrah! The wall's half finished already!" The joyous cry echoed through rubble-filled Jerusalem and bounced off the Temple's outer walls.

"There came up a healing on the walls of Jerusalem" is a literal wording of Nehemiah 4:6.[8] What a wonderful thought about *our* broken walls as well! For those who choose to heal, staying broken is not an option.

In the midst of national euphoria, however, came disturbing news about serious enemy movements. Not just sarcastic insults this time but a dangerous military threat. To the north of little Jerusalem, Sanballat (with his Samaritan troops) was more firmly in alliance with Tobiah and the Ammonites to the east. These two enemy leaders had now enlisted the support of Geshem (see Neh. 2:19) with his Arabians to the south of Jerusalem as well as the Ashdodites [Philistines] to the west (see Neh. 4:7, 8). Enemies surrounded Jerusalem on all sides and were conspiring to invade.[9]

Have you ever felt as if you were surrounded by enemies on all sides? Financial enemies to the north? Health crisis enemies to the east? Relationship enemies to the south? Spiritual enemies to the west?

If you've ever felt surrounded, then you can relate to . . . Mama Kitty.

## The Mother of All Cats

Given to us by a U.S. Embassy official because she was destroying his satin brocade furniture, Mama Kitty arrived with two identifying characteristics. First, she produced kittens faster than any other cat on the mission compound. Hence, her name.

Second, she was the most watchful creature I've ever seen. Nothing—no inanimate object, no creature, no human being—inside the house or out ever escaped her notice.

Using her nest in the bottom of Kent's closet as a launching pad, Mama Kitty noticed—and dealt with—beetles, large spiders, flies, black vipers, cockroaches, tall human newcomers, and especially dogs.

One afternoon Kent and Elisse, an African friend, were trying to help push Turtle, our large yellow watchdog, off the front porch and into the pickup truck for a trip to the vet. Terrified of vehicles, Turtle refused to budge from the porch, and set up a terrific howl.

From her hideout in the bottom of the closet, Mama Kitty watched through Kent's bedroom window and waited. When Turtle's howling modulated to his highest pitch ever, Mama Kitty must have assumed her babies were in danger.

Out of the closet she shot—straight down the newly waxed linoleum hallway toward the front door. Turning the corner at the entryway, she lost her footing for an instant and slid aimlessly on the floor, her feet doing a vain "dog paddle" for traction. This unexpected setback to her plan only heightened the pressure in her adrenaline tank.

When she finally regained traction, she zoomed straight through the open door. Turtle's loud yelping, voices shouting orders, and three pairs of human legs shuffling about the tiny porch might have intimidated a lesser cat. But not Mama Kitty.

No, she knew what she had to do. Attack! Attack whatever was closest to her. With a yowl of rage, she leaped through the air, front claws extended, and sank them deeply and directly into the calves of Elisse's plump legs. I thought my left eardrum would never be the same again!

Mission accomplished, Mama Kitty returned directly to Kent's closet to resume watch over her small world once again. Meanwhile, I rushed Elisse up to the medical dispensary at the top of the hill for first aid.

## An Essential Trait

What made Mama Kitty such a zealous protector of her kittens was the same trait Nehemiah manifested as he dealt with the latest enemy threat. He was watchful.

When news of enemy maneuvers arrived, Nehemiah recorded that "we made our prayer unto our God, and set a watch against them day and night" (verse 9). Prayerful watchfulness is how Nehemiah chose to deal with the potential danger.

But for what does God want us prayerfully watching? Or is that: prayerfully watching . . . out?

## Prayerfully Watching . . . Out

Watching out for what? Our principal reason for needing to keep watch we find in Christ's own words. "Watch and pray, that ye enter not into temptation: the spirit indeed is willing, but the flesh is weak" (Matt. 26:41).

If you're like me, you're tempted about something every time you turn on the television or pick up a magazine or remember something someone said or go shopping or feel tired or overworked or like "rewarding" yourself with a big old chocolate bar. Why, I can't even wake up in the morning without being tempted, for temptations come from within and without.

That's why Jesus tells us to watch, to be on our guard.

But *how* does one watch?

## Side Dishes to Watchfulness

Yesterday was Thanksgiving. Our family ate with the next-door neighbors, who prepared a wonderful meal. Their family's traditional entrée was magnificent. But a variety of side dishes enhanced its flavor even more. One was wild rice spiced with pieces of dried apricot, cranberries, and tiny round onions.

Watchfulness is like an entrée enhanced by a variety of side dishes, the most important being *prayer*. Why? Because even if I'm really alert in my watchfulness—identifying temptations as they show up on my brain's "in box"—that doesn't mean I will automatically resist "opening" them.

That's why Jesus said, "Watch and pray." Prayer will help me make the decision to "discard" the temptations in my in box.

Paul knew the importance of the prayer side dish. "Continue in prayer," he cautioned, "and watch in the same with thanksgiving" (Col. 4:2). Only prayer can bring out the full, effective "flavor" of watchfulness by giving me the strength to resist temptation at the thought level.

Another delectable side dish my neighbors crafted in their kitchen was a shallow bowl filled with alternating slices of baked butternut squash and Granny Smith apples. Cinnamon and nutmeg flavored them. Delectable!

Another enhancement to watchfulness is *faith*. Paul, in 1 Corinthians 16:13, wrote, "Watch ye, stand fast in the faith." Faith in God's power to keep us from sinning brings fruitfulness to our watching.

Now let me tell you how my neighbor lady put together the prettiest side dish of the whole meal. She first slowly sautéed long strips of bright-red pepper. Next she added sliced almonds and seasonings of her choice. When the pepper slices were adequately cooked and the almond slices slightly browned, she stirred in freshly cooked (previously frozen) green beans. This vegetable sidedish looked like the whole holiday season in a bowl. Talk about a wonderful blend of flavors!

"Chef" Paul, in 1 Thessalonians 5:6, added another side dish to watchfulness. "Let us watch and be *sober [self-controlled]*." Being sober includes taking control over our environment. It's far easier to be watchful against a chocolate addiction if one isn't standing at the counter of a See's candy store. It's far easier to make pure thought choices if one isn't watching two soap opera stars disrobing one another.

See what I mean?

## Higher on the Wall

Jesus told those who wanted to know about signs of His second coming to "watch" (see Matthew 24, Mark 13, and Luke 21). John echoed Christ's instruction when years later, in the context of the end time, he wrote, "Blessed is he that watcheth" (Rev. 16:15).

Like Nehemiah, Paul prayed that the early church members set up a watch "day and night" (see Acts 20:31) against the incursions of the enemy. A watch bathed in prayer (see Col. 4:2), a watch grounded in faith (see Col. 1:23), a watch protected by the exercise of self-control in all things (see 2 Tim. 4:5).

Then, in conjunction with praying about these spiritual side dishes, Paul did "not cease to pray" that they would "be filled with the knowledge of *his will*" for their lives (Col. 1:9).

That too is my prayer for each of us as we make Nehemiah's choice to set up a watch.

# UNDER THE BANANA-LEAF CHRISTMAS TREE

## REMEMBER . . . GOD

**(Based on Nehemiah 4:12-23)**

*"To all who are reaching out to feel the guiding hand of God, the moment of greatest discouragement is the time when divine help is nearest."* [10]
**—Ellen G. White**

Just as Nehemiah was getting the watchmen stationed in their guard positions, something else attacked progress on the wall: Nehemiah's own countrymen began mouthing off. "And Judah said, The strength of the bearers of burdens is decayed, and there is much rubbish; so that we are not able to build the wall" (Neh. 4:10).

Disgruntled individuals from *within* the ranks were trying to discourage Nehemiah by exaggerating their problems. Notice that they didn't say the burden bearers were "tired" or "getting weak" or "needing a break." They said their strength was "decayed." Used up! Kaput! They also pointed out the continued presence of "much" rubbish.

I'm embarrassed to admit how many times I've brought discouragement into my own life—as well as the lives of others—by doing this very thing: exaggerating the problem. Especially that first Christmas in Africa.

## Crummy Christmas

With the banana plantation just outside the front window, it was hard to get into the spirit of Christmas. We had only three months of African mission work behind us and another long two years and nine months to go before our first furlough.

I hoped Christmas wouldn't be the disaster Thanksgiving had been.

# No More Broken Places

We'd both been in bed with a particularly severe strain of flu that was raging through the isolated mountains of northern Zaire. We turned on the *Voice of America* to cheer us up. But the radio announcer's voice sounded so much like my father's that soon we were heaving great sobs of homesick discouragement into our pillows. Home was still on the other side of the world.

Now it was Christmas Eve. How do you generate a cozy Christmas mood when village drums are beating across the road and the broken school generator won't let you play Christmas carols on the phonograph? How do you go Christmas shopping in the bush when your first pay-check is four months overdue?

I'd borrowed enough money to pay our only American neighbors to bring me chocolate chips, cinnamon, and powdered sugar from Kampala, Uganda, 17 hours away. And from a small lemon a child had sold me at the front door, I'd squeezed enough juice for two tiny tarts—which would be Christmas dinner's centerpiece.

Along the mantel, I finished hanging the few ornaments our two-year-old family owned. They reflected the flames of an unnecessary fire. Under the makeshift banana-leaf Christmas tree, the small package Mother had sent was waiting to be opened.

The accompanying card we'd already unsealed and displayed on the mantel. I picked it up and read her heart-tugging message at the bottom: "We miss you so very much. You are in our prayers, and we are looking forward to the time we can all be together again."

The next few words brought a lump to my throat.

"Your father says to tell you that he loves you and is lonely without you here. But when your work there is done and you finally come home, he says we're really going to celebrate Christmas!" She'd under-lined the word "really."

My husband and the jovial student missionary arrived from another vain attempt to repair the school generator. The three of us, by candle-light, offered thanks for the best that I could manage with current provi-sions—an egg omelet, small boiled potatoes, a tiny tomato sliced three ways, and my newly baked cinnamon rolls.

## Gift Exchange

After supper we sat—perspiring—before the crackling fire and exchanged gifts.

I gave my husband a giant stalk of bananas and a crude wooden desktop file for organizing his school papers. Our neighbor had helped me construct it from scrap plywood. My husband gave me a charcoal-burning iron he had walked eight miles round-trip to purchase (on borrowed money) at the nearest outdoor market. Our gift to John was a small woven basket and chocolate chip cookies. His gift to us was the promise of continuing repairs on our temperamental Belgian toilet.

Trying to ignore homesickness, the three of us munched cookies and made sure the conversation stayed light. But I sure missed home!

When the conversation lapsed, my husband looked at me with a special glow in his eyes and said, "Carolyn, shall we tell Jonathan the latest news?"

I smiled self-consciously and admitted, "We're going to have a baby." Then we couldn't resist relating the response of an African acquaintance earlier in the day when we'd shared our news with him.

"Of course you're going to have a baby," he'd countered with a condescending air. "The way your wife stood visiting so long that day in the shade of the fertility tree in your backyard . . . I knew then it was just a matter of time."

In the dancing light of our unnecessary fire, laughter died, and lest the ensuing silence and loneliness grow too heavy, I suggested we close the evening with a reading of Luke's Christmas story. There, beside our banana-leaf Christmas tree, we began the ancient story of another young couple—centuries ago—who were expecting their first Child in a far-away land.

## A Reminder

Blinking back tears of self-pity, I listened as the familiar story unfolded. For years I'd viewed the Child's coming in general terms: God's Gift to the world. Tonight—perhaps because I was in Zaire—I heard about a Baby born in a foreign country, a tiny Missionary who gave up unspeakable comforts of His homeland to travel to a dark, underdeveloped culture and live in sinful surroundings, which were so foreign to His divine nature.

As time passed, how He must have missed His heavenly family! He was separated from His Father for 33 years—before being killed by those He had come to serve.

As I reflected on my discouragement and doubts over the past three months, the brightness of Bethlehem's star suddenly shone on a new perspective. It showed me that any service I offered would be effective only if I sheltered *anew* the Babe in my drafty heart and allowed His spirit of *willing* and *joyful* sacrifice to become my own.

## Disdaining Discouragement

By concentrating on the negatives that first holiday season in Africa, I had brought on discouragement. I'd taken my eyes off the reason for my being there.

Thank God for individuals such as John the Baptist and Mother Teresa, who didn't focus on the impossibilities of their circumstances and succumb to discouragement!

Neither did Nehemiah. His response to the attack of discouragement from within Jerusalem was to redirect the eyes of his countrymen away from the obstacles and back to the reason for their rebuilding the wall. His rallying cry was "remember the Lord" (Neh. 4:14)!

Sometimes—even in our own families or churches—we hear, report, and exaggerate difficulties, thereby sowing the seeds of discouragement. Others of us may half-believe or even act on these discouraging reports, thereby weakening not only our own faith but also the efforts of those among us who are trying to focus on the task at hand.

Let us not be caught in either party but rather "go steadily forward, doing His work with unselfishness, and committing to His providence the cause" for which we stand.[11] Like Nehemiah, in times of internally caused discouragement, may we also be able to say, "we returned all of us to the wall, every one unto his work" (verse 15).

Is discouragement threatening to take you from your place on the wall? Perhaps you're having remorseful second thoughts about "filing" diapers instead of company memos. Yet remember God, His love, His strength—and take courage in faithfully doing the task closest at hand.

Perhaps failing eyesight or painful arthritis now keeps you from the energetic, ambitious, rewarding work you once did. Remember God and focus on the task closest at hand: an encouraging phone call to a friend struggling with cancer or a caring note dropped in the mail to a newly widowed relative.

(I'll let you in on a little secret: The previous paragraph is actually about my mother. As her daily prayer list grows longer, her sweet life continues to touch others despite her growing physical limitations. She eludes discouragement by *remembering* the reason for living life to the fullest.)

## Back on the Wall—And Armed!

Remembering that God was with the construction project on Jerusalem's wall, Nehemiah commanded the people to work in close family groups (think about the wisdom of that injunction); to be ready to fight for the welfare of each other (see verse 17); to go to the defense of their neighbor (see verses 18-20); and to stay within the parameter of the walls (see verse 22). Fighting discouragement within the safety of loving family and church support is much easier than fighting discouragement when you've wandered close to the enemy.

## Gift Exchange

Knuckling under to discouragement that holiday season in Africa, I had forgotten . . . to remember. Now as we knelt for prayer on that first Christmas Eve in Africa, my gift to the Christ Child was my heart—but this time more thoughtfully wrapped.

In exchange, the holy Child's gifts to me poured down in abundance—adaptability, learning to make do with what I had, perseverance, a sense of humor, and the beginning of a nine-year love affair with God's children of another culture.

A few days later, while carefully packing away our sparse Christmas ornaments from off the mantel, I picked up the Christmas card from home and reread it.

There—in Mother's loving words—I discovered the holy Child's greatest gift of all . . .

"Your father says to tell you he loves you and is lonely without you here. But when your work there is done and you finally come home, he says we're really going to celebrate Christmas!"[12]

Don't forget . . . to remember.

# DON'T COUNT YOUR CHICKENS—DISHONESTLY

## LIVE LIFE TRANSPARENTLY

**(Based on Nehemiah 5)**

*"Happiness is not the end of life; character is."*
—*Henry Ward Beecher*[13]

*"Live in such a way that when death comes,
the mourners will outnumber the cheering section."*
—*Anonymous*

*"Let integrity and uprightness preserve me."*
—*King David, in Psalm 25:21, NASB*

"Everyone always went on red alert when old man Perkins drove his Model T onto Dad's property," recalled my uncle. (Perkins is not his real name.)

He and my dad were reminiscing about their boyhood days growing up on a farm in western Kansas. An old Kansas wheat farmer, Perkins would occasionally drop by my grandfather's farm for a brief chat.

"Wasn't he the one who'd park his car next to the windmill?" asked my dad.

"Yep," my uncle nodded. "He'd park it right in the front yard there where the chickens were pecking around in that mound of grass next to the water. Remember how Papa, early on, discovered the real reason for Perkins' neighborly visits?"

"Yeah," answered my father, "but it wasn't too neighborly, was it!"

As the story unfolded, I learned why everyone in the neighborhood went on "red alert" whenever old man Perkins came to call. The old man followed a pattern of parking his car right next to chickens, wherever they were in someone's barnyard. He'd open his trunk under some pretext, such as sharing a little farm produce. Cracked corn previously scattered in his trunk made it appear as if a grain sack had recently overturned back there.

Then, while Perkins steered the conversation—and his hosts—away from his car to another area of the barnyard, the ever-hungry chickens, sooner or later, would spot the corn in the trunk and fly up into it. Upon seeing this, Perkins would remember an urgent "appointment" he needed to keep. Hurrying back to his car, he'd slam down the lid of his trunk, crank up the motor, and peel out of the barnyard a few chickens richer.

"At first he got away with it," recalled my uncle, "until Papa later counted our chickens. Imagine that—stealing from people right in their own front yards!"

## In *Your* Front Yard

It's in your front yard too—deception, cheating, lying, mixed messages, and veiled motives. In other words, dishonesty. This near-total breakdown of personal and corporate integrity comes in many forms. Stealing checks to credit card companies from a rural mailbox. HMOs padding surgical bills to MediCare. Cheating on a spouse. Car repairs costing three times the repair shop's estimate. The same weight package costing a dollar more to mail this week than it did last week. Guess what! All of the above have happened either to me or to individuals I know—just within the past month.

## In Nehemiah's Front Yard

Have you ever felt as if everyone were just waiting to cheat you out of what was rightfully yours? Ten-year-old Patrick must have felt that way when he left this message on the Internet: "Never trust a dog to watch your food." That's exactly how a large segment of Jerusalem's Hebrews felt the day they came to Nehemiah for help.

Though labeled public enemy number 1 by his enemies (first threat) . . . giving his builders a crash course in guerrilla warfare defense (second threat) . . . combating discouragement from within his own camp (third threat), Nehemiah had steadfastly focused on restoring the broken wall. But this latest threat brought Nehemiah flying down from his construction site post with righteous fire in his eyes.

Families in dire straits came to Nehemiah with the desperate report that some of the more wealthy exiles had been financially preying on them—in complete opposition to Mosaic law provisions that allowed for relieving financial distress of the needy. Among other practices, the offenders were lending money at high interest rates, taking land mortgages from the poor, and even forcing some to sell their children into bondage (see Neh. 5:1-5).

Obviously God has always had very strong feelings about the integrity issues at stake in this latest attack. After all, three of God's ten commandments (the seventh concerning adultery, the eighth concerning theft, and the ninth concerning misrepresentation) deal with living life in holy transparency. In Isaiah 58:6, 7, 10, God enumerates specifics concerning how He wants us to take care of one another.

Like God, Nehemiah had some pretty strong feelings about the issues at stake, for the Bible records that he became "very angry" (Neh. 5:6). Next, he strongly rebuked the influential individuals who had been getting wealthier by oppressing the less fortunate (see verse 13).

## Nickel Quiz

Can you answer this quiz question? Which New Testament stature-challenged tax collector (whose name begins with a Z) does this event in Nehemiah's story bring to mind? (See Luke 19:1-10 for a clue.)

Yes, Zacchaeus was living proof of the old proverb "He who walks in integrity walks securely, but he who perverts his ways will be found out" (Prov. 10:9, NASB). Yet, notice that Jesus had a very special response to this man who chose to repent, make restitution to those he'd hurt, and start living an upright, transparent life. Christ invited Himself home to do lunch with the tax collector!

Wouldn't you love to have the Master's feet under your supper table? It can happen, you know. Zacchaeus showed us that it can happen in the same amount of time it takes to make just one choice.

Nehemiah's rebuke to the offenders led them to make this choice as well: to mend their dishonest ways and make restitution for the misery they'd caused (see Neh. 5:14).

## Do as I Do

Yet Nehemiah's most authoritative response to the breakdown of integrity in Israel was nothing he really *had* to say. For he was already *living* his response—living it in love and transparency with nothing for which to be ashamed (verses 15-19).

Both before and after the time of Nehemiah, individuals with nothing shady to hide could boldly state that truth. Said Job: "Let me be weighed in an even balance, that God may know mine integrity" (Job. 31:6).

H. L. Mencken stated that "conscience is the fear that someone will see you." But know what? You won't ever be caught in the wrong place . . . if you never go there. You won't ever be discovered in a sinful act . . . if you don't commit it. Of His own life Jesus said, "The prince of this world cometh, and hath nothing in me" (John 14:30).

It's our duty to walk in integrity as well (see Prov. 20:7) if we claim to represent Jesus. "Be careful how you live," someone once wrote, "for you may be the only Bible some people will ever read." [14]

Wouldn't you like transparency to characterize your life? Good for you! Then may we talk frankly for a minute?

## Sensually Speaking . . .

Paul lived his life in such a way that before a public assembly he could matter-of-factly state, "I have lived in all good conscience before God until this day" (Acts 23:1).

A child's history report stated that "Oliver Cromwell had a large red nose, but under it were deeply religious feelings." This bit of information suggests that the schnozz on Cromwell's exterior didn't suggest what really comprised his interior.

Take a minute to look in the mirror. How do your interior and exterior match up?

In an age of underwear-as-outerwear fashion, does your public appearance reflect—or stand in juxtaposition to—your private desire to be a reflection of Jesus? Before going out into public, do you put yourself together as someone who wants to be *loved* for Christlike attractions, or as someone who wants to be *coveted?*[15]

We began this chapter on transparent living with a discussion of old man Perkins and Grandpa's chickens. Playing off the barnyard theme, let me warn my fellow chickens in the flock to watch out for those subliminal fashion mag, sitcom, and silver-screen implications that being a sexy "chick" is the highest attainment a woman can achieve. The bottom line for these industries is money, not morals. Fashion show producer Maryanne Grisz stated, "You can't regulate an industry based on morality."[16]

Most screenwriters and women's magazine editors obviously overlook Solomon's statement of fact: "As a ring of gold in a swine's snout, so is a beautiful woman who lacks discretion" (Prov. 11:22, NASB). It's all too true that as a woman "thinketh" in her heart—and readeth and vieweth and imitateth—so she most certainly will become (see Prov. 23:7).

## Squeaky Clean

Someone once said that if you take care of your character, your reputation will take care of itself.

Jesus said, "Blessed are the pure in heart" (Matt. 5:8). Perhaps it was His way of gently reminding us that whatever takes place on the inside will show up, sooner or later, on the outside. Christ Himself chose not to live "in the flesh to the lusts of men, but to the will of God" (1 Peter 4:2).

Jesus, the spotless, transparent Lamb of God, calls us to make the choice of living in holy transparency . . . in every area of our lives.

# BUG OFF!

## RESIST TEMPTATION

**(Based on Nehemiah 6:1-4)**

*"Unless there is within us that which is above us,
we will soon yield to that which is around us."*
**—Anonymous**

Jesus *"faced down the tempter in the desert,
focusing His mighty power on the energy of restraint."* [17]
**—Philip Yancey**

*"Jesus does not desire those who have been purchased at such a cost
to become the sport of the enemy's temptations."* [18]
**—Ellen G. White**

"Bug off!" is what we used to say as kids when we wanted one of our cohorts to quit harassing us. And "Bug off!" is what I *should* have said to the temptation presenting itself at my back door that afternoon in Africa. Doing so would have saved me a lot of frustrating animal antics.

## Monkey Business

I'd been working hard on the task at hand—getting supper ready—when the smiling Zairean stranger knocked at my door.

"Nice monkey," said the man, holding a tiny-faced creature up for me to see. "I sell him to you—cheap."

A monkey in the house was the last thing we needed. Looking into the soulful eyes of the cowering creature, I fully intended to say, "Thanks but no thanks."

However, I hesitated.

"OK, you take him—free! 'Bye!" As if vaporized, the man disappeared after having shoved the monkey into my arms.

Though I hadn't wanted the monkey, I chuckled at the thought that now I could always say I'd once been the owner of an "exotic pet." Feeling a tinge of pleasure that I'd not resisted the temptation strongly enough, I thought, *I'll play with the monkey for a couple days, then humanely release him back into the jungle.*

I carried the trembling creature into the living room for a brief session of rocking chair bonding. His tiny hands tightly grasped my wrists and his little head pushed against my stomach. Before I could fully get into the lullaby mode, however, something warmed my lap and began running down my left leg.

Uh-oh! The monkey's former owner hadn't mentioned the little creature wasn't house-trained. I tried to set the monkey down so I could clean things up, but he snapped to my ankle like a wraparound magnet.

Ouch! The previous owner hadn't told me the monkey was a *biter,* either! I limped into the kitchen for a cleanup rag.

Sighting Missy, our kitten, the monkey screamed, unsuctioned himself from my ankle, and pounced. Then, like lightning, the monkey flew onto the counter, slurped up a bowl of Pablum I was cooling for the napping baby, and dived through the pantry door. There he planted himself on a hanging stalk of bananas. Between bites, he continued screeching while I ducked the banana peels he slung through the doorway.

Yep! My slight hesitation to say "No" to the monkey temptation had left me with a big problem on my hands. The man at the back door had lied to me—big-time. This was no "nice monkey." In fact, the more I gave into the creature's whims, the more he wanted. Before a fellow missionary could get the monkey back out into the jungle, my little "indulgence" had turned into a monster-sized problem that nearly took over my home and my life.

## Hard at Work and Then . . .

Have you ever been hard at work when an unexpected situation came along and, despite your better judgment, you were tempted to compromise? That's what happened to me that day—and that's what happened to Nehemiah.

His construction crew had just completed repairing the wall so that "no breach remained in it" (Neh. 6:1, NASB). His now-familiar antagonists—Sanballat, Tobiah, Geshem, and the rest of Israel's self-appointed enemies—heard about this rapid progress on the wall. They were concerned that once the massive doors were hung in the various gate entrances, the newly fortified city would forever bar them access to either it or Nehemiah. How could they lure Jerusalem's focused leader away from his followers in order to capture or kill him? He hadn't been hurt by their ridicule. He hadn't retaliated in anger to their threats of attack.

Ah, but what about . . . compromise?

"Come, let us meet together," the confederation of enemies cordially invited Nehemiah through a messenger, "in one of the villages on the plain of Ono" (verse 2, NIV).

But Nehemiah, sensing ill will behind the seemingly friendly invite, sent back a message of his own: "I am doing a great work and I cannot come down. Why should the work stop while I leave it and come down to you?" (verse 3, NASB).

Phillip Keller notes the necessity of not allowing distractions to draw us from our God-given duties. "It is essential for each of us to examine our lives and ascertain what it is that diverts us from the highest duties to which God calls us as His co-workers."[19] Keller says that when we follow these diversions, "our energies are wasted, our strength is expended—yet really the benefit either to God or His flock is nil."[20]

Not easily put off, Nehemiah's enemies extended their deceptive invitation three more times. Nehemiah reports that each time "I answered them in the same way" (verse 4, NASB), knowing that giving in to temptation could land him in deep, troubled waters.

## Vicious Cycle

I once heard a radio preacher succinctly identify the vicious-cycle problem with giving in to temptation.[21] He said that giving in to temptation leaves us wanting more of it. Most certainly, then, the temptation will return . . . wanting more of us. In the end, we will never have control over the temptation, but it will definitely have control over us.

How true! Had I stayed focused on my task in the kitchen that afternoon in Zaire instead of "hesitating myself" into a compromise, I wouldn't have ended up with a literal monkey on my back. And the monkey salesman would have gone away.

That's what Nehemiah's enemies did after his repeated "Bug off!" responses.

Peter counsels us to "resist" the adversary (1 Peter 5:9), while Paul warns, "Do not give the devil an opportunity" (Eph. 4:27, NASB). Nehemiah sets us an example on both counts.

But how, specifically, do we "get" the power to resist temptation? One way is through imitation.

## Midnight Nightmare

One summer our family attended an African language school to study Kinyarwanda, the local language. Kim, the German shepherd watchdog, was the terror of the mission compound. Because this animal was so vicious, mission officials kept Kim caged up during the day. But after 10:00 p.m. the huge canine had free run of the compound because of the severe burglary problem in that part of the city.

Each language student stayed in a sparsely furnished single room with a bed, unsanded shelves, and a small sink. My husband, our 3-year-old son, Kent, and I shared one of these rooms. Unfortunately, the only restroom/ shower facility was at the end of a long, covered, outdoor corridor. When, on occasion, ferocious barking and frantic cries for help awakened us, we knew that some fellow student had risked a nocturnal trip to the restroom, only to be run up one of the metal roof support poles by Kim.

"Mommy, I need to go to the restroom!" Kent called out one night. I rolled over in bed and looked at the luminescent hands of my wristwatch: 1:00 a.m. That meant Kim would be out and about. My husband snored loudly.

I located our heavy-duty flashlight. Then after helping Kent out of bed, I quietly opened the heavy wood door. The chirping of a thousand crickets crackled through the tropical air. Cautiously, my little boy and I began tiptoeing down the long breezeway.

Suddenly the sound of large animal feet pounded toward us across the dry lawn, and my body went cold. Familiar, ferocious barking sliced through the darkness, then went silent. Frozen in place, we next heard a deep, guttural growl come from somewhere nearby.

"It's Kim!" my terror-stricken son gasped quietly as, from the *opposite* direction, another growl rolled. Kim was circling us in preparation for an attack. "Mommy, help me!" Kent pleaded in a terrified whisper. Scooping my defenseless and trembling child up in one arm, I clumsily juggled the big flashlight. Its strong, steady beam soon located the wild, red eyes of Kim. I could clearly see his foam-flecked lips curled back over long, ivory incisors.

## That Powerful Little Word

Call it maternal instinct . . . call it a big adrenaline rush . . . call it stupidity. Whatever the cause, a single word suddenly resounded through my head, and I verbally slung it at Kim.

"No! No! No! *No! NO!*" I barked back, advancing on the crouched canine.

The huge dog held its ground but turned its head ever so slightly before the bright glare of the flashlight.

Then, without warning, Kent came to life in my arms. He pointed a short—but authoritative—finger at the big German shepherd, and his childish voice rang out clear in the black night. "No!" he repeated. "No, bad dog! Go away!"

An amazing thing happened. At the sound of Kent's voice, Kim's snarl turned to a whimper, and the huge animal slunk off into the shadows.

"He's gone!" said Kent triumphantly. "You can put me down now. Just keep hold of my hand, and let's go potty." We completed our journey to the restroom in peace.

My demonstration of "courage" gave my little boy strength to imitate my example. He simply repeated the word exactly as he'd heard me use it: No! Likewise, we can imitate the example of Jesus just prior to His public ministry. In His Father's strength, He met the temptations by repeating His Father's words as recorded in Scripture. As Kent repeated my words to rebuff Kim, we can imitate Christ's example and repeat His words to rebuff the tempter of our souls.

## Heaven's Pretemptation Help

Heaven puts us at an advantage during times of temptation if we have previous and prayerfully "observed" Christ's example in the Scriptures.

In addition, we can go to the same place both Nehemiah and Jesus went when assailed by their enemies. "When temptations and trials rush in upon us," wrote Ellen White, "let us go to God and agonize with Him in prayer. He will not turn us away empty, but will give us grace and strength to overcome, and to break the power of the enemy."[22]

One thing God cannot do, however, is make a decision for us. All He can do is offer His help through His Spirit and through a Bibleful of defense strategies, such as "Resist the devil, and he will flee from you" (James 4:7) and "If sinners entice thee, consent thou not" (Prov. 1:10).

Shakespeare might have had Hamlet say, "To be, or not to be: that is the question." But God says, "To resist, or not to resist: that is your choice."

# PERMANENT WAVE
# WITH GUITAR ACCOMPANIMENT
*PRACTICE A POSITIVE MIND-SET, PART 1*

**(Based on Nehemiah 6:5–9)**

*"My job is to choose what kind of day I am going to have. . . .
I can complain because the weather is rainy or I can be thankful
that the grass is getting watered for free."*
**—Author Unknown**

*"We live in an age characterized by the power of negative thinking and a
constant (and carefully calculated) sense of personal dissatisfaction."*[23]
**—W. Bingham Hunter**

In his masterpiece on the survival of the human spirit, *Man's Search for Meaning,* Viktor Frankl penned this profound truth.

"We who lived in concentration camps can remember the men who walked through the huts comforting others, giving away their last piece of bread. [Those men] may have been few in number, but they offer sufficient proof that everything can be taken from a man but one thing: . . . to choose one's attitude in any given set of circumstances."[24]

You and I have within us the power to choose a positive mind-set. Unfortunately, I have sometimes rationalized that hard times give me the right to choose otherwise. One of those times was a Christmas Eve a few years back.[25]

## Connie and Friends

It was the afternoon of December 24, and I was having a "bad hair day." Actually, I'd been having a bad hair year. The divorce I thought would never happen to me was almost final. I was feeling worthless, depleted on every level, and—most of all—ugly. Really ugly.

Oh, sure, I'd still be "celebrating" Christmas with my family: that's Mom *with* Dad; brother *with* wife; aunt *with* uncle; and son *with* girlfriend. I, on the other hand, would not be part of a couple—for the first time in 23 years.

As if that weren't painful enough, probation had just run out for my last permanent wave. In the late December fog my hair looked like a stringy mop. All the beauty shops I'd called in the southern California town where my parents lived were fully booked. Only Connie and Friends, way down the street, could take me.

Warm air, rancid with the odor of a dozen strong hair chemicals, struck my nostrils as the door swung closed behind me. Static-punctuated mariachi music played through speakers while a foil banner reading "Feliz Navidad!" fluttered in the air blowing from an overhead heater vent.

*Oh, great,* I thought sarcastically. *The one year I need the familiar warmth of home I end up in "Little Mexico."*

A short, middle-aged Hispanic woman approached me. Red Christmas-ornament earrings peeked out from under her short-cropped hair.

"I'm Connie," said the woman with a thick accent and warm smile. She extended her hand. I shook it. "How can I help you?" she asked as if she really meant it.

*Well, for starters,* I wanted to say, *you can put my marriage back together for me.* But instead I answered, "I have an appointment for a perm at 4:00."

A quick glance told me I was the only non-Hispanic in the shop, which was fine. I followed Connie toward the shampoo bowl. Occasional words I'd learned in a long-ago Spanish high school class reached my ears from snatches of conversations. We passed three customers under hair dryers, two beauticians hard at work on holiday hairdos, and low tables strewn with back issues of *The National Enquirer*.

But it was the big, wavy-haired man with a five-o'clock shadow seated on a stool in the corner that I wasn't expecting to see. Totally out of context in a beauty salon—and totally oblivious to what was going on around him—he plucked away at an old guitar.

When I did a double-take, Connie explained, "That's Pico, Maria's husband. They have only one car, and he works an early shift on Thursdays. So he comes here and waits for her until she's finished with her last customer."

## Misery Loves Company

Except for Connie's pleasant patter in two languages (which gave me tacit permission to check out mentally), the next hour was sheer misery. Dozens of sticky green, tightly pulled rollers stretched my hair. Cold, smelly solution ran down my scalp. Inside my head I kept going to a bank of dark emotional clouds with no silver linings.

At one unidentifiable point during this hour someone shut off the mariachi music, and I began hearing strains of Pico's guitar. I had to admit he had a rather nice voice—and an amazing repertoire. For someone playing in a beauty shop, anyway. I had to give him credit for being so sweet and patient about waiting for Maria. She looked tired, if not a bit haggard, for her obviously young years. Things must be tough for them. But, hey, times were tough for all of us—especially for *me* right now.

Connie's cheerful voice drew me from my heavy thoughts: "Time to come to the shampoo bowl. It won't be long now."

I glanced outside. It was already dark. All but one other client had gone. Maria was sweeping the floor by her work station. In a halfhearted effort to manifest the Christmas spirit (despite my chosen *bah-humbug!* state of mind) I mumbled to Pico as I passed him, "Your music sounds good."

Almost as soon as Connie started rinsing the solution out of my hair, Pico rolled his stool to the other side of the shampoo bowl, guitar in hand. "What kind of music do you like, uh—"

"My name's Carolyn," I said, suddenly wishing I hadn't spoken to him.

"Pico," he introduced himself, pushing his hand into mine. "I'm Maria's husband. What kind of music do you like?"

## Blue Christmas

"It really doesn't matter," I answered, speaking truthfully. *Nothing matters much anymore,* I thought miserably.

"Well, then, here's a little ballad Elvis Presley came out with in the late fifties—or was it the early sixties?" Pico strummed once to get the key and started tapping his foot before beginning with a characteristic Presley growl. "'It'll be a [pause] bu-lue [tap, tap, tap] Cuh-ris-mas [tap] without you.'" Connie, still spraying warm water through the rollers on my head, started humming.

The lyrics should have depressed me, but the thought of personalized live entertainment at the shampoo bowl on Christmas Eve somehow got in the way. The weirdness of the whole situation unexpectedly buoyed me.

"Country!" Pico guessed excitedly when he'd finished the Elvis song. "I'll bet you like country." Before I could respond, Pico cleared his throat. "This one was recorded smack in the middle of the folk song era. It's called 'Cotton Fields,' and it climbed right to the top of the charts."

"Yeah, I know that one," I answered, in spite of myself. "I sang harmony on it years ago with a folk group at a youth camp one summer."

"Great!" he responded. "I hope you'll still enjoy it!"

He tapped his foot and enthusiastically exploded, "Two . . . three . . . four . . . 'When I was a little bitty baby my mama would rock me in the cradle . . .'"

Maria, finished now with her cleanup, had pulled on her coat and was standing behind Pico, ready to go. The third beautician brought the other customer to the bowl beside mine. I couldn't get over the fact that everyone in here acted as if a guitar performance were a normal everyday occurrence. The whole scenario was so ludicrous that for a minute I honestly didn't care how ugly I looked or how bad I was hurting.

Maybe that's why I suddenly decided to make a choice about my attitude. A choice to be upbeat in my "given set of circumstances," as Viktor Frankl would have called it. Despite the cold shampoo bowl pushing those sticky green rollers into the back of my neck, despite the neutralizer dripping from my soggy scalp into my ears, despite my imminent divorce and aching loneliness, I made a choice—a very uncharacteristic choice.

Taking a deep breath, I relaxed my neck against the shampoo bowl and belted out a loud alto. "'But when those cotton balls get rotten, you can't pick very much cotton—'"

"Oooh," cooed the other customer, beginning to snap her fingers.

Connie put down the rinsing hose and clapped in time to the guitar's rhythm. When Pico and I finished, everyone cheered and applauded.

As Connie led me back to her work station, Pico and Maria followed, situating themselves to our right. They seemed in no hurry to leave. Maybe they wouldn't be going home to much Christmas cheer. Soon the other customer was seated in the adjacent chair to our left. In the mirror I watched as Connie blew a new style into my hair—and even a few dark thoughts out of my head.

## Feliz Navidad

"Feliz Navidad," Pico suggested, and burst into song once again. This preceded "O Little Town of Bethlehem" and "God Rest Ye Merry, Gentlemen"—all in Spanish.

Then the shop fell silent except for the heater snapping the little foil "Feliz Navidad" banner against the wall. As Connie directed final spurts of hairspray at my bangs, Pico said, "Before she goes, let's all sing a song that Carolyn can sing with us. We've got her trapped right in the midst of us anyway."

With that, he strummed once and took a deep breath. "'Si–i–lent night . . .'" His rich baritone voice filled and sweetened the air. Standing behind him, Maria put her arms lightly about his neck. Then giving me a weary smile, she added her soft harmony. "'Ho-o-ly night . . .'" I was about to join in when Connie leaned over, gave one final flick to the back of my new, soft curls, and whispered, "You look beautiful!"

"'All is calm . . . ,'" the others sang.

Then I heard my own wavery voice join with "'All is bright . . .'"

Connie slipped an arm around my shoulder and, at that instant, so did Someone else. Someone else who also told me I was beautiful. Someone else who would be my Partner and consolation—not only on that Christmas Eve, but on every Christmas Eve until He, as a Bridegroom, comes back to take me home to be with the heavenly family.

A moment of silence reigned at the end of the song. When I got up to leave, they all shook my hand. I hadn't felt so accepted, loved, and lighthearted in a long time.

"Can you come back next Thursday afternoon?" asked Maria. "Pico comes early that day, too."

"No," I answered, sincerely touched. "I'll be back home by then."

"Too bad," said Pico, playfully accenting his broad smile with a quick strum of the guitar.

Pulling on my coat after paying Connie for the perm, I dared hope I'd soon be having a few more "good hair days" than I'd had during recent months.

I paused with my hand on the doorknob and wished everyone a merry Christmas.

The last thing I heard as I stepped confidently into the gray Christmas Eve night was Connie and Friends wishing me "Feliz Navidad!" Their warmth—and His—would stay with me.

## Changing the Mind

Maya Angelou wrote, "What you're supposed to do when you don't like a thing is change it. If you can't change it, change the way you think about it."[26]

Paul recognized the importance of mind-set when he wrote, "Set your *mind* on the things above, not on the things that are on earth" (Col. 3:2, NASB).

## Mind control

If a positive, determined mind-set is so important, why are many of us depressed so much of the time? Exactly *how* can we have a more positive outlook and cheerful attitude about our lives?

Nehemiah's response to his enemies' next "attack" provides the answers to these questions . . . and even more.

# SURVIVING THE COYOTES
## PRACTICE A POSITIVE MIND-SET, PART 2

**(Based on Nehemiah 6:5–9)**

*"Physically, we are what we eat.*
*Spiritually and emotionally, we are what we think."*
**—Author Unknown**

*"The power of the will can resist impressions of the mind,*
*and will prove a grand soother of the nerves."*[27]
**—Ellen G. White**

*"Gird your minds for action, keep sober in spirit,*
*fix your hope completely on the grace*
*to be brought to you at the revelation of Jesus Christ."*
**—Peter, in 1 Peter 1:13, NASB**

"It's all in your mind!"

That was essentially the message Nehemiah sent back to Sanballat, who was more and more resembling a wily coyote. Four times Nehemiah had sent his broken-record message to the enemies: "I will not come down."

Sanballat now changed his strategy. He sent a fifth message—but this time in the form of an open letter for all Jerusalem to read.

It contained three main accusations: (a) that Nehemiah and the Jews were plotting to rebel against the king (Neh. 6:6); (b) that Nehemiah was rebuilding the wall for his own glory—since he was supposedly planning to make himself king of the Jews (verse 6); and (c) that Nehemiah had appointed prophets to proclaim he was setting himself up as king (verse 7).

Then the message got downright frightening. It stated that news of Nehemiah's intentions would soon get back to Persia where the king (under whose authority Nehemiah was rebuilding the wall) would retaliate for Nehemiah's duplicity. Jerusalem would be crushed once again.

Sanballat ended his open letter with the supposedly urgent plea to Nehemiah: "We've got to talk about this!"

Like a pack of coyotes circles a potential victim, Sanballat and his cronies had been circling Jerusalem.

## Coyote Attack

I lay awake in the darkness that night, allowing them—those old "tapes" with their accusatory, negative messages—to encircle me, to make darting lunges at my most susceptible vulnerabilities. My mouth grew dry, my stomach knotted, my chest felt as if a huge weight were crushing it.

Then a howl pierced the oppressive silence, stabbing a sharp chill down my spine. Another howl followed, coming from the direction of the upper pasture. Soon a chorus of short yips and more prolonged yelps joined that first piercing voice, causing me to pull the quilt tighter about my neck.

I remembered someone once told me that when a coyote pack spots a lone jack rabbit or some other hapless creature out on a nocturnal feeding mission, it puts a fatal plan into action. One coyote will surprise a jackrabbit with an initial terrifying howl, taking it off guard. While the poor rabbit is nearly immobilized by the cries of the one coyote, others in the pack quietly surround it.

When all are in place, they simultaneously set up such a ruckus that the victim is psychologically paralyzed. At that point, flight and escape are virtually impossible. The pack moves in for the kill.

Reflecting on their strategy as I listened to the coyotes' howling, I suddenly realized I'd been allowing myself to become the victim of a mental coyote pack. Instead of doing something positive about that initial negative thought when it first "howled," I'd *focused* on it, giving opportunity for related negative scenarios to "sneak up on me" until I felt surrounded and helpless.

Do you ever do that? Nurse a negative mind-set until the resulting "downward spiral" starts siphoning away your emotional, spiritual, physical, and creative energies?

## Sam's Counterattack

Sam, our black lab-greyhound mix, responds to the local coyotes with a very positive mind-set. Since he considers them an exciting challenge, he's ready for them when they come around.

One day a huge black coyote, the leader of the local pack living in the nearby woods, ran up behind Sam while he was contemplating a ground squirrel's hole. Sensing the coyote's approach, Sam looked over his shoulder, saw the wild animal approaching, and started to run—*toward* the coyote!

Taken off guard, the coyote turned tail and headed for the woods. Sam kept gaining on him. Just before the coyote reached the safety of the woods, Sam reached the coyote. After giving him a playful nip on the rear end, Sam joyfully turned and galloped back home.

Sam was well within his rights to counterattack. The leader of the coyote pack has his own domain, and therefore no right to any of the territory that Sam patrols.

Nehemiah knew that Sanballat, the leader of the enemy pack, had no right to any part of what God was accomplishing in Jerusalem. Nehemiah had already previously stated to Sanballat and his cronies, "Ye have no portion, nor right, nor memorial, in Jerusalem" (Neh. 2:20) or in the work of rebuilding the wall.

Neither does Satan, the leader of our enemy pack, have any portion, right, or memorial in our lives. He has no right to deceive us or discourage us. He has no right to distract us from pursuing a clearer knowledge of God's will for our lives. Yet he untiringly tries to "wear out" those who have determined to rebuild brokenness (see Dan. 7:25).

Our archenemy has two especially mesmerizing howls that—if we listen to them—can result in a chronically negative and debilitating mind-set. These howls can sound like (1) the "replaying of old tapes" from the past and (2) the steady, wearing mantra: "I'm not worth anything."

But Nehemiah shows us three ways to stifle the howlings of the enemy, turning a negative mind-set into a positive one.

## 1: Turn Off the Old Tapes

Nehemiah went on the offensive lest Jerusalem's inhabitants be worn down by a recital of past failure, present weakness, and future hopelessness.

*He exposed the source of his enemies' accusations as being lies.* He counter-attacked with the accusation "Everything you've accused me of comes from your mind—it's all made up" (see Neh. 6: 8). God's faithful history with Israel had proven that as long as His children chose to cooperate with Him, the enemy would have no power over them.

Our archenemy is the "father of lies" (John 8:44, NASB) and the "accuser of [the] brethren" (Rev. 12:10). Like Nehemiah, we may be unable to do anything about the *origins* of our tapes, but we can make the choice to recognize how they're the result of the enemy's *past* work. He delights in distracting us from wall-rebuilding by drawing our minds to past hurt, disappointment, and injustice that we've experienced.

The second thing we can do about past tapes is ask God to help us listen to new tapes—ones that have to do with *the present and the future.* I know all too well the emotional strength it takes to turn one's thoughts from the familiar painful past and to look for a silver lining in the present and beyond. But Nehemiah, once again lifting his gaze toward heaven, asked God for the strength to do just that. "O God, strengthen my hands" (Neh. 6: 9), he prayed.

Only Jesus can give us strength to redirect our thoughts. Only He can heal our depressed state of mind, show us how to redirect our mental and emotional energies, and take care of past injustices.

When Candy Lightner's teen daughter was killed by a repeat-offender drunk driver, she allowed herself a time to grieve. After that she turned off the "old tapes," channeling her residual outrage, frustration, and loss into the formation of a foundation, Mothers Against Drunk Driving (MADD). This national support group for grieving mothers has also evolved as a key player in major law changes having to do with drunk driving.[28]

Let's do what Nehemiah did about old tapes. He recognized their source. Then he gave them to God so he could live for the present and the future. Besides, who would you rather listen to: the father of lies or your heavenly Father?

"We need not keep our own record of trials and difficulties, griefs, and sorrows. All these things are written in the books, and heaven will take care of them." [29]

## 2: Send "Poor Little Me" Packing

Another very successful "howl" of the archenemy is "You aren't worth anything." How many of us have bought into this lie, as well. You've heard the following statements, I'm sure, if not even thought or spoken them yourself.

"Oh, you're so talented [or beautiful]—I'm not."

"She has such a gift for working with children—I don't."

"They had all the breaks of a good upbringing [or marriage or education or money]—but I didn't."

Some individuals' chronic theme seems to be "I just can't speak badly enough about myself, my problems, or my inadequacies."

But not Nehemiah. Focusing on God—instead of on others—reminded him of his value in God's sight. Focusing on his commitment to the building project gave him hope for better things in the future.

In his book *Encourage Me* Charles Swindoll reminds us that nobody is a "nobody." He asks:

"Who found the Dead Sea scrolls?"

"Who were the parents of the godly and gifted prophet Daniel?"

Though we don't know their names, Swindoll points out that God is the Somebody who knows how to select just the right "nobodies" in order to accomplish His grand designs. [30] In God's sight, therefore, everyone is a somebody "redeemed . . . with precious blood, as of a lamb unblemished and spotless, the blood of Christ" (1 Peter 1:18, 19, NASB).

Contemporary studies actually demonstrate that individuals with a sense of self-value and commitment to a cause are happy, successful. In *The Self-Healing Personality,* Howard S. Friedman tells about a survey taken on 157 lawyers. The survey assessed recent stressful life challenges, recent illnesses, and individual personalities. The lawyers scoring healthiest were those who "felt a greater sense of personal power [self-worth] and who were involved with and vigorously committed to their work."[31]

Nehemiah's positive mind-set, like the lawyers', seemed to be related to his value in God's family and his being committed to God's cause (see Neh. 6:9).

## 3: Adopt the Mind-set of the Master

Nehemiah took charge of the coyote attack, and so can you. Here are a few pointers from coyote counterattackers.

David: "Let the words of my mouth and the *meditation of my heart* be acceptable in Thy sight, O Lord, my rock and my Redeemer" (Ps. 19:14, NASB).

Paul: "Let us also *lay aside every encumbrance,* and the sin which so easily entangles us, and let us *run with endurance* the race that is set before us, fixing our eyes on Jesus" (Heb. 12:1, 2, NASB).

Timothy: "For God hath not given us the spirit of fear; but of *power, and of love, and of a sound mind"* (2 Tim. 1:7).

God: "For I know the plans that I have for you . . . , plans for welfare and not for calamity *to give you a future and a hope"* (Jer. 29:11, NASB).

Your mind-set may have had you down in the dumps, yet with God's help, you have nowhere to go but up! A negative mind-set, one "set on the flesh is death, but the mind set on the Spirit is life and peace" (Rom. 8:6, NASB).

Adopting the mind-set of the Master will eventually lead to an understanding of "the plans" He has for you. And this positive mind-set will be able to survive any coyote attack.

# THE MONSTER CRICKET'S IMAGINARY VICTIM

## FEAR . . . SINLESSLY

**(Based on Nehemiah 6:10-14)**

*"What the wicked fears will come upon him,
and the desire of the righteous will be granted."*
**—Proverbs 10:24, NASB**

*"We do not know what will come. But we know who will come.
And if the last hour belongs to us,
we do not need to fear the next minute."* [32]
**—Helmut Thielicke**

*"Fear not, little flock; for it is your Father's good pleasure
to give you the kingdom."*
**—Jesus, in Luke 12:32**

A counselor-pastor once shared that of all the issues people bring to his counseling sessions, around 90 percent are fear-based. Fears that can be traced back to the (realistic or unrealistic) expectation that some basic need of theirs—physical, emotional, or spiritual—is not going to be met.

We all have deep-seeded fears, don't we? For many years the issue of physical safety was a magnet for my most primal fears. Then once, in the middle of Africa, I had to confront them all.

## It Was a Dark and Stormy Night . . .

The dying embers in the fireplace reddened briefly as the kitchen cuckoo clock struck midnight. I stood before the hearth, enjoying a final moment of warmth before retiring. An almost imperceptible flutter of the African-print living room curtains caught my eye.

*That's strange,* I mused. *The wind usually doesn't blow on a foggy night.*

I drew my Java pagne (cotton cloth used as a skirt or shawl) closer about my shoulders and shivered slightly.

Suddenly a flash of lightning seared the thick darkness as a clap of thunder exploded overhead. After a moment of unearthly silence, a light rain started falling. Wind gusts billowing the thin curtains threatened to extinguish my candle.

I stepped over to the window and swung it shut, suppressing a growing sense of uneasiness. From the direction of the red brick hearth, a cricket began to chirp. As I made my way down the hallway toward my bedroom, I first checked the lock on the front door and then peeked into the first bedroom, where our baby lay asleep in his crib. The wind howled mournfully as it rounded this corner of the house.

Involuntarily I shuddered. I never really had been the courageous type. As a child I was so easily frightened that once Aunt Jemima's sweet smile from a box of pancake mix on a low grocery store shelf sent me into uncontrollable hysterics. On another shopping trip with my parents, I happened to see five seconds of an old Godzilla movie in a Sears-Roebuck TV showroom. For some time afterward, Godzilla remained one of the major mental antagonists lurking in the outskirts of my mind.

No wonder a number of my childhood acquaintances referred to me as Scaredy Cat.

## Mysterious Tales

Earlier in the evening Yunis and Baluku, two Zairean students staying with us through the summer, had been swapping stories over cups of hot chocolate. My husband was 2,000 miles away in Kinshasa purchasing textbooks for the upcoming school year. Since the other American family on campus was on furlough in the United States, I had appreciated having company on this unusually wet and windy night.

Yet my mind went back to our earlier conversation. At one point Yunis had spoken, her voice hushed with apprehension after Baluku commented on the storm outside. "You know, they say that on nights like this mysterious tongues of fire sometimes appear in that big fertility tree on the top of the hill."

"I've heard of such a thing in my region too," responded Baluku, serving as nightwatchman during my husband's absence. "But have you heard that . . ." What followed was a recital of strange stories, indeed, with frequent references to the unhappy spirits of deceased ancestors.

The increasingly dark turns of conversation had eventually compelled me to remind us all of the Bible's teaching regarding the state of the dead and the true identity of evil spirits. By the time the hour grew late, the hot chocolate pot empty, and our eyelids heavy, the conversation had ended on an upbeat note.

Yawning, Baluku had thanked Yunis and me for our hospitality and bidden us good night before slipping outside to take up his post on the large covered back porch.

"*Murara halyana,*" Yunis had said in Kinyarwanda, as she wished me a sleep so deep that I wouldn't feel the bedbugs bite. Then, with her candle, she had disappeared down the shadowy hallway to the guest bedroom.

That's when the cuckoo clock struck midnight—and the cricket had begun to chirp.

## A Growing Terror

In the back bedroom I read my nightly chapter from the Bible. Yet the incessant chirping of the cricket kept strangely distracting me. It didn't pause in its raspy grating like other crickets I'd heard.

I slid down onto my knees to say my prayers and then crawled between the cool sheets. As I lay there in the flickering candlelight, I decided that the insect sounded friendly enough. So I leaned over the nightstand and blew out the flame of the candle, plunging the room into complete darkness.

## Godzilla Meets Scaredy Cat

*What was that?* I wondered, holding my breath to listen.

The very instant I extinguished the candle's flame, the cricket chirping had doubled in volume. Then, in a few seconds, tripled! Then quadrupled!

*What's going on?* A sense of panic formed a tight knot inside my chest. Involuntarily, my mind pictured a cricket the size of a department-store Santa Claus emerging from the fireplace and slowly—but intentionally—crawling down the long hallway. Now the chirping swelled until the far end of the house seemed filled with its rhythmic waves of sound.

Bizarre scraping noises started a counter-cadence with the familiar chirps. Then abruptly an eerie cry, like the cawing of some ghostly crow, added to the cacophony rolling down the hallway. My ever-active imagination now pictured a *giant* cricket with cruel, sinister pincers advancing, robotlike, toward my open bedroom door. My body suddenly felt cold, as if all the blood had drained from it.

In that instant every fear I'd ever known seemed to rush into my consciousness. Those fears—including Godzilla, along with the evening's earlier flaming-tree and ancestral spirit tales—filled me with terror.

Just when I thought it couldn't get any worse, a deep grating noise sliced through the air and a high-pitched chattering nearly numbed me with nameless horrors. I exhaled in shallow gasps but couldn't get much air back into my paralyzed lungs. The weight of overbearing fear seemed to push me down into the mattress and press the breath out of me.

With great effort I mustered what was left of my depleted physical and emotional energies. Spasmodically I flung myself over and buried my face in the thin down pillow.

*God, save me!* I cried wordlessly from somewhere deep within.

## The Morning After

The next thing I knew I was lying on my back and struggling to open heavy eyelids against bright sunlight. Outside, sparkling raindrops from the previous evening's storm still clung to the tall elephant grass. I sprang from bed and bounced into the baby's room, joyfully lifting him from his crib. *What a beautiful day to be alive!* I thought with no recollection of the previous night's terrors. Two hours later, while whistling through my morning chores, I suddenly remembered . . .

"Yunis," I asked abruptly over the clothesline where we were hanging out the wash, "did you hear anything, uh, *strange* last night?"

"Oh, yes," she replied quickly, her eyes widening. "But it's bad luck to bring up that subject, so I was waiting for *you* to say something."

From where he was cutting elephant grass with a machete, Baluku overheard our conversation.

"So," he called, "you heard the sorcerers last night with their noisemakers?"

"The what?" gasped Yunis.

"Yes," he continued. "In this part of the country local sorcerers often try to frighten people so they'll stay inside their houses. Then they're free to rob the chicken coops undisturbed. They use chicken parts to cast spells, you know, and of course they like the tender meat."

He chuckled. "Crafty old fellows. They're often out on stormy nights to diminish the risk of running into travelers on the road as they carry their loot home. Fortunately, I was here to shine my big flashlight in their direction, so they left without taking any of our chickens."

Suddenly the magnitude of what God had done for me was almost more than I could comprehend.

Within five seconds of my anguished midnight prayer, I'd fallen into a deep, peaceful slumber. (Didn't Christ tell his followers that they "ought always to pray, and not to faint" [Luke 18:1]?) So peaceful was my sleep, in fact, that on this morning after, I'd barely remembered the night before! In the midst of my sheerest terror, God had dealt, in one instant, with many of my deepest fears.

Someone once said, "Courage is fear that has said its prayers."[33]

Since the night of my frantic prayer, I don't much worry about being alone in the dark. Aunt Jemima's just another pretty face on a box of pancake mix. And best of all, Godzilla and Scaredy Cat will never meet up again . . . for neither one exists anymore.

## The Sin of Fearfulness

Fear. Nehemiah's enemies knew how devastating it could be. That's why Tobiah and Sanballat hired Shemaiah—a spinmeister of a false prophet—to come up with some threatening predictions. Nehemiah's archenemies paid Shemaiah to fabricate some bogus "prophecies"—

prophecies concerning Nehemiah's imminent death if he didn't immediately leave his responsibilities on the partially restored wall and run to the "safety" of the Temple (Neh. 6:10). His enemies obviously hoped to trap Nehemiah within its confines and kill him.

But Nehemiah knew the Temple was a holy place where God had ordered that only members of the priesthood could enter. Nehemiah was not a member of the priesthood. Therefore, he would not go into the Temple.

Moreover, Nehemiah flat out accused his enemies of hiring Shemaiah so "that I should be afraid, and do so, and sin" (verse 13).

Sin? Was Nehemiah saying that being *afraid* would have opened the door to sin? Evidently so, for John (in Revelation 21:8) resoundingly supports this concept when he lists "the fearful" as being among those who will be excluded from heaven!

The first time I read this text it angered me. *It's not fair,* I thought, *that "the fearful" won't qualify for heaven's housing list. After all, fear is a basic human emotion. What can be so bad about fear that it could keep me out of heaven?* Annoyed, I put the matter aside for a time.

Since then an encounter with a couple hard-core bikers, a cattle stampede, and meeting Nehemiah have helped me better understand why being fearful could become a sin. I've also learned about some strategies for combating human fearfulness (our topic of the next three chapters).

## Your Current Fear Quotient

Is fear part of your present "foggy place"?

Has your archenemy recently "hired" a Godzilla or two to intimidate the scaredy cat in you?

Is some type of fear tempting you to take your focus from the restoration project on your personal wall?

Like me, do you find your own meager inner reserves of courage to be no match for recurrent fears, generated either from within or without?

Worst of all, is the attention you give to fear distracting you from discerning God's will in certain areas of your life?

If you've answered "Yes" to any of the above questions, then our man in Jerusalem, Nehemiah, has some suggestions for you!

# OF BIKERS AND CATTLE STAMPEDES

### *FEAR . . . APPROPRIATELY*

**(Based on Nehemiah 6:10-14)**

*"When your knees are knocking, kneel on them."*
**—Anonymous**

*"It is the Lord of hosts whom you should regard as holy.*
*And He shall be your fear. . . .*
*Then He shall become a sanctuary."*
**—Isaiah 8:13, 14, NASB**

*"For God hath not given us the spirit of fear;*
*but of power, and of love, and of a sound mind."*
**—2 Timothy 1:7**

When I first started putting into practice the principles Nehemiah taught me in just five short verses (Nehemiah 6:10-14), they began slicing through my fears (real and imaginary) almost immediately. I'm praying Nehemiah's example will have the same positive impact in your life.

## What Gives?

Let's back up for just a minute and reword an earlier question: How can it be sinful to fear when the Bible contains express *commands* to fear?

For example, Nehemiah requested that God listen to the prayers of those who "desire to fear thy name" (Neh. 1:11). Centuries later John wrote, "Fear God, and give glory to him" (Rev. 14:7). Jesus, on the other hand, said several times during His earthly ministry, "Fear . . . not."

A contradiction? No. The key to resolving the seeming contradiction is to look at the *object* of fear in these texts.

Let's clarify what Nehemiah suggested and John told us to do: fear God. Did they mean we were to be afraid of God?

No again, for Moses went out of his way to assure Israel they were not to be *afraid* of God. "Do not be afraid; for God has come . . . in order that the fear of Him may remain with you, so that you may not sin" (Ex. 20:20, NASB). Moses wanted Israel to understand that "fearing" the Lord meant a "reverential trust in God that makes us want to please and obey Him. And yet there is a wholesome feeling of being sure that we do not disobey or displease Him."[34]

Comparing a number of "fear" and "fear not" texts helps us understand that the *object* of "fear" (the energizing fear of God or the energy-sapping fear of man) determines whether or not we are dealing with fear in a spiritually healthy or sinful manner.

## Biker Threat

One summer afternoon during my final graduate quarter in college, I decided to go for a walk. Most of my friends had gone home that weekend to be with their families.

Twenty minutes into my pleasant stroll along a narrow, isolated southern California road I heard the distant rumble of an exposed vehicle motor. Since the road zigzagged through fruit-laden orange orchards, I had no way of seeing what might be approaching in the opposite lane. Imagine my chagrin when one Harley-Davidson—and then another—rounded the corner bearing two sweaty, leathered, and tattooed Hell's Angels.

Taken completely off guard, I mechanically kept walking and looking straight ahead. The ponytailed duo slowed down in an attempt to engage me in conversation. When I ignored their lascivious come-ons, they chose to continue traveling down the road (much to my relief). Yet I picked up my gait in spite of the green leather, loose-fitting pumps and rather narrow skirt I was wearing.

Then I heard the fading motorcycle engines decelerate . . . reaccelerate . . . and rev loudly as the bikers wheeled back in my direction! Soon

I could hear the explicit, if not obscene, invitations they once again called out to me, addressing me as "Mama."

Panic city!

At that moment a curve in the road led me out of orange orchard territory and beside a freshly plowed field. On the opposite side of the field were what looked like some low-income duplexes.

A dry-ice terror formed in my stomach as the bikers approached me once again. Suddenly my lower extremities felt like lead. (You've had those nightmares, haven't you, when you couldn't escape some nameless horror because your legs wouldn't move?)

## Fighting Fear (of Bikers) With Fear (of God)

At this point I had to make a choice between what *object* I would fear.

One option was to focus helplessly on the leering *bikers* as the object of my fear. Innately I sensed this response would paralyze my ability to be proactive, rendering me a victim of my pursuers.

My other option was to focus prayerfully on *God* as the object of my fear in the hope that He'd help me reach safety among those distant duplexes.

My decision was instantaneous. A desperate prayer, adrenaline-pumped calf muscles, a slightly hiked-up skirt . . . and this "Mama" was on her way!

## Go, Baby, Go!

At first the duplexes didn't appear to get any closer. Sinking deep into the fluffy dirt clods with each quick but labored stride, I struggled across the loamy soil (miraculously retaining both shoes). A glance over my shoulder revealed two frustrated bikers quickly turning their Harleys onto the shoulder of the road in preparation for the chase.

The next thing I knew they were cursing angrily and screaming some very, very impolite untruths about me. (My feelings might have been more hurt if I hadn't been in such a hurry to get where I was going.) Thank God, my two pursuers, unable to ride their Harleys over the loose, deep soil, had to turn their mean machines back onto the road.

By the time I reached the cement stoop of the nearest duplex, the thwarted bikers, ponytails at half-mast, were burning rubber around the bend on the distant road from which they'd first emerged. Soon all that remained from this frightening encounter was a dissipating poof of tailpipe exhaust.

## No Fear!

Centuries before my moment of decision, Nehemiah faced—in a sense—the same type of choice. He could have feared—inappropriately—Shemaiah's prophecies. In that case, however, he would have fled to the Temple—and been killed. But by fearing God (both in his choice of object and in his prayerful response to danger), Nehemiah saved himself, the wall he was restoring, and his people.

Let's take a quick look at Nehemiah's response upon hearing Shemaiah's doleful prophecies and bogus counsel. His exact words were "Should such a man as I flee? . . . I will not go in" (Neh. 6:11).

In other words, Nehemiah intended to stay on the wall, not go to the Temple. His first declaration—"Should such a man as I flee?"—indicates confidence that he was within God's will. His second declaration—"I will not go in"—shows that Nehemiah was choosing to fear God through *obedience* by neither entering the Temple nor leaving his heaven-appointed post of labor.

Nehemiah also feared God through *trust*. He asked God to deal with "Tobiah and Sanballat . . . and the rest of the prophets, that would have put me in fear" (verse 14). (More about fearing God through obedience and trust in the next two chapters).

## Godly Versus Ungodly Fear

Notice that godly fear always sends a person running *toward* God and, therefore, toward spiritual safety. Bible characters making this choice include Jehoshaphat (2 Chron. 20); Daniel (Dan. 9); Peter and the other apostles (Acts 5:29); and, of course, Jesus (John 16:32).

By contrast Bible characters who exhibited *ungodly* fear were always running—or attempting to hide—from whomever or whatever was frightening them. In responding to fear in this manner, they were also running away from God. This group includes individuals such as Elijah fleeing Jezebel and ending up in a cave; Jonah fleeing perceived failure and ending up in a big fish; and our first parents hiding from God and ending up behind a clump of bushes.[35]

Earlier we established that fear is a sin when we *focus on the wrong object* and respond in kind. We also see that that fear is a sin *when we allow it to separate us from God.*

Finally, being fearful is a sin when it *undermines the courage of those around us.* Fear can be very contagious—as the following neighborhood incident illustrates.

## Danger to the Herd

Only one half-grown Limousin steer in Rancher Jim's herd of 16 noticed the skinny yellow dog circling the pasture. The other peacefully munching cattle seemed oblivious to the curious canine. The dog sensed the steer's uneasiness, however, and slipped under the lowest strand of the barbed wire fence, working its way through the tall grass. The calf turned to face the approaching dog. This brief eye-contact standoff ended when the young bovine made a nervous gesture with its head.

Sensing its advantage, the derelict dog let out a tentative yip. The spooked steer bolted between two nearby cows. Seeing their heads jerk up, the dog barked confidently.

When the frightened steer and its two now nervous companions pushed their way into another trio of grazing steers, one of them saw the dog. The dog made a slight lunge in the direction of the cattle.

Now, one swift cow kick would have sent that dog sailing into eternal oblivion. Instead, the whole herd of hefty bovines, eyes wide and nostrils flaring, suddenly made a mad rush for the far end of the pasture, fleeing before a dog less than one quarter the size of any of them.

By the time the chaotic stampede ended, the cattle had burst through two tough barbed-wire fences and ended up in a pasture filled with neighbor Mike's cattle. It took the two ranchers—and several of their neighbors—the better part of a day to calm the cattle, sort them, treat the injured ones, return them to their respective pastures, and repair the damaged fences.

## Danger to the Shepherd's Flock

As that one little steer panicked the whole herd, so one fearful voice on a committee can undermine everyone else's courage. Why do you think the Mosaic law dictated that a "fearful and fainthearted" man be sent home before a battle even began (Deut. 20:8)? Answer: "lest his brethren's heart faint as well as his heart."

Why did God postpone the children of Israel's entrance into Canaan an additional 40 years? Answer: because they *feared* the giants of the land (see Num. 14:9). Years later God was still telling commanders (in this case, Gideon) to send back the soldiers who were "fearful" (Judges 7:3).

Ungodly fear saps corporate courage as well as individual energy; God didn't design us to function efficiently on a consistently high level of adrenaline.

## Fear—God's way

By listening to our own answers to the following four questions, we can know if we are fearing—God's way.

1. What is the *object* of my fear? (Am I fearing a sin-produced scenario, or am I fearing God by talking to Him, obeying Him, and trusting Him?)

2. What is my *response* to my fear? (Am I responding to the saving power of God or to the victimizing power of my fear?)

3. In *which direction* am I "running" with my fear? (Is my response nurturing my relationship with God or eroding it?)

4. Is fear *affecting my courage?* (Is my courage to live for God intact, or is fear contaminating the spirit of "power, and of love, and of a sound mind" God has promised me in 2 Timothy 1:7?)

Personally, I praise God for Nehemiah's righteous response to fear. His example has given me the necessary weapons for overcoming it. Proverbs 1:29 assures me that fearing God is a choice I have the power to make. Choosing to fear God will empower me to deal with any earthly fear that may ever come my way.

What about you? Right now . . . why not start replacing a debilitating fear in your life with the fear of God?

# DRIVER ANT DILEMMA

## FEAR . . . OBEDIENTLY

**(Based on Nehemiah 6:10-14)**

*"Now these are the commandments . . .*
*which the Lord your God commanded to teach you . . .*
*that thou mightest fear the Lord thy God."*
**—Moses, in Deuteronomy 6:1, 2**

*"The fear of the Lord is the beginning of knowledge:*
*but fools despise wisdom and instruction."*
**—Proverbs 1:7**

*"Practice makes perfect, so be careful what you practice."*
**—Anonymous**

The Ecclesiast wrote, "Fear God, and keep his commandments" (Eccl. 12:13). When Nehemiah chose to stay at his post on the wall instead of hiding in the Temple from his enemies, he was fearing God . . . by obeying Him. Solomon stated that "the fear of the Lord is the beginning of knowledge" (Prov. 1:7).

I saw this principle at work dramatically in a traumatic experience my son and I once shared.

## Enemy Invasion

"Coming immediately when you're called is still one of our family's safety rules—even if you are getting older," I reminded my 7-year-old late one morning after he'd chosen to do otherwise. "Obeying right away is so very, very important. Will you please try to remember that?"

Nodding his head in silence, Kent sulked off to his room to put a Lego car together.

Two days later, next-door-neighbor boys Josh, 5, and Marc, 3 (not real names), were playing with Matchbox cars in Kent's room. Mathilde, a student helper at the mission school where my husband and I taught, came rushing through the back door into the kitchen. Her eyes were wide with fear.

"Madamu!" she exclaimed, "the driver ants have come!"

I hurried out onto the covered back porch, where we did most of the cooking on a large wood-burning stove. There, along the sidewalk below the last step of the concrete staircase, was an endless three-inch-wide ribbon composed of thousands upon thousands of shimmering red ants. They were coming from around the corner of the house and disappearing over the far side of the lawn in the direction of the garden on the next terrace below.

"Are you sure they're really driver ants?" I asked anxiously. I'd once read that a phalanx of driver ants has been known to strip a cow's carcass to its bare skeleton in just minutes.

Mathilde stepped outside, where she picked up a thick twig that had fallen from one of the eucalyptus trees overhead. Descending the eight steps, she gingerly placed one end of the twig into the ant "ribbon." When she pulled it up, hundreds upon hundreds of wiggling ant bodies clung to it—and each other—like tiny carpet tacks to the end of a powerful magnet.

Before the swarming insects could reach her end of the stick, she dropped it down onto the moving beltway. In horror I watched as the ants partially raised the long twig and carried it along with them. Yes, they were driver ants.

## Intercepted Warning

I ran up the stairs toward the kitchen to warn Kent and his two little visitors. But before I got to the far side of the kitchen I heard the voice of my next-door neighbor calling from the front hallway.

"Josh! Marc! It's time to come home for lunch!" I heard their giggles and suddenly remembered my neighbor had been trying to break her boys of a bad habit—the habit of running the opposite direction when she called them.

I heard the boys run toward the front door. Good! They'd be safe. Then I heard her sternly call, "Boys! I don't have time to play!"

Before I could call out my driver ants warning, Josh—followed by Marc, and then Kent—rounded the dining room door to the kitchen and dashed past me toward the back porch.

"Boys!" I yelled at the top of my lungs. "Stop this *instant!*"

With a disgusted groan Kent stopped in his tracks, wheeled around to glare at me, and then stamped his foot in anger. Just as his foot hit the tan linoleum, Josh's and Marc's first screams of pain and terror pierced the air.

"Driver ants!" I screamed. Kent's face blanched. Soon we two mothers and Mathilde were yanking off Marc's and Josh's little shirts and shorts, already covered with the ants. For the next five minutes we pulled the swarming ants from their bodies. Each pair of ant pincers carried off a tiny hunk of flesh, leaving behind great open pits and ugly red welts on the boys' skin.

After saying goodbye to the sobbing boys and their sober mother, I leaned over to hug Kent. "I'm so proud of my big boy for obeying when I asked him to!"

"Oh, Mom," responded Kent, his lower lip quivering. "That family rule about coming when I'm called? *Now* I understand why we have it."

"The fear of the Lord is the beginning of knowledge," said Solomon.

When we fear God through obedience, He begins to help us better understand His will for our lives, as well.

## Knowing God's Will Through Obedience

In these words "The steps of a good man are ordered by the Lord" (Ps. 37:23), David tells us that God reveals His will to the obedient.

One of the most dazzling women to put this principle into practice was Queen Esther.[36] From the time she was an orphaned child, she was obedient to Mordecai, her elder cousin and legal guardian. She respected him both as a parent and spiritual adviser.

Obedient to his counsel, she did not reveal her Jewish heritage to her husband (see Esther 2:10), and helped convict two would-be assassins (see verses 22, 23). Eventually risking her life, Esther obeyed Mordecai's request that she make preparation to plead the Jewish nation's case with her despotic husband, King Ahasuerus (see Esther 4:8).

Shocking the king by her untimely entrance into his throne room, Esther nervously waited to see if he would extend the scepter of welcome (or the sword of disapproval). When the king finally smiled on his lovely, young queen—and extended the golden scepter—Esther had all the assurance she needed to know she was being obedient within God's will.

Then—and only then—did she *act* to assert her newly empowered authority, thus saving her people from genocide.

## The "Other Side" of Obedience

The best way to "fear" God is simply to love Him. Jesus said, "If anyone loves Me, he will keep My word" (John 14:23, NASB). Loving children of God will be obedient children. Two special blessings await our choice to fear God by obeying Him.

The first is His help—for He doesn't put all the responsibility of obedience upon our shoulders alone. He is in this earthly walk with us. Through Paul He says, "Work out your own salvation with fear and trembling." But in the next verse He explains the balance of responsibility: "For it is God which worketh in you both to will and to do of his good pleasure" (Phil. 2:12, 13). The secret of obedience is being connected to Him (see John 15:5).

The second blessing on the other side of the obedience choice is the indwelling of the Holy Spirit "whom God hath given to them that obey him" (Acts 5:32). And it is this Spirit that will convict us, empower us, and guide us (see John 16:13) into a clearer understanding of God's will for our lives.

What mighty miracles God works on the other side of obedience! Both Nehemiah and Esther proved God on that point. And because of Heaven's abundant promises and provisions, so can you!

# CLINGING TO THE ROPE

*FEAR . . . TRUSTINGLY*

**(Based on Nehemiah 6:10-14)**

*"Ye that fear the Lord, trust in the Lord."*
**—Psalm 115:11**

*"The fear of man bringeth a snare: but whoso putteth his trust in the Lord shall be safe."*
**—Proverbs 29:25**

*"Not a doubt nor a fear . . .*
*Can abide while we trust and obey . . .*
*Never fear, only trust and obey."*
**—snatches of a song I sang as a child**[37]

What gave Jeremiah courage to prophesy fearlessly even when his own countrymen turned against him?

Why did Nehemiah stay on the wall instead of running for the temple?

How did Mary find the courage to slip into the home of Simon (a man who had defiled her) in order to anoint the feet of Jesus?

What held the apostles true to their mission in an age of Roman-colosseum, Christian-devouring lions?

What kept generations of Waldenses translating the Scriptures, even at the risk of a brutal martyr's death?

What was the secret for fearlessness in the lives of all these individuals? Their secret was replacing the fear of man with the fear of God—through a faithful prayer life (see 1 Thess. 5:17); through obedience to God's commands (see Rev. 14:12); and especially through trust (see Ps. 115:11).

King David worded it well: *"What time I am afraid,* I will trust in thee." In a nice turn of phrase, he added, *"I will not fear* what flesh can do to me" (Ps. 56:3, 4).

## Frankly, My Dear, Rappelling Repelled Me

Mike, a strawberry-blond ninth grader with rebellion in his eyes, walked into my English class the first day of school and announced that English was his most hated subject. I told him I didn't much blame him and then asked him to sit down and remove his cap while in the school building. Objecting loudly, he complied with my request. The remainder of the class period he was a study in defiant boredom.

One morning during the second week of school, Mike burst through the door. "Mrs. R, do you know how to rappel?"

*Rappel?* I'd heard that word somewhere before. Ah, yes. Unpleasant memories filled my head as I suddenly remembered Joshua Tree National Monument. There I'd done a little rappelling with my brother, sliding down a skinny little rope to reach terra firma after a nerve-racking cliff climb. No wonder I was having so much trouble remembering the word—it was one I'd tried to forget.

"Well, do you?" Mike quizzed me. "Do you even know what *rappelling* means?" Of course I knew what it meant. It meant queasy stomach, body-immobilizing fear, and admitting I wasn't cut out for the adventurous life.

"Oh, yeah, I know what it means," I answered nonchalantly. "I've done it a few times."

"I rappel all the time," he informed me. During the next two minutes Mike revealed that his favorite pastime was rappelling 180 feet into Moaning Cavern, a natural wonder and popular tourist attraction in Vallecito, California. Although my stomach knotted involuntarily as he described his subterranean descent, I was amazed that he was such an articulate conversationalist.

## Lower and Lower

Somewhere near the end of our brief dialogue, I was horrified to hear myself agree to try it sometime. Whoa! Where had *that* come from? I hoped Mike hadn't picked up on it. But he had, for later that week he asked if I'd be free the following weekend to rappel with him over at the cavern.

Quickly I made up a halfway legitimate excuse—and continued to do so for the next two months. The time arrived, however, when I knew that for the sake of integrity I needed to "either put up or shut up," as the old saying goes. Most reluctantly, I decided to "put up."

The Sunday before Thanksgiving found me nervously eyeing the harness into which an efficient and jovial cavern guide was about to strap me. I'd persuaded my husband and son to come along—for moral support. Even as Mike helped me into a pair of nondescript coveralls, I couldn't believe the incredible fix into which I'd gotten myself.

Glancing out the gift shop window, I noticed how very normal the world out there seemed: a robin hopped across a rock, pecking at some dry grass seeds. I sighed deeply, musing that many people die on normal days like this one. Was establishing a rapport with just one student, in hopes of raising one grade—for a class he didn't even like—worth risking my life? At this point I seriously doubted it was. Besides, the rappelling ropes were *so* thin!

With unspeakable anxiety gnawing at my insides, I watched the guide give instructions to my husband and son on how to handle their respective ropes before lowering themselves into the gaping mouth of the cavern. Mike and I would get on the ropes once they were off.

I closed my eyes to blot out the sight of the dark entrance hole leading to the yawning chasm directly beneath me.

"The ropes are free now." The guide's friendly voice jolted me back from an increasingly dark reverie. "You can start down first, Carolyn. Soon you'll hit [I wished he had chosen a different word] a limestone floor. Wait there for Mike. He'll guide to the window leading to the Main Room entrance."

I tightened the strap on my helmet. Mechanically, I stepped under the other ropes and held to the rail while the guide locked my harness into the J-rack, through which that ever-so-thin rope had been threaded.

"Drop in again sometime," he joked as I stepped backward—and into the first part of my descent toward that bottomless pit.

## A Matter of Survival

As I slowly inched my way down the initial drop, a tour group entered the room.

"Quick," said their guide, "step over this way, and you'll be able to watch a rappeller just starting down!"

*Oh, great,* I thought wryly. *Just prior to my untimely death, I get to become a tourist attraction.*

One of them exclaimed, "Look at that tiny little rope she's holding on to! That can't be very safe!"

*[Duh!]*

"Yeah," Mike cut in unexpectedly above me, "but that rope's sure holding her!" Mike gave a backward push and gracefully glided down his rope, dropping softly beside me. There he instructed me to switch on my headlamp.

Squeezing past, he led the way through a short, dark passage to the upper entrance of the Main Room. Then he beckoned. Looking through a three-foot-wide "window," I contemplated—for the first time in my sheltered life—just how far down 165 feet really is. Why, my husband and teenage son looked like two ants down there on the cavern floor!

Numb with terror, I followed Mike out onto the first six-inch ledge, refused to look down, and silently prepared to meet my Maker.

"Nervous?" Mike asked, unnecessarily. "I've been noticing your legs shaking. Kinda like I sometimes feel before an English test," he mused, good-naturedly.

"OK, guy," I said. "You're the teacher now. I'm trusting you."

"Well, I haven't lost anyone yet," he assured me. Then he added, "But don't trust me. You gotta trust your rope."

To make an incredibly long story short (and it was a long story because it took me *forever* to get down), I clung to my rope, and it . . . held!

It held when I brushed a streak of mud from off my face and when I adjusted my helmet.

It held when I slipped from a foothold and swung out over the cavern floor still 130 feet below. It held when I got a bit of confidence and tried a little jump off a lower ledge closer to the floor.

It held when I opened my eyes to see the crystalline ceiling formations from a magnificent eye level.

It held! It held! It held! I could trust the rope! It gave me freedom and mobility. I could explore. I could enjoy—because I could trust the rope. (Evidently Mike found out he could trust me. For during the next quarter he raised his D– in English to a B–.)

Learning I could trust the rope gave my life a new dimension. I returned to the cave to rappel eight more times . . . that is, eight more times *before* I joined the staff as a cave guide and could then, during my 10-minute breaks, rappel all I wanted to—for free! Yes, rappel on the rope that I could trust!

## You Can Trust the Rope

Have you ever put your trust in someone only to find out his or her promises were like ropes of sand? We've all experienced hurt because someone or something failed our expectations or needs. As a result, we fear that some future need (physical, spiritual, emotional) will not be met. That makes us hesitant to trust again.

And with good reason. Because even a person who cares about me is not capable of meeting all my needs. My pastor can't. My sibling can't. My spouse can't. My college roommate can't. My accountant can't. Why not? Because only "my God" can supply *all* my needs "according to his riches in glory by Christ Jesus" (Phil. 4:19).

In other words, Jesus is the only rope to which we can cling with complete assurance of all our needs being met. We can trust the Rope.

Remember all those individuals at the beginning of this chapter? What was their secret for facing the threats of a fear-producing world?

First of all, they knew that "the fear of man bringeth a snare: but whoso putteth his trust in the Lord shall be safe" (Prov. 29:25). They expected only God to meet their needs. They had learned to cling to the Rope that connected them with heaven by putting all their eggs into God's basket.

And what they got in return (even those who suffered martyrdom) was far more than courage. We can receive those same benefits from fearing God—through trust.

Here are a few of them: Not only will we receive courage, we will also receive perfect peace (Isa. 26:3); a great night's sleep (Ps. 4:8); more energy for meeting life's daily demands (Prov. 19:23); fulfilled desires (Ps. 145:19); and, best of all, a deeper spiritual intimacy with God (Ps. 25:14).

## Finding God's Will Through Trust

As with a number of other choices we've discussed, this choice also has a "connection" with finding God's will for our lives.

Here's what the Bible has to say about the Trust-and-God's-Will Connection: *"Trust* in the Lord with all thine heart; and lean not unto thine own understanding. In all thy ways acknowledge him, *and he shall direct thy paths"* (Prov. 3:5, 6).

What will keep a God-loving remnant standing by their Bible-based faith at the end of earth's history in the face of potentially overwhelming fear? The same thing that gave courage to Jeremiah, Nehemiah, and the Waldenses. By replacing the fear of man with the fear of God . . . through a faithful prayer life, through obedience, and through trust.

> *When we walk with the Lord*
> *In the light of His word,*
> *What a glory He sheds on our way!*
> *When we do His good will,*
> *He abides with us still,*
> *And with all who will trust and obey.*[38]

# THE TOPPING-OFF PARTY

*THANK AND SERVE*

**(Based on Nehemiah 6:16–8:12)**

*"He who spreads the sails of prayer
will eventually fly the flag of praise."*
**—Anonymous**

*"It's nice to know that when you help someone up a hill
you're a little closer to the top yourself."*[39]
**—Anonymous**

*"The joy of the Lord is [my] strength."*
**—Nehemiah, in Nehemiah 8:10**

"We've topped off the highest floor!" called one of the construction workers reporting to the approaching foreman. Two of the worker's buddies temporarily removed their hardhats and, with forearms, mopped the perspiration from their brows.

"That must mean it's about party time!" the foreman grinned back at the workers. They cheered.

Soon news reached us down in the construction site office. The new wing of the hospital had been "topped off." The project manager beamed as he strode through our temporary office and announced, "After work tomorrow we'll have the topping-off party. Come prepared to eat a lot. Everyone's worked hard!"

## Preparing for the Party

Jerusalem was preparing for a topping-off party, as well. Flags un-
furled. Trumpets sounded. On the twenty-fifth day of Elul (sixth month
in the sacred year) deafening cheers resounded along the wall and echoed
from one corner of the city to another.

Jerusalem's broken wall was restored at last. Mission accomplished!
And in just 52 stressful, but short, days!

Outside the city wall enemies retreated in shame while the nearest
intimidating enemy nations "lost their confidence; for they recognized
that this work had been accomplished with the help of our God" (Neh.
6:16, NASB).

Inside the city wall the prayerful, methodical Nehemiah left nothing
to chance midst the frenzied joy and excitement. For the next few days
he continued tying up loose ends.

In quick succession, he hung city gates, hired gatekeepers, and appointed Hananiah, "a faithful man [who] feared God . . ." (Neh. 7:2,
NASB), as secretary of defense to oversee national security. Next, with the
help of official aides, Nehemiah updated the Returned Exiles Census
Records, recording a grand total of 42,360 Hebrew citizens in the newly restored nation—not including household servants and musicians. (With his
usual eye for detail, Nehemiah also noted "their horses were 736; their
mules, 245; their camels, 435; their donkeys, 6,720" [verses 68, 69, NASB]).

Then there was the Wall Street response! The restored wall and
Zion's apparently bright future caused Jerusalem's stock market to soar as
donations of precious metals and expensive clothing poured into the
Temple treasuries (verses 70-72). Yes, it was time for Jerusalem's topping-off party! The invitation stated the party would start early on the
first day of the seventh month (see Neh. 8:2), just one week after the actual completion of the wall.

## Thanksgiving and Service

To a vast expectant assembly gathered in the great square before the
Water Gate the morning of the celebration, Ezra the scribe, who'd brought
a group of exiles to Jerusalem 13 years earlier, took his place behind a

*149*

wooden podium. Out of respect for the venerated spiritual warrior—and for the sacred Book of the law in his hands—the people rose to their feet.

There, with the help of Nehemiah, interpreters, and Q&A men, Ezra once again shared from the writings of Moses God's timeless instructions, faithfulness, mercy, blessings, and plans for His people.

Then the lights came on, so to speak. The people finally "understood the words which had been made known to them" (verse 12, NASB). And it was almost more than they could bear. The memories of their sinful, destructive responses to God's great goodness, patience, and mercy reduced them to uncontrollable "weeping when they heard the words of the law" (verse 9, NASB).

But the wise Nehemiah knew there would be time enough for serious reflection. Today, he told them, he wanted the focus to be on God's goodness, on second chances, and on new beginnings. As the Levites were still calming the distressed people (see verse 11), Nehemiah joyfully announced, "Let the festivities begin!"

He told them two ways they should celebrate God's goodness. "Go, eat of the fat, drink of the sweet, and send portions to him who has nothing prepared" (verse 10, NASB). In essence he told them (1) to thankfully partake of God's blessings through sanctified reveling with their families and (2) to serve those who were less fortunate than themselves.

Then, in what have become Nehemiah's most famous words, the now beloved leader reminded God's chosen people that "the joy of the Lord is your strength" (verse 10, NASB).

## A Double Cure

Let's look at the first directive Nehemiah gave the people—to thankfully partake of God's blessings to them.

W. Bingham Hunter wrote, *"Praising* his greatness and perfection . . . means living a life characterized by *thanksgiving."* [40]

Many helpful books explore the dynamics and benefits of praise and thanksgiving so convincingly that I won't pursue this aspect of Nehemiah's topping-off party. Suffice it to say that if God "inhabitest the praises of Israel" (Ps. 22:3), then what a wonderful means is thanksgiving to invite Him into our hearts!

Dr. Laraine Day found a most surprising—and positive—side effect to thanksgiving: vastly improved health. In a television interview Dr. Day, who successfully overcame breast cancer by natural means (natural foods, water intake, exercise, etc.), stated that she didn't experience a lasting improvement in health until she made the conscious decisions to adopt a spirit of "praise and beneficence" in her lifestyle.

Another person who discovered that helping others improved her own condition was an elderly woman given to isolation and depression. When Dr. Milton Erickson, a psychologist, went to visit her, he noticed that the only bright spot in her dingy existence was a well-kept greenhouse, where the woman had rows of African violets.

Instead of probing the reasons behind the woman's depression, he "prescribed" that she get a membership list from her church as well as regular copies of the church newsletter. "Whenever there was an announcement of a christening, an engagement, an illness, or a death, she was to send one of her violets."[41]

The woman followed the doctor's orders and emerged from her depression. When she eventually died, a local newspaper ran this headline: "African Violet Queen Dies, She Will Be Missed by Thousands."[42]

Thankfulness and service are two aspects of spirituality that are very complementary. Thankfulness to God invites Him into our hearts, while service takes us directly to His. Jesus said, "Inasmuch as ye have done it unto one of the least of these . . . , ye have done it unto me" (Matt. 25:40).

Paul reminds us that when we do serve others, we should do so in a nongrudging manner, "for God loveth a cheerful giver" (2 Cor. 9:7). The *attitude* in which one serves another can make all the difference in the world.

## Downer Dentist

"Ooooh! My tooth is killing me!" I awoke one morning in central Africa miles from anyone professionally trained in dentistry.

"I heard there's a French dentist in Ruhengeri," said my sympathetic neighbor. "That's six hours by bus, but he could probably help you."

Six *miserable* hours later I weakly pushed my way through the tiny aisle space between two large women holding chickens and staggered off the bus. At the other end of town outside a tiny clinic I took the last place in the patient line. Soon I would find relief for my screaming tooth.

"Just say 'A-a-a-a-ah!'" ordered the tall blond dentist in a dingy white coat.

I did.

"Ugh! Your dental work is primitive and looks horrible!" he exclaimed. "Looks like something they'd do over in America."

"Excuse *me!*" I felt like saying. Instead I started explaining that my dental work had been done by a highly—and professionally—respected relative of mine, but the dentist cut me off.

"Oui, I can sure tell *you're* American by that 'cowboy' accent with which you're trying to speak French. French with an American accent is truly lamentable!"

I'd come to this dentist assuming he was an altruistic expatriate. Instead his grudging assistance made the time I spent with him most miserable—in more ways than one. Though he eventually filled my tooth, I, to this day, have a hard time fully appreciating the help he gave me.

Only one kind of service is pleasing to God. Cheerful, openhearted service. "Restore to me the joy of Thy salvation, and sustain me with a *willing* spirit" (Ps. 51:12, NASB).

Near death, university professor Morrie Schwartz passed on this bit of life observation to former student Mitch Albom: "If you're trying to show off for people at the top, forget it. They will look down at you anyhow. And if you're trying to show off for people at the bottom, forget it. They will only envy you. Status will get you nowhere. Only an open heart will allow you to float equally between everyone."[43]

## Thermostats, Not Thermometers

Join the club if you don't feel either thankful, cheerful, or generous *all* the time. None of us does. But that's all right because Jesus doesn't ask us to be thermometers *reflecting* the temperature around us. Rather, He asks us to be thermostats, *setting* the temperature around us.

Nehemiah has told us how to be thermostats: by continually thanking God for His unmerited goodness and mercy to us. And the joy God will bring when He comes to "inhabit" our praises will provide the enabling strength to reach out to those who need us.

The resulting cheerful spirit will bring a topping-off party into the lives of everyone with whom we come in contact.

Choose to let the joy of the Lord be your strength!

---

[1] Ron Halvorsen, *Prayer Warriors,* p. 135.

[2] *The Seventh-day Adventist Bible Commentary* (Hagerstown, Md.: Review and Herald Pub. Assn., 1977), vol. 3, p. 396.

[3] Max Lucado, *No Wonder They Call Him the Savior* (Portland, Oreg.: Multnomah Press, 1986), p. 24.

[4] From *Parade* magazine, as cited by Michael Warren in "The Factory," *Guide,* Aug. 9, 1997, p. 32.

[5] Corrie ten Boom in *Prayer Powerpoints,* p. 21.

[6] W. Bingham Hunter, *The God Who Hears* (Downers Grove, Ill.: InterVarsity Press, 1986), p. 203.

[7] In *Prayer Powerpoint,* p. 57.

[8] *The Seventh-day Adventist Bible Commentary,* Vol. 3, pp. 409-410.

[9] *Ibid.,* map between pages 416 and 417.

[10] Ellen G. White, *Promises for the Last Days* (Hagerstown, Md: Review and Herald Publishing Assn., 1994), p. 47.

[11] ———, *Prophets and Kings* (Mountain View, Calif.: Pacific Press Pub. Assn., 1917); p. 645.

[12] Story adapted from *Christmas in My Heart,* ed. Joe Wheeler (Hagerstown, Md.: Review and Herald Pub. Assn., 1995), book 5.

[13] Quoted in *Cornerstone Connections,* January 1998, p. 38.

[14] In *14,000 Quips and Quotes,* p. 45.

[15] One of several related concepts discussed in Daniele Starenkyj, *Woman's True Desire* (Richmond, Quebec: Ulverton House Publications, 1996).

[16] Cited in "That's Outrageous," *Reader's Digest,* March 1997, p. 92.

[17] Philip Yancey, *The Jesus I Never Knew* (Grand Rapids: Zondervan Pub. House, 1995), p. 78.

[18] Ellen G. White. *Promises for the Last Days,* p. 133.

[19] Phillip Keller, *Lessons From a Sheepdog* (Waco, Tex.: Word Books, 1983), p. 95.

[20] *Ibid.,* p. 94.

[21] An October 1998 sermon by a radio preacher who never identified himself on the air while I was listening.

[22] White, p. 132.

[23] Bingham Hunter, *The God Who Hears* (Downers Grove, Ill.: InterVarsity Press, 1986), p. 113.

[24] Viktor E. Frankl, *Man's Search for Meaning* (New York: Washington Square Press, 1984), p. 86.

[25] Adapted from "Feliz Navidad," *Christmas in My Heart,* book 7, pp. 31-34.

[26] Quoted in Jack Canfield and Victor Hansen, *A Third Serving of Chicken Soup for the Soul* (Deerfield Beach, Fla.: Health Communications Incorporated, 1996), p. 234.

[27] Ellen G. White. *Selected Messages* (Hagerstown, Md.: Review and Herald Pub. Assn., 1986), book 2, p. 432.

[28] As discussed in Howard S. Friedman, *The Self-Healing Personality* (New York: Henry Holt and Co., 1991), pp. 77, 78.

[29] Ellen G. White, *Promises for the Last Days,* p. 47.

[30] Charles R. Swindoll, *Encourage Me, Caring Words for Heavy Hearts* (Portland, Oreg.: Multnomah Press, 1982), pp. 27-29.

[31] Friedman, p. 104.

[32] Helmut Thielicke, *The Silence of God,* p. 9.

[33] *The Complete Book of Practical Proverbs and Wacky Wit,* p. 77.

[34] *Evangelical Dictionary of Theology,* ed. Walter A. Elwell (Grand Rapids: Baker Book House, 1984), p. 409.

[35] Fast facts about godly fear: It's clean (Ps.19:9); it's the beginning of wisdom (Prov. 9:10); it prolongs life (Prov. 10:27); it begets confidence, providing a place of refuge (Prov. 14:26); it's a source of life (Prov. 14:27); it leads us away from sin (Prov. 16:6); it puts us on God's side, giving us courage not to be afraid of what man can do to us (Ps. 118:6); and tends toward "riches, and honour, and life" (Prov. 22:4).

[36] Cathy O'Malley (writer and international speaker) shared these insights on Esther with me during a January 3, 1999, coast-to-coast telephone conversation.

[37] J. H. Sammis, "Trust and Obey," *The Seventh-day Adventist Hymnal* (Hagerstown, Md: Review and Herald Pub. Assn., 1985), No. 590.

[38] *Ibid.*

[39] From *The Complete Book of Practical Proverbs and Wacky Wit,* p. 108.

[40] W. Bingham Hunter, *The God Who Hears,* p. 111.

[41] Michele Weiner-Davis, *Fire Your Shrink!* (New York: Simon and Schuster, 1995), p. 28.

[42] *Ibid.,* p. 28.

[43] Mitch Albom, *Tuesdays With Morrie* (New York: Doubleday, 1997), pp. 126, 127.

*Section Three*

# TALL ON THE WALL

*"Always labouring fervently for you in prayers,*
*that ye may stand perfect and complete in all the will of God."*
**—Paul, in Colossians 4:12**

Nehemiah could finally take time to stand tall on the wall, for the broken wall was now rebuilt. Through a series of continuing choices, the Persian king's humble cupbearer had brought Jerusalem's latest reconstruction project to a resounding and successful conclusion.

And his enemies? For the time being, anyway, they were lying low—very low. All their efforts to divert Nehemiah from duty, to take his focus off God, had failed.

With the wall restored (Neh. 1-7) Nehemiah was now free to turn his attention to the primary concern of his heart—the restoration of his people's walk with God (Neh. 8-13).

In this section we will first look at how Israel renewed her covenant with God, as well as the amazingly relevant implications this choice has for us at our particular time in earth's history.

Next, we'll let Nehemiah give us some helpful pointers for coping with the realities of walking in God's will while living on a sinful planet.

Finally, we'll end our Nehemiah story where all good stories should end: in the context of "happily ever after." Which reminds me . . . I promised to tell you about the "other man" in my life, didn't I? And about how Nehemiah helped me find God's will concerning his possible upcoming marriage proposal . . .

Before going any further in Nehemiah's story, then, let me make good on that promise right now!

# KNOWING GOD'S WILL AT LAST

## PRACTICE THE PRINCIPLES, PART 1

### (Based on Nehemiah 1-7)

*"Interpret your own personal experience
in the light of Scripture—and not vice versa!"*[1]

After the divorce I taught four years in the San Francisco Bay Area. Although I loved my students and colleagues, my eventual dream was to settle in a more rural area. I was thrilled, therefore, when God put me in a southern Oregon classroom—and I was determined to stay put in this lovely spot until Jesus returned.

Once in Oregon, I began praying about which constituent church to join. I wanted to be a member of a congregation (a) that I could serve in some way and (b) that contained no identifiable single males. After all, hadn't I told God to take my heart and just keep it? Hadn't I told Him it was going to be "just the two of us" all the way to the kingdom?

Eventually I transferred my church membership from California to a small church tucked among the tall pines in the northern end of the Rogue River Valley. In this little church my pathway crossed Jim's.

Jim was a blue-eyed, silver-haired rancher several years my senior who had recently experienced devastating family and financial losses because of his newly acquired faith. As with a number of other friendly people in the church, we became casual friends. Nothing more.

## What, God? Not Another Move!

But my stay in Oregon was to be a brief one, for God made it very clear, just three short months after my arrival, that He had plans for me at a religious publishing house—in Maryland, of all places!

Long before I left—I later learned—Jim had begun to seek God's will concerning "us." In fact, the night before I drove out of Oregon, he phoned me with a question. When visiting relatives in Tennessee sometime in the future, could he "fly up" and take me out to dinner? Not sure this would ever happen, I nonchalantly answered, "Maybe."

A year and a half later the dinner date happened. When Jim returned home to Oregon, his phone bill quickly mounted, and two Hallmark stores in Grants Pass, Oregon, suddenly found themselves doing a thriving business. When he could, Jim would visit me.

I'm not sure when I first started expecting a possible proposal, since I'd made it abundantly clear during innumerable conversations that we would always be "just friends, nothing more." Perhaps it was Jim's long-distance kindness—the occasional flowers and encouraging words. Perhaps it was his prayers for wisdom in how to deal gently with a woman's low self-esteem following the greatest devastation of her life. Perhaps it was the fact that he finally told me in a choked-up voice over the phone one night, "I've told God that if it's His will, I'd like to spend the rest of my life helping to heal a heart I didn't break."

I knew that I either needed to end this friendship or offer the poor man some hope. And that dilemma, as I explained earlier, was my foggy place.

But could I risk being hurt again? The thought terrified me. Besides, hadn't I told God it would be just Him and me all the way to the kingdom?

Ah, there it was! *I* had told *Him* how it was going to be—not the other way around. I hadn't even really asked Him what *His* will was for my marital status. With fear and trembling, I realized I'd better find out. That's when I began an all-out search for God's will. And that's also when—as I explained in the first chapter of this book—I met Nehemiah.

Several months passed as I immersed myself in Nehemiah's story and his choices. Beyond family members, I now quietly confided my foggy place to a few godly friends in various parts of the country. They began fervently praying that I would be able to discern God's will concerning Jim—and have the courage to follow it.

## Applying the Principles

I want to tell you how applying the Nehemiah principles to my situation helped me make needed choices that led to a clear indication of God's will for my foggy place.

First, let me remind you that, should you be noting some similarities between my dilemma and your own, your life is not mine, and my life is not yours. Jesus told Peter that His journey with him would be different than His journey with John. God gives us all the same choice opportunities Nehemiah had, but our individual journeys with the Lord are never exactly the same. How God leads you to apply the Nehemiah principles to your situation will be unique from my or anyone's else's experience. For His journey with you will be unique from His journey with anyone else.

All right—here we go . . .

*Principle 1: To acknowledge a Higher Authority and look for Him*
Realizing I'd been dictating to God that I wanted to remain single, Nehemiah helped me understand I must let Christ be the master and I the follower. So I swallowed my pride, shouldered my dilemma, and went looking anew for God with the intention—this time—of letting Him lead out in this particular dialogue.

*Principle 2: To submit all areas of my life to God*
Regardless of the risks I might have to take and consequences I might experience, I finally chose to surrender the sensitive marital status area (which I'd overprotected for years) to the Keeper of my heart.

*Principle 3: To realign my soul*
Prayerful soul-searching revealed some murky pockets that needed a good spring cleaning—through confession and repentance. With God's help I worked especially hard on areas such as resentment and harbored hurts. I also double-checked that, where necessary, I'd made things right with any individuals concerned.

*Principle 4: To wait on God*
When one waits on God, she doesn't have to rush either into—or

out of—anything. God will reveal when and how to move. Jim, who didn't want to rush ahead of the Lord either, assured me he wouldn't push me to make any rash decisions. "If this relationship turns out to be something that either you or God doesn't want, then we'd never be happy," he repeated in more than one telephone conversation. "Maybe God wants this to stay a simple friendship. Time will tell, so take all the time you need."

*Principle 5: To measure prayer requests*

I took some time to restudy the biblical principles concerning divorce and remarriage. I wanted my prayers and choices to "measure" appropriately with what God had already revealed in the Bible. Over a period of about three years, I also double-checked my understanding of these principles with four pastor friends and read many Bible-based books on that topic. I wanted to be very certain that a "Yes" response to a marriage proposal would, in my case, be biblically appropriate.

*Principle 6: To do my homework*

A number of Christian manuals on dating and premarital counseling gave me many helpful guidelines in getting to know someone better, avoiding pitfalls, and making a second marriage work. Jim and I spent hours on the telephone sharing our lives and as much time as possible together. Each visit was prefaced by reassurances from him that his expectations for the visits were just to get to know me better, not to pressure me in any way toward a commitment to him.

Having the time and space to do my homework took a lot of potential pressure off the situation.

*Principle 7: To proceed with prudence*

Since both Jim and I needed adequate privacy to quietly study and learn God's will for our friendship, we were guarded in what we said about it—and to whom. We asked selected family members and friends to pray about the potential life-changing decision that might lie ahead of us. We asked them for their no-holds-barred impressions, observations, opinions, and counsel—which we certainly got.

Neither Jim nor I, however, felt we needed inquisitive, personal incursions from individuals with loose tongues or with tendencies toward busybodyness or matchmaking. Nor did we need off-the-wall input from those not making God's will for our situation a matter of prayer.

*Principle 8: To act on the obvious*

When Nehemiah, after four months of prayer, stood before the king, he was able to act on the obvious—even if the obvious was to wait and pray more.

When Jim finally got my "permission" for that first visit, he used frequent flier miles to get him as far as his family. His plan was to purchase a ticket for the final leg of the trip once he got to Tennessee. Two days before he was to arrive in Maryland I began to panic about the visit. There were just too many things I was unsure of.

The "obvious" became glaringly clear: I was not ready for this friendship to go any further just then. So I acted—down on my knees that Sunday morning.

"Help, God!" I prayed. "I'm not ready for this yet, but I told Jim he could come visit. What do we do here?"

An hour later the phone rang. It was Jim in Tennessee. "Carolyn, I don't know how to tell you this," he said in a tentative voice, "but at this late date I can't get any ticket to Maryland below $1,500. I don't know what's going on. I'm so sorry, but I'm afraid I won't be able to come see you this time around."

I hung up the phone and dropped gratefully to my knees. After thanking God for relieving my anxiety, I asked, "So what do You want me to do now?"

As always, He was ready with an answer.

# YOU WANT ME TO DO *WHAT?*

## PRACTICE THE PRINCIPLES, PART 2

**(Based on Nehemiah 1-7)**

*"If God bolts the door, do not climb through the window."*[2]

*"There are four answers to prayer—yes, no, wait awhile,
and you've got to be kidding!"*[3]

For the next several months I continued to study, pray, and wait. Jim's first visit occurred, and then a few others followed.

As time passed, however, I began to realize that some emotional issues I'd simply swept under the rug needed to be hauled out and dealt with. They'd been nonissues as long as I was planning never to be in a relationship again. Now they began to almost eat me alive, affecting my sleep. I started having some serious second thoughts about my involvement with Jim.

Finally I asked God what to do about the situation. Later that week a former pastor called from northern California to check on my well-being. In the course of the conversation he asked, "Are you following the advice my wife and I gave you more than three years ago—to start dating around?"

I hesitated, "No, not really."

Two days later a former principal/pastor phoned me from southern California to check on my well-being. In the course of the conversation, he asked, "Did you take my advice to date around so God can show you who He has in mind for you?"

Again I answered, "No, not really."

The next day a colleague at work (whom I'd asked to pray about my foggy place) dropped by my office and put the business card of a Christian counselor under my nose. "Just a suggestion," she said kindly and left.

The next week the Christian counselor asked me, "Have you thought about dating around so that you can perhaps get a better perspective on God's will for this area of your life?" This same question three times in 10 days sent shivers down my spine!

## More Unwelcome Advice

*H'mmmmm,* I wondered. *Is God trying to tell me something here? I hope all this advice I've been getting is just coincidental, because I certainly don't want to follow it.*

Later that week my current pastor dropped by the office to check on my well-being. He also was praying about my foggy place. In the course of the conversation he suddenly brought up Jim and asked, "Don't you think maybe you should be dating around?"

I guess God thought I was suffering from Gideon's Need-for-Excessive-Signs Syndrome. A day later, during a long-distance conversation, Jim said—out of the blue—"I sense real hesitation on your part at this point in our friendship. If you feel you need to date around or something, then do it. I'll still be here."

Whoa! I felt as if God were suffocating me. The same unwelcome suggestion from five godly people who didn't even know one another—and within a two-week period! I had no choice but to act on the obvious—again.

If dating around was stressful enough at the age of 18, it certainly wasn't my bag at 52, believe me! Yet, after more prayer, and feeling more distraught than ever, I phoned Jim the following week to suggest our friendship be put on hold. (Unfortunately, I neglected to remember the three-hour time difference, so the ringing phone awakened him at 4:45 in the morning.) I told him I needed some time and space.

Though quietly hurt, Jim respectfully told me to do what I felt was best. His only request was that I promise to phone him if I ever needed anything. Before hanging up, he tried to jokingly say, "You sure know how to start a fellow's day!" Yet I heard the tears in his voice when he added, "Take care of yourself."

Heartsick and confused, I hung up the phone and cried. It almost felt as if God were jerking me around. Later that week I prayed, "God, You know my comfort level, but I'm willing to do what You're obviously pushing me into. But . . . with whom am I supposed to go out?"

Almost immediately the phone started ringing, and invitations came out of the woodwork.

*Principles 9-12: To bury the hurt in Jesus, to deal with anger, to be watchful, and to remember God*

The next four Nehemiah principles I worked on simultaneously. My counselor was a godsend at that point, being especially insightful in helping me bury the vestiges of past hurt and lingering anger. In an upbeat—yet spiritual—manner, she guided me through an assessment of the present (be watchful) and an examination of possible future scenarios (remember that God holds the future).

*Principles 13 and 14: To live transparently and to resist temptation*

These two principles require ongoing choices no matter what else is going on.

*Principle 15: To practice a positive mind-set*

Applying this principle was a special challenge for me. Because of the earlier divorce, my mental tendency was to assume that a subsequent marriage would end prematurely and painfully. I needed God's help to turn my negative thought patterns around. This took much time, much prayer, and much, much effort.

*Principle 16: To fear God (through prayer, trust, and obedience)*

In the end, the repeated application of this principle became my most potent antidote to the fear of risking love again. I found that making the choice to fear God through prayer, trust, and obedience automatically focused my mind on His power, His promises, and His plans.

Fear of God eventually roto-rootered its way through the muck of accumulated relational-failure fears and cleared out the channels through which love might once again flow.

During the months of counseling and of enjoying other friendships with a variety of new friends, I finally saw God's specific will for my foggy place. He did this suddenly, after years of waiting on my part. And

He did it through nearly immediate answers to private concerns and requests I laid out before Him. I will mention just one, for it was pivotal, leading directly to . . .

## The Proposal

Two weeks prior to Christmas that year, Jim finally phoned "to see if you need anything" and to let me know he had no plans over the upcoming holidays. He hastened to add that if he came, it would be just another visit to "get to know each other better—no pressure to make a decision and no conversation about anything heavy."

I had been feeling a strong burden that should God lead me into another marriage, I would want some heavy-duty premarital couples' counseling. Yet many men are adverse to this type of thing. I prayed, therefore, that if God was directing me toward Jim, one of the divine indications would be his being open to counseling.

Within 48 hours Jim called to verify his flight times. Then, completely out of context, he asked, "You apparently feel your counselor has helped you figure some things out, right? Well, I think I'd like to talk to her when I'm back there."

"As a couple?" I asked in astonishment.

"Well, maybe later—but just me for now. Maybe she could help me figure some things out too."

I nearly dropped the phone. *Dear God, I guess You've answered this one—pronto!*

When Jim phoned the counselor, however, she told him she was going away with her family for the holidays and was booked until the day of her departure. He phoned her again when he arrived in Maryland. She told him she'd had a cancellation and could see him the next morning.

"How was the counseling session?" I asked Jim later that day.

"Very helpful," he answered. "But she gave me some homework, and I'm not quite sure what to do about it."

I didn't pursue the subject any further.

The following evening, Saturday night, we'd accepted an invitation to eat out with my pastor and his wife. Jim returned from his hotel to pick me up and take me to the restaurant. We had about an hour before we needed to be there.

"I haven't done my counseling homework yet," he informed me. "I think I'll need your help, but first let's just have a little worship and a prayer so I can organize my thoughts."

We sat on the couch together and opened the Bible to the Christmas story. After reading it, we knelt side by side. He took my hand before praying.

"OK," he said, taking a deep breath when we were seated again. "The counselor and I talked about my past and about my life now. We talked about prayer and looking for God's will. She reminded me that He gives us the opportunity to make choices within His will. So my homework is this: I'm supposed to figure out what I want for the rest of my life. Then, if what I want involves another person, I'm supposed to go to that person and find out what she wants. Then I'm supposed to ask, 'How do we get there from here?' I think you know by now that my desire is to spend the rest of my life with you. So how do we get there from here?"

His face suddenly turned very red. "Oh, dear!" he said. "I think I just asked you to marry me—oh, no, I'm so sorry. I promised I wouldn't do anything like that on this visit—oh, my goodness. Should I get down on my knees? Have I blown it?"

Jim's voice was distressed, his face flushed. One part of me wanted to laugh, but the other part of me was off in a quick search for Nehemiah: *Hey, guy! We're finally down to the wire here! What are we going to do about this?*

As if reading my mind (or simply seeing shock register on my face), Jim answered my unspoken question to Nehemiah. "If I was out of place, forgive me. Though the question is on the table, you don't have to answer it right now . . . or in two weeks . . . or even before Jesus comes. Just know I'm not going anywhere you can't find me."

## My Answer

"Thank you for the lack of pressure," I responded, letting out a sigh of relief. "As soon as I'm sure of the answer, I promise you'll be the first to know."

Over dinner Jim and the others engaged in animated conversation. Joining in enough to avoid appearing detached, I was simultaneously racing my mind over the past two-plus years: God's leading through closed windows, open doors, unanswered prayers, answered prayers, and Nehemiah's choices.

Mentally, I quickly went down Nehemiah's list to see where I stood:

Submission of situation to God . . . check.

Realignment through confession and repentance . . . check.

Waiting on God . . . check.

Proceeding with caution . . . check.

Trying to live life transparently . . . check.

Dealing with hurt, anger, and fear . . . check.

Doing one's homework . . . check.

Far from perfect yet in any of these areas, I at least knew that with God's help, I'd done everything I could to uncover His will—when He was ready for it to be revealed.

Trying not to choke down nachos too quickly, I reflected on something else. Though my life was productive and rewarding, I had begun to notice over the past few months a small and gnawing vacancy in my life. The busier and more involved I'd become at work, at church, in travels, the larger the vacancy had been growing.

By the time Jim phoned a couple weeks prior "just to make sure you're all right" and to let me know he had "no plans for the upcoming holidays," I had a strong suspicion that the quickly growing vacuum in my heart might be Jim-shaped.

Like Nehemiah, I'd been hard at work rebuilding the earlier brokenness in my heart. Though the job wasn't quite finished, Jim had promised to spend the rest of his life helping to heal the heart he hadn't broken.

By the time the dessert course was over, God had led me to the final choice I would make. It was yet another application of Nehemiah's principle: *Act on the obvious.*

# JUST WHAT PART OF "THOU SHALT NOT" DON'T YOU UNDERSTAND?

## KEEP COVENANT WITH GOD

**(Based on Nehemiah 9-12)**

*"The existence of the church is not to restore rules but to restore relationship."* [4]

*"Bad doctrine usually leads to bad living."*
**—Anonymous**

*"I delight to do thy will, O my God: yea, thy law is within my heart."*
**—Psalm 40:8**

Back at my little townhouse after dinner, I asked Jim, "Could you come in and talk for a bit before going back to your motel?" By now I knew what my answer to his marriage proposal would be. But first, because of prior hurts, I needed final reassurance. So I asked him, "Can you promise me a relationship held firm by a covenant of mutual love and faithfulness?"

With tears in his eyes, Jim assured me, "Because of God's grace, I can."

"Well, then," I responded, blinking back tears of my own, "will you marry me?"

And the engagement period began.

## Who Broke the Covenant?

On a large Fort Lauderdale, Florida, billboard last year, this burning question and author reference caught commuters' eyes:

"Just what part of 'Thou shalt not' don't you understand?—God."[5]

This message, as well as 16 related ones from "God," was anonymously sponsored by someone who evidently had a deep concern about present-day society's near-complete failure to keep covenant.

Evidently Nehemiah and Ezra implied the billboard's same question to Israel the morning after their topping-off party. What Nehemiah had done in his realignment prayer back in Persia he now led Israel to do as a nation. Their recommitment of loyalty to God's covenant was essential not only for getting on with their national life after exile, but also for keeping the city wall intact while they waited for the promised Messiah.

For the next week Ezra publicly read to the people—from the writings of Moses—reminders of God's love in His past dealings with them as well as reminders of His character as reflected in the law. These two realities seem to have been the bases for Nehemiah's earlier prayer (see Neh. 1) when he renewed his personal covenant with God.

Why was renewal of covenant so critical at this point in Jerusalem's history? Because Nehemiah knew all too well that Israel's entire history could be "divided according to the nation's obedience or disobedience to God's conditional covenant: blessings from obedience and destruction from disobedience."[6]

Only after the people had renewed their covenant with God was the rebuilt wall finally dedicated in an elaborate round of memorable ceremonies that included brass bands, antiphonal choirs, and a joyous converging parade on top of the wall (see Neh. 12:27-47).

## God's Covenant With Us

If we believe that the Bible was written for our "admonition, upon whom the ends of the world are come" (1 Cor. 10:11), then we must certainly believe that God has made—and is keeping—His covenant with us. His covenant was validated at Calvary. In exchange for Christ's living a perfect earthly life—and dying—in our place, God asks our return love for Him (see Matt. 22:37, 38) and for others (see verse 39). "On these two commandments hang all the law and the prophets," Jesus stated (verse 40). Jesus told explicitly how He wants

*169*

us to express this love: "If ye love me, keep my commandments" (John 14:15).

God asks us to keep His commandments because they provide a continuing protection around individuals, relationships, families, the church, and society. God's commandments are a clear revelation of His will concerning how He wants us to treat Him and our fellow human beings. (If you need a quick review, refer to Exodus 20:1-17. Notice that Exodus 20:20 tells us why He gave the commandments in the first place—so that we could know the difference between right and wrong.)

When we stay within His revealed will, God can provide for all our needs and ever so much more (see Mal. 3:10).

## Covenant With the Cows

The unpredictable cows in our pasture help me understand the primary benefits of God's covenant with me. Jim and I have a "covenant" with the four cows—and their babies—in our mini-herd. The basic covenant is this. We are committed to providing for all their needs—and then some: food, water, shelter, salt licks, veterinary services, vermin control, new-grass pastures, protection from mountain lions, a handsome bull for occasional social interaction, and enriched grain on Christmas Day.

The cows' part of the covenant is simply this: to stay within our property limits so that we can continue providing for them. That's all we ask.

So far Gloria, Miss Lori, Cutie, and Dakota have kept their part of the covenant, by not running beyond the boundaries of our care. As a result, they—and their babies—experience the benefits of keeping covenant with us. These include having their physical needs met, being contented, having excellent health, and staying safe.

And what wonderful benefits result from our keeping covenant with God!

## Benefits of Covenant Keeping

1. Keeping covenant *puts us in a position in which God can be with us.* Until the end of time He has promised, "When thou art in tribulation, and all these things are come upon thee, even in the latter days, if thou

turn to the Lord thy God, and shalt be obedient unto his voice; (For the Lord thy God is a merciful God;) he will not forsake thee, neither destroy thee, nor forget the covenant of thy fathers which he sware unto them" (Deut. 4:30, 31).

2. Keeping covenant *leads to victory* (see how it worked for Israel in Deuteronomy 11:22, 23).

3. Keeping covenant *prepares us for the crises in life.* "Commit thy works unto the Lord, and thy thoughts shall be established" (Prov. 16:3). David said that when the law of God is in someone's heart, "none of his steps shall slide" (Ps. 37:31; also see Ps. 40:8, 11).

Before rappelling into caves, it is absolutely necessary that cavers check the condition and operation of their equipment. How often attention to details pays off—and even saves lives.

Once when being the first caver of the day down into a vertical cave known as Dragon's Breath, I noticed the rappel rope below me had somehow knotted up when the leader threw it down this tortuous passage. Halfway through my descent, I found myself squeezed between the walls without enough room to unhook the rappel rack and hook up the ascending gear.

I couldn't go back up. Yet my rack couldn't go over the large knot below me, either.

Because I'd paid close attention to the details of my equipment, I could rely on them to hold me as I slid a few yards down the rope to where the vertical pit widened.

There I started swinging myself back and forth. My goal, as I swung in widening arcs, was to eventually cross above a flowstone saddle on a tall, narrow "bridge" to the right.

Momentum eventually swung me in a wide enough arc to place me directly above the saddle. Slightly (but quickly) releasing tension on my rack, I dropped directly onto the limestone saddle, straddling it.

From there I secured myself, pulled up the rope, untangled it, dropped it, and continued safely to the floor. As soon as I was off the rope, the next caver could descend into Dragon's Breath.

Remember that the devil has been called a dragon too (see Rev. 20:2). Someone once said, "Pay as close attention to your spiritual life as if your very mortal life were at stake." Paying close attention to the details of God's covenant protects us from that dragon's "breath" as well.

4. Covenant keeping *brings happiness.* Solomon tells us "he that keepeth the law, happy is he" (Prov. 29:18).

5. Finally, *covenant keeping ensures a loving relationship with God.* "If ye love me," He said, "keep my commandments" (John 14:15). In showing us how to love Him (first four commandments) and how to love others (last six commandments), God gave us a revelation of His own loving self.

## Breaking God's Heart

If the law is a reflection of God's love for us, then when we knowingly break a commandment, I suspect that *we don't just break covenant. We also break God's heart,* for His character and personhood are closely bound up in His covenant with us.[7]

"Yeah, but if God is so loving, what about the judgment?" someone asks.

Many consider God to be a tyrant, accusing Him of keeping detailed records in heaven so that on the day of judgment He can use His cosmic eternal-death zapper on anyone who hasn't kept covenant with Him. The simple fact of the matter is that when we stray from His will, we remove ourselves from the domain of His care.

So in response to this what-about-the-judgment question, I again point you to the pasture and to . . .

## Phoebe Filet

That wasn't always her name. When the little horned heifer mysteriously showed up in the pasture one morning, we couldn't figure out how she'd gotten there. We alerted our neighbors, Animal Control, and the brand inspector. None of them knew anything about the renegade heifer or her origins.

But we *did* know that she was trouble from the moment she first arrived. A neighbor had been grazing his 50 head of peaceful cattle in the front pasture. Peaceful, that is, until Phoebe showed up. After her arrival, we could instantly spot her whereabouts just by looking for the latest guerrilla-warfare "hot spot" in the pasture.

She'd attempt to drive her short horns into the bellies of nursing calves. She challenged various cows—all larger than she—to head-butting duels. If one of them ignored her peevishness, Phoebe would attempt to gore it from behind. Occasionally she even tried to take on the bull—but would usually give up after his massive black head tossed her aside a few times.

Catching sight of the goats, Phoebe would come charging across the pasture as if planning to burst through the barbed-wire fence in an all-out attack. She'd lunge at Sam the dog (though minding his own business), or she'd snort and paw in anticipation of trampling Billy Bob, the resident barn tabby.

After the neighbor moved his cattle to other property—leaving Phoebe behind, of course—we still couldn't get near her for purposes of vaccination, deworming, or anything else. She chose to keep herself away from where we could help her. We could have handled that. But then she took to bellowing all hours of the day and night, disturbing us as well as the neighbors.

Phoebe did want one thing from us, however: the crushed corn and freshly mown grass hay we provided. Yet she used the resulting good health and energy to endanger other animals and disrupt the neighborhood. Very soon it became obvious that neither we, nor the neighbors, nor the rest of the ranch animals—nor especially Phoebe—could go on like this forever.

So judgment day came for Phoebe. The sad truth, however, is she brought judgment upon herself by her own willful choices. She had chosen neither to mend her wild ways nor to have faith in us so we could take proper care of her.

No, we don't avoid the judgment—or earn salvation—by keeping covenant. But as one Southern radio preacher put it, "we are saved by the kind of faith that produces good works." And God's commandments (with amplification by Christ in Matthew 5-7) help define what those "good works" are.

## How Do We Keep Covenant?

So how do we keep covenant, obeying what God has asked us to do, when doing so is not our natural human tendency? Ezekiel 36:26, 27 provides the clear answer. God Himself gives us the *heart* to keep covenant with Him. Jesus lived this reality when He said, "The Father that dwelleth in me, he doeth the works" (John 14:10).

Christ promised to be our partner in helping us keep covenant when he said, "He that believeth on me, the works that I do shall he do also" (verse 12). Again, the final choice is up to us, for as someone said, "God alone can change our desires; but we alone can change our behavior."

## Covenant Keeping and Knowing God's Will

Finally, how does covenant keeping help us know God's will?

First, *keeping covenant with God sharpens our discernment,* one choice at a time. David said to God, "Through thy precepts I get understanding" (Ps. 119:104). "Thy word is a lamp unto my feet, and a light unto my path" (verse 105; see also Prov. 16:3).

Second, *keeping covenant is one of the principal conditions for our prayers being heard.* "If I regard iniquity in my heart," David admitted earlier, "the Lord will not hear me" (Ps. 66:18). Does it make sense to pray for a revelation of God's *specific* will when we, at the same time, choose not to walk within what He's already revealed as His *general* will?

Mr. Anonymous was very right when he said, "A patient cannot accept the physician and, at the same time, reject his remedy."

## Marriage Made in Heaven

Back to Jim. I'll fill in some of the missing details later, but for now I'll try not to sound too schmaltzy as I attempt to describe what it's like . . . being married to someone who makes family decisions only after considering what is best for *me*. Being married to someone upon whose word I can always count. Being married to someone whose love for me and fidelity to the relationship are foregone conclusions. Being married to someone who proves again and again that he's willing to pull out all the stops—even to his own discomfort or detriment—to give assurance that he will never, ever break the covenant he set up with me in the beginning.

Knowing I'm so loved and cared for makes keeping covenant with

Jim an easy choice. In fact, I hardly notice that it's a choice at all. It's more like a natural, joyful response. I truly feel that ours is a marriage made in heaven.

And know what else? Everything in the preceding paragraph—and so much more—is the kind of relationship Jesus wants to have with you and me. "I have loved you with an everlasting love," He tells us.

If our covenant with God gets broken, it's because we have left Him. He doesn't abandon us. And, as Jim used to remind me when I couldn't make up my mind about our relationship, God also reminds us, "I'm not going anywhere you can't find Me."

In His graciousness He has prolonged the opportunity for us individually to renew that covenant. But, as always, it's our choice.

# COPING WITH "HOW IT IS"

*COPE WITH REALITY . . . BY BEING THE BEST YOU CAN BE*

**(Based on Nehemiah 13)**

*"Some days I feel like coping with my current problems*
*by committing suicide. But the reality is, I know*
*I'm too lazy to ever get around to doing it."*
**—A phlegmatic friend going through a divorce**

*"One thing you can learn by watching the clock*
*is that it passes the time by keeping its hands busy."*[8]

*"Whatsoever thy hand findeth to do, do it with thy might."*
**—Ecclesiastes 9:10**

We've explored a number of choices Nehemiah made. He based his choices on God's generally revealed will, which led him into a revelation of God's will for the specifics of his life. I've shared how in my own small sphere, but in a similar manner, God also led me through a foggy crossroads and into His lighted will.

Because of God's track record of faithfulness through millennia, I can confidently say to you—in the words of Ananias, who was speaking to Saul of Tarsus (also searching for God's will in *his* life)—"The God of our fathers hath chosen thee, that thou shouldest know his will" (Acts 22:14).

Let's pray for each other that we "may stand perfect and complete in all the will of God" (Col. 4:12) as He reveals it to us.

That brings us to the final few choices we'll discuss in this book. Whether you're in the process of searching for God's will in a foggy

place or whether you've already found it, you still—in the meantime—
have to cope with "how it is."

## Reality

*Reality* is another word for "how it is."

Reality: We all have different ways of coping with it, don't we!
Here's how one writer playfully claims she coped with it. "Reality," she
wrote, "is the leading cause of stress amongst those in touch with it. I
can take it in small doses, but as a lifestyle I found it too confining. It
was just too needful; it expected me to be there for it all the time, and
with all I have to do—I had to let something go. Now, since I put reality on a back burner, my days are jam-packed and fun-filled."[9]

Wouldn't it be nice if we *could* put reality on a back burner whenever it started sapping the joy from our journeys? But we can't, can we!
We can't just *ignore* shaky financial uncertainties or failing health or loneliness or an unreasonable boss or a difficult teenager—or a foundering
marriage. Reality doesn't just go away.

So here's the question: Even when we know God's will and are
doing our best to walk in it, how do we hang in there—make those
godly choices—when those old uncertainties are still part of our lives?
How do we cope with . . . how it *really* is.

Again, Nehemiah has several answers to this question.

## How Nehemiah Coped With Reality

For 12 years Nehemiah stayed in Jerusalem with his people before
returning to the Persian court. In that time, as you well know, he rebuilt
Jerusalem's wall in record time. Then he and Ezra led the people to
renew their covenant with God before dedicating the newly rebuilt wall.
When everything—including Jerusalem's economy—seemed to be going
smoothly again, Nehemiah returned to Persia.

After "certain days" (Neh. 13:6) spent back in Persia, Nehemiah returned to Jerusalem to check on how his people (whom he'd left waiting
for the Messiah) were coping with reality. The hard-edged realities he
found back in Jerusalem must have nearly crushed him!

For starters, God's people had actually allowed one of their worst enemies, Tobiah, to set up housekeeping in their midst—within the holy precincts of the Temple, of all places (verses 4-9)!

Furthermore, Nehemiah found his people no longer supporting the national/temple treasury but rather using money for their own selfish purposes (see verses 10-14).

In addition, he found them blatantly breaking covenant with God in their desecration of the fourth commandment's Sabbath day (see verses 15-22).

Finally Nehemiah found the Israelites engaged in unholy matrimony (see verses 23-29). In other words, the children of Israel were violating the *exact points* on which they had specifically promised to keep covenant with God (see Neh. 10:28-39).

Pause a moment here, will you, to reread the preceding paragraph. Notice the frightening similarities between Israel's choices and those pervading contemporary society and churches. Friendly toleration of the enemy, supremacy of self, absence of true worship, and immorality dictate the majority of individuals' choices today. Yet we too are supposed to be living in a state of readiness for the return of the Messiah—the second coming of Christ.

Are you beginning to understand, then, why the choices set forth throughout the entire book of Nehemiah are so very relevant for the times in which we live? Our reality forces us to make choices, and these choices carry eternal significance.

Though it might have appeared to Nehemiah that all his previous efforts in Jerusalem had been expended in vain, he chose to cope with reality. In fact, he chose to *confront* it head on, taking it by the horns, so to speak.

His first coping strategy will be the subject of the remainder of this chapter.

*Coping Strategy 1: Be the best you can be . . . and leave the rest to God*
No matter what else is going on about you, by God's grace be the best that you can be. Do this by making only those choices that honor God. Then, any deficiency on your part, He will make up. "Seek ye first the kingdom of God, and his righteousness," He instructs us. Then He promises: "and all these things shall be added unto you" (Matt. 6:33).

"All these things" includes the power to be our best.

## Climbing Power

As assistant director of a summer camp one year, I somehow let the rock-climbing instructor (appropriately named Cliff) convince me to literally drop into his climbing class one morning.

The rappel wasn't too bad. At the base, however, my strategy was to let everyone else climb back up, leaving no one to witness my clumsy struggle against gravity. But two 9-year-old boys—and their counselor—politely insisted that I go up before they did.

So I carabinered my harness to the line, took a deep breath, and called up to Cliff, "On rope!"

From above the ledge somewhere, Cliff called back, "On belay!" I got about 10 feet up the 35-foot incline when I ran out of footholds and handholds. Knowing that the campers below were about to discover my true identity—a rather clumsy, middle-aged person—I braced myself for a humiliating fall.

Just as I said something like "Whoa-o-o-o-o!" I felt a sudden—and comforting—tension on the rope. Then, through no effort of my own, I literally rose two inches and then four more. I continued to hug the side of the rock without really holding on to anything. Yet I was slowly moving upward.

"Wow," said one of the campers below. "She's really good!"

"I'm getting help from Cliff," I called back.

"No, you're not—you just keep going up."

So, like a spider at the end of its filament, my arms and legs continued making random movements against the side of the granite slope while the still-out-of-sight Cliff continued pulling me up.

The last comment I heard from below was "Whoa, look at her go! She's so good—it looks like she just *floats* up." They, of course, couldn't see Cliff, perspiration dripping from his chin and overstrained muscles, as he continued to drag me up the last few yards.

Back at camp, word got around that I was pretty hot stuff on a vertical granite slope—that my masterful climbing technique made it appear that I just levitated up sheer rock surfaces. But I knew better, and so did Cliff.

I had the reputation, but Cliff had the experience and the strength. What Cliff did for me at the end of my climbing rope God will do for us when we're at the end of our coping rope.

Yes, as Paul said, "I *can* do all things." But never on my own. Only through the unmerited grace of "Christ which strengtheneth me" (Phil. 4:13). It was through God's strength and wisdom that Nehemiah brought about great changes.

The same is true for us. Kay Coles James states that "for godly women to bring about change . . . we must recognize that we cannot be good wives and mothers apart from the saving grace of God."[10]

## Being the Best He Could Be . . .

Like a divinely energized human tornado, Nehemiah coped with his reality through wise, energetic action. How? Hold on to your hat for the specifics.

First, he "cast forth" Tobiah and his "stuff" from the Temple apartment (Neh. 13:8). Next he "contended . . . with the rulers" (verse 11), who'd not been setting an example of financial support for God's work. Nehemiah himself quickly brought "tithe" (verse 12) and "made treasurers" (verse 13) to restore order.

Next, Nehemiah "contended" (verse 17) with the nobles for not having honored all of God's law.

In short order Nehemiah turned his energy toward the people who had permitted blatant commerce within the walls of Jerusalem during the Sabbath hours. He "commanded" that changes be made. He "set" his own servants in charge of guarding the gates during the Sabbath hours and "testified" (verses 19-21) about the mandated reform.

But all the preceding was *nothing* compared to the housecleaning of immoral marriages into which the people had once again fallen. Nehemiah was especially troubled upon learning that a member of the very priesthood had become a son-in-law to Jerusalem's archenemy, Sanballat.

"Look out! Here comes Nehemiah!" the offenders must have warned one another as the returned leader karate-chopped his way through this latest national outrage. Nehemiah records that he "contended," "cursed," "smote," "plucked off their hair," and "chased" away those persisting in this sin (verses 25-28).

"Whatever it takes to put God's honor first": that seemed to be Nehemiah's motto. He pulled out all the stops to be the best builder-turned-reformer he could be.

## Being the Best You Can Be . . . in Your "How It Is"

You too can be your best . . . no matter what your reality.

In the midst of her humble "how it is," little orphaned Hadassah chose to be the best housemaid she could be . . . before becoming the best Queen Esther she could be.

Joseph was the purest, most honest steward and prisoner he could be . . . before becoming the best prime minister of Egypt he could be.

Mary was the most upright single girl she could be . . . before becoming the most upright mother of God's Son she could be.

In your "how it is" and by God's grace, you too can be the best you can be. You can be the best mother you can be, the best daughter-in-law you can be, the best deaconess, the best lawyer, the best neighbor, the best grandmother, the best real estate agent, the best retirement-home visitor, the best wife, the best X-ray technician, the best teacher, the best nurse you can be.

Like Nehemiah, you can cope with the cold, sharp-edged realities of life through wise, energetic action. Do you know what happens to people's foggy places when they make this choice? "Those who accept the one principle of making the service and honor of God supreme, will find perplexities [foggy places] vanish, and a plain path before their feet."[11]

Why not choose to cope with *your* reality by being the best you can be? Then let God lead you more clearly into *His* reality . . . for your life.

# WALL MAINTENANCE

## COPE WITH REALITY . . . BY PRAYER POWER

**(Based on Nehemiah 13)**

*"God's Word is known at the throne.
Use it every time you pray. It is your prayer language."* [12]
**—Armin Gesswein**

It seems that nearly every time Nehemiah turned around he was praying. In private. Before the king. On the wall. During attacks by enemies. In front of a vast assembly renewing their allegiance to God.

Even during his four final reforms, Nehemiah prayed four specific prayers (recorded in Nehemiah 13:14, 22, 29, 31). And the book of Nehemiah ends exactly how it started: with a prayer.

Prayer is the second strategy by which Nehemiah coped with hard reality. But Nehemiah's prayers weren't one-sided monologues directed at God. Both his private prayer (in Nehemiah 1) and the public prayer (in Nehemiah 9) attest to his intimate knowledge of the Scriptures, which recorded both God's character and His care for individuals. Through the Scriptures, Nehemiah "listened" to God.

This same communion can be ours. Through prayer we talk to God; in turn, He reveals Himself to us through His Word. As Andrew Murray put it, "God's listening to our voice depends upon our listening to His voice." [13]

## Empowerment at the Florist Shop

During our engagement Jim and I decided that we would get married in Maryland. Since it was across the country from Oregon, where he was living, he told me to plan the wedding.

Not having been involved in wedding plans for many years, I was astounded at how much fresh flowers cost at the local florist shop. I phoned Jim, telling him I thought we should get a bare minimum of flowers—even artificial ones—because that's all I could afford. He said, "I like *fresh* flowers, and I know you do too. I'll pay for them, so get whatever you want."

Since Jim said "Get whatever you want," I could say to the florist: "Give me two table arrangements, one pulpit hanging arrangement, nine boutonnieres, 10 corsages, and three bouquets."

This is also a prayer principle. What God has told us in Scripture, we are perfectly free to say back to Him. "By bringing God's Word directly into our praying," says Dick Eastman, "we are bringing God's power directly into our praying."[14]

Paul gives an example of this principle in Hebrews 13:5, 6: "He hath said, 'I will never leave thee, nor forsake thee.' So that we may boldly say, The Lord is my helper, and I will not fear what man shall do unto me."

## Backlash

The most unusual "He-said-so-I-can-say"[15] experience I ever had was 14 years ago. Sparing you the hows and whys of my back injury, I'll just tell you that, at that point in my life, it was taking me five minutes to complete the painful process of getting out of a rented orthopedic bed so I could get in position to use a walker. Even the simple gesture of lifting a toothbrush to my mouth caused excruciating pain from neck to ankle.

After months of chiropractic and physical therapy an orthopedist put me in a local hospital. Following two additional weeks of intense physical therapy, my doctor prescribed morphine for the pain and recommended surgery—in spite of a back surgery 20 years prior. Then, for whatever reason, he moved me to a corner room of the hospital to decide whether or not to undergo another surgery.

The new academic year had just started in the school, which was located almost next door to the hospital. And I, the upper-grade language arts teacher, was stuck in a solitary, pain-filled corner of the community hospital.

Every morning for the next five days hushed voices of my

schoolchildren, who'd sneaked in through a side door, would awaken me from my drug-induced sleep. Like little angels in groups of threes and fives, students would be standing at the foot of the bed clutching homemade get-well cards or handfuls of newly picked wildflowers. They'd tell me they'd been praying for me.

Every morning the question was always the same. "When will you be back in school to teach us?" I didn't have the heart to tell them I suspected it would be . . . never.

After much prayer and counsel with my family, I reluctantly consented to surgery. Lying alone in that corner hospital room the night before the operation, I prayed that all was right between God and my soul—you know, should the surgeon's knife slip or something. Desperately needing assurance, I painfully maneuvered myself into a position to reach for my Bible. It fell open to Isaiah.

Now, don't get me wrong here. I believe in *consistent* Bible study to obtain encouragement. As a general rule, I do *not* subscribe to the close-your-eyes-and-put-your-finger-on-the-random-text "method." Yet I am well aware that sometimes, when we need it most, God provides an occasional shortcut to hope.

Evidently I needed a shortcut that night, for my eyes fell on the words of Isaiah 30:20. I read, "And though the Lord give you the bread of adversity, and the water of affliction, yet shall not thy teachers be removed into a corner any more."

No-o-o, wait. I read it again. This was just too weird. You see, *I* was a teacher, and the text said "teacher." *I'd* been moved by my doctor to a corner room of the hospital. But the text said that the teachers wouldn't be removed into a "corner" anymore. Certainly God couldn't be telling me—you know, in black and white—that my hospital corner room stay was almost over.

Besides, the context of Isaiah's words was that of a merciful God assuring the wayward Israelites that He had not forgotten them. Isaiah was stating that the Hebrew teachers would be brought out of their "corners" to instruct the Hebrew children: "This is the way, walk ye in it" (verse 21).

Yet, in Isaiah 30:20, *He had said . . .*

So that night in the hospital bed, *I* could say, "Lord, the teachers about whom You made this promise long ago are dead and gone—and so are the Hebrew children who needed those teachers. But right next door is a school with some other children who need their teacher to come out of this corner. More than anyone, You know the desires of my heart, yet . . . Thy will be done."

The next day a team of surgeons performed a spinal laminectomy. Three days later the head surgeon, after telling me I was experiencing "remarkable recovery," released me from the corner room of the hospital, sending me home. Three weeks later this teacher, virtually pain-free, was back in her classroom.

## Saving Data on Your "Hard Drive"

Allowing God to speak to us through the pages of His Word and claiming His promises back to Him are wonderful tools for empowerment along the Christian journey. But God asks us to do more. He asks us to commit to our mental "hard drive" what we need in order to "give an answer to every man that asketh you a reason of the hope that is in you" (1 Peter 3:15). Moreover, He asks us to hide His Word in our hearts in order to give us power over sin in our lives (see Ps. 119:11).

People of numerous denominations believe a testing time is soon to be upon us. Again and again the Bible warns us to be ready to defend ourselves against overwhelming deception (see Matt. 24:4, 24).

For what personal beliefs are you not yet biblically able to "give an answer"—or a "reason" for your hope?

Why not get ahold of some succinct Bible studies on two or three key doctrines that you hold close to your heart? Why not schedule some personal study time to commit their main points and biblical references to memory? Why not make some simple self-study cards (easily and inexpensively laminated with clear, see-through contact shelf paper) to slip in your pocket or purse for serendipitous study during doctor office waits, etc.?

If you haven't put the necessary data on your mental "hard drive," how can the Holy Spirit "retrieve" it to your memory—either for your own benefit or for the benefit of someone you might encourage?

## A Final Thought on Prayer and Coping

Every person who chooses to cope—God's way—will experience those times when it seems as if their fervent prayers about broken walls and foggy places are going unheard.

Yet theologian Helmut Thielicke reminds us: "Behind the silence are His higher thoughts. He is fitting stone to stone in His plan for . . . our lives, even though we can see only a confused and meaningless jumble of stones heaped together under a silent heaven." Then he reminds us: "The cross was God's greatest silence."[16] It was also His most eloquent proclamation of love.

Whether you are presently experiencing God's obvious answers to your prayers or whether you are experiencing His silence, remember to dialogue with Him by reading and praying His Word back to Him. Like Nehemiah, you can remind Him of His promises, including the one in which He's promised to "guide us until death" (Ps. 48:14, NASB).

Know that whatever you're going through, He suffers with you (see Isa. 63:9). And He is continually with you: "I will not fail thee, nor forsake thee" (Joshua 1:5). His request that you "pray without ceasing" (1 Thess. 5:17) expresses His deep desire that you be continually with Him, as well.

Praise God that His Word and your prayers will go hand in hand to unleash divine power—power that will enable you to cope with your reality, whatever it is.

# FATHER KNOWS BEST

## HAVE FAITH IN GOD'S REALITY

**(Based on Nehemiah 13)**

*"Remember you're never too old to hold your father's hand."*
**—Author Unknown**

*"Our God turned the curse into a blessing."*
**—Nehemiah, in Neh.13:2**

*"Since we have a Father, we are not adventurers. We are those
who live by the surprises and miracles of God."* [17]

The first time I saw those computer-generated holograms was in a
mall display. I just thought they were a new type of weird art or something. Then a stranger walked over to me, pointed to the one I was
looking at, and asked, "See it yet?"

"See what?" I responded cautiously.

"Why, the military bomber—in the picture," he answered matter-
of-factly. "And there's a school of dolphins in that blue one there and
tropical flowers in the red one."

About then the thought occurred to me that this man might be on
drugs and therefore dangerous. I quickly left the display and resumed
my shopping.

But in the months that followed, some people I knew (and even respected) started telling me they were seeing 3-D pictures in holograms.
So I kept looking.

Then one day about four years later when my son and I were staring
at a green hologram in an art shop, my eyes relaxed, or something.
Suddenly, almost bursting through the borders of the shiny black frame

was a huge dinosaur. It appeared so real it was scary! I was right there in the picture—and so was a grazing brontosaurus in the distance and a pterodactyl flying overhead.

Then a friend gave me my own hologram. I hung it on my office wall. When my eyes got tired of looking at the computer screen, I'd glance up at the thousands of computer-generated color fragments. In a matter of seconds I was in the picture hidden within my hologram— standing at the foot of the cross. The cross was flanked by the Bethlehem manger in the lower left-hand corner and an empty tomb in the right.

*Coping Strategy 2: Have faith in God's "big picture"*

Just as Christ emerges in the disarray of seemingly random color spots on my hologram—*to those who know how to look for Him*—so He emerges as the power working through the myriad, fragmented life pieces that make up our earthly realities.

Nehemiah had the ability to look beyond the burdens, the fatiguing demands, and the discouragements of his reality—and to have faith in God's reality.

Let's briefly refer to three individuals we mentioned two chapters back. In her "hologram," the little orphan girl, Hadassah, saw nothing but a lifetime of servitude in an older relative's house. But through these fragmented pieces of submission and patient servitude, an unseen Power was shaping the spiritual development of a queen—the same Queen Esther whose courageous prayers and actions would someday save God's people from genocide.

Several centuries earlier the Hebrew slave Joseph's "how it is" con-sisted of an unjustly sullied reputation, four dungeon walls, and probable death at Pharaoh's hand. But that same unseen Power-behind-the-scenes was training a prime minister who would save two nations from starvation.

Looking at the fragmented pieces of her hologram, Mary, the mother of Christ, saw her fondest Dream tortured and nailed to an old rugged cross. But three days later God's Reality emerged from the tomb as the risen Hope of the world.

I consider one text—more than others—in the Bible to be God's hologram principle. You know it well, I'm sure: Romans 8:28. "All things work together for good to them that love God, to them who are the called according to his purpose." This hologram principle—this promise—assures us that God is at work not only behind the scenes but also in the very fragmented scenes that make up our lives.

## Coping—Day by Day

Here is what I find so amazing—and so encouraging—about Nehemiah's choices. Unlike many other Bible characters, God never once spoke to Nehemiah in person . . . or through an angel . . . or by the high priest's Urim and Thummim . . . or in vision . . . or through a dream . . . or by means of a contemporary prophet. As we've discussed several times earlier, Nehemiah had only past absolutes on which to base his life choices: God's character or personhood (who God is as revealed in earlier scriptural writings) and God's track record of faithfulness with His people (how God operates).

Nehemiah clearly saw these absolutes as God's reality. In God's reality Nehemiah chose to put his faith. And look what He accomplished: the miraculous rebuilding of a broken wall and the restoration of a people's relationship with God.

How often we forget that God has a "big picture" that we don't see! How often we forget to "look not at the things which are seen, but at the things which are not seen: for the things which are seen are temporal; but the things which are not seen are eternal" (2 Cor. 4:18)!

## Seeing God's Reality

I was certainly not seeing the big picture when, after my divorce, the random pieces of my life found me in a rural Oregon classroom (not that I was complaining, mind you). Then there was that burdensome, unanticipated cross-country move to Maryland.

On moving day I kept wondering, *Why only 10 short months in beautiful Oregon, God?* I wept all the way to the state line. Yet the scattered pieces on my hologram, which made no sense to me at the time, were making perfect sense to God smiling down on His big picture for my life—and Jim's.

Excerpts from our wedding program will perhaps explain it best. The following two entries were included under the section entitled "The Wedding Party."

"The bride moved to Oregon intending to remain forever single under the care of her heavenly Father who owns the cattle on a thousand hills (see Ps. 50:10).

"The groom was the Oregon cattle rancher who fervently prayed she'd change her mind (his prayers were answered)."

The program section entitled "Brief History of a Friendship" explained how God's reality had unfolded.

"More than two years ago Jim met Carolyn in a little Oregon church she'd joined because, among other reasons, there were 'no identifiable single men.' They became casual friends, but Carolyn moved to Maryland anyway.

"Meanwhile, back at the ranch . . . Jim was causing both Hallmark and AT&T stock to soar. The coast-to-coast friendship eventually deepened. Carolyn credits this turn of events to Jim's faithful prayers, his patient wait, the separation, and the Lord's revealing His will to them both—one small step [choice] at a time."

## The Wedding

The little mountain-church wedding experienced a few last-minute glitches and sweet memory-making surprises, as every wedding does.

When the canned background music failed, a dear friend graciously agreed to push the "On" button of the organ she'd never seen before in her life and start playing hymns from the hymnal.

Since I'd overlooked arranging for someone to light the two lone candles, our sons faked it with a box of Diamond matches they found downstairs in the church kitchen.

The soloist had to sing a cappella. The bride played her banjo while the groom cried. The groom's son was the best man, and the bride's son proudly gave his mother away.

The preacher, who was a few minutes late, wore cowboy boots in honor of the rancher groom.

The food at the reception was superb. The bride and groom atop the elegant three-tiered confection were a couple of dressed-up cows, while the thoughtful caterer allowed a few candy cows she'd made to graze blissfully on the nearby heart-shaped, pasture-green cake.

A 10-year-old guest with stars in her eyes asked me if I was going to throw a bouquet. I asked her if she could catch. The bouquet was all hers.

In the end, everything added up to—in Jim's words—"a perfect wedding."

## Faith in the Puzzle Solver

Faith is relying on the great Puzzle Solver to piece together one nonsensical life fragment after another—and being assured that someday we will see the big picture.

Between now and eternity, we—like Nehemiah—will still have to cope with those difficult people, nagging pains, overwhelming temptations, heart-crushing disappointments, and draining uncertainties. That's our "how it is" on this old planet.

But here's God's "how it is." When we, through His strength and despite our reality, choose to be the best we can be, utilize Word-based prayer power, and put our faith in God's reality . . . then we can rest in the knowledge that our heavenly Father is continuously moving among the puzzle pieces that make up our lives. And we can have the assurance that, as sung in the old hymn, "We will understand it better by and by."

One writer said, "Instead of wondering, 'Why me, God?' I simply say, 'Thank You, God.' Then I wait until all of the evidence rolls in."[18]

But until it does we can *still* cope—because of Calvary. Helmut Thielicke words this reality so beautifully: "There hangs here One on whom our burden rests and on whom we may lay it—our care, our anxious fear of the future, our guilt, our broken homes, the many bankruptcies we experience in life. Here hangs One who bears all that we find intolerable and who knows all that we dare not know. And here also hangs One who for us has burst open, or rather prayed open, the way to the heart of the Father . . . the way is open; One has gone before."[19]

When God's timing is right, you will stand with your hand in the Father's, looking at the perfect panoramas of His big picture for your life. And you will joyfully acknowledge another reality that He's been wanting you to understand all along: Father knows best!

# GRACE IN AN ENVELOPE
## USE THE CREDIT CARD

*"My grace is sufficient for thee:*
*for my strength is made perfect in weakness."*
**—2 Corinthians 12:9**

So Jim and I were married, even though we knew it would necessitate living apart for a time until God revealed which one of us should relocate. Jim still lived in Oregon and I in Maryland.

Two weeks after the honeymoon (and after he'd returned to his farming responsibilities back in Oregon) my thoughtful new husband sent me an envelope containing a credit card with a note. It read, "I don't want you to be worrying so much about struggling with your bills. We're in this together now. Use my card."

Believe me, that credit card was a tremendous relief! It couldn't have come at a better time! I carefully tucked it away in my desk—and continued wrestling with my bills.

Five weeks later my husband commented during a phone conversation. "Incidentally, I got the credit card bill; you didn't charge anything. Have things really eased up for you or something?"

"No," I admitted sheepishly.

A long silence ensued. He broke it by asking, "Then why aren't you letting me help you?"

My very lame answer was "I don't know—I guess I'm just in the habit of trying to figure it all out by myself." The credit was there for me to use. I was the one choosing not to use it.

Our heavenly Husband (see Isa. 54:5) gives us a credit card too. And there's no maximum limit on His grace.

We charge our *sins* to His account; He covers them with forgiveness.

We charge *impurity;* He covers it with righteousness.

We charge *problems;* He covers them with answers.

We charge *temptations;* He covers them with strength and victory.

We charge *pain;* He covers it with peace.

We charge our *loneliness;* He covers it with Himself.

Amazing grace . . . that through Christ Jesus, the riches of the universe are at my disposal—and *yours!*

And when you make the choice to use God's credit card, you can finally stop trying to figure it out—all by yourself.

---

[1] Concept from Dwight Hill, adapted from Jerry White, "To the Navigators," *Fax of the Matter* (a weekly Internet ministry to professional men and women *[http://www.bpnavigators.org]*), Dec. 16, 1998.

[2] From *The Complete Book of Practical Proverbs and Wacky Wit,* p. 217.

[3] *Ibid.,* p. 190.

[4] Victor dela Vega, lay pastor.

[5] From a forwarded e-mail.

[6] From preface to book of Nehemiah in the study edition of the *New American Standard Bible* (Nashville: Thomas Nelson Publishers, 1990), p. 545.

[7] Concept from Steve Marshall, *Blessed Assurance* (Arroyo Grande, Calif.: Concerned Communications, 1979), pp. 22, 23.

[8] From *The Complete Book of Practical Proverbs and Wacky Wit,* p. 247.

[9] Jane Wagner. *The Search for Signs of Intelligent Life in the Universe* (New York: Harper and Row, 1986), p. 18.

[10] Kay Coles James (wife, mother, and dean of the School of Government at Regent University), in *Focus on the Family,* January 1999, p. 7.

[11] Ellen G. White. *The Desire of Ages* (Mountain View, Calif.: Pacific Press Pub. Assn., 1940), p. 330.

[12] In *Prayer Powerpoints,* p. 171.

[13] *Ibid.*

[14] *Ibid.*

[15] A term Ron Halvorsen uses in *Prayer Warriors.*

[16] Helmut Thielicke, *The Silence of God,* p. 14.

[17] *Ibid.,* p. 57.

[18] Robert G. Allen, adapted as quoted on Gibson Greeting Card from *Chicken Soup for the Soul,* p. 214.

[19] Thielicke, pp. 75, 76.

# *Epilogue:*
# WAITING FOR THE BRIDEGROOM
## RECEIVE A LOVE

**(Based on Nehemiah 13:31)**

*"And I John saw the holy city, new Jerusalem, coming down from God out of heaven, prepared as a bride adorned for her husband."*
**—John the revelator, in Revelation 21:2**

*"And what I say unto you I say unto all, Watch."*
**—Jesus, in Mark 13:37**

Before we close the book on Nehemiah's story, I want to look back at the importance of the engagement period before a marriage. Essentially, that's where Nehemiah and Israel were in their relationship with God.

Jerusalem had a restored wall. She had a temple. She had a renewed covenant with God. She even had a kingly lineage still intact. She had everything—except a King. Four hundred years later her King came, but few recognized Him.

While here, Jesus told a story about a wedding and 10 bridesmaids waiting for the arrival of the bridegroom. Only half were ready when he appeared.

As Nehemiah's Jerusalem, we too are in an engagement period. We too are awaiting the arrival of the Bridegroom-King. Concerning His arrival, Christ asks us to "watch therefore: for ye know not what hour your Lord doth come" (Matt. 24:42). As in the story of the 10 bridesmaids, only some will enter into the marriage feast. Those remaining outside will have "received not the love of the truth, that they might be saved" (2 Thess. 2:10).

Our final choice, then, is to receive a love—of the truth. Jesus said, "I am the truth, no man cometh unto the Father, but by me" (John 14:6).

It is our love of the truth about Jesus that will keep us in a watchful state. Let's look at some principal implications of the word W-A-T-C-H.

## W: Watch—Big-Time!

Watch. Watch what's going on—*in the world.* Recognize the signs in politics, in natural disasters (see Matt. 24:7), in lawlessness (see verse 12), and in the heavenly bodies (see verse 29). Watch, said Jesus, but don't be overwhelmed with what's going on, or it will take your focus off Him and you'll be caught unready (see Luke 21:34).

Watch what's going on *in your life and in your attitudes.*[1]

But most of all, watch what's going on in your mind because that's where you make your choices.

"Have you had to struggle with your thoughts today? That's what the battle at the end of earth's history is all about. It's a battle for the mind. A battle against false ideas, a battle against the power of the enemy, a battle for self-control."[2]

## A: Anticipate the Celebration

One of the best parts of the engagement period is that it's a time to *anticipate the marriage celebration.* All activities—selecting flowers, planning the guest list and refreshments, planning for future years together—somehow still revolve around the wedding day.

Let's use this engagement period as a time to put things in order, to take care of unfinished business, to plan ahead. "Forgetting those things which are behind," says Paul, "and reaching forth unto those things which are before, I press toward the mark for the prize of the high calling of God in Christ Jesus" (Phil. 3:13, 14).

With unreserved excitement we can anticipate the wedding celebration . . . without fear (Matt. 24:6; Luke 21:9), with foreknowledge (Matt. 24:25), with trust (Luke 21:18), with the assurance of salvation (Matt. 24:13; Luke 21:19), and with great joy (Luke 21:28).

## T: Talk to the Bridegroom

During our engagement period Jim and I talked nightly on the telephone even though nearly 3,000 miles separated us. During this engagement period, get to know—really know—your Fiancé. *Talk frequently With the Bridegroom.* Setting aside time to really get to know someone takes effort and planning. It's no different with our heavenly relationship. "Knowing God is work. Any deep relationship takes great effort." [3] But we all know that solid relationships don't just happen.

## C: Choose—God's Way

The engagement period is a time in which to learn how to make only those *choices that honor God.* "No good marriage or friendship is ever formed by people who do strictly what they want when they want." [4] Jesus said, "Ye are my friends, if ye do whatsoever I command you" (John 15:14).

## H: Hold Hands

You have two hands. Let one hold the hand of the Bridegroom. Let the other be outstretched in a continual offering of comfort and help to those in need. Remember that when the disciples asked Jesus how to "watch," He gave His answer in four parables (see Matt. 24:32-Matt. 25:46) demonstrating simultaneous covenantkeeping with God and fairness and compassion for our fellow human beings.

True, it's necessary for us to embrace a "love of the truth," as Paul puts it. But God wants that commitment to be evident in a love that is "willing to work." [5]

## Reminder

Remember that though the engagement period doesn't last forever, choices made during that time have "forever" consequences.

"The most sobering aspect of the teaching of Revelation is its assertion that the decision cannot be put off forever." [6] "To day if ye will hear his voice, harden not your hearts" (Heb. 4:7).

Someone once said, "Not to choose is to make a choice." Either we receive a love of the truth by our choices, or we don't. It's impossible, Jesus reminded us, to serve two masters (see Luke 16:13).

John tells us that the day will soon come when those that are "unjust" will remain so, and those who are "righteous" and "holy" will remain eternally righteous and holy (Rev. 22:11).

## The Bridegroom's Specific Will for You

The Bridegroom stated His specific will for you: "Father, I will that they also [that includes *you*, fellow wall builder], whom thou hast given me, be with me where I am; that they may behold my glory, which thou hast given me" (John 17:24).

Oh, how Jim and I longed to be together during those long months of separation! When God made His will known concerning which one of us should move (me), Jim flew into Baltimore to help me pack and move.

I'll never forget the thrill of seeing Jim walk off that plane and knowing that neither of us would have to get back on a plane alone and fly away for more prolonged waiting. So excited were we over the prospect of finally being together for good that I got the directions jumbled on the way home and had us going the wrong direction on the beltway. It was a minor inconvenience compared to the sweet fulfillment of being together at last—forever!

Someday soon Jesus is coming to "pack us up" and take us home. Can you even imagine the joyful excitement you'll feel as He lifts you out of sin's foggy miasma? The sense of lightness sweeping over you as He restores any lingering brokenness, puts pain in the past, rights every wrong?

In the vast fiery chariot in which He carries home His church-bride, I suspect He might give the front-row seats to those of you hurt most deeply—"so that you'll be the first to see it," He whispers cryptically.

Then, in the midst of a million angel voices singing your welcome home, and through the blinding bolts of lightning flashing before the mighty chariot, you see it . . . and it takes your breath away!

The great rainbow wall of the New Jerusalem comes into view on the distant horizon. It rises slowly from out of the billowing silver-lined mists ahead. Escorted by the hosts of heaven, the chariot carries you ever nearer.

Suddenly a man seated beside you can contain himself no longer. "Spectacular!" he cries out, though his voice is nearly lost in the mighty angel anthem resounding through the skies.

You tear your eyes from the rising wall long enough to glance at the young man whose excited outburst has momentarily stolen your attention. Looking down, you notice that his thick arms and muscular hands attest to a life of energetic labor. Oblivious to anything but the approaching wall, he continues, his voice trembling with emotion. "How unlike the brick-mortar wall I restored down there! Oh, the good hand of my God is yet upon me. He has remembered me for good!"

Though you've never seen him before, you suddenly know exactly who he is. "Nehemiah?" you cry out. "You're Nehemiah, right?"

The man's quick side-glance wordlessly answers your question.

"Oh, Nehemiah," you say, with a growing lump in your throat, "thank you—thank you for showing me how to rebuild *my* wall too!"

He looks at you quizzically, but you just wave your hand, nearly unable to speak. "I'll explain later."

For the magnificent wall, whose appearance is of jasper laid upon foundations of precious stone, rapidly approaches. (See Rev. 21:18-20.) The dazzling sapphire, emerald, topaz, and amethyst foundations of heaven's great wall have once again absorbed your complete attention.

Then, with joy unspeakable, you look anew at the Lamb of God escorting this victorious group to His kingdom. Beaming over His church-bride, His smile resembles the morning sun. Incredulous, you realize that God's church is made up of millions. Yet, just by looking into His loving eyes, you have a deeper understanding of God's reality: Had you been the only sinner on Planet Earth, Christ would *still* have come to die in your place so that you could be going home with Him at this very moment. Just as He prayed you would.

Memories have already dimmed in the glory radiating from the golden domes of the Holy City now coming into view from inside the spectacular wall. Yet you try to recall the efforts you expended in making those earthly choices that honored the Bridegroom. Those choices to submit, to wait, to resist temptation, to fear God. . . . In the radiance of the unspeakable reward on the quickly approaching horizon, your best efforts in the past now seem, well, tawdry.

## Wedding Invitation

As the city's wall—imposing in its bejeweled magnificence—looms overhead, the Lord speaks directly to Nehemiah . . . and to you.

"Children, choice by choice, you sought My will. Come, let Me take you to where your choices have led."

At that very instant strong arms bear you both upward. In amazement you realize how *familiar* they feel! Suddenly, you recognize—and lean back into—the everlasting arms that have supported and empowered you to trust . . . and obey . . . and watch . . . and receive true, faithful, unfailing love.

Nehemiah knows them too, for with a deep laugh he suddenly exclaims, "These joyful arms of the Lord have indeed been my strength!" (see Neh. 8:10).

A warm blast of spring air rushes into your face as the Bridegroom carries you up, up, ever upward, toward the top of Jerusalem's wall. Then, gently, He sets your feet down on its lofty heights. Dizzying heights—from whence you can see the glorious panorama of the starry universe as the singing wind playfully billows out the diaphanous train of your radiant robes.

There stand the three of you: Jerusalem's wall builder of so long ago . . . the Bridegroom to whom he so faithfully pointed . . . and you.

"Old friend," the Lord smilingly observes to Nehemiah, "you should feel right at home up here on the wall!"

Then He turns to you with a reassuring twinkle in His eye. "Don't worry, child; you'll soon get used to the altitude." With those words, you begin to understand your true worth in Heaven's sight.

"My precious children!" exclaims the Lord as He joyfully extends His nail-scarred hands. "Never again will you know what it feels like to be forsaken or desolate. I am naming you, 'My Delight.' The empty places of your hearts I will eternally fill. At last! As a bridegroom rejoiceth over his bride, so will your God *ever* rejoice over you" (see Isa. 61:11; 51:3; 62:4, 5).

Those words—the weight of their eternal beauty is almost unbearable. Yet the Saviour adds, "Fear not. Here you will find no more broken places. For the world has passed away, and the lusts thereof; but those who have done *the will of the Father* will abide forever" (see 1 John 2:17, italics supplied).

"Come now, children. Give Me your hands. And I'll give you a tour of your new home. I think we can best see it from up here . . . *walking on the wall.*"

---

[1] See parable in Matthew 24:45-51.

[2] Jon Paulien, *What the Bible Says About the End-time* (Hagerstown, Md.: Review and Herald Pub. Assn., 1994), p. 137.

[3] Tim Stafford, *Knowing the Face of God* (Colorado Springs, Colo.: NavPress, 1996), p. 233.

[4] *Ibid.*

[5] *Ibid.,* p. 236.

[6] Paulien, p. 137.